Thinking About Law

Thinking About Law

Perspectives on the history, philosophy and sociology of law

Edited by Rosemary Hunter, Richard Ingleby and Richard Johnstone

LONDON AND NEW YORK

First published 1995 by Allen & Unwin

Published 2020 by Routledge
2 Park Square, Milton Park, Abingdon, Oxon OX14 4RN
605 Third Avenue, New York, NY 10017

Routledge is an imprint of the Taylor & Francis Group, an informa business

© This collection, Rosemary Hunter, Richard Ingleby and Richard Johnson, 1995
The copyright in individual pieces remains with the authors

All rights reserved. No part of this book may be reprinted or reproduced or utilised in any form or by any electronic, mechanical, or other means, now known or hereafter invented, including photocopying and recording, or in any information storage or retrieval system, without permission in writing from the publishers.

Notice:
Product or corporate names may be trademarks or registered trademarks, and are used only for identification and explanation without intent to infringe.

National Library of Australia
Cataloguing-in-Publication entry:

Thinking about Law
    Bibliography.
    Includes Index.
    ISBN 1 86373 842 8..

    1. Law—Australia—History. 2. Law—History
    3. Law—Australia—Philosopy. 4. Law—Philosopy.
    1. Hunter, Rosemary. II. Ingleby, Richard.
    III. Johnstone, Richard, 1957-.

340.1

Set in 10/11pt Times by DOCUPRO, Sydney

ISBN-13: 9781863738422 (pbk)

Contents

Acknowledgments	vii
Tables and figures	viii
Contributors	ix
Introduction	x
Rosemary Hunter, Richard Ingleby and Richard Johnstone	

PART ONE

1	Law and history in black and white	3
	Penelope Mathew, Rosemary Hunter and *Hilary Charlesworth*	

PART TWO

2	Themes in liberal legal and constitutional theory	41
	David Wood, Rosemary Hunter and Richard Ingleby	
3	Economic and sociological approaches to law	61
	Richard Johnstone	
4	Objecting to objectivity: the radical challenge to legal liberalism	86
	Gerry J. Simpson and Hilary Charlesworth	

PART THREE

5	Explaining law reform	135
	Rosemary Hunter and Richard Johnstone	
6	Invocation and enforcement of legal rules	157
	Richard Ingleby and Richard Johnstone	
7	Judicial decision making	174
	Richard Ingleby and Richard Johnstone	

Notes	189
Bibliography	230
Index	249

Acknowledgments

In their famous socio-legal study (see chapter 6) Felstiner, Abel and Sarat discuss the factors which may operate to transform injurious experiences into disputes. They identify three stages of transformation, which they label 'naming, blaming and claiming'. This seems an appropriate framework for an acknowledgments page.

First we must name the people who have assisted in bringing this book to fruition. We are indebted to Mark Tredinnick, whose interest in the History and Philosophy of Law course at the University of Melbourne led to the commissioning of the book, and whose expectations we hope we have lived up to. Jenny Morgan was involved in the development of the initial proposal. Michelle Jarvis and Gordon Innes provided research assistance on parts of chapters 1 and 4. Many colleagues, friends and our respective partners offered encouragement and support, read parts of the manuscript and helped us refine our ideas. We particularly thank Don Anton, Sarah Biddulph, Deborah Cass, Maddy Chiam, Sean Cooney, Laurie Duggan, Ian Duncanson, Andrew Goldsmith, Charles Guest, Dan Hunter, Jane Kelsey, Carolyn Last, Richard Mitchell, Vanessa Mitchell, Wayne Morgan, Di Otto, Murray Raff, Megan Richardson, Kim Rubenstein, Lisa Sarmas, Loane Skene, Maureen Tehan, David Tucker, Susie Wein and Phillip Williams. The editors owe a vote of thanks also to the other contributors for being remarkably responsive to deadlines and editorial suggestions.

For blaming, we can find no cause at all. Our quality controllers should not be blamed for any errors that remain—these are claimed as the exclusive responsibility of the authors.

Tables and figures

Figure 3.1 A summary of Parson's theory 83
Table 6.1   Naming, blaming and claiming framework
            (Felstiner, Abel and Sarat) 167

Contributors

Hilary Charlesworth teaches Australian legal system, human rights law and international environmental law at the University of Adelaide. She researches and writes in the areas of international law, human rights and feminist theory.

Rosemary Hunter teaches history and philosophy of law and discrimination law at the University of Melbourne. Her research interests lie in discrimination law, women's work and Australian legal histories.

Richard Ingleby is a solicitor with Gadens Ridgeway, Melbourne. He also researches and teaches in the areas of family law and dispute resolution.

Richard Johnstone teaches employment and labour relations law at the University of Melbourne. His research interests are in labour law, corporate crime and legal education.

Penelope Mathew teaches history and philosophy of law, international law and human rights law at the University of Melbourne. Her research concerns human rights law, particularly as it relates to refugees and indigenous peoples.

Gerry J. Simpson teaches history and philosophy of law and international law at the University of Melbourne. His research interests cover the areas of sovereignty, free speech and war crimes.

David Wood teaches jurisprudence and criminal law at the University of Melbourne. He has written on legal and constitutional theory and on criminal justice.

Introduction

*Rosemary Hunter, Richard Ingleby
and Richard Johnstone*

This book is an introduction to the history, philosophy and sociology of law. Its three parts mirror this broad division of subject matter, with Part 1 dealing with legal history in Australia, Part 2 introducing a range of Western theories of law, and Part 3 examining a variety of socio-legal case studies. The divisions between the three parts are not sealed, however. Indeed, the attempt to demonstrate their permeability is one of the things that (we hope) makes this text distinctive. It differs generally from other recent contributions to the field—both introductory and specialist jurisprudence texts—in its breadth of coverage, its range of authors, and the conversations generated between them.

The book is primarily directed towards first year law students, and its enterprise is to lead students to reflect on the nature and operation of the legal phenomena they are studying. As a teaching text it is designed to be supplemented by cases, legislation and other materials which expand on or illustrate the various points being made. Different teachers will have different preferences amongst the constellation of material that might be used for this purpose. The book is also written for the many practising lawyers who went through law school without encountering legal theory.[1] Some may have been introduced to traditional legal history and jurisprudence, but may have less familiarity with contemporary critical or social theories or with socio-legal research. We have tried to present this material in an accessible way, and to demonstrate the 'relevance' of legal theory to legal practice. We hope, too, that anyone else with an interest in law will read the book and find it illuminating.

Because of its introductory nature, the book does not purport to be a comprehensive survey of all legal theoretical and empirical work. We have tried to represent the major strands of contemporary legal thought, but of

Introduction

course our judgments about what is 'major' proceed from our own particular perspectives. Our editorial decisions about what cannot (and can) be ignored[2] would not necessarily command widespread assent among lawyers, legal academics, or even our own contributors. Such diversity of views is partly a product of the recent proliferation of theoretical influences upon and the fragmentation of legal discourses—a trend which could be seen as part of the postmodern condition (chapter 4) but which in any case, we believe, makes studying law more challenging and interesting. One of the main themes of the book is the construction and partiality of legal knowledge. We introduce a range of different perspectives from which law can be studied, and seek to place the various approaches and theories in historical and political contexts, to expose their assumptions and methods as well as their substance, and to show their limits as well as the insights they offer.

One feature of the book's construction is that we have attempted to give more or less equal time to different perspectives. Among other things, this meant choosing the authors of chapters for the particular expertise they could bring to their subject. Inevitably, then, the authors have different preferences among the theories discussed. This does not mean that overall we balance each other out, nor that we attain a position of collective objectivity. It would be absurd to suggest that the book neutrally represents the various theories and suspends judgment. Nevertheless, the juxtaposition of historical, philosophical and sociological approaches itself produced some interesting effects as each offered an implicit critique of the other, raising questions which might go unasked when the approaches are considered in isolation.

Most obviously, the book is a critique of legal formalism—the notion that law is a closed and autonomous system of rules, that legal rules are determinate, and that they can be discovered and applied by the use of specialist techniques of legal reasoning.[3] If we reject formalism, the question arises as to what we take law to be. The constitution of the field of inquiry is not easy to define. Each perspective has a particular view of its subject, resulting in a series of answers throughout the text. But while the book is organised around perspectives—for logistical reasons and in the interests of clarity—its project and themes may be illustrated via a selection of issues which are of both topical and enduring relevance: judicial independence; gender bias in the legal system; Aboriginal land rights; IVF and surrogacy; police accountability.

Judicial independence requires that the decision making processes of judges are not subjected to political pressures to reach particular decisions in particular cases. A judiciary which is not constrained by the interests of governments is generally considered a necessary protection for individuals against the various manifestations of state power (chapter 2). But where does this requirement come from? Why is it considered so important and how is it enforced? What are the consequences when judges who were appointed with tenure have their appointments terminated by the abolition of the tribunal of which they were members, as happened in 1988 to Justice

Staples of the former federal Conciliation and Arbitration Commission, and in 1992 to the judges of the Victorian Accident Compensation Tribunal? Does the principle of judicial independence extend to statutory office holders, such as the Director of Public Prosecutions or the Commissioner for Equal Opportunity? Whose interests are protected and whose denied in the name of judicial independence?

It has been argued that judicial independence is threatened by attempts to make the judiciary aware of the extent to which their decisions may be influenced by gender bias (chapter 7). It is easy to demonstrate the extent to which the higher echelons of the legal profession remain a male enclave. The appointment of a woman judge is still sufficiently novel to make the front page of a newspaper. Statistics on the destinations of law graduates indicate that women are clustered in the lower status areas of the legal profession, if they remain in practice at all.[4] Many women practitioners feel that their career advancement will be threatened by any acknowledgment of exclusionary practices within the profession. But of what relevance is the gender of judges? Does it affect judicial decision making?

Judges deal with the facts of the case before them, legislative provisions, and decisions in previous cases. If one accepts that different judges may make different interpretations of these materials, what causes the difference in the interpretations (chapter 7)? If differences are attributable in any way to the values of the decision makers, then the contexts from which those values have arisen become highly relevant to the field of inquiry. Are judges inevitably out of touch? How can the independence of the judiciary be sustained without preserving undesirable anachronisms? What is (or should be) the relationship between judicial values and social values (chapter 7)? Whose interests are protected and whose denied in the name of social values (chapters 1, 3, 4)? Is the answer for judges simply to promote economic efficiency (chapter 3)?

Like judicial independence, equality before the law is a fundamental tenet of our legal system (chapter 2). All legal persons are deemed to be equal, even if they are far from being equal in real life. An uninformed lay person who signs a contract with BHP is deemed to be aware of the terms which are incorporated into the contract by various legal doctrines. Except in extreme circumstances, the reasons why the parties may have entered into the contract are not directly relevant (chapter 3). But how can the claim of legal equality be reconciled with social inequalities based on class, gender and race (chapter 4)? Socio-legal studies have shown, for example, that the ways in which occupational health and safety offences and rules governing public drunkenness are enforced are affected, respectively, by the class and race of the objects of the regulation (chapter 6).

The High Court's decision in the Murray Islands case and the enactment of the *Native Title Act 1993* (Cwlth) go some way towards ameliorating the legal oppression of Aboriginal people, by beginning to recognise the Aboriginal legal systems which existed before the European invasion of Australia (chapter 1). Yet this development involves suspension of the principle of

Introduction

strict equal treatment before the law. Rather, Aboriginal people and Europeans are treated differently because of their different histories (chapters 1, 5). What are the philosophical justifications for this differential treatment (chapter 2)? And how far can law be of use in producing greater social equality (chapters 2, 4) or social cohesion (chapter 3)? Is law part of the solution or merely part of the problem, and therefore to be eschewed by activists (chapter 4)?

The question of how far law can be of use as a tool of social reform involves consideration of the law in action. If the enactment of a law was enough to achieve its purpose, we would live in a society without physical violence, discrimination, tax avoidance and many other antisocial activities. It is easier to demonstrate that this is not the case than to explain why it is not. Some of the reasons why law does not always do what it (at face value) tries or claims to do include the indeterminacy of language (chapter 7), the existence of 'non-legal' factors such as class, race and gender (chapters 4, 6), the existence of other norms besides law which seek to govern human behaviour (chapter 3), the interactional aspects of the circumstances in which law is applied to particular situations (chapter 6), the incompatibility of legal forms with some of the ends to which the law is directed and law's role as ideology (chapters 4, 7).

Another reason why law's use as an instrument of social reform may have been less profitable than some legislators might have wished is that the society in which laws are applied is not static. Even if, for the sake of argument, the legislation governing the adoption process had managed to be a unique example of legislative aims being implemented in precisely the intended manner, the changing nature of the world means that this aim could not be sustained for ever. Advances in reproductive technology mean that the legal concepts of parent and child require redefinition. But what is the relation between social/economic/scientific change and legal change (chapters 3, 5)? Do necessary law reforms follow smoothly from other changes? What factors determine when and what kind of legal changes are made? Who has a say in this process (chapter 5)?

The rules governing advances in reproductive technology raise another set of questions about law. Certain areas of human life have been regarded uncritically as private and beyond the concern of the law (chapters 2, 4). The public/private distinction has a tendency to become blurred in practice, however. For example, a woman's decision to have a child has generally been considered a private matter, especially if she wants to combine it with a career or claim a tax rebate for child care expenses. Yet Aboriginal women and women with an intellectual disability have not enjoyed the same private right to make reproductive choices. Any woman's decision to have an abortion is more problematic. Is it a matter of merely private or of wider public concern? And what about surrogacy arrangements? Is the woman who agrees to act as a surrogate mother presumed to be an individual of full capacity freely entering a contract (chapter 3)? Or should the state intervene to prevent such arrangements in the interests of women (chapter 4), children, or 'the public' (chapters 2, 3)?

Another example of the public/private distinction is the criminal law's tolerance, until very recently, of rape within marriage. Now some States have passed legislation and the High Court has decreed that the anomaly should be removed. Why did this change occur when it did (chapter 5)? And what effect has it had? Predictably, legal change has not brought about wholesale change in social or legal practices. The notion of the sanctity of the private sphere remains deeply rooted within the minds of judges and law enforcement officers. Thus some judges appear to have difficulty in taking rape in marriage seriously,[5] and research into police responses to family violence has shown a continued unwillingness on the part of police to intervene in this area.[6] Thus the meaning of law may be determined by the attitudes of law enforcement officials as much as it is by the text of a statute (chapters 6, 7).

Concerns about the behaviour of law enforcement officials bring us full circle to the first of the questions raised in this introduction, that of judicial independence. Even on this brief analysis, the principles justifying the contemporary Australian legal system seem to be challenged by contemporary reality. Paradoxically, the legal system is the site for many contemporary political struggles. On the one hand the law is not what it appears to be. But on the other its importance is rarely questioned. The view may be different from stage left (chapter 4), stage right (chapter 3), backstage (chapter 5), the dress circle (chapter 2) or the stalls (chapters 6, 7). But only some marxist and postmodernist theorists (chapter 4) have sought to dislodge law from its position in the spotlight at centre stage.

Part one

1

Law and history in black and white

Penelope Mathew, Rosemary Hunter and Hilary Charlesworth

Where did Australian law begin? According to traditional legal historiography the origins of Australian law are found in England, around the time of the Norman conquest in 1066.[1] The English law that developed in the succeeding centuries was ultimately imported to Australia by the British colonists, laying the foundation for an Australian law which grew to have a separate existence from its English parent. This account assumes that the history of law in Australia, like all other Australian histories, began only with the 'discovery' of Australia by Captain Cook in 1770.

For most of the past two hundred years, the very idea of a history of Australia before Cook ('BC', as many Aboriginal people say) has been denied. Indeed, the period before colonisation has been persistently classified as 'pre-history'. The physical existence of the original inhabitants of Australia was undeniable, but the generic Latin name *ab origine* bestowed by the European invaders on over two hundred distinct language groups obscured their identities,[2] and their understandings of the past were categorised and dismissed as 'myths' and 'legends'. 'History' was all about civilisation and progress. In the perceived absence of change or progress in Aboriginal societies, 'Aboriginal history was an impossibility'.[3]

Just as European historiography saw Australia BC as lacking history, the Anglo-Australian common law held that Australia BC was devoid of law. Aboriginal societies did not include institutions of the kind which characterised law in European states.[4] In particular, they had nothing recognisable to English lawyers as a form of land tenure. Thus the legal fiction was established that Australia was *terra nullius*—literally, land belonging to no one. Accordingly, the land was open for settlement by the British, who brought their own law to the new colonies of New South Wales, Western Australia and South Australia, and made the indigenous people subject to it.

Recent years have seen the establishment of 'Aboriginal history' as a field of study, but Aboriginal law remained largely invisible to the Anglo-Australian legal system. It was not until 1992, with the High Court's decision in *Mabo v Queensland*[5] (the Murray Islands case[6]), that legal knowledge finally shed its colonialist blinkers. In a claim by the Meriam people of the Torres Strait concerning their rights to land under their own law, the High Court held that the Anglo-Australian common law is capable of recognising and giving effect to 'native title'—that is, title to land derived from the legal systems that existed in Australia BC. The Murray Islands case signals that, even in the eyes of the imported legal system, the history of law in Australia began long before Cook.

In order to comprehend the Murray Islands case and other Aboriginal claims, lawyers need some understanding of Aboriginal law and societies BC. Such an understanding will not be gained from traditional legal materials. Disciplines such as history, anthropology and archaeology can contribute to understanding, though they too have been associated with the colonialist enterprise. The perspectives of Aboriginal people themselves are a vital element in understanding the indigenous past. Again, however, Aboriginal people have often been compelled to translate their knowledge literally and metaphorically 'into English', in order to be heard at all.

This chapter examines representations of Aboriginal societies and law Before Cook. It focuses particularly on the representations made by the Anglo-Australian legal system up to and including the Murray Islands decision. The chapter concludes by looking at the prospects for further accommodation between Aboriginal and non-Aboriginal legal systems.

Representations of Aboriginal law and society BC

According to Koori[7] activist Gary Foley:

> Aboriginal society and European society are diametrically opposed. European society, if you want a really simplistic analysis, is essentially competitive. It is laughably referred to as a free enterprise society. It holds up materialism and individualism as being the great things to aspire to. And its basic unit is the nuclear family. Aboriginal society is different at all levels. Aboriginal people reject the concept of individuality, of materialism. Ours is a non-competitive society; for want of a better term, it is a socialist society. And the basic unit of our society is the extended family. As far as we are concerned, we lived here in perfect harmony with each other and with the total environment.[8]

Here Foley uses European concepts to convey a favourable view of Aboriginal society in comparison with European society. The success of his argument depends on the extent to which the reader is prepared to accept that a 'non-competitive', 'socialist' and harmonious society is better than a competitive, materialistic and individualistic one. Such comparative language has more often been used to demonstrate the worth of European cultures and the lack of worth of the societies they displaced in the process of colonisation. Indigenous people have consistently been portrayed as the negative of the colonisers.[9] They have been described as static while colonisers are active, as primitive while colonisers are civilised, as roaming the land while colonisers put it to good economic use. It has been argued that indigenous cultures were doomed to 'wither away' after contact with the more aggressive and progressive cultures of European settlers.[10]

Such European representations have been defended as objective human knowledge, based on observed historical facts. Yet the claim to objectivity is open to question, as the evaluation and interpretation of historical evidence ultimately rest upon a system of beliefs. Non-Aboriginal history, 'based on beliefs about the basic importance of time and space, and the scientific predictability of the physical processes governing the world and its occupants . . . satisfies those who believe in its view of the world'.[11] The following examination of accounts of Aboriginal law and societies BC, from early colonial, archaeological and anthropological perspectives, draws attention to the worldviews, systems of beliefs and disciplinary preoccupations from which the accounts were generated, and which European readers may share. The section begins, though, with an attempt to represent Aboriginal views of the past. Of course, non-Aboriginal writers cannot speak for Aboriginal people. But neither can Aboriginal perspectives be excluded, as that would simply perpetuate their invisibility.

Aboriginal histories

All Aboriginal languages were and are spoken languages, so Aboriginal histories are oral, pictorial and performative rather than written. Important knowledge is passed down the generations through dance, art, song and stories. Most significant are Aboriginal creation stories. Europeans have regarded these stories as 'myths' and 'legends' from the 'Dreamtime', but for Aboriginal people they are the foundations of religious-moral-legal systems. The stories tell of travelling spirit ancestors who, in the course of their journeys, formed and marked out the earth and the sky and established the law, mapping it onto the country. These ancestral beings fought with each other, and struggled with other forces. They became transformed, into rocks, landforms, animals and birds, the stars.

While Western historians might determine the truth of an historical account by checking the author's sources, Aboriginal people use a different set of indicators to establish the truth of their stories.[12] Firstly, the location of a story in 'Dreaming' time (before the beginning of human time, or out of time) provides it with an eternal verity. Secondly, proof of the story exists so long as the physical landmarks representing the transformed ancestors remain. Place, rather than time, is central to Aboriginal histories. Thirdly, the story is known to be true if it is told by an acknowledged custodian, to whom it has been entrusted by generations of past custodians.[13] For example, in the following preamble to an historical account of Captain Cook (not a creation story) the storyteller establishes the place of the story and his own source of knowledge. The story, *Captain Cook*, comes from the south coast of New South Wales, and was related by Percy Mumbulla of Ulladulla and 'recorded' by the poet Roland Robinson:

> Tungeei, that was her native name.
> She was a terrible tall woman
> who lived at Ulladulla
> She had six husbands
> an' buried the lot.
> She was over a hundred, easy,
> when she died.
> She was tellin' my father
> They were sittin' on the point
> that was all wild scrub.
> The big ship came and anchored
> out at Snapper Island
> He put down a boat
> an' rowed up the river
> into Batemans Bay.[14]

Aboriginal creation stories deal not just with the sources of the land and its people but also with the sources of the law. Thus storytellers and ceremonies renew links with the Dreaming and reinforce the law. Aboriginal law is understood as a transcendent rather than temporal phenomenon. It is said to have been established in the Dreaming rather than being created by human agents, hence it is not susceptible to alteration by humans to suit their needs at particular times.[15] Moreover, law does not exist in a compartmentalised area of life, but is pervasive and all-encompassing.[16] In particular, law and the land, having been created together, are closely connected. In Pat Dodson's words, law forms part of 'a complex intimacy between Aboriginal people and their country'.[17]

Aboriginal societies flourished on the Australian continent for tens of thousands of years. Today's descendants of those societies are justifiably proud of their history. In the years following the colonisation of Australia, however, that history was subjected to sustained assault. The physical and cultural genocide of Aboriginal peoples resulted in the loss of languages, stories, land and law. Aboriginal attempts to have their laws and rights to land recognised (as discussed in later sections of this chapter) are only now meeting with some success. At the same time, Aboriginal people are concerned to record the languages and oral histories that remain[18] as an important source to set alongside the extensive and readily available European accounts of the past. These efforts are inevitably interconnected. As the later discussion of the Murray Islands case makes clear, while European accounts of the past have been used by the Anglo-Australian legal system to deny claims for the recognition of Aboriginal laws and land rights, Aboriginal oral histories have become essential evidence required to support such claims.

Non-Aboriginal perspectives

Since the time of colonisation the indigenous people of Australia have been relentlessly observed and studied by Europeans. Indeed the study of indigenous peoples was a key aspect of colonialism.[19] As the historian Chris Healy points out, 'The white invasion of this continent can be written as the story of Aboriginal people being made subjects by twin forces of domination and documentation'.[20]

The earliest European observers of the Aborigines were sailors, soldiers and convicts, settlers, explorers, missionaries, amateur ethnographers and Protectors.[21] These early observers wrote about social organisation and relationships in Aboriginal societies, education of children, ritual and economic activities, relationships to land and the natural world, and crime and punishment.[22] They explained, for example, the way in which Aboriginal law was internalised through education, obviating the need for elaborate political or judicial systems.[23] They represented senior males as the locus of authority and power in Aboriginal groups, although in this respect it is difficult to tell whether they were being descriptive (reflecting the actual situation) or normative (reflecting what they expected and desired to see, in their own cultural terms).[24]

The construction of Aboriginal societies as strongly patriarchal was one of the many ways in which European interpretations were inevitably coloured by their particular interests and preconceptions. Explorers, for example, were most interested in the prospects of the land they were 'discovering'. Natives were an inconvenient intrusion, both on the land and in their narratives of discovery. As Gary Foley points out: 'When I went to school, I was told that Blaxland, Lawson and Wentworth discovered the route across the Blue Mountains; they neglected to tell us that an Aboriginal person showed them the way across, because Aboriginal people had been doing it for thousands of years'.[25]

The pastoralists who followed the explorers had an overwhelming interest in ensuring that local Aborigines did not interfere with their livestock or grazing land. Thus it was against their interests to accord the Aborigines an equal humanity or an attachment to the land.[26] Missionaries were there to Christianise and civilise, so were likely to characterise indigenous customs as barbaric. In addition, early European observations of Aboriginal societies were distorted by the fact that they were observing the situation post-contact rather than pre-contact.[27] Reports of warfare between Aboriginal groups, for example, may have been more a reflection of the dislocation of some groups, forcing them to trespass on others' land, than an accurate indicator of a way of life before the coming of the Europeans.

The often self-interested observations of Aboriginal societies by early European settlers may be contrasted with the 'detached' approach of archaeology. Archaeologists confine themselves to material evidence—sites and artefacts. Archaeological research has demonstrated that there was great diversity among Aboriginal societies BC, and that those societies changed and altered their environment over time. The fact of diversity contradicts the essentialised and undifferentiated view of Aborigines taken by European settlers, who named and treated Aboriginal groups across the continent as if they were all the same, defined primarily in terms of their race.

Archaeologists can offer opinions about population and technological changes and about economic and ritual activity, and can draw relevant material comparisons. The noted Australian archaeologist D. J. Mulvaney points out, for example, that 'Aboriginal people in 1788 actually exploited the resources available with great efficiency and ate a better-balanced diet than most European town- or Asian country-dwellers of the time. Their way of living also demanded less labour, allowing them more time for creative activities.'[28]

Archaeological methods do, however, produce a focus on some aspects of life while ignoring others. The evidence they use yields no direct information about law, oral traditions or knowledge, about the dynamics of social and spiritual relationships, or about the interrelationship between various aspects of life. The limits of archaeological knowledge are particularly acute in relation to cultures which do not leave written records.

Nevertheless, the science of archaeology has taken precedence over Aboriginal histories as the authoritative form of knowledge about Australia's past. '[W]hite Australia has found an independent source of information about the human history of the continent, and this information is not couched in hard-to-get-at concepts like the Dreamtime.'[29] Archaeological 'discoveries' mirror explorers' 'discoveries',[30] enabling white Australians to take possession of the past as well as the country. For example, contrary to Aboriginal views about the length of their occupation of the continent, archaeologists at first insisted that Aboriginal people had been in Australia for only about 15,000 years. Then, in the 1970s, a burial site at Lake Mungo in southern New South Wales produced evidence of human habitation and sophisticated social practices over 30,000 years old. This new archaeological evidence set the new parameters for the 'known' period of Aboriginal settlement. From an Aboriginal perspective, 'Now the experts' research techniques have caught up with the teachings of Aboriginal oral culture'.[31]

The significance of physical evidence for an archaeologist may be qualitatively different from its significance in Aboriginal history. The ritual use of an object or the personal ancestral associations of physical features such as rocks may not be appreciated. Interpretations of physical objects and speculations about the Aboriginal society in which a particular object was used are necessarily influenced by other sources of evidence, such as the observations of early European settlers, the archaeologist's own cultural assumptions and values, or anthropological studies of the social practices of particular Aboriginal groups. Yet filling in the gaps of archaeology with anthropological data tends to militate against the notions of change and diversity in Aboriginal societies.[32] Anthropological conclusions about one group at a particular time are not necessarily applicable to other groups at other times.

Because it is concerned with the distant past, archaeological knowledge has not generally been relied upon in the assessment of Aboriginal legal claims. Anthropologists, on the other hand, have assumed a central role in land rights cases, both in compiling the kind of evidence that courts require and as expert witnesses able to present a structured view of Aboriginal tradition[33]—generally on behalf of the claimants. Thus anthropological knowledge affirms rather than denies the existence of Aboriginal law.

Nevertheless, as a means of interpreting indigenous societies to colonising powers, the social science of anthropology has a long association with colonialism. It has been a prominent force by which Aboriginal people have come to be 'known' by Europeans. The method of anthropology is 'fieldwork', a form of participant observation.[34] Anthropologists study their subjects at close range, often living among them for an extended period of time. In Australia, anthropologists have generally studied remote Aboriginal communities in the central and western deserts, Arnhem Land and north Queensland where 'traditional' culture remains strong.[35] This emphasis in the research tends to create the impression that these are the 'real' Aborigines, even though urban Aboriginal communities also have their own distinct cultures and laws governing behaviour.[36] Anthropological studies also tend to be ahistorical, thus perpetuating the notion that indigenous societies are timeless and unchanging.

One of the strengths of anthropological study is that it enables the anthropologist to construct a very detailed portrait of a particular community. Anthropologists can add to white Australians' understanding of Aboriginal law. The following passage, for example, helps to explain Pitjantjatjara relationships to land:

> For Pitjantjatjara men and women, their land is the central and inseparable part of their being. Their entire lives are spent understanding its nature and how they must relate to it in a proper fashion . . . The land is not owned or valued in a European proprietary sense; the Pitjantjatjara do not see the land as a 'thing', separate from themselves. They 'grow up the country' just as they 'grow up the kids', with deliberate care and affection. They see themselves as the land's inherent and perpetual custodians.[37]

Of course, anthropologists' interpretations may be coloured by their own cultural assumptions. This has proved to be a particular issue in relation to male anthropologists' interpretations of gender relations in Aboriginal societies, which have tended to reflect Western patriarchal views and expectations.[38] The problem has been compounded by the fact that male anthropologists do not have access to many women's activities. As Diane Bell explains, on the basis of her fieldwork in central Australia:

> The Law is termed 'business' and is made up of 'women's business' and 'men's business' . . . Within their own ritual domain women exercise complete autonomy and totally exclude men . . . it is little wonder that men are vague about women's ritual activity. Moreover, Aboriginal men will not and cannot discuss women's business: male anthropologists may not be made

aware of the activity, let alone be invited to attend. As a result the image of women as lacking any important ritual responsibilities has been perpetuated by the male orientation of research . . . Women's ritual activity . . . has been seen as of concern to women only, while that of the men is seen as of concern to the whole of society . . . Such an interpretation of ritual misreads the way in which women state their role and the way in which that role is evaluated by Aboriginal men and women.[39]

The frameworks within which anthropologists order their observations and analyse their subjects are determined by current debates in their discipline.[40] One anthropological debate has concerned 'disputing behaviour', and some legal anthropologists have used the medium of disputes to examine the nature and content of Aboriginal law. Yet the Eurocentric notion of the centrality of disputes to the determination of law may not be a useful way of analysing Aboriginal societies,[41] where knowledge of and obedience to the law means that in many matters it is unlikely that there will be disputes needing a third-party arbitrator. 'For example, the ethnographic record does not suggest that Aborigines went in for disputation over land, but not even the most dispute-oriented legal anthropologist could conclude that there is no customary land law.'[42]

Lawyers have sometimes expressed impatience that anthropologists tend to use 'law' as a synonym for 'traditional culture', and have consequently regarded anthropologists' conclusions about Aboriginal law as unhelpful to lawyers concerned to discover whether Aboriginal societies BC had anything like 'legal' law.[43] Yet such concerns indicate the limits and preconceptions of the discipline of law. From the previous discussion it is clear that Aboriginal societies had a very different conception of law from the one with which Anglo-Australian lawyers are familiar. Rather than being imposed by external authorities it came from the Dreaming in connection with the land, and it permeated life.

The discussion has also shown that different disciplines construct knowledge on different bases. They ask different questions, look at different evidence and make different interpretations in order to produce their own 'truths'. This applies equally to the discipline of law. The law imported by the British settlers of Australia asked questions, looked at evidence and made interpretations in such a way as to deny the existence of Aboriginal law. When Aboriginal people began to make claims under non-Aboriginal law, it was necessary for them to present those claims in terms wholly dictated by the imported legal system.[44] The next section examines how non-Aboriginal law came to occupy its dominant position in Australia.

The legal basis and consequences of European settlement in Australia

From the perspective of Aboriginal people, the colonisation of Australia was arbitrary, forceful and catastrophic. From the perspective of colonising powers in the late eighteenth century, the situation was governed by legal principles derived from two sources. Firstly, there were international legal rules, which justified the exercise of European power in the acquisition of colonies regardless of the wishes of their indigenous inhabitants. Secondly, England, as a colonising power, had developed its own rules and practices regarding the founding of colonies and the application of the common law in the colonies. The complementary operation of these international and English legal principles provided the basis for the English acquisition of Australia and the introduction of English law in Australia.

International law and colonialism

Modern international law is said to date from the Peace of Westphalia in 1648 which marked the end of 30 years war between Catholic and Protestant princes, the demise of the Holy Roman Empire and the emergence of European nation states. Thus international law has its roots in the philosophy and customs of the coterie of 'civilised' European states. International law theory gradually moved from natural law philosophy, based on the idea that there are universal laws of nature deriving either from God or from human reason, to a positivist emphasis on observable conduct of states in their relations with each other as the basis from which to extract rules of law.[45] The influences of both natural law philosophy and positivism can be seen in the legal justifications for European subjugation of non-European peoples and the acquisition of their territories. Natural law philosophy tended to confirm European perceptions of racial superiority while positivism's emphasis on actual conduct appeared to justify whatever powerful states could achieve in their relations with other states and peoples.

At the time of European colonialism international law permitted the use of force in international relations. Thus the international legal rules regarding the acquisition of territory essentially validated the title of any sovereign who came to be in effective control of territory. Prior to the United Nations Charter (1945), which outlawed the use of force, international law permitted the acquisition of territory by conquest or by forced or voluntary cession of territory by treaty. Title to uninhabited territory, *terra nullius*, was open to all states under the doctrines of discovery and occupation.

As European knowledge of the world increased, other peoples and territories encountered by European explorers became a factor in the relations between European states, though frequently only as the objects of colonialist aspirations for new markets and the display of power beyond national borders. The motives for acquisition of new territories are well illustrated in the Admiralty's instructions to Captain Cook regarding the acquisition of the great South land:

[T]he making discoveries of countries hitherto unknown, and the attaining of a knowledge of distant parts which though formerly discovered have yet been imperfectly explored, will redound greatly to the honours of this nation as a maritime power, as well as to the dignity of the Crown of Great Britain, and may tend greatly to the advancement of the trade and navigation thereof . . .[46]

From the first wave of Spanish and Portuguese colonisers who took their authority for acquiring territory from Papal Bull,[47] colonialism was justified by a view of indigenous peoples as 'backward'[48] and thus not fit to be members of 'the family of nations'. In the case of Australia, the perception of 'backwardness' was so extreme that colonisation was justified on the basis of an expanded version of the rule permitting acquisition by occupation.[49] Although the territory was inhabited, the British did not accord the Aborigines the limited recognition of sovereignty inherent in colonisation by conquest or cession.[50]

The view of indigenous peoples as backward and therefore objects, rather than subjects, of international law was supported by interrelated religious and philosophical arguments. For example, Europeans had a duty to Christianise these peoples. Alternatively, the societies of indigenous peoples had little or no social and political organisation, let alone law, thus Europeans had a duty to bring them to the level of European civilisation. Further, 'newly discovered' land was open for European settlement because the indigenous population had no recognisable European-style system of property law, or because their laws were not Christian, or because they did not cultivate and thus own the land.[51] The requirement of cultivation was prominent in the work of the Swiss jurist Vattel, whose advocacy of the application of the doctrine of occupation to uncultivated territories was influential in the categorisation of Australia as *terra nullius*.[52]

International law has now retreated from its support for colonialism. The concept of 'self-determination of peoples',[53] which holds that peoples have the right to determine their political destiny, has become a major aspect of United Nations work. In the Western Sahara Case,[54] the International Court of Justice denied the validity of title to territory claimed as *terra nullius* because it was inhabited by a nomadic indigenous people. This case confirmed self-determination as a legal principle. Many former colonies have gained independence and become full members of the 'family of nations' under the banner of self-determination. In addition, a body of international human rights law has developed based on the idea that certain rights inhere in the human person, regardless of any distinction such as race, gender or religion, thus eschewing colonialist perceptions of superiority.

Self-determination has not, however, delivered much to the indigenous peoples of independent states and they have not gained status as subjects of international law. They are guaranteed the protections of international human rights law as nationals of the state which has been created around and despite them. But title to territory of those states remains largely unchallenged as states refuse to extend the phenomenon of decolonisation to indigenous peoples within the territories they govern. Thus self-determination in its 'external' form would appear to be an unreachable aspiration. States also resist proposals for 'internal' self-determination in the form of greater autonomy for their indigenous peoples. The issue of self-determination in relation to Aboriginal people in Australia is discussed further in the last section of this chapter.

Law and history in black and white

English law and practice in the Australian colonies

The English common law paralleled the international legal rules regarding the acquisition of territory. It also developed its own rules regarding the application of English law within the colonies established in the newly acquired territories. Blackstone's *Commentaries on the laws of England* explains the application or 'reception' of English law in the colonies as follows:

> Plantations or colonies in distant countries are either such where the lands are claimed by rights of occupancy only, by finding them desart and uncultivated, and peopling them from the mother country; or where, when already cultivated, they have been either gained by conquest, or ceded to us by treaties. And both these rights are founded upon the law of nature, or at least upon that of nations. But there is a difference between these two species of colonies, with respect to the laws by which they are bound. For it hath been held, that if an uninhabited country be discovered and planted by English subjects, all the English laws then in being, which are the birthright of every subject, are immediately then in force. But this must be understood with very many and very great restrictions. Such colonists carry with them only so much of the English law, as is applicable to their own situation and the condition of an infant colony . . . But in conquered or ceded countries, that have already laws of their own, the King may indeed alter and change those laws; but, till he does actually change them, the antient laws of the country remain, unless such as are against the law of God, as in the case of an infidel country.[55]

The concept of a 'settled colony' in English law mirrors the international legal notion of *terra nullius*. In these colonies it was supposed that there was a legal vacuum, which would be filled by the automatic application of English law. It was accepted by English political and legal authorities that the Australian colonies were 'settled', as opposed to conquered, colonies. Cook's failure to conclude a treaty with any of the Aboriginal peoples suggests that he simply ignored his instructions to take possession of land in Australia 'with the consent of the natives'.[56] Cook's log records that he took possession through the symbolic acts of planting a flag and firing a gun, ignoring some Aboriginal people, 'who follow'd us shouting'.[57] His actions appear to have been based on his and Sir Joseph Banks' conclusions that there were few inhabitants, living only in the coastal area, who could not be in possession of the land as they did not cultivate it.[58]

The historian Henry Reynolds argues that, regardless of the first impressions of Cook and Banks, it became clear to the British settlers who followed that the Australian colonies were not *terra nullius*. On the basis of a detailed examination of historical evidence he argues that the Imperial government was prepared to accept that, while English law applied in the Australian colonies, that law could and should recognise Aboriginal title to land. Reynolds contends that the colonists failed to observe Imperial instructions by continuing to ignore the Aborigines, and the common law followed suit.[59]

The British settlers of Australia brought with them an entire legal system which, from the moment of settlement, applied (at least in theory) to settlers and indigenous inhabitants alike. Reynolds reproduces one legal historian's interpretation of this event, and offers a different interpretation from the perspective of the indigenous people:

> In 1937, R. T. Latham, a prominent legal scholar, remarked that when the first settlers reached Australia, 'their invisible and inescapable cargo of English law fell from their shoulders and attached itself to the soil on which they stood. Their personal law became the territorial law of the Colony.' It is a graphic image. What was not mentioned was that in transit from shoulder to soil the inescapable cargo struck the Aborigines such a severe blow that they have still not recovered from it.[60]

The English law received in the colony of New South Wales ultimately consisted of all statute and common law in force in England on 25 July 1828, so far as it was applicable to the conditions of the colony.[61] After that date a Legislative Council was established to amend or supplement the body of received law as local conditions dictated, though restrictions on the competence of colonial legislatures remained for many years.[62] Disputes as to whether particular laws had been received or not arose from time to time during the colonial period, including disputes between colonists and the Crown about applicable land law.[63] In one such case in 1889, *Cooper v Stuart*, the Privy Council confirmed that New South Wales was a settled colony and stated that '[t]here was no land law or tenure existing in the Colony at the time of its annexation to the Crown'.[64] Although these property disputes did not involve specific consideration of the position of Aborigines, their decisions were invoked in the major Aboriginal land rights cases to establish that Aboriginal title remained unrecognised by the common law.

The consistent adherence to the legal fiction of *terra nullius* had disastrous consequences for Aboriginal people. The notion that indigenous peoples were not fit to be members of the 'family of nations' was reflected in the treatment of Aboriginal people by the Anglo-Australian legal system. Though nominally British subjects,[65] Aborigines effectively became second class citizens.

In the first hundred years of settlement the Aboriginal population dropped from an estimated 300,000 to 60,000.[66] Aboriginal land was appropriated as settlement expanded, and violence often resulted.[67] Official policies towards Aborigines slowly changed from tolerance of exploitation of them to paternalism and protection. These protectionist policies, which operated in various forms from the mid-nineteenth century until the 1950s, involved the isolation of 'full-blood' Aborigines on reserves and the 'assimilation' of Aborigines of 'mixed blood'.[68] By the 1950s the assimilation of all Aborigines into white society was the generally accepted policy.[69] This assumed that Aborigines would merge into a single Australian community, 'enjoying the same rights and privileges, accepting the same customs and influenced by the same beliefs as other Australians'.[70] One particularly destructive aspect of assimilation policies was the taking of Aboriginal children from their families and placing them in institutions or with white families.[71]

Aborigines were not able to vote in federal elections until 1962. In 1967 the Constitution was amended to allow Aborigines to be counted in the census and to enable the federal government to legislate on Aboriginal issues. By the mid-1970s the policy of assimiliation gave way to an integrationist approach, which offered formal equality between Aboriginal and non-Aboriginal Australians, with some concessions to Aboriginal heritage.

The Aboriginal population continues to be distinguished, however, by a stark set of social indicators.[72] The Aboriginal community is the major object of racist violence in Australia.[73] Aborigines continue to be among the very poorest in Australian society, with an average income half that of Australians generally.[74] Their unemployment rate is three times higher than that of white Australians;[75] their health is much weaker than the Australian average, with infant mortality almost twice as high;[76] their life span is twenty years shorter.[77] They are 15 times more likely to be in prison and 29 times more likely to be held in police custody[78]—a phenomenon dramatically recorded in the reports of the Royal Commission into Aboriginal Deaths in Custody. The Commission argued that the dispossession of Aboriginal people from their lands had resulted in a loss of identity and hope which contributed greatly to their disproportionate numbers in the prison population.[79]

Aboriginal people have taken a number of initiatives to regain control of their lives and land. In particular, Aboriginal groups have litigated to secure recognition by the common law of their rights to land. The two major Aboriginal land rights cases prior to the Murray Islands case were *Milirrpum v Nabalco*[80] (otherwise known as the Gove land rights case because it concerned land on the Gove peninsula in the Northern Territory) and *Coe v Commonwealth*.[81] In these cases the Aboriginal plaintiffs took different approaches to the task of confronting and reconciling the common law with Aboriginal interests in land, but in each case the plaintiffs were unsuccessful in their claims.

The Gove case involved a claim submitted by the Rirratjingu and Gumatj clans of north-east Arnhem Land regarding land over which the Commonwealth government had granted a mining lease to Nabalco. In order to have any hope of success the plaintiffs had to adduce detailed evidence to prove their historical attachment to the land and to demarcate its boundaries. This was a formidable task given the Australian property system's framework of written records of property interests and transactions. The plaintiffs also had to explain their relationships with the land in a language that Australian property lawyers could understand. Thus they claimed that the Anglo-Australian common law recognised 'communal native title'—the interests in land held by Aboriginal communities in accordance with their own law, such interests generally being held communally rather than individually. It was argued that these interests remained in existence under the common law unless and until they were expressly extinguished by the Crown.

Blackburn J, in the Northern Territory Supreme Court, found that the plaintiff clans did have a system of law, which he defined as 'a system of rules of conduct which is felt as obligatory upon them by the members of a definable group of people'.[82] His Honour observed that he did not think that it was possible to devise a universal definition of law and rejected the defendants' positivist contention that there was a requirement for 'some recognized sovereignty giving the law a capacity to be enforced'.[83] Indeed, he noted that the international community had no supranational sovereign authority, but this did not mean it was lawless.[84] Nevertheless, Blackburn J found against the plaintiffs on several interrelated grounds.

His Honour first noted that British colonies were often not expressly categorised as conquered, ceded or settled and that there was sometimes confusion about the status of particular colonies although '[o]ne would have thought that the question depended on matters of plain fact'.[85] If so, the finding that the plaintiff clans had a system of law cast doubt on the rationale for categorising the Australian colonies as settled colonies. However, Blackburn J proceeded to hold that the categorisation of a colony was a question of law,[86] to be decided on the basis of precedent regardless of its incompatibility with the facts. As a result, he found himself bound by the Privy Council's ruling in *Cooper v Stuart* that the Australian colonies were settled colonies.

Blackburn J's central decision was that the common law which was received in the Australian colonies by virtue of their settled status had not developed to include a doctrine of communal native title.[87] His interpretation of history was crucial to this decision. After examining authorities in other common law countries, he concluded that recognition of native title in other jurisdictions had not been achieved through the common law but by express executive action or legislative provisions. Finding no executive acts or legislation which recognised native title in Australia,[88] he moved to an alternative position:

> If the approach is made to the question of the existence of a doctrine of communal native title, on the assumption that it may have been the law notwithstanding that no court applied or declared it, then it is reasonable to ask a question which is rather a historian's than a lawyer's question—'Did people say or do anything which suggests that it was the law?' To the lawyer the answer cannot be decisive whatever it is, but it need not be insignificant.[89]

His Honour considered that the colonial policy of ignoring Aboriginal interests showed that communal native title did not exist under Anglo-Australian law.[90] He noted that there had always been an official policy of concern for Aboriginal people in Australia but that it took the form of protection and did not include recognition of native title. Indeed, he found that the protective attitude adopted was necessitated by the fact that Aboriginal interests in land had not been recognised.[91] In particular, he construed one action which *could* be taken as a recognition of Aboriginal title—the creation of reserves on which Aboriginal people were to reside—as the manifestation of an intention to dispose of all Australian land without regard to Aboriginal interests.[92] The forcible removal of Aboriginal people to reserves, regardless of the location of their ancestral lands, and the oppressive regulation to which they were there subjected, could support his Honour's conclusion.[93] On the other hand, Reynolds points to a significant body of material which shows that the Imperial government had intended the reserves to be a recognition of Aboriginal title rather than its negation.[94]

Blackburn J also considered the official reaction to the 'treaty' concluded by John Batman with several Aboriginal 'chiefs' for acquisition of the site of Melbourne. Governor Bourke proclaimed Batman's treaty 'void and of no effect against the rights of the Crown',[95] effectively denying Aboriginal people the ability to alienate land to private individuals. Once again, this event may be interpreted in two different ways. Blackburn J construed the response to Batman's treaty as a denial of the existence of any Aboriginal title, hence they had nothing to alienate to anyone.[96] The alternative construction is that the proclamation was consistent with common law recognition of native title, which was extinguishable only by the Crown, with English settlers able to acquire land only from the Crown, not through direct transactions with Aborigines.

Despite his detailed examination of the Australian historical material, Blackburn J noted that he was 'not here concerned to give a balanced historical account of the relations between the aboriginal [sic] and white races in Australia'.[97] This stance may help to explain why he interpreted historical facts such as the reserve system and the repudiation of Batman's treaty in a way which confirmed the traditional legal story of *terra nullius*. In 1979 the High Court took a similar stance when it delivered its judgment in *Coe v Commonwealth*.

In *Coe*, the plaintiff, a well-known Aboriginal lawyer, submitted a statement of claim against the Commonwealth on behalf of all Aboriginal people. He later sought to amend the statement of claim but his application to amend was dismissed by Mason J (as he then was) of the High Court. Coe appealed. In the amended statement of claim Coe made several different arguments.[98] He argued that British sovereignty had been wrongly proclaimed over Australia in the face of Aboriginal sovereignty. The majority of the High Court responded that the acts by which Cook took possession were acts of state and therefore were immune from examination by the courts. In the words of Jacobs J, '[t]hese are not matters of municipal law but of the law of nations and are not cognisable in a court exercising jurisdiction under that sovereignty which is sought to be challenged'.[99] Coe also argued that Australia was acquired by conquest, which would mean that Aboriginal people retained their law and rights to land. Gibbs CJ, with whom Aickin J agreed, replied that earlier cases held decisively that the Australian colonies were settled colonies.[100] Both Jacobs and Murphy JJ were prepared to hear argument on this point, noting that the available precedents did not bind the High Court.[101] Coe further argued that even if the Australian colonies were settled colonies the common law recognised Aboriginal people's interests in their land. Again, both Jacobs and Murphy JJ were prepared to hear argument as to whether, contrary to the ruling in *Gove*, this was the case.

Gibbs CJ, however, declared that as the claim did not specify particular lands it was impossible to decide.[102] As the Court was tied as to whether or not to allow the appeal, the decision of Mason J was allowed to stand. The question did not come up for reconsideration until the Murray Islands case, when the relationship between law and history was critically examined in the light of modern standards of justice and human rights.

The Murray Islands case

The Murray Islands case was brought by a group of Meriam people from the islands of Mer, Waier and Dauer in the Torres Strait. Torres Strait Islanders are ethnically and culturally distinct from mainland Aboriginal groups. Under the Meriam method of land holding, land on the islands is divided into small family parcels: house plots on the sea shore, garden plots in the middle of the island, and reef plots for fishing and gathering shellfish. Garden plots are intensively cultivated. Plots are handed down from father to son, and there have been a number of recorded disputes over the ownership of particular pieces of land.

The Murray Islands were annexed by the Colony of Queensland in 1879, and in 1882 the Islands were 'reserved' for native inhabitants. Since that time missionaries, 'blackbirders' and adventurers have come and gone, but overall the Meriam people have remained relatively undisturbed by Europeans. Innovations such as Christianity, a local government structure and a school have been assimilated into the Meriam way of life, which is still regulated, in the eyes of the Meriam people, by their own laws.[103]

In 1982 the Queensland government sought to alter the legal basis of the Murray Islands reserve to bring it within the new land management scheme for Queensland's indigenous population, the Deed of Grant in Trust (DOGIT). Under this scheme reserve lands were granted to local Aboriginal or Islander communities and held in trust by the Community Council. Communities had only limited rights of control over resources on the land and no control over access for tourism or mining purposes. Community Councils were encouraged to lease parts of their land to individual community members for economic development.[104] The DOGIT system was inimical to Meriam methods of land holding, and the Queensland government's action prompted some of the Islanders to seek common law recognition of their traditional title to their land. In doing so the plaintiffs, like those in the Gove case, were faced with the problem of confronting the legal system imposed by the colonial power and making their own cultural and legal concepts understood within it.

Overcoming evidentiary barriers

The plaintiffs faced two substantial tasks in translating their claims into a form likely to succeed in the Anglo-Australian courts. They had to make a legal case against the doctrine of *terra nullius* and for recognition of their interests in land in the face of contrary precedents. Even before they reached the legal argument, they encountered substantial evidentiary barriers concerning the facts of their occupation of the islands. As the parties could not reach an agreed statement of facts which would enable the case to go directly to the High Court, it was remitted to the Queensland Supreme Court to make findings of fact. The Supreme Court proceedings were lengthy and complicated by the incompatibility between Meriam forms of knowledge and Anglo-Australian legal methods of discovering 'truth'.

The rules of evidence applied in Anglo-Australian courts have developed over several centuries to complement the courts' adversarial procedures and to ensure that no party gains an unfair advantage in the adversarial contest. Moreover, they developed in a culture which preserves material evidence of legal activities. One of the rules of evidence, known as the hearsay rule, holds that witnesses may ordinarily only give evidence of matters within their direct personal experience. Thus X may give evidence that she saw Y doing something, in order to prove that Y did that thing. But she may not give evidence of something Y said to her, in order to prove that what Y said was true. Such evidence of what someone else said (hearsay) is generally inadmissible.

In a culture where knowledge is transmitted orally rather than in written form, almost any information about tradition will contravene the hearsay rule. Hence the defendants in both the Gove and Murray Islands cases sought to exclude most of the plaintiffs' evidence about traditional land ownership (e.g. 'My father told me that this was our land') as hearsay. In seeking to establish their version of the facts it was necessary for the plaintiffs' counsel to make detailed arguments that their evidence fell within various exceptions to the hearsay rule, and thus could be admitted.[105]

Ultimately, the Supreme Court judge in the Murray Islands case, Moynihan J, decided to admit all of the evidence, though some pieces were accorded less weight than others. He found insufficient evidence to support the plaintiffs' claims to some plots of land.[106] But he made sufficient positive findings to enable the case to proceed to the High Court for legal argument.

The rejection of terra nullius

In the High Court the plaintiffs argued that, contrary to previous authorities, the doctrine of communal native title was part of the Australian common law. The Court found in their favour by a majority of six to one.[107] The decision, handed down in June 1992, had taken ten years, during which time three of the original five plaintiffs had died.

On the question of sovereignty the High Court maintained, as it had in *Coe*, that the acquisition of Australia by the British Crown was an act of state, an exercise of political power constitutionally beyond the scrutiny of the courts. Thus the decision operated within a limited framework in which the basic fact of colonisation remained both morally and legally unchallenged, and the imposition of European social and legal structures was taken as given. However, the legal consequences for Aborigines flowing from the act of colonisation, and the place of Aboriginal societal structures within the imposed system, were critically examined by the majority in the Murray Islands case.

The majority found that the notion that the Australian colonies were *terra nullius* accorded neither with historical fact nor with modern standards of justice and human rights. As Murphy and Jacobs JJ had pointed out in *Coe*, none of the precedents concerning the Australian colonies was binding on the High Court, and the Court declined to follow authorities which rendered the Aborigines 'intruders in their own homes and mendicants for a place to live'.[108] The majority considered that the common law must be developed in accordance with modern values and that international law, particularly in relation to indigenous peoples and human rights, could be evidence of these values. Brennan J used an anatomical metaphor to explain that new rules which 'accord with contemporary notions of justice and human rights' may be adopted, if they do not 'fracture the skeleton of principle which gives the body of our law its shape and internal consistency'.[109]

Analysis of this argument reveals its circularity: if justice, a moral concept, determines the content of the law, then surely it determines which are the skeletal principles as well.[110] Indeed Brennan J conceded that, in deciding which cases espouse a skeletal principle and which do not, 'no case can command unquestioning adherence if the rule it expresses seriously offends the values of justice and human rights (especially equality before the law) which are aspirations of the contemporary Australian legal system'.[111]

But, while the majority saw a need to revise the law in accordance with justice and human rights, the dissenter, Dawson J, felt constrained by the traditional historical view, previously espoused by Blackburn J in the Gove case, that the Australian colonies were settled purposefully without regard to Aboriginal interests in land—indeed on the positive understanding that Aborigines had no interests in land. Like Blackburn J, Dawson J found evidence for this view in colonial laws and policies from the inception of New South Wales.[112] Consequently:

> [H]owever insensitive the politics [of colonisation] may now seem to have been, a change in view does not of itself mean a change in the law. It requires the implementation of a new policy to do that and that is a matter for government rather than the courts. In the meantime, it would be wrong to attempt to revise history or to fail to recognise its legal impact, however unpalatable it may now seem. To do so would be to impugn the foundations of the very legal system under which this case must be decided.[113]

Dawson J's historical picture better reflects colonial reality than the suggestion of some majority judges that native title holders could have defended their title in the courts from the earliest days of colonisation.[114] However, as shown in the discussion of the Gove case, Dawson J's interpretation of history was not the only one available. Although he claimed that the policies of the past presented him with a fait accompli, his position did involve a choice among the possible meanings that may be ascribed to the 'facts' of colonisation.

The view accepted by Dawson J of the policy and law adopted at the time of settlement allowed him to avoid consideration of whether the Aborigines had any interests in land and whether *terra nullius* was really applicable. These questions were addressed by the majority. Acknowledging, as Blackburn J had done, that there was pre-existing indigenous law in the Australian colonies, the majority recognised that British colonial practice had blurred the factual basis for the distinctions between conquered, ceded and settled colonies. Accordingly, they turned to the available authorities from conquered and ceded colonies, where native title had been recognised, to decide what principles should apply to the recognition of native title in Australia.[115]

Legal basis and nature of native title

From its examination of precedents from conquered and ceded colonies the High Court drew the following conclusions about the doctrine of native title.

In legal systems derived from the British legal system there is a conceptual split between 'radical title' over land and 'beneficial ownership' of that land. According to the doctrine of tenure, a theory dating from the Norman conquest of England and part of the English law received in the Australian colonies, radical title vests in the sovereign while beneficial ownership, the right to use and enjoy the land, is granted by the sovereign to his or her subjects. The split between radical title and beneficial ownership allows for the reconciliation of the fact of pre-existing rights in land with a change in sovereignty. Where unoccupied territories were acquired, both radical title and beneficial ownership vested in the sovereign. In the case of conquered and ceded colonies, however, only radical title vested in the sovereign while the pre-existing indigenous rights to land (beneficial ownership) continued. According to the High Court, the same rules applied to colonies that were categorised as settled despite the presence of indigenous peoples. The one important effect of the change in sovereignty was that a thin layer of ultimate Crown title slipped between the indigenous peoples and their land.

It follows that the content of pre-existing native title is determined by reference to indigenous legal systems. This will be a matter of evidence in each case.[116] Native title in Australia will generally be held communally rather than individually, since that is the usual pattern of Aboriginal relationships to land. In addition, native title will generally be inalienable, since disposing of land is antithetical to the connections between people, ancestors, land and law outlined in the first section of this chapter.

The indigenous origins of the rights recognised under native title result in a unique status in relation to other land titles. A key factor in the High Court's decision was its preparedness to look to indigenous legal systems without making unfavourable comparisons with Anglo-Australian property interests.[117] This may be contrasted with Blackburn J's decision in the Gove case that one of the obstacles to recognition of the plaintiff clans' rights in the land was the fact that their ties to the land did not conform to Eurocentric notions of property, such as the right to exclude anyone from the land and the right to alienate it.[118]

As well as according protection to indigenous property rights, the High Court in the Murray Islands case carefully avoided drawing distinctions between different indigenous groups based on their varying relationships to land or any other aspect of their different cultures. While the facts of intensive cultivation and undisturbed occupation may have made the Murray Islands a special case, the majority judges set down principles applicable throughout Australia and available to all Australia's indigenous people. The Court expressly acknowledged that to 'apply the existing authorities and proceed to inquire whether the Meriam people are higher "in the scale of social organisation" than the Australian Aborigines whose claims were "utterly disregarded" by the existing authorities'[119] would be to perpetuate the racist mentality which allowed the treatment of occupied lands as *terra nullius*.

However, in one crucial respect the Murray Islands judgment did accord a lower level of protection to native title than to other interests in land. That is, native title is subject to unilateral extinguishment by the Crown.

Extinguishment of native title and the debate over compensation

A fundamental question considered by the High Court was whether any native title rights have managed to survive the last 200-plus years. All members of the majority agreed that continuous occupation of the land is a necessary condition for recognition of native title, although there was disagreement as to the extent to which traditional laws and customs relating to the land must continue to be observed.[120] This aspect of the judgment raises difficult questions about the maintenance of culture in the face of colonisation, and who should be the ultimate arbiter of whether indigenous culture is still alive. Even those judges who required continuity in traditional laws and customs accepted that cultural changes will not be fatal to claims for recognition of indigenous rights to land.[121] This acknowledges both the impact of white settlement and the fact that Aboriginal cultures have never been static.[122] However, in the light of history, the requirement of continued occupation means that the potential group of claimants will be rather small. One estimate puts it at less than 20 per cent of the Aboriginal population.[123] At least one commentator has questioned the validity of the continuous occupation requirement given the spiritual nature of Aboriginal ties to the land.[124]

Apart from the requirement of continuous occupation, native title must not have been extinguished by subsequent Crown dealings with the land. Since radical title to the land vests in the Crown, native title is as vulnerable to extinguishment as it is subject to protection by the Crown. Native title may be extinguished in theory by voluntary surrender or sale of the land to the Crown. The more likely scenario is that the Crown may extinguish native title by using the land in a way that is inconsistent with the continued enjoyment of native title, or by granting to someone else an interest in the land that is inconsistent with the continued enjoyment of native title.[125] The exercise of the power to extinguish native title must reveal a clear and plain intention to do so.[126]

The judges gave some examples to illustrate these principles regarding extinguishment. The granting of a freehold title (the most complete form of land ownership in Anglo-Australian property law) would certainly have the effect of extinguishing native title.[127] On the other hand, the creation of a national park would not necessarily extinguish native title existing within that area,[128] while the creation of an Aboriginal reserve would not have the effect of extinguishing native title subsisting within its boundaries.[129] Brennan J considered that the granting of a lease would have the effect of extinguishing native title, though Deane and Gaudron JJ considered that this would be the case only where the lease conferred the right to exclusive possession.[130] In relation to leases that had been granted over a small part of the Island of Mer and the whole of the Islands of Dauer and Waier, the High Court judgments were inconclusive. Three of the judges thought the leases had extinguished native title, but three did not find it necessary to make a decision on the question.[131]

The Court did not have occasion to consider the specific effect of the grant of pastoral or mining leases on native title, since no such interests had been created on the Murray Islands. This issue is discussed further below.

Members of the Court also disagreed as to whether unilateral extinguishment of native title by the Crown gives rise to a claim for compensation. Compensation is a major issue not only because of the question of the present status of native title but because of past extinguishment of title. While only a few Aboriginal communities across Australia are still able to maintain a native title claim, compensation for those who have been dispossessed has been a longstanding political demand of Aboriginal people. The issue of compensation must also be seen within the framework of protection for property interests in the Anglo-Australian legal system. Section 51(xxxi) of the Constitution provides that the federal parliament may make laws with respect to 'the acquisition of property on just terms'. In effect, when the federal government compulsorily acquires property from any person it must pay a fair price. Section 51(xxxi) binds only the Commonwealth, although the States and Territories, which are the main land management authorities, all have similar legislative requirements to provide 'just terms' when they compulsorily acquire private property.

Despite the desire of the six members of the majority to place the issue of recognition of native title within the parameters of human rights and equality before the law, only Deane, Gaudron and Toohey JJ were prepared to accept that the Crown's power to extinguish native title should be subject to the same 'just terms' requirements as apply in all other cases of compulsory acquisition.[132] Brennan J, on the other hand, held that only interests in land derived from the Crown are subject to such protection. Native title is not granted by the Crown, and hence is not so protected. Rather, it is an incident of the Crown's acquisition of sovereignty that it may freely extinguish pre-existing titles, without any obligation to pay compensation.[133] This view of the Crown's power is not far removed from the general tenor of Dawson J's judgment, that the might of the coloniser equals right in legal terms. Indeed Brennan J (with whom Mason CJ and McHugh J agreed) joined with Dawson J to form a 4–3 majority against the proposition that there is any obligation to pay compensation for unilateral extinguishment of native title.

The decision against compensation was tempered, however, by the effect of the *Racial Discrimination Act 1975* (Cwlth), which provided some degree of protection for native title holders whose title still existed at the date of its enactment (31 October 1975). This was illustrated by the High Court's decision in *Mabo (No. 1)*.[134] In 1985 the Queensland government attempted to circumvent the Meriam people's claim by passing legislation to extinguish retrospectively (from the date of annexation) any native title they may have had. The High Court held that this legislation was inconsistent with s. 10 of the Racial Discrimination Act, which prohibits the arbitrary deprivation of the property rights of persons of one race. Section 109 of the Constitution provides that where a State law is inconsistent with a federal law, the federal law prevails and the State law is invalid to the extent of the inconsistency. Thus any State legislation which attempted to extinguish native title in contravention of the Racial Discrimination Act would be invalid. Section 9 of the Racial Discrimination Act also rendered unlawful any non-legislative action by any person or government that had the effect of extinguishing native title without compensation (such as issuing an incompatible title over the same land), after 31 October 1975.

Past extinguishments of native title that might have been rendered invalid by the operation of the Racial Discrimination Act are now validated by the *Native Title Act 1993* (Cwlth) (see below). But the Act also entitles the former native title holders to compensation for such extinguishment, and it provides for compensation for any future extinguishment or impairment of native title. According to the Act's preamble, 'Justice requires that, if acts that extinguish native title are to be validated or to be allowed, compensation on just terms . . . must be provided to the holders of the native title'. Thus, while the High Court invoked modern standards of justice to justify the common law's recognition of native title, the parliament has extended this justification to cover the payment of compensation in some circumstances.

Significance of the Murray Islands case

The discernible shift in the relationship between Australian law and history is one of the most significant features of the Murray Islands decision. In the words of Brennan J:

> To treat the dispossession of the Australian Aboriginals as the working out of the Crown's acquisition of ownership of all land on first settlement is

contrary to history. Aboriginals were dispossessed of their land parcel by parcel, to make way for expanding colonial settlement ... [I]t is appropriate to identify the events which resulted in the dispossession of the indigenous inhabitants of Australia, in order to dispel the misconception that it is the common law rather than the action of governments which made many of the indigenous people of this country trespassers on their own land.[135]

In rejecting the version of history expounded in *Cooper v Stuart* and followed by Blackburn J and Dawson J, the majority in the Murray Islands case bestowed legal force upon a new historical story. Critics of the decision have labelled the majority's view of Australian history as 'unusual', arguing that it was based on 'prejudice and misguided research',[136] or on the work of 'propagandist historians'.[137] By contrast, in the passage above Brennan J suggests that there was a need to bring the law into line with a widely acknowledged historical reality. Indeed, it proved easier for the Court to renew the law's legitimacy by reconciling it with the 'facts' of history than to provide redress for the dispossession of Aborigines in the form of compensation.

The Murray Islands decision has also been criticised on the basis that recognition of native title constitutes 'special treatment' for Aborigines because it is a right to property which is unavailable to non-Aboriginal Australians.[138] This argument ignores history. Native title is unavailable to non-Aboriginal Australians because it predates the arrival of Europeans in Australia. Far from amounting to special treatment, recognition of native title is an expression of equality, as Aboriginal property rights are acknowledged in the same way as Anglo-Australian property rights.[139]

Another response to the Murray Islands case was concern about its impact on the status of non-Aboriginal land titles and hence on investment and economic development.[140] The main sites of uncertainty were pastoral leases, mining leases, and titles issued since the date of the Racial Discrimination Act.[141] The extent of uncertainty was undoubtedly exaggerated,[142] particularly since resource developers have been dealing with native title holders in Canada and the United States for many years, and native title has formed the basis for effective relationships between indigenous peoples and settlers in the rest of the common law world.[143] Nevertheless, Australian State and federal governments saw a need to legislate to clarify the relationships between native and non-Aboriginal titles. The Victorian *Land Titles Validation Act 1993* is discussed in chapter 5.

The federal Native Title Act, as noted above, validates all non-Aboriginal titles issued by the Commonwealth before 1 January 1994 (to the extent that they were invalid due to the Racial Discrimination Act or for any other reason pertaining to the existence of native title), and allows the States and Territories to do the same for titles issued by them.[144] Freehold titles and residential, commercial, agricultural and pastoral leases issued before 1 January 1994 extinguish any native title that might have existed over the same land.[145] The only exception is where such titles contain reservations for the benefit of Aboriginal people.[146] Existing mining leases, on the other hand, simply have the effect of 'submerging' any native title for the duration of the lease.[147] Lesser interests that have been created in land exist alongside any native title.[148] If an Aboriginal group can show that it had native title to any land or waters, prior that title being extinguished or impaired by a validated non-Aboriginal title, compensation on 'just terms' is payable by the government that issued the validated title.[149]

In order to establish that they had, or still have, native title, Aboriginal groups must, in line with the High Court's decision, prove their continuous association with the land since before white settlement.[150] Claims for compensation, or to establish and register existing native title, may be made in an appropriate State or Territory court or the National Native Title Tribunal established by the Native Title Act.[151] Claims which are contested and which cannot be settled by agreement or mediation are decided by the Federal Court.[152]

Native title can only be extinguished by future acts of governments in accordance with the Native Title Act.[153] If extinguishment occurs under a compulsory acquisition Act, compensation on just terms is required.[154] Many other proposed activities on native title land, such as the issue of a mining lease, do not have the effect of extinguishing native title.[155] Such proposals must be negotiated with native title holders[156] and if necessary determined by the National Native Title Tribunal or other appropriate arbitral body.[157] But native title holders do not have a veto over mining. Moreover, tribunal decisions may be overridden by governments in the State, Territory or national interest.[158]

This regime preserves the unique status of native title in that the content of native title continues to be determined by reference to Aboriginal laws, and there is an attempt to accommodate Aboriginal relationships to land in the determination of compensation (which may take the form of land rather than money).[159] However, the denial of a right of veto over mining and the privileging of the State or national interest represent derogations from the full enjoyment of Aboriginal rights to their land.

A final concern that was expressed in the debate over the Murray Islands case was that, by virtue of the decision, Aborigines would gain control over a disproportionate amount of land in Australia.[160] One flaw in this argument is that the principle that land should be distributed proportionately amongst the population, whether on an individual or a group basis, has never been applied to non-Aboriginal people. Secondly, the argument assumes that land is of equal value to all groups and, in particular, that economic value is of primary concern. Thirdly, the argument rests on the colonialist view, outlined earlier in the chapter, of 'Aborigines' as an undifferentiated category. A crude division of the amount of land currently held by Aborigines by the number of Aboriginal people, to produce a *per capita* Aboriginal land holding, ignores the fact that many Aboriginal groups are not aided at all by the Murray Islands case, the Native Title Act or previous land rights legislation (discussed below). While the Pitjantjatjara or Yolgnu or Jawoyn people may have gained statutory title to (part of) their ancestral lands, many Aboriginal people remain irretrievably dispossessed. This point underlines the importance of the land acquisition fund, also established by the Native Title Act, to benefit Aboriginal communities who are unable to claim native title.[161]

The Murray Islands decision and the Native Title Act are initiatives which attempt to establish a new relationship between the white legal system and Aboriginal law and history. The following section examines other initiatives towards this end, and assesses the terms on which further accommodation might take place.

Towards accommodation?

The Murray Islands case has undermined one of the pillars of the white legal system's account of European 'settlement' of Australia. The rejection of *terra nullius* paves the way for a wider ranging recognition of Aboriginal law. Other former colonies have developed pluralist legal systems in which (to a greater or lesser degree) imported and indigenous laws co-exist. Indigenous laws may apply within defined geographical areas, or they may apply as the 'personal' law of the members of particular ethnic or religious communities. Malaysia is an example of the latter model, where the imported English law operates alongside Islamic law and Malay customary law (*adat*).[162]

The terms on which indigenous laws are recognised in pluralist legal systems may also vary. At one extreme, indigenous laws may be treated as subordinate, with the imported legal system defining the extent to which and the conditions on which they will be recognised.[163] A more complete form of pluralism might be based on the notion of self-determination, which would allow indigenous peoples themselves to determine how their traditional laws should relate to the imported legal system.

In Australia, even the most limited form of pluralism has been elusive. The view of the New South Wales Supreme Court in 1883 in *R v Cobby*[164] that Aborigines had 'no laws of which we can take cognisance' has been remarkably durable. It underpinned a great range of injustices, from the non-recognition of traditional marriages to the denial of land rights. The failure to recognise Aboriginal laws has been supported by official failure to acknowledge Aboriginal history before European settlement, for fear of potential legal consequences. Proposals put forward during the 1980s to include reference in the Constitution,[165] or in a legislative preamble,[166] to Aboriginal prior ownership of Australia were not proceeded with. The first substantive motion carried in the new federal Parliament House, acknowledging the nation's Aboriginal history and the significance of its Aboriginal heritage, failed to gain bipartisan support.[167]

The Murray Islands case has largely removed the cause for reticence in acknowledging prior Aboriginal occupation and ownership. The High Court has taken the problem out of the hands of politicians by establishing the doctrine of native title as part of the common law. This change may account for the unusual frankness of Prime Minister Keating's speech delivered in

Redfern Park in December 1992, at the start of the United Nations' International Year for the World's Indigenous Peoples. The prime minister echoed Brennan J's words in the Murray Islands case in calling for:

> ... an act of recognition: recognition that it was us who did the dispossessing. We took the traditional lands and smashed the traditional way of life. We brought the diseases, the alcohol. We committed the murders. We took the children from their mothers. We practised discrimination and exclusion.[168]

Now, too, the preamble to the Native Title Act acknowledges that:

> The people whose descendants are now known as Aboriginal peoples and Torres Strait Islanders were the inhabitants of Australia before European settlement.
> They have been progressively dispossessed of their lands. This dispossession occurred largely without compensation, and successive governments have failed to reach a lasting and equitable agreement with Aboriginal peoples and Torres Strait Islanders concerning the use of their lands.

In this context the Native Title Act 'is intended to further advance the process of reconciliation among all Australians'. This follows from the establishment in 1991 of the Council for Aboriginal Reconciliation, to 'promote a process of reconciliation between Aborigines and Torres Strait Islanders and the wider community' through educating the Australian community about its indigenous culture and the dispossession suffered by the indigenous people over the last 200 years.[169] The reconciliation process might also create a more favourable climate for legal pluralism. The following section looks at the forms that pluralism might take in Australia.

Recognition of customary law

Although some statutory recognition of Aboriginal law has occurred in some contexts, such as in cultural heritage and sacred sites legislation,[170] overall recognition has been 'particular rather than general, has been confined to particular jurisdictions, and has often depended upon the exercise of discretion rather than existing as of right. It has been a piecemeal approach to the problems facing Aboriginal people rather than a reasoned response on the part of the general legal system'.[171]

In 1977 the question of the recognition of Aboriginal customary law was referred to the Australian Law Reform Commission. It published a major report on the issue in 1986 recommending that the Anglo-Australian legal system recognise Aboriginal customary law in a variety of ways in particular contexts. The Commission decided against a general codification or direct incorporation of customary laws, and argued instead for a 'functional' approach on an issue-by-issue basis.[172] The problem of a general incorporation of traditional laws into the white legal system identified by the Commission was that it may deprive Aborigines of control over their laws and constitute an intrusion into traditionally secret matters. A functional approach, by contrast, allowed Aboriginal people to remain in control. Some recommendations of the Commission, such as those relating to traditional marriages, involved the translation of customary rules into Australian law in order to give them effect in the latter system. Others, such as those relating to the exercise of discretion in sentencing, were for legislation to ensure that the criminal justice system took Aboriginal laws into account. The Commission also recommended the strategy of using exemptions to legislation to recognise customary laws in some areas such as hunting and fishing rights.[173]

Although the Commission's report was relatively conservative, recommending the limited incorporation of Aboriginal customary laws into the Australian legal system, rather than viewing the former as independent systems of laws, its recommendations have never been implemented. The reasons for this seem to be simply lack of commitment on the part of the Commonwealth and States and resistance of some officials within the Aboriginal affairs bureaucracy. The Council for Aboriginal Reconciliation could usefully encourage implementation of the report.

Land rights

Recognition of land rights, whether through the common law or by legislation, offers a limited but important form of recognition of Aboriginal customary law by the white legal system. Both because of the centrality of land to Aboriginal and Islander identities and a growing sense of injustice at non-Aboriginal exploitation of traditional lands, a land rights movement gained momentum in the late 1960s. Around this time Land Trusts were established in most States to administer remaining Aboriginal reserves. The more contentious issue, however, was rights to other land that had been traditionally owned by Aboriginal groups.

The unsatisfactory outcome of the Gove case and the reluctance of the federal government to enact land rights legislation led to the setting up of an Aboriginal Tent Embassy in front of Parliament House in 1972, which drew national attention to the issue. The newly elected Labor government established an Aboriginal Land Rights Commission in 1973, with A. E. Woodward QC as Commissioner. His reports eventually resulted in the *Aboriginal Land Rights (Northern Territory) Act 1976* (Cwlth). Under the legislation Aboriginal reserves could be directly transferred to local Land Trusts. Land claims can be made only to vacant Crown land on the basis of 'traditional ownership'. Title to land granted under the legislation is held communally and vested in Land Trusts, which hold the land for the benefit of all traditional owners. Title can only be passed to other Aboriginal groups. Disputed land claims are decided by an Aboriginal Land Commissioner. The Act also provided for the establishment of regional Land Councils with important functions in the negotiation and administration of land claims and mining applications, including the exercise by the traditional owners of the right to veto mining exploration on Aboriginal land. The mining veto was considered by Commissioner Woodward to be essential to the full recognition of Aboriginal peoples' relationships to their land.[174]

Most of the Australian States now have some form of land rights legislation.[175] These laws vary greatly in their scope and procedures, disparities which emphasise the need for a national approach. Although the Hawke Labor government made an election commitment in 1983 to uniform national land rights legislation, it eventually abandoned this promise in the face of pressure from the Western Australian Labor government, which was concerned by the prospect of an Aboriginal veto over mining on Aboriginal land, negative public opinion polls and a potent campaign by mining and pastoral interests.[176] The themes of this campaign were repeated in the responses of mining companies and pastoral associations to the Murray Islands case, discussed earlier.

The High Court's adoption of the doctrine of native title as part of the common law succeeded in providing the basis for a national approach to Aboriginal land rights, which is now embodied in the federal Native Title Act. It also achieved a form of recognition of a central aspect of Aboriginal law in the spirit of the Australian Law Reform Commission's recommendations. The Murray Islands decision, land rights legislation and the Law Reform Commission's proposals all represent versions of legal pluralism in which the dominant, white legal system bestows recognition on some aspects of the subordinate, indigenous law. But the granting of land rights does contain the potential for a more extensive form of pluralism. Land rights provide Aboriginal people with the potential for control of activities on their land, enabling them to develop an economic base, protect sacred sites and exercise their own laws, and opening the possibilities of self-management and self-determination.

Self-management

The current policy of the federal government towards Aborigines encourages 'self-management'. While this term is sometimes equated with 'self-determination', it must be carefully distinguished from the international legal principle of 'self-determination' (discussed earlier and further below). 'Self-management' in the Australian context means simply some degree of Aboriginal involvement in decisions affecting them, rather than the right to choose a particular political destiny.[177] The creation of the Aboriginal and Torres Strait Islander Commission (ATSIC) in 1989 was presented as the central element in the government's 'self-management' package.[178]

ATSIC is composed of representatives of Aboriginal and Torres Strait Islander people elected through 36 regional councils. It has the power to allocate funding and to determine national and regional indigenous priorities. Its creation and operations have been controversial in indigenous communities because some groups see it as lacking real independence from government and unable to properly represent Aboriginal and Islander concerns.[179] One criticism is that it has absorbed the same public servants who worked in the former Department of Aboriginal Affairs, and that they are not directly answerable to the ATSIC Commissioners. Another concern (though one not universally shared) is that ATSIC is not directly involved in important areas of service delivery contained in ministerial portfolios such as community services, social security and employment, education and training.[180] Indeed, some observers have queried whether the ATSIC structure is any advance on the policy of integration.[181]

The blurring of the line between 'self-management' and integration is particularly noticeable in the ATSIC election process, which superimposes Western notions of democracy and individualism upon Aboriginal group identities and authority structures. The representative framework of ATSIC takes no account of cultural and historical differences among Aboriginal groups.[182] The election process can also have the effect of disempowering significant decision makers in some communities, when young educated people are elected rather than 'elders'. Furthermore, because ATSIC is part of the federal bureaucracy, regional Councils are required to operate in an accepted bureaucratic way rather than according to the decision-making arrangements of particular Aboriginal communities. Finally, because of its centralised nature, ATSIC may not be the most appropriate forum for the determination of particular questions regarding the relationship between Anglo-Australian and Aboriginal laws. Such questions require attention at the local level.[183] But ATSIC does have the capacity to establish a national policy and to direct resources towards the issue, something it has not yet done.

As a national representative body, however, ATSIC has played a key role in major issues affecting indigenous people, such as the monitoring and implementation of the recommendations of the Royal Commission into Aboriginal Deaths in Custody[184] and the negotiation of the Native Title Act. Through its funding policies it has ensured that legal services, alcohol and drug projects and family reunion initiatives have been implemented by Aboriginal and Torres Strait Islander community-based organisations rather than by non-Aboriginal bureaucrats or social welfare organisations. It has also promoted economic development for Aboriginal communities through the administration of funding for land acquisition and land management, community development employment programs, housing and industry strategies.

In addition to the forms of Aboriginal self-management fostered by ATSIC, there is some scope for community self-management through the use of local government structures.[185] One model has been implemented in the Northern Territory by providing for a specific form of Aboriginal community government under the *Local Government Act 1978* (NT). However, this approach has been criticised as actually limiting Aboriginal decision making rather than expanding autonomy.[186] In Western Australia some Aboriginal communities have chosen to seek access to and control of local government funds through participation in the mainstream local government system.[187] It may be possible to establish self-managing regimes through the interaction between local government and land rights legislation.¹⁸⁸ In Canada, Aboriginal governments in defined territories are recognised as a third order of government alongside the federal and provincial governments, and the Canadian Constitution recognises that 'the Aboriginal peoples of Canada have the inherent right of self-government within Canada'.¹⁸⁹ These Canadian self-government structures also provide models for Aboriginal self-management in Australia.

Aboriginal claims of sovereignty

Some Aboriginal groups have argued that an appropriate accommodation of white and black cultures in Australia would include the recognition of Aboriginal sovereignty. Because Aboriginal people never ceded their land, the argument is that they retain their sovereignty, although it is not always clear whether the claims are made in respect of a single Aboriginal nation or in regional or local groups. As noted above, Paul Coe tried unsuccessfully to have the High Court consider this issue in 1979, and the High Court refused to consider it again in the Murray Islands case. Michael Mansell, a Tasmanian Aborigine, has taken the bold move of simply declaring the existence of an Aboriginal state within Australia and establishing an Aboriginal Provisional Government.¹⁹⁰

The political wisdom of such claims has been hotly debated. Frank Brennan SJ, a former adviser to the Australian Catholic Bishops on Aboriginal issues, has argued that '[t]he claim to Aboriginal sovereignty is a political claim, not a justiciable legal claim in either international or domestic courts. It will be sterile ground to continue the debate . . . as to whether sovereignty was asserted by settlement, conquest, cession or prescription'.¹⁹¹ On the other hand, Mansell's claim has struck a deep chord in the Aboriginal community because it 'articulates the stark alienation of Aboriginal people from the Australian nation, something with which Aboriginal people from throughout the continent can identify'.¹⁹² The lack of recognition of Aboriginal history, land rights and laws by the dominant culture has contributed significantly to this alienation. Nevertheless, Noel Pearson of the Cape York Land Council has argued that the rhetoric of sovereignty, without detailed proposals on how it might be accomplished, is unrealistic and capable of harming the Aboriginal cause. Pearson questions whether the international legal notion of sovereignty is appropriate in the Aboriginal context: 'the concept of sovereignty developed in western legal tradition to describe nation states is artificial if applied to the Aboriginal relationship to land which is at the core of the indigenous domain'.¹⁹³ He suggests instead the recognition of 'local indigenous sovereignty' based on a spiritual relationship with land.

Another, less radical, form of recognition of Aboriginal sovereignty would be for the Australian government to negotiate a treaty with the indigenous population, setting out the terms of co-existence between European and indigenous culture. Talk of a treaty or 'makarrata' has waxed and waned over the years.¹⁹⁴ It was given renewed impetus by a statement made by Prime Minister Hawke at Barunga in the Northern Territory in 1988 in response to a call by the Central and Northern Land Councils for recognition of indigenous rights.[195] The prime minister affirmed the federal government's commitment to work towards a negotiated treaty and promised support for Aboriginal consultations on the content of the treaty. He later described it not as a treaty in the international legal sense of the term, which implies the existence of two sovereign states, but as a 'national declaration of shared principles and common commitments'.[196] Since 1988, however, no progress has been made on this issue, both because of lack of consensus within the Aboriginal community on the mechanisms for treaty negotiation and the lack of resources to develop the notion.[197] The treaty issue has now been assigned to the Council for Aboriginal Reconciliation.[198]

The use of international law

While the Australian political and legal scene has been unreceptive to Aboriginal demands that white Australia recognise and make amends for its usurpation of indigenous culture, some Aboriginal groups have attempted to use the international legal arena to bring pressure on the Australian government.[199]

Indigenous peoples may make use of the international human rights mechanisms available to all citizens of those states which adhere to international human rights treaties. Australia has recently accepted three different procedures by which individuals can make direct appeal to United Nations human rights monitoring bodies.[200] The three treaties which can be used as the basis of such claims are the International Covenant on Civil and Political Rights (ICCPR), the Convention on the Elimination of All Forms of Racial Discrimination, and the Convention Against Torture.

Article 1 of the ICCPR provides that all peoples have the right to self-determination and, on its face, appears to hold great potential for claims by indigenous groups. However, there are both substantive and procedural problems in the application of the traditionally accepted notion of self-determination to indigenous peoples. In the context of decolonisation, the colonised people has the right to choose from several options including the formation of an independent state, integration with the colonising state or a loose form of association with that state. But indigenous minorities are rarely in possession of a discrete area of territory so as to attract the operation of the principle as it is known in this context. Furthermore, there is no body in the international legal system to which claims of self-determination can readily be referred. Aboriginal groups have considered the International Court of Justice as a possible forum for resolution of their claims against white Australia, but the Court is only empowered to adjudicate claims between recognised nation states.[201] In 1978, after Mason J struck out his statement of claim, Paul Coe formally requested the International Court of Justice to intervene to prevent the Commonwealth from failing to protect Aboriginal lands on which the Queensland government had allowed bauxite mining. The response from the Registrar of the Court was simply that Coe had no standing to bring the action under the Court's Statute.[202]

Even the advent of the First Optional Protocol to the ICCPR, which provides a mechanism for individuals to bring complaints concerning violations of the Convenant, has not solved these problems. The ability merely to raise the question of what the principle of self-determination might entail for indigenous minorities is currently precluded. The Human Rights Committee, which considers communications brought by individuals under the First Optional Protocol, has decided that it cannot consider communications alleging violation of the right of self-determination under Article 1, on the basis that the Protocol only provides a mechanism for bringing complaints concerning violations of *individual* rights.[203] It is possible, however, for complaints to be brought on behalf of groups, if the individual rights of members of the group have been breached. Thus, for example, while the Committee refused to hear the issue of self-determination raised by a communication submitted by the Chief of the Lake Lubicon band of Indians from Alberta, Canada, it stated that the Chief could represent the band in complaints concerning breaches of Article 6 (the right to life), Article 7 (the prohibition on torture), Article 14 (criminal procedural rights) and Article 26 (equality before the law).[204] The Committee also found that the Chief could make complaints on behalf of the band for violations of Article 27,[205] which provides that 'In those States in which ethnic, religious or linguistic minorities exist, persons belonging to such minorities shall not be denied the right, in community with the other members of their group, to enjoy their own culture, to profess and practice their own religion, or to use their own language'. This article deals with rights which are held by individuals, although they are held in common with other members of a minority. It is therefore not subject to the Committee's concerns regarding Article 1.

Although Aboriginal and Islander groups have not yet used these international complaint procedures, they offer the possibility of direct international scrutiny of the failure of the Australian legal system to respond to Aboriginal claims and concerns. As Aboriginal rights campaigner Helen Corbett argued in the Boyer Lectures in 1993, international standards remain a 'safety net' for Aborigines, given the Australian tradition of recalcitrance over indigenous rights.[206]

Apart from the provisions of international human rights instruments, there is one formal international agreement which explicitly deals with the rights of indigenous peoples. International Labour Organisation (ILO) Convention 107, 'Protection and Integration of Indigenous and Other Tribal and Semi-tribal Populations in Independent Countries', was adopted in 1959. This instrument reflected contemporary approaches to indigenous minorities: its goal was to allow rapid assimilation of such groups into the non-indigenous population.[207] Australia never became a party to this Convention and was active when moves were made in the 1980s to revise it. Aboriginal groups also participated in the revision. The revised Convention, No. 169, 'Indigenous and Tribal Peoples of Independent Countries', respects the right of indigenous groups to maintain their culture and identity. It also recognises the importance of indigenous peoples' control over their own institutions and economic development.[208] The Australian government, along with other governments, insisted on the inclusion of a provision to prevent the use of the word 'peoples' in the Convention from bolstering any indigenous claims to self-determination at international law.[209] Australia has yet to ratify the Convention, although ratification was one of Australia's national objectives in 1993, the International Year of the World's Indigenous People.

Alongside the development of ILO Convention 169, the United Nations' Working Group on Indigenous Populations (UNWGIP) has been working for a decade to produce a Declaration on the Rights of Indigenous Peoples. Although the Declaration will not bind nations in the way that a treaty does, it will be an important development in the rights of indigenous peoples.[210] The latest available draft of the Declaration defines the right of self-determination for indigenous peoples as the right to 'freely determine their political status and institutions and freely pursue their economic, social and cultural development'.[211] The fullest form of 'external' self-determination, being the right to form an independent state, appears to be an impossibility for indigenous minorities. However, it may be that the Declaration will provide the basis for an agreement by the international community to an 'internal' right of self-determination, and help to define the content of such a right, which would entail some sort of control over health, education, land and resources and some measure of political autonomy.[212]

An 'internal' right of self-determination could also include some form of control over applicable laws and a measure of legal autonomy. This would produce a form of legal pluralism beyond the model of dominant and subordinate legal systems. As Frank Brennan has pointed out, the notion of legal self-determination requires much further thought and elaboration, including an accurate delimitation of its scope. Brennan is particularly concerned about the position in urbanised and some fringe-dwelling communities, where 'traditional' laws and authority structures have broken down under the assaults of white culture. He is also concerned about the ability of young people to reject the strict dictates of custom, regarding arranged marriages or initiation, for example, in favour of the greater freedom offered by modern Western culture.[213] This concern reflects the commonly raised question as to whose voices are included in the notion of self-determination.[214] Because of these difficulties Brennan offers only qualified support for the recommendations of the Royal Commission into Aboriginal Deaths in Custody, which identified as central to any strategy designed to improve the position of Australia's indigenous people the relinquishing of non-Aboriginal control over many aspects of Aboriginal life.[215]

Nevertheless, a move towards greater legal pluralism in Australia seems inevitable. The Murray Islands case took a first step in rejecting the legal fiction of *terra nullius* as the basis for the introduction of the English legal system. Both the Australian Law Reform Commission report on recognition of customary law and the Royal Commission into Aboriginal Deaths in

Custody made detailed recommendations on how Anglo-Australian law might better accommodate Aboriginal law and culture. Domestic moves towards reconciliation, the continuing evolution of overseas models of indigenous self-government and international legal norms concerning the rights of indigenous peoples, and the possible application of a form of 'internal' self-determination to indigenous minorities, all serve to move Australia to implement and build on those recommendations.

Further reading

Representations of Aboriginal law and society

Maddock, Kenneth *The Australian Aborigines: a portrait of their society*, Penguin, Ringwood, 2nd edn, 1982

The legal basis and consequences of European settlement

Cassidy, Julie 'A reappraisal of Aboriginal policy in colonial Australia: imperial and colonial instruments and legislation recognising the special rights and status of the Australian Aboriginals' (1989) 10 *Journal of Legal History*, 35

Gilbert, Kevin *Living black: blacks talk to Kevin Gilbert*, Penguin, Ringwood, 1977

Hocking, Barbara 'Does Aboriginal law now run in Australia?' (1979) 10 *Federal Law Review*, 16

Hookey, John 'The Gove land rights case: a judicial dispensation for the taking of Aboriginal lands in Australia?' (1977) 5 *Federal Law Review*, 85

Jennings, R.Y. *The acquisition of territory in international law*, Manchester University Press, Manchester, 1963

Miller, James *Koori: a will to win: the heroic resistance and triumph of black Australia*, Angus & Robertson, Sydney, 1985

The Murray Islands case

Lumb, R. D. 'Native title to land in Australia: recent High Court decisions' (1993) 42 *International and Comparative Law Quarterly*, 84

Symposium: Indigenous peoples: issues for the nineties (1993) 16(1) *University of New South Wales Law Journal*

Symposium: *Mabo v the State of Queensland* (1993) 15(2) *Sydney Law Review*

Towards accommodation?

Bird, Greta *The process of law in Australia: intercultural perspectives*, Butterworths, Sydney, 2nd edn, 1993

Blay, S. K. N. 'The international covenant on civil and political rights and the recognition of customary law practices of indigenous tribes: the case of Australian Aborigines' (1986) 19 *Comparative and International Law Journal of South Africa*, 199

Maddock, Ken *Your land is our land: Aboriginal land rights*, Penguin, Ringwood, 1983

McLachlan, C. 'The recognition of Aboriginal customary law: pluralism beyond

the colonial paradigm' (1988) 37 *International and Comparative Law Quarterly*, 368
Peterson, N. and Langton, M. eds *Aborigines, land and land rights*, Australian Institute of Aboriginal Studies, Canberra, 1983
Wright, J. *We call for a treaty*, Collins/Fontana, Sydney, 1985

Part two

2

Themes in liberal legal and constitutional theory

David Wood, Rosemary Hunter and Richard Ingleby

One of the major themes of chapter 1 was the tension between the legal systems in existence in Australia before Cook and the system which was introduced with European settlement. This chapter examines some of the important features of the Anglo-Australian legal system. This issue can be approached on a number of levels. The first level, that of political philosophy, involves consideration of fundamental moral and political values, such as justice, liberty, autonomy, privacy, tolerance, prosperity, welfare, efficiency, stability, security and order. The second level, that of constitutional theory, involves consideration of the constitutional features that safeguard and promote these chosen values, such as the separation of powers, responsible government, parliamentary sovereignty, a bill of rights, judicial review and federalism. The third level is the level of functions, structures and design of institutions such as the political executive, the bureaucracy, the legislature and the judiciary. The most important question at the third level is that of the legal regime which best ensures the continuity, health and vitality of the political regime recommended by theorising at the previous two levels. Finally, Australian constitutional lawyers have devoted much attention to a fourth level, examining particular legal rules, constitutions, legislation and court decisions. This is the level where technical legal skills become most relevant. The previous levels have tended to fall within the realm of 'jurisprudence', which requires a different set of skills in abstract reasoning (described further below).

The approaching centenary of Federation has focused attention on the levels of political philosophy and constitutional theory. In the past the failure of proposed constitutional amendments and difficulties over constitutional interpretation and reform have been related to the lack of an overall constitutional philosophy to provide context and justifications. For instance, the debate over the Senate's blocking of supply in 1975 raises questions about the varying roles for the Senate suggested by different theories of democracy. Likewise, questions about the scope of the Commonwealth's legislative powers, for instance the extent to which the external affairs power can be used to protect the environment and human rights, and the corporations power to introduce a national scheme of business regulation, might arise from rival models of federalism.

The dominant political philosophy in Western democracies such as the United Kingdom, the United States and Australia is liberalism. Liberal political philosophy is a product of the Enlightenment or 'age of reason', a period in the European history of ideas which spanned the late seventeenth and eighteenth centuries. That period marked the secularisation of Western societies, a shift from faith in divine revelation to faith in human reason as the basis of knowledge, the rise of scientific method, a belief that the natural world could be understood and mastered for human ends, and a corresponding belief in the idea of progress.[1] This chapter examines some of the implications of these ideas at the levels of political, legal and constitutional theory. It looks at the values that constitute liberalism, the concepts of the rule of law and equality, the relationship between law and morality, the separation of powers, responsible government and federalism.

What is a liberal?

The term 'liberalism' encompasses a spectrum of philosophical positions, ranging from 'laissez faire' liberalism and libertarianism, through rights-based liberalism and utilitarianism, to 'welfare' liberalism.[2] Laissez faire liberalism, which developed in Western Europe from the mid-eighteenth to the mid-nineteenth century, was primarily concerned with the protection of the individual[3] against the state. It viewed the state as the main threat to individual freedom and autonomy. Until well into the nineteenth century, many European states were made up of a monarchy and/or a landowning elite, whose authority derived from inherited wealth and social status. As emerging middle classes struggled for political power corresponding to their economic position, they began to invoke individualistic concepts of democracy, which were at odds with status-based assumptions about individual worth which had previously prevailed. In 1859, in his famous treatise *On Liberty*, the English philosopher John Stuart Mill articulated the principle that:

> ... the only purpose for which power can be rightfully exercised over any member of a civilised community, against his will, is to prevent harm to others ... The only part of the conduct of any one, for which he is amenable to society, is that which concerns others. In the part which merely concerns himself, his independence is, of right, absolute.

Modern libertarians are closest to the laissez faire liberals of the nineteenth century in seeing the state as, at best, a necessary evil, to be limited to such functions as maintaining order, punishing crime, protecting property, enforcing contracts and perhaps providing a minimum level of social infrastructure such as roads, drains and ports.[4] Libertarians place a strong emphasis on property rights, seeing in property the main bulwark against oppression by the state.[5] The right to personal property appears most prominently in the writings of the United States theorist Robert Nozick. Nozick argues that individuals cannot be justly deprived by the state of anything which they have justly acquired. For example, it is wrong for the state to finance hospitals through taxation of personal earnings. For Nozick, too, the right to property refers to *private* property. As illustrated in the discussion of the Murray Islands case in chapter 1, however, private ownership is not the only possible form of property.

Utilitarianism, which dates from the late eighteenth century and whose leading exponent was the English philosopher Jeremy Bentham, is concerned primarily with the maximisation of happiness. Bentham urged the application of his 'felicific calculus' in evaluating the action to be taken in any particular situation. That is, one should calculate the totality of the consequences of a proposed action in terms of the happiness and unhappiness of every person who might be affected by it, and decide what action would produce the greatest overall happiness.[6] Utilitarianism remains highly influential in the arena of political decision making. Australian governments frequently invoke utilitarian considerations in developing policy and framing legislation,[7] and often seek to justify decisions in terms of overall community welfare.

There are three common objections to utilitarian liberalism. The first is that it is purely aggregative, that there is no direct concern with the distribution of happiness. For example, would we prefer a society where 999,999 people had one notional unit of happiness and one person had two million units, or a society where one million people each had two units? Utilitarians reply that, because each person counts equally in their calculus, gross inequalities are unlikely to occur. Yet this concedes that unequal distributions *may* occur (however unlikely). Should we admit this, or should we refuse to permit any inequalities at all? The second objection is that the calculus itself is a fiction, that happiness (or any other single currency) cannot accommodate the great number of criteria that might be relevant to a decision. For example, some of the values mentioned in the introduction to this chapter, such as justice, tolerance, efficiency and order, cannot easily be subsumed under the notion of happiness. Does this mean that these values should be ignored in decision making? The third common objection is that the calculus treats individuals instrumentally; there is no concept of individual rights to protect an individual against the majority. What if the happiness of 17,000,000 Australians would be increased by the death of the 17,000,001st? Concerns about the effects of majoritarianism are relevant, for example, in the context of the Native Title Act, discussed in chapter 1. Is it a sufficient objection to the legislation that it decreases the happiness of a greater proportion of the population than the proportion whose happiness it increases?

Before proceeding with the description of liberalism, it is possible to make an observation about jurisprudential method. The previous paragraph is a typical example. It begins by enumerating the points to be made ('three common objections'). The discussion then outlines each argument and tests one of them by setting a counter-argument against it. Hypothetical examples are used to illustrate the consequences of particular points being accepted or denied. By the end of the paragraph all of the arguments and counter-arguments have been worked through, leaving the impression of a complete system of reasoning (there are no *other* arguments available). Having exhausted the issue of utilitarianism, the next point is taken up.

The last criticism of utilitarianism objected to its lack of respect for individual rights. While utilitarianism is primarily concerned with the common good or general welfare, rights-based liberalism is based on concepts of individual rights and treats some basic principles of justice as non-negotiable. John Rawls' 'theory of justice' is one of the most influential modern conceptions of rights-based liberalism. Rawls constructs his model by using the method of hypothetical reasoning referred to above. He uses the concept of the 'original position' where individuals have to decide the basic assumptions under which society should be organised and continue to be organised, while having no knowledge of the position which they will occupy or the attributes they will possess in that society. Rawls argues that the principles which would emerge from that position are:

> First: each person is to have an equal right to the most extensive basic liberty compatible with a similar liberty for others.
> Second: social and economic inequalities are to be arranged so that they are both (a) reasonably expected to be to everyone's advantage, and (b) attached to positions and offices open to all.[8]

For Rawls, the basic liberties are:

> political liberty (the right to vote and be eligible for public office) together with freedom of speech and assembly; liberty of conscience and freedom of thought; freedom of the person along with the right to hold (personal) property; and freedom from arbitrary arrest and seizure as defined by the concept of the rule of law.[9]

Rawls' basic liberties are all classic civil and political rights which have been invoked and referred to on countless occasions. The right to freedom of speech and the concept of the rule of law are considered further below. Rawls does admit that there will be social and economic inequalities but, according to his second principle, measures will not be adopted unless they provide some advantage to the least well off.[10] Welfare liberals go further in their concern with the position of the least well off, seeking to reduce social and economic inequalities rather than accepting them as unavoidable.

While also concerned with the threat to individual autonomy posed by state power, welfare liberalism holds that the negative liberty of laissez faire liberalism, the absence of interference and coercion by the state, is a limited ideal. Negative liberty ignores those who lack sufficient property or resources to fulfil their plans and projects, to lead meaningful and satisfying lives.

Welfare liberalism is concerned as much with well-being and equality of life chances as with negative liberty. It attacks laissez faire liberalism for taking existing distributions of property as given, and so ignoring the need for redistribution by taxation, social security, equal opportunity or even affirmative action legislation. Whereas laissez faire liberalism provides little for those poorly positioned by the existing distribution of property, welfare liberalism offers the promise of a better life in a more egalitarian society. In reply, laissez faire liberals argue that they, too, are concerned with a better life for all, but that this is more likely to be achieved in a free market than by the redistributive efforts of a welfare state.

Secondly, welfare liberalism is concerned with concentrations of power in the private sector as well as in the state.[11] It recognises the need to protect individuals as much from the former as from the latter. In particular, it is concerned with the power of the modern business corporation. The use and enforcement of legislation in such areas as industrial relations, consumer affairs, safety and environmental matters are rejected by laissez faire liberals as an interference with the rights of individual producers, consumers, employers and employees. A welfare liberal would question the extent to which consumers and employees have genuine freedom of choice in the contexts of purchasing and employment. An implication of these two points is that welfare liberalism takes a less suspicious attitude towards the state. While the state's capacity to oppress individuals is recognised, it is seen more as an instrument of social justice, having the capacity through taxation to redistribute wealth into such areas as education, health and social welfare. It is also viewed as a concentration of power which can be used to protect individuals against exercises of power within the private sphere of civil society.

Differing conceptions of the state and individual rights are reflected in the judgments of members of the High Court in *Australian Capital Television Pty Ltd v The Commonwealth*.[12] The case concerned the validity of legislation regulating the use of electronic media for political broadcasts. The *Political Broadcasts and Political Disclosures Act 1991* (Cwlth) sought to prohibit most forms of political advertising during an election period. One of the questions the Court had to consider was whether the Commonwealth Constitution, by establishing a system of representative government, also established an implied right to freedom of expression in relation to political affairs. Mason CJ found that freedom of communication was 'so indispensable to the efficacy of the system of representative government for which the Constitution makes provision that it is necessarily implied in the making of that provision',[13] a view which was broadly supported by Brennan, Deane, Toohey, Gaudron and McHugh JJ.[14] The majority therefore used the concept of individual rights to prevent Parliament from legislating to regulate access to the electronic media.

The contrary view was expressed by Dawson J, who saw the rights implied by the majority as derogating from the fundamental principle of parliamentary sovereignty:

[T]hose responsible for the drafting of the Constitution saw constitutional guarantees of freedom as exhibiting a distrust of the democratic process. They preferred to place their trust in Parliament to preserve the nature of our society and regarded as undemocratic guarantees which fettered its powers.[15]

The decision illustrates the liberal paradox. The holding of the majority relies on the notion of freedom of communication, but in practice enables communication to be bought and sold by a limited number of actors—those individuals who can afford to purchase radio and television stations, and those political parties that can afford to purchase advertising time. A libertarian would approve of the decision, but a welfare liberal might be more concerned about the distribution of media ownership and funding for political parties.

In his dissent Dawson J emphasised the separation of powers (a liberal constitutional principle discussed further below) and referred to the absence in Australia of a Bill of Rights. In the United States, a series of Constitutional Amendments have enshrined a set of constitutionally guaranteed individual rights. The framers of the Commonwealth Constitution, however, chose not to follow the United States model of constitutionally guaranteed rights. The possibility of enacting an Australian Bill of Rights in some form has become a topic of debate in recent years. The question at the level of consitutional theory is: would it be better to have a constitutionally entrenched Bill of Rights, or to leave it to the High Court to find implied rights in the existing Constitution, or, as Dawson J suggests, to trust in parliamentary democracy to safeguard individual rights and freedoms?

A final concern of liberals of all shades is the so-called 'public/private' distinction.[16] As noted earlier, liberals have observed the historical tendency of states to intrude oppressively into all aspects of people's lives. In order to check this tendency liberals see a need for some positive protection of individuals' private activities from state interference. The notion that the state ought not to intrude into individuals' private affairs assumes some kind of demarcation between a public sphere, which may be regulated, and a private sphere, which ought to be free of regulation. One attempt to draw this line involves a distinction between the state (the public sector) and civil society (the community and private enterprise). Another version involves a demarcation between what goes on outside the home (the market and political life) and inside the home (the family). The public/private distinction in liberal thought raises a number of questions. For example, is it possible, or desirable, to enforce a sharp dichotomy between public and private? What are the consequences of designating an area as private? These questions are considered further in the critiques of liberalism—in particular the feminist critiques—discussed in chapter 4.

The rule of law and the concept of equality

In addition to individual liberty (whether positive or negative) and the public/private distinction, a central tenet of liberalism is the rule of law. And, just as there is no single definition of liberalism, the phrase 'rule of law' is elusive.[17] The standard comparison is between the rule of law and 'the rule of men', between the supposedly stable, impartial, general, measured and ordered nature of the former and the idiosyncratic, arbitrary or capricious nature of the latter. Three interpretations of the 'rule of law' are considered here: law and order, the 'inner morality' of law, and formal equality before the law.[18] This last concept may be contrasted with substantive equality,[19] which is also discussed in this section.

The first interpretation of the rule of law refers to 'any state of law and order as opposed to anarchy'.[20] The rule of law in this sense is identified with the mere existence of law. Indeed, it may be asked why 'law *and order*' is required. The answer seems to be that the emphasis is on 'order' rather than 'law'. It is 'order' not 'law' that is the antonym of 'anarchy'. It is with order rather than law that those enamoured with the phrase 'law and order' are most concerned. Faced with a stark choice between order without law and law with some degree of disorder, their preference is for the former.[21] For example, law and order proponents would argue that it is better for police to be given sufficient flexibility to fight crime in the most effective way than to have police investigations fettered by numerous rules concerning the rights of suspects and accused persons.

By contrast, the United States legal philosopher Lon Fuller put forward one of the most influential arguments elaborating the rule of law in terms of the *obligations* of law makers and law enforcers rather than their *powers* to ensure social order. Fuller argued that if law was to fulfil its purpose of subjecting human conduct to the governance of rules it must necessarily adhere to a number of principles,[22] which constitute the 'inner morality of law'.[23] First, laws must consist of general rules which are addressed to the population at large, rather than to particular individuals. Second, laws must be publicly promulgated so that individuals may be aware of their existence. Third, laws must be prospective. Laws can only regulate conduct if they are directed to future behaviour.[24] It is unfair for actions that were lawful at the time they were taken to be rendered unlawful at a later date.[25] Fourth, laws must be clear so that individuals can be aware of the extent of their obligations. Fifth, laws must be free from contradiction, so that people are not compelled to break one rule in complying with another. Sixth, laws cannot require the humanly impossible. Seventh, laws must be reasonably constant through time so that people can plan their lives with some degree of certainty. Eighth, the law should be enforced as it is enacted and promulgated. In other words, legal officials such as judges and police should perform their functions according to law—and legal redress should be available if they fail to do so. This constitutes an important safeguard for individuals against arbitrary exercises of state power.

Fuller saw these principles as a set of moral requirements, concerned not with substantive legal rules[26] but with the just operation of the legal order. Fuller did not claim that it was essential for a legal system to fulfil all the requirements in order for it to be classified as a legal system. He drew a distinction between the morality of duty, 'the basic rules without which an ordered society is impossible',[27] and the morality of aspiration, a morality 'of the fullest realisation of human powers'. Failure to meet a morality of aspiration was 'shortcoming, not . . . wrongdoing'.[28] Fuller regarded the inner morality of law, with the exception of the requirements relating to the promulgation of law, as a morality of aspiration.

An implication of this is that there is no clear dividing line between systems that do and do not conform to Fuller's notion of inner morality. There are various legal values and principles which are instantiated to varying extents by different systems of rules. Below an unstated threshold level such systems do not warrant the appellation of 'system of law', but only 'system of government'.

The English philosopher H. L. A. Hart, whose aim of separating the definition of law from questions of morality is considered later in this chapter, questioned whether there was any value to the rule of law in Fuller's sense. He argued that one may as well refer to instructions for a poisoner as the 'morality of poisoning' and suggested that Fuller was blurring the distinction between efficiency and morality.[29] The modern English natural law theorist John Finnis agrees with Hart to the extent that a tyrant could pursue pernicious ends in accordance with the inner morality of law. For example: clear, general and prospective laws could be enacted which required children to inform the authorities if they heard their parents criticising the government. But Finnis argues that there is a deeper sense in which Fuller's concept of a reciprocity between governer and governed does have a moral value:

> A tyranny devoted to pernicious ends has no self-sufficient *reason* to submit itself to the discipline of [the inner morality of law] granted that the rational point of such self-discipline is the very value . . . which the tyrant . . . holds in contempt. Adherence to the Rule of Law . . . is always liable to reduce the efficiency for evil of an evil government, since it systematically restricts the government's freedom of manoeuvre.[30]

Another objection to Fuller's principles is that they do not go far enough. The eight principles do not necessarily guarantee equal access to the law, or that like cases will be treated alike. This leads to consideration of the third sense accorded to the rule of law, that of equality before the law.

The idea of equality before the law derives from the liberal insistence on the equal value of individuals. Formal equality before the law requires that official decisions be free from bias, and that they should only be made after a fair hearing. Decisions must not be arbitrary, like cases must be treated alike, and there must be rights of appeal to correct any errors in applying these principles. The adversary system of procedure embodies this version of the rule of law by constituting all litigants as formally equal. In court, all parties, be they wealthy individuals, poor individuals, corporations or governments, appear as equal 'legal persons', with responsibility for presenting their own case to an impartial adjudicator.

Allan Hutchinson illustrates the notion of formal equality with the story of a swimming carnival in which the swimmer who was declared the winner of one race was subsequently disqualified. The rules stated that the winner of a race is the first swimmer to touch the end of the pool with both hands. The swimmer who was disqualified had only one arm. Applying the rules equally to all contestants meant that he could not be a winner.[31]

The requirement of formal equality under the law excludes laws which discriminate against particular groups. To take an extreme example, it rules out slavery, at least as a matter of a distinct legal status, if not of brute social and economic fact. Formal legal equality also rules out special measures designed to assist disadvantaged groups. This narrow view of equality does not distinguish between the use of the law to strengthen further the position of already advantaged groups (for example apartheid laws) and the use of the law to help accelerate de facto equality (for example affirmative action laws to improve the employment prospects of the former victims of apartheid). Thus positive or benign discrimination in favour of disadvantaged groups is in principle contrary to the notion of legal equality, and hence to the rule of law, in the same way as invidious discrimination.

This formal view of equality is consistent with libertarian liberalism, which holds that any form of discrimination derogates from the rights or entitlements of individuals adversely affected by it. For example, affirmative action laws for the benefit of women and/or racial minorities who have been disadvantaged in the past are unfair to the white males whose current employment opportunities are thereby diminished. A welfare liberal's understanding of equality, by contrast, would positively require special measures to assist disadvantaged groups, especially where the effects of past discriminatory treatment cannot be expected simply to dissipate, but are likely to persist for a considerable time into the future unless strong action is taken. The same principle of equality which justifies equal treatment in the standard case justifies unequal treatment or special measures in exceptional cases.[32] This contrast highlights the tension within liberalism between liberty and equality. The libertarian desire to maximise liberty may involve sacrificing some equality, while the welfare liberal desire to maximise equality may result in the sacrifice of some liberty.

In this light, formal equality before the law represents no more than a minimum agreed standard. Like the law and order sense of the rule of law it ignores the fact that, far from being a bulwark against subjugation, the law 'may degenerate into a positive implement of oppression'[33] when despotically minded people can harness legal authority and institutional structures to achieve their ends. For example, a law which enables complaints about discrimination to be presented to a tribunal could be rendered useless if a million dollar filing fee were imposed, or if claims were required to be drafted in Latin.

In other words, it is difficult to discuss the question of equality before the law unless one directs attention to the social and economic context in which law is applied. Procedural justice and formal equality are only sufficient to secure substantive equality where there is background social equality. Indeed, formal equality is often a questionable good, because of its capacity to mask and perpetuate unequal social practices, as illustrated by famous aphorisms about the majesty of French law prohibiting both the rich and the poor from sleeping under the bridges of the Seine, and the English courts being open to all, like the Ritz Hotel.[34] Formal equalities may function for the benefit of all, but background social inequalities mean that they do not function for the *equal* benefit of all. Social and economic rights, as well as civil and political rights, are needed in order to achieve substantive equality. Feminist debates about the adequacy of the model of formal equality before the law, and other possible meanings of equality, are discussed further in chapter 4.

The relationship between law and morality

Fuller's attempt to define the rule of law in procedural terms, outlined in the previous section, was also an attempt to provide an answer to one of the major jurisprudential questions, that of the relationship between law and morality. Fuller's argument that his eight requirements constitute an 'inner morality of law', and that at least some of those elements must be present in a legal system in order for it to be valid, steers a course between the traditional positions of natural law theorists, who argue that human law is only valid if it conforms to natural law, and positivists, who argue that no element of moral value enters into the definition of law. These opposing positions are examined here.

Positivists such as H. L. A. Hart have been anxious to distinguish questions about the existence of a legal rule from questions about its moral value. As noted in the previous section, Hart disagrees even with Fuller's limited attempt to link law and morality. Positivists centrally hold that law is identified solely according to its source or pedigree. What makes a legal rule valid is that it has a certain history; for instance, its being contained in a statute passed by a competent legislature or its status as precedent. It is not identified by reference to moral considerations. As John Austin succinctly put it: 'The existence of law is one thing; its merits or demerits another'.[35] This is not to say that a legal rule cannot specifically provide for direct appeal to moral considerations. For instance, as noted in the previous chapter, s. 51(xxxi) of the Commonwealth Constitution requires that the compulsory acquisition of property by the Commonwealth be on 'just' terms. Another example occurs in the Family Law Act, which requires Family Court judges in resolving maintenance disputes to take account of 'any fact or circumstance which, in the opinion of the court, the justice of the case requires to be taken into account'.[36] The vital difference is that moral considerations are relevant in such circumstances not in their own right but only by virtue of a relevant legal rule.

Positivist philosophers defend the conceptual separation of law and morality because they fear that blurring the distinction can hamper the vital task of moral assessment and criticism. Hart argues, for example, that 'the elucidation of the concept of law, without reference to the moral values which it may be used to promote, seems to me to offer better guarantees of clear thought'.[37] The 'separation thesis' makes it possible to state that laws can be immoral, that there can be laws (conscription laws, for example) which generate no moral obligation to comply but on the contrary can create a moral obligation of non-compliance or even resistance. The separation thesis also serves the pragmatic function of enabling legal practitioners and law teachers to say what (they think) the law *is*, without committing themselves to a judgment of its merits.

Hart does not deny that there are general facts of the human condition (human vulnerability, approximate equality, limited altruism, limited resources and limited understanding and strength of will) from which follows 'a natural necessity' for certain minimum forms of protection for persons, property and promises.[38] However, he insists that the connection between law and morality is merely empirical, that although there historically have been relationships between particular laws and particular moral precepts, this is quite distinct from a conceptual connection.[39] Laws may express moral values, or they may bear no relation to moral values. Either way, their status as laws is unaffected.

By contrast, natural law philosophers hold that there is an unequivocal conceptual connection between law and morality. Natural law theory was referred to as one of the foundations of international law in chapter 1, but it has a much longer history.[40] Classical natural law doctrine was based on the idea of a law of nature, which was discoverable by reason and was universal and immutable. Its status as 'higher' law made it morally binding. Human laws were morally binding to the extent that they incorporated principles of natural law, and were not valid laws at all if they conflicted with those principles. The Roman orator Cicero summarised classical natural law doctrine as follows:

> True law is right reason in agreement with Nature; it is of universal application, unchanging and everlasting; it summons to duty by its commands, and averts from wrong-doing by its prohibitions . . . It is a sin to try to alter this law, nor is it allowable to attempt to repeal any part of it, and it is impossible to abolish it entirely. We cannot be freed from its obligations by Senate or People, and we need not look outside ourselves for an expounder or interpreter of it. And there will not be different laws at Rome and at Athens, or different laws now and in the future, but one eternal and unchangeable law will be valid for all nations and for all times . . .[41]

Natural law theory was later adapted by the Christian church, which incorporated the claim that natural law was God-given. In the late eighteenth century, natural law theory was used as a powerful political tool by the

American and French revolutionaries. In the Declaration of Independence (1776), the American colonists avowed:

> We hold these truths to be self evident: that all men are created equal; that they are endowed by their Creator with certain inalienable rights; that among these are life, liberty and the pursuit of happiness; . . . that whenever any form of government becomes destructive of these ends, it is the right of the people to alter or abolish it, and to institute new government, laying its foundation on such principles, and organising its powers in such form, as to them shall seem most likely to effect their safety and happiness.

The French revolutionaries, too, insisted that liberty and equality were fundamental 'rights of man'. The international law of human rights and concepts such as 'crimes against humanity' have developed from this natural law basis. The emphasis on individual rights and equality suggests that a close association has grown between natural law theory and liberalism.

Yet the author of the most recent formulation of natural law theory, John Finnis, draws on earlier classical and Christian models, such as Aristotle and St Thomas Aquinas, rather than on liberal principles or thinkers.[42] Finnis's starting point is the existence of a number of 'basic goods'. These are life, knowledge, play, aesthetic experience, friendship, religion and practical reasonableness. Practical reasonableness is the type of reasoning we should use to make decisions about how to act and to order our lives. Hence it is the means by which we should pursue the other basic goods. Finnis argues that these seven items are the basic forms of human flourishing and that, as such, they are universal and unchanging. The value of these goods is not something that can be established by scientific proof. Rather, their value is self-evident to any human being who engages in reasoned reflection upon human existence.

Finnis then argues that a system of legal rules is needed to ensure the existence of a society in which human beings can co-operate and co-ordinate their activities in pursuit of the basic goods. Law is the only alternative to unanimity or anarchy. The uniqueness of each human being makes unanimity impractical, while anarchy is not a condition in which basic goods can be pursued. Law is therefore a system of rules which (inter alia) is 'directed to reasonably resolving any of the community's co-ordination problems . . . for the common good of that community'.[43] Lawmakers must act in accordance with practical reasonableness, but this restriction still leaves them with considerable discretion in routine matters, such as which side of the road motorists should drive on, or whether to impose a goods and services tax. So long as law fulfils the purpose of enabling pursuit of the basic goods in a rational way, it is implicit in Finnis's argument that the law should be obeyed.[44] The obligation to obey the law exists up to the point when a particular law or legal system is so unjust that it no longer serves the purpose of enabling pursuit of the basic goods, in which case it no longer deserves the name of law.[45]

The separation of powers

Earlier sections of this chapter have considered some of the assumptions which underlie the Anglo-Australian legal system at the levels of political philosophy and constitutional theory. A further constitutional doctrine, which is often considered to be as much a defining characteristic of liberal legal and political systems as the rule of law, is that of the separation of powers. The doctrine of the separation of powers is usually taken to refer to a system of government where different aspects of governmental power are dispersed between different bodies. Two main questions concerning this doctrine are its justification and its definition.[46] Neither of these questions has a simple answer. The specific justification put forward influences the particular shape of the doctrine.

This section considers various justifications for the standard form of the doctrine of the separation of powers, which distinguishes between executive, legislative and judicial power. The most obvious justification lies in the dangers inherent in concentrating the totality of the power of the state in one person or organisation or institution. In the words of Lord Acton's famous dictum, 'Power corrupts, and absolute power corrupts absolutely'. The implicit idea is that the more widely state power is distributed the better. Institutional arrangements which disperse power are to be preferred to arrangements which centralise it. The argument which arises from the desirability of power being dispersed supports not just the separation of powers but other divisions of power. It is equally an argument for a federal system of government, and temporal restraints on the accumulation of power which prevent certain political officers, for example United States presidents and governors, from holding power for more than a certain period.

The doctrine of the separation of powers relies on and helps to create distinctions between different types of political power (which require different types of institutions and personnel). As noted above, it is standard now to distinguish between legislative, executive and judicial power, but there is nothing magical about this trinity. With the tremendous growth of the modern state, some suggest a further distinction between the political executive and the administration or bureaucracy.

But, to remain with legislative, executive and judicial power, the obvious question arises of how each type of power is to be defined. Executive power is sometimes viewed as raw power. It exists in its purest form in the case of the absolute ruler or tyrant. It is central to the idea of the rule of law, however, that executive power should exist only if it has a firm legal basis—whether this lies in a constitution, legislation, judicial decisions or some combination of these. An alternative and more limited view of executive power sees it as the administrative and bureaucratic power to apply and enforce rules, in contrast with the legislative power to make general rules. The separation of executive and legislative power therefore requires an institutional separation between the executive and legislature.[47]

One problem with this formulation is the place of executive 'policy', which is a form of rule making. Another is the problem of subordinate legislation, where the legislature delegates its law-making power to the executive, so as not to be overwhelmed by the sheer volume of legislation required by the modern state. For example, the *Migration Act 1958* (Cwlth) contains the bare bones of Australia's immigration scheme, and enables detailed criteria to be specified in regulations. The Migration Regulations 1993 determine the entitlements of people in a way which is difficult to conceive of as being anything other than legislative. Moreover, the regulations are supplemented by a *Procedures Advice Manual, Policy Control Instructions*, and *Administrative Circulars*, for use by decision makers. In this situation the separation of powers between legislature and executive has become hopelessly blurred. Giving different names to legal rules emanating from the legislature and the executive does not disguise the fact that they are both making law. The claim that only the legislature has an inherent or primary right to make legal rules, and that the legal rule-making capacity of executive bodies is delegated, derivative or secondary, does not entirely solve the problem either. The increasing tendency for executive bodies to legislate has been identified by Roberto Unger as a feature of the 'post-liberal' state. Unger's argument is included in the discussion of critical legal studies in chapter 4.

Judicial power is usually described as the power to adjudicate disputes according to the pre-existing legal rights of the parties concerned. In order to adjudicate, it is inevitable that courts are required to interpret legal rules, whether made by parliament, the executive or another court. This raises the question of where the line lies between applying existing law and making new law.[48] Judicial law making may be questioned on the grounds that it is an exercise of legislative rather than judicial power, and therefore infringes the separation of powers. One rationalisation of this problem is to treat the legislature as having tacitly delegated certain law-making power to courts but retained the final say in its capacity to legislatively overrule judge-made law. Of course, this is not applicable in the case of constitutional adjudication, where courts make decisions about parliaments' legislative competence. It may be suggested that in such cases the final say lies with the people, through their capacity to amend the constitution. However, this is not necessarily a convincing reply. Procedures for amending the Commonwealth Constitution, for example, are cumbersome and militate against change.[49]

The doctrine of the separation of powers contains somewhat contradictory notions of independence and checks and balances. In the case of the judiciary, the notion of independence is given prominence, and an independent judiciary is held up as an ideal. It is much less usual to think there is any need to 'check' or 'balance' the power of the judiciary, although growing demands for judicial accountability, and calls for legislatures to override controversial judicial decisions, must be noted. By contrast, the independence of the executive is never set up as an ideal. Far from being independent, it is the power of the executive that pre-eminently needs to be 'checked' and 'balanced'. Checks and balances on the power of the legislature may take several forms. Firstly, there are constraints to maintain the representative nature of the legislature, which is usually achieved by means of a constitutional or legislative requirement for regular elections. Secondly, there are 'bill of rights' restraints to protect the infringement of individual and minority rights from a possible 'tyranny of the majority'. As noted earlier, while liberal democracies such as Canada and the United States do have constitutionally entrenched bills of rights, such restraints do not exist in written constitutional form in Australia, although the High Court has recently found some such restraints implicit in the Constitution or the common law. Thirdly, there are federal restraints, to protect the legislative power of legislatures at one level (e.g. regional) from encroachment by the other (e.g. central). The checks and balances imposed on the executive by the doctrine of responsible government are considered in the following section, while Australian federalism is discussed in the final section of the chapter.

Responsible government

The doctrine of responsible government holds that the executive is responsible to the legislature, which in turn is responsible to the electorate. The doctrine is otherwise known as the Westminster system of government, since it is based on the model of the English parliament at Westminster. In Australia, there is some debate as to whether the executive is responsible only to the lower house of parliament or to both houses. On the one hand, both houses are elected (unlike the English House of Lords). On the other hand, the government is formed from the party having a majority of seats in the lower house. Government ministers are responsible to parliament for their portfolios, through the capacity of members of parliament to call ministers to account by directing questions to them during question time. The government as a whole is collectively responsible to parliament by the requirement that it have the confidence of the lower house. If the government loses a no-confidence motion in the lower house it is obliged to resign.

Executive power in Australia is technically vested in the Crown (the Governor-General and the State Governors).[50] The theory of responsible government requires, however, that the Crown act only on and in accordance with the advice of ministers who are responsible to parliament.[51] The theory bestows on the legislature the function of controlling the executive. If the Crown could act as it wished there would be no democracy.

The theory of responsible government is embodied in constitutional conventions rather than in formal legal rules. That is, the practices of responsible government are carried out by all concerned by convention rather than by positive law. This raises questions regarding the precise scope of the conventions, and the extent to which they are binding. These questions were raised sharply by the events of 11 November 1975, when the Australian Governor-General, Sir John Kerr, 'sacked' the Labor prime minister, Gough Whitlam, and replaced him with a caretaker prime minister, the Liberal Malcolm Fraser, until a general election could be held. Kerr argued that he was obliged to act in a situation of constitutional crisis, in which the Senate was refusing to pass the Labor government's supply Bills, raising the possibility that the government would soon have no money to run the country. On the other hand, the government still had the confidence of the House of Representatives, and when Malcolm Fraser was installed as prime minister a vote of no-confidence was immediately passed against him in the House of Representatives, which the Governor-General refused to acknowledge. Moreover, rather than acting only on the advice of responsible ministers (Whitlam and his government), Kerr acted independently in taking advice from the Chief Justice of the High Court, Sir Garfield Barwick, and also in acting on the advice he sought from Fraser to call an election.

One interpretation of these events is that Kerr was acting legally in accordance with the written Constitution.[52] This interpretation elevates the written Constitution over the unwritten conventions that surround it. The preference for written rules derives from the positivist emphasis on rules that have the requisite pedigree to count as law. Another interpretation is that Kerr staged a revolution in blatant disregard of constitutional conventions.[53] On this view, Kerr's action was a breach of the rule of law. A third interpretation is that Kerr's actions had the effect of *modifying* the existing conventions.[54] That is, after 1975 the theory of responsible government must be taken to mean that the Crown must ordinarily act in accordance with the advice of responsible ministers, but may do otherwise in exceptional circumstances. This interpretation is also consistent with a positivist approach which determines rules by reference to actual events. For example, in international law one source of legal rules is the actual practice of states in relation to a given matter (such as the 'modified' version of *terra nullius* discussed in chapter 1). Here, then, the practice of relevant actors is allowed to shape the meaning of responsible government. A criticism of this approach is that it simply provides a justification for what happened, and avoids difficult moral questions about the correctness of Kerr's actions.

Apart from the problem of the role of the Crown in the theory of responsible government, the main criticism of responsible government is that the huge growth of government in recent decades has meant that government departments have in reality become quasi-autonomous bureaucratic empires, beyond the effective control of ministers.[55] The traditional means of parliamentary scrutiny of executive action, such as committees and question time, and judicial review of administrative decision making to prevent unlawful action by the bureaucracy, are insufficient. There have been strenuous attempts to remedy the problem through the various elements of the 'new administrative law', which include expanded grounds of judicial review,[56] administrative appeals tribunals, grievance mechanisms such as ombudsmen, and freedom of information provisions. The most effective mix of political and legal controls is a continuing question.

Federalism

It was mentioned above that underlying the doctrine of the separation of powers is the fear of undue concentration of the power of the state. Separating different types of state power—executive, legislative, judicial—is one method of dispersing power. Another method is geographical, through a system of different levels of government, for instance national, regional and local. There are also reasons of efficiency for such 'vertical' as well as 'horizontal' dispersal of state power. More importantly, it can be supported by democratic considerations. Federalism is more a matter of constitutional design than political principle. It takes as given goals such as dispersal of state power, citizen participation in state decision making, and administrative efficiency, and is concerned with the means to achieve these ends.

The liberal concept of democracy requires that political decisions are wherever possible made by those affected by them, which in turn requires that decisions be made at the appropriate level, whether national, regional or local. Of course, this raises the question of how political issues and decisions are to be classified. Very few can be neatly fitted into one of these three categories. Indeed, to draw the line at three categories itself smacks of arbitrariness. Most decisions have ramifications at different levels. The decision to locate a chemical incineration plant, or a prison, in a particular locality is obviously a matter which affects that locality. But the issue of where to locate it arises only on the assumption that there is a regional or national need for such facilities.

Once a distinction between different levels of government is granted, the question arises of the relation between them. For convenience (at the risk of compounding the arbitrariness), attention in this section is restricted to the levels of national and regional government.

Three very different models may be proposed. According to the unitary model, the national government is dominant. It has total control over regional governments, which function very much as 'branch offices'. There are no regional legislatures or separate regional courts. New Zealand and the United Kingdom are both examples of unitary models of government. In contrast, according to the federal model, national and regional governments are to a certain extent independent from each other. Each has a distinct constitutional existence. There are separate legislatures and courts. The United States, Canada and Australia all have federal forms of government. In the third model, regional governments are dominant although there is a point at which a federation ceases to exist, and becomes a confederation if it does not completely disintegrate. The former Soviet Union and former Yugoslavia are obvious examples of disintegration. The European Union, by contrast, is an example of national governments moving closer to federation.

The crucial question for a federal system is the nature of the independent constitutional levels of government, of the safeguards against government at one level from encroaching on government at the other levels. Some form of constitutional entrenchment of the legislative powers to be exercised at each level is required, which in turn requires a written constitution to set out the distribution of powers, and a central court to interpret the constitution. This makes judicial review of legislative action an inescapable feature of federal systems. The political broadcasts case discussed earlier in this chapter is an example of the High Court finding that a particular piece of legislation was beyond the legislative power of the Commonwealth.

One question raised by the need for a constitutional court is where that court is to stand in the hierarchy. On the one hand, it must be a national court, which means that it is not surprising that constitutional courts in federal systems tend to favour central as against regional governments. On the other hand, because it has to adjudicate between national and regional interests and concerns, it must be independent.[57]

A further, though not essential, feature of many federal systems is representation of the regions in the central parliament. For instance, the Australian Senate was established, in part, as a States' house, each State being provided with equal representation.[58] In fact, the domination of a national party system has been such that the Senate has never performed this role. However, some argue that, from the point of view of federalism, this is not necessarily a fact to be lamented. Representation of the regions in the central parliament is no more required by or even consistent with federalism than representation of the centre in regional parliaments.[59] The democratic underpinnings of federalism are also compromised by equal representation of the States in the Australian Senate, as equal representation gives greater value to the votes of citizens of the smaller States than to those of citizens of the more populous States. The Senate may be more democratic than the House of Lords, but it is less so than the House of Representatives which is elected on the basis of 'one person one vote'. This point leads back to the question raised in the previous section as to whether the theory of responsible government in Australia requires the federal executive to be responsible to both houses of the federal parliament, or only to the House of Representatives.

The third ground for federalism noted above, that of efficiency, is also open to question in Australia. Clearly, even in unitary systems there is always more than one layer of government. In the United Kingdom, for example, local government plays a significant role in the delivery of a range of services. Nevertheless, it seems grossly inefficient to have so many parliaments and bureaucracies in such a small country as Australia. It is far from efficient to have the operations of national businesses governed by six different laws in six different States (for example, different defamation laws applying to the media), to be unable to develop a national strategy on some issues (such as the environment), to have constant disputes between the States and the federal government over their respective responsibilities—which might only be resolved by expensive High Court challenges (for example legislative responses to the Murray Islands case)—and to have the federal and State governments passing the buck to each other on other matters (such as implementation of the Australian Law Reform Commission's report on the recognition of Aboriginal customary law or the recommendations of the

Royal Commission into Aboriginal Deaths in Custody). Again, new structures have been put in place to deal with these problems, such as mutual recognition between the States in certain areas of regulation and regular meetings between State and federal ministers to arrive at consistent strategies. In practice, then, some areas of decision making are removed from the local level in the interests of efficiency.

It appears that the federal model adopted in the 1890s by the founders of the Australian Constitution is not able to achieve very effectively the goals of dispersal of state power, citizen participation in state decision making and administrative efficiency. Any revision of the federal system or broader rewriting of the Constitution should involve a rethinking and re-evaluation of its underlying philosophical principles and values. The next chapter considers legal philosophies that are consistent with but have different emphases from the dominant liberal paradigm. Rather than pursuing the political values of liberty, equality, the rule of law and the separation of powers, these theories are interested in the values of economic efficiency and social cohesion respectively.

Further reading

Liberalism, the rule of law and the concept of equality

Berlin, Isiah *Four essays on liberty*, Oxford University Press, Oxford, 1969
Bottomley, Stephen, Gunningham, Neil and Parker, Stephen *Law in context*, Federation Press, Sydney, 1991
Dworkin, Ronald *A matter of principle*, Harvard University Press, Cambridge, Mass., 1985
Ely, John Hart *Democracy and distrust*, Harvard University Press, Cambridge, Mass., 1982
Gaze, Beth and Jones, Melinda *Law, liberty and Australian democracy*, Law Book Co., Sydney, 1990
Tucker, David *An essay on liberalism: looking left and right*, Kluwer, Dordrecht, 1994

The relationship between law and morality

Davies, Margaret *Asking the law question*, Law Book Co., Sydney, 1994
Hart, H. L. A. *Law, liberty and morality*, Oxford University Press, Oxford, 1963
Honore, Tony 'The dependence of morality on law' (1993) 13 *Oxford Journal of Legal Studies* 1
Fuller, Lon L. 'Positivism and fidelity to law—a reply to Professor Hart' (1958) 71 *Harvard Law Review* 630
MacCormick, Neil 'Natural law reconsidered' (1981) 1 *Oxford Journal of Legal Studies*

The separation of powers, responsible government and federalism

Archer, Jeffrey and Maddox, Graham 'The 1975 constitutional crisis in Australia' (1976) 14 *Journal of Commonwealth and Comparative Politics* 14

Detmold, M. J. *The Australian Commonwealth: a fundamental analysis of its constitution*, Law Book Co., Sydney, 1988

Galligan, Brian ed. *Australian federalism*, Longman Cheshire, Melbourne, 1989

Sawer, Geoffrey *Australian federalism in the courts*, Melbourne University Press, Melbourne, 1967

—— *Modern federalism*, Pitman Australia, 1976

3

Economic and sociological approaches to law

Richard Johnstone

The previous chapter examined liberal approaches to law and legal philosophy. This chapter discusses approaches to legal phenomena which have their roots in two other disciplines, economics and sociology. It provides a basic introduction to the economic approach to law; and it examines the work of two of the most important figures in the development of sociology as a discipline—Durkheim and Weber. It then discusses the functionalist theories of Talcott Parsons, who tried to integrate the work of Weber and Durkheim.

One concern of this chapter is the assumptions underlying the economic and sociological approaches to law, concerning the nature of the individual, the nature of society and the relationship between the individual and society. A uniting theme of the approaches examined in this chapter is their construction of models of human action which refer to people's intentions and goals, and their selection of what appears to be appropriate means to achieve these intentions and goals. Each approach works, either explicitly or implicitly, within an accepted idea of social structure which is built upon the actions and interactions of individuals. The chapter also outlines the methodologies utilised within each perspective to analyse the behaviour of individuals and their relationship with society and law. It further examines the role of the state and of law within each perspective. Durkheim and Parsons, for example, envisaged law as a stabilising institution within society, providing an integrating mechanism which promoted order, cohesion and justice. The law and economics school, on the other hand, emphasises the law's role in promoting economic efficiency. Approaches which are more sceptical of law's capacity to achieve these ends are discussed in chapter 4.

One of the characteristics which the economic approach and Weberian sociology have in common with liberalism is the importance of rationality. The postmodernist critique of rationality is also examined in chapter 4.

Law and economics

Closely linked with liberalism as discussed in chapter 2 is the law and economics school, which has emerged as an influential movement within Western legal scholarship. The economic analysis of law involves the application of economic theory to examine the formation, structure, processes and impact of the law and legal institutions. This section will describe the importance of the economic approach, its assumptions and its central techniques, as well as different schools of law and economics.

The economic approach and its relevance to law

Economics is concerned with the 'process of providing for the economic well being of society'.[1] Societies need to devise institutions that will assure the production of enough goods and services for their survival, and distribute the fruits of production so that more production can take place.[2] Economics is the study of rational behaviour in the face of scarcity.[3] It looks at the way in which individuals and societies choose to employ scarce productive resources that could have alternative uses. It analyses the costs and benefits involved in changing the way resources are allocated in society. Economists argue that the most efficient choices are those which tend to maximise the wealth of society.

As a scholarly discipline,[4] economics dates back to the work of the English writers Petty and Locke in the 1660s. Up to the end of the nineteenth century, economics existed principally as a branch of moral philosophy. The leading economic writers were Enlightenment[5] scholars such as John Locke (England), Cesare Beccaria (Italy),[6] David Hume (Scotland), Adam Smith (England),[7] and later Jeremy Bentham and John Stuart Mill,[8] who were interested in both economic analysis and the law. With the emergence of economics as a distinct discipline in the 1880s and 1890s, economics became detached from moral philosophy. The Institutionalists of the 1920s and 1930s wished to integrate economics with other social sciences and to give economics a sounder empirical basis. But, with this exception, the economic analysis of law was largely neglected until the work of the Chicago School in the 1940s and the law and economics movement's rapidly increasing influence in the United States from the 1960s on.

The economic analysis of law in the 1960s was concerned principally with the economic effects of regulation on industry and with the application of economic theory to the analysis and reform of accident liability and tort law. This development was part of an extension of economics into the domains of other social sciences. Economic analysis was applied to sex and race discrimination, crime, education, the family, and health. Public Choice theory applied economic principles to explain political behaviour as the outcome of rational pursuit of self interest.[9]

During the 1970s law and economics established itself within legal scholarship. Economic concepts were applied to all areas of law, from contract to criminal law, to explain and rationalise legal doctrine and procedural rules by reference to the concept of economic efficiency.[10] By the 1980s the law and economics movement had a toehold in Australia.[11]

The law and economics school can help to answer two basic questions: what effects do legal rules have on society; and how do economic forces shape and determine the law? Economics can assist lawyers with technical economic aspects of legal decision making, such as discount rates in the calculation of damages.[12] Economics can also assist legal policy makers to structure the legal framework in regulatory systems and institutions to ensure that they function in the most efficient manner, by showing the costs of alternative policies and by showing the most efficient means to achieve particular policy objectives. Economists can evaluate the impact of alternative frameworks on industry, consumers, the economy in general and on the overall distribution of wealth. They can also re-examine legal problems from an economic perspective and pose alternative explanations and solutions.[13]

This last role of economists in thinking about law is the most important. For example, accidents and injuries do not just have medical and legal consequences. They also have economic consequences because the measures designed for the prevention of accidents and the compensation and rehabilitation of the injured consume resources. Moreover, the amount of resources consumed may vary depending on who is required to bear the cost, an issue which is discussed later in this chapter. This suggests that the rules of law which determine what happens after an accident should not only be just; they should ensure that resources are used efficiently. For example, Calabresi argued that the person who could avoid the accident or reduce the risk at the lowest cost (the 'cheapest cost avoider') should be made liable, because this would minimise the costs of avoiding accidents. If a motor vehicle driver collides with a pedestrian, the driver should be made liable if the cost to the driver of avoiding the collision (for example, by improving the brakes of the car) is less than the damages suffered by the pedestrian. A rule imposing liability on the driver in these circumstances would provide the driver with a strong incentive to seek the most efficient solution, which is to repair the brakes of the vehicle. Economics also helps to explain why few accident compensation cases are resolved by court decisions.[14] It is cheaper and more efficient for cases to be settled out of court, even though settlements may compromise the rights of plaintiffs. In settling cases, lawyers use economic principles within the shadow of the legal rules.[15] For example, plaintiffs will choose to settle for a smaller sum rather than seek final adjudication for a greater level of compensation if they believe they will be better off with a certain outcome rather than the risks involved in litigation. Any process which involves, as the legal process does, choices between different courses of action in the face of scarce resources must, by definition, have an economic aspect to it.

Assumptions behind economic thinking

'Legal reasoning' relies on drawing principles from statutes or cases and then applying them to new fact situations using inductive and pragmatic reasoning, analogies, argument and extrapolation.[16] Lawyers use legal rules in this fashion to determine rights in disputes. Economics, on the other hand, systematically balances up the advantages and disadvantages in problems of choice.

Economists think in terms of models which are simplified by basic assumptions to make them more manageable and useful in understanding the real world. As Veljanovski argues, *'theory must be simple and unrealistic*. Its value lies in revealing connections hitherto unknown and in giving its possessor a compass to guide him [sic] through the (mostly irrelevant) complexity of the real world'.[17] Very simple models can be made more complex by removing the more unrealistic assumptions. There are, however, certain basic assumptions at the heart of all economic analysis of law.

The first and most basic assumption made by economists is about human nature. It is that individuals generally behave in a *rational* manner to promote their self interest. Individuals are 'utility maximisers'. Economists use the term 'utility' to describe the combination of monetary and psychological satisfactions that an individual derives from engaging in a particular activity. People choose their desired ends (which may include emotional needs or altruistic concerns), and then work purposefully to achieve them in the face of constraints and the limited resources at their disposal. 'Rationality implies no more than a good fit between means and ends'.[18] It does not suggest that people are passionless calculating robots, but assumes that people do, on the whole, behave in certain predictable ways, with differences in individual responses. It also assumes that, after a while, rational ways of doing certain things will emerge, so that those who eschew these approaches will not be successful in the marketplace.

It follows from the first assumption that individuals will respond rationally to *incentives*. Whereas lawyers envisage law as a set of rules and procedures, 'economists see law as a system for altering incentives'.[19] They assume that if individuals can increase their satisfactions by altering their behaviour they will do so. The incentive to do something will, all things being equal, increase if the cost of doing it decreases or if the rewards for doing it increase. Economists conceive of law as a system of constraints, penalties and rewards, imposing costs and benefits so as to influence human behaviour. A change in the law can result in a changing of incentives or disincentives, costs or constraints. For example, if the penalty for a certain offence increases, on balance we would expect fewer people to participate in that activity. If other activities are decriminalised, on balance we would expect more people to engage in those activities. Law, therefore, can be used to channel human activity in certain directions through the use of incentives.

Economists assume that individual preferences or tastes do not change much over time, nor do they vary much between rich and poor individuals. This assumption of the *stability of preferences* enables economists to make predictions about human responses in the face of changing variables, such as price, quality of product or change in penalty. Economists make no attempt to disqualify preferences that are morally unacceptable or self-destructive.

Other assumptions underlying the economic approach to law show its liberal heritage. As the principal three assumptions suggest, there is a heavy emphasis on *the individual as an economic unit*. Moreover, the economic approach assumes the existing structure and hierarchy of society. It has no interest in changing the underlying social and political structure. In particular economists tend to ignore power differentials and structural inequalities within society and the market. All individuals are treated as being formally equal, and as free, autonomous and responsible economic actors. Economics is individualistic and subjectivist. Individuals are in the best position to make choices about what is best for them and what is required to satisfy their needs and preferences. The approach emphasises the primacy of market mechanisms, even in apparently non-market activities such as pollution, marriage, driving a car and so on. In effect, there is a focus on economic efficiency rather than on equity or justice, although economists would argue that an efficient use of resources is central to any equitable solution.

Basic tools of the economic approach to law

This section introduces the basic concepts of economics: opportunity costs, transaction costs, supply and demand, marginal analysis, and positive and normative economic analysis.

The concept of *opportunity cost* is central to the economic way of thinking. Most people think of cost as the price paid for a good or service. An economist, however, would argue that the true cost of choosing to do something should be measured in terms of the opportunities that are sacrificed to do it. This sacrifice of something else is called the opportunity cost. So, the cost of using a good is the benefit foregone by not using that good in its next best use. The cost of being a law academic, for example, is the benefit foregone in employment in a law firm or at the bar. Law academics, therefore, are willing to trade money for the attractive features of the job, such as the satisfaction of intellectual curiosity, opportunities for travel, and the freedom to be involved in research of one's own choosing rather than at the request of a client. The cost of being a law student is the lost opportunity, during university study, of full-time employment, together with the benefit foregone in using resources to study rather than in their next best use.

The calculation of opportunity cost, therefore, involves asking what an individual is willing to pay to get the benefit sought. This may be more than the financial cost of the benefit. Rather it is a quantitative indication 'of an individual's intensity of preferences'.[20] The economist measures the monetary value that an individual assigns to that benefit.

In the economic analysis of law the concept of opportunity cost is central to the consideration of whether, for one legal rule or a social or educational policy or program, there is another rule, policy or program that achieves the same outcome or consequence at a lower cost or achieves a better outcome or consequence at the same cost. Rationality demands that the opportunity costs of any course of action should be minimised. For example, will it cost society less to reduce road injuries and fatalities by increasing the penalties for dangerous driving, by increasing the number of traffic police on the roads (rather than policing other types of crime), by publicising the consequences of dangerous driving, by reconstructing intersections and parts of roads where traffic accidents regularly occur (rather than devoting these resources to other uses), by regulating the design of motor cars to maximise driver and passenger safety, or by relying on the law of negligence?

An example of the application of opportunity cost analysis is the famous Coase theorem.[21] It holds that in a world where there are no *transaction costs* the initial assignment of a property right will not affect the ultimate use of the property. Transaction costs include all the costs incidental to the transaction, such as the time and resources consumed in gaining information, identifying and getting together the other parties to a negotiation, and enforcing the bargain. Assuming transaction costs are zero, property rights will be transferred to those who value them the highest or, in opportunity cost terms, are prepared to pay the most for them.

For example,[22] assume that if a factory pollutes a river each of the five residential landowners downstream will suffer $500 damage. The pollution can be minimised by the factory owner spending $250 on filtering equipment or by each residential landowner purchasing a water purifier for $80 each. The Coase theorem argues that it does not matter whether the relevant legal rule protects the residential landowner's right to clean water or gives the factory owner licence to pollute. The most efficient solution is for the factory to install the filtering equipment—it is cheaper than the other solutions. If pollution is illegal, the factory will pay $250 for equipment rather than $500 damages to each of the landowners. If there is no rule outlawing pollution the landowners will club together to pay the factory $250, which is less than the total cost of each installing a water purifier. If, however, there are transaction costs of $60 for each residential landowner and the rule prohibits water pollution, the factory owner will still install the equipment for $250. But if the rule allows water pollution, it is cheaper for each landowner to purchase a water purifier, because of the transaction costs involved in their seeking to have the factory owner install the filtering equipment. Hence the transaction costs prevent the efficient solution being implemented irrespective of the legal rule. To achieve the efficient solution in a world of transaction costs the legal rule would need to prohibit pollution.[23] This discussion of opportunity costs and transaction costs shows how economics is not concerned with equity or fairness in any abstract sense. Its notion of equity is concerned with looking at the opportunity costs of different legal rules, programs or policies, and trying to achieve the maximum benefit at minimal cost.

Individuals can measure their own costs and benefits in private transactions, but the question remains as to how economists calculate the costs of social policies. To an economist, this is done not by policy makers themselves determining costs and benefits, but rather by asking how people want policy makers to spend their money.[24] An example usually given to illustrate this point is the value that should be placed on a human life. How much should society spend on saving human lives? Economists suggest that this is not the way to ask the question. Instead of asking what society ought to spend to preserve someone else's life, the question should be what individuals would be prepared to pay to make their lives safer. How much do individuals value a reduction in risk as compared to other things that money can buy? Would they prefer to spend $100 on making their cars safer or on food for their families? It is clear from this that people with lower incomes in this situation will value their safety less than people with higher incomes. That is because the economist always asks what is the alternative? What is being given up? Instead of spending $100 per capita on improving everyone's safety, the economist argues that it would be more efficient to give everyone $100 and let them decide what they would do with it.

Unlike lawyers, who typically think backwards (*ex post*) in terms of resolving existing disputes (generally by apportioning fault), economists generally like to think forwards (*ex ante*) in terms of the broader consequences of legal rules and their enforcement on all individuals likely to have contact with them. The law should be seen as a tool to be considered long before any particular dispute arises, and as a method of allocating losses so as to provide incentives to other individuals to reduce harm and use resources more efficiently. As noted earlier, economists assume that individuals will change their behaviour as a result of changes in legal rules, whether these rules be made by the legislature or by the courts in resolving disputes between other parties.

To understand the effects of a change to a legal rule or its enforcement, economists look at the people who change their behaviour. If there is an increase in the level of the fines that negligent drivers will have to pay, economists are concerned with predicting whether this will give rise to a change in the number of drivers who drive carelessly. Analysis should be focused on the margin, the *rate of change* in behaviour. Will the road toll fall at a greater rate if fines for dangerous driving are increased, if the licences of dangerous drivers are confiscated, or television advertisements show vividly the consequences of dangerous driving?

By focusing on the marginal effects of legal changes, economists are forced to consider *substitution effects*. If the price of tea increases, to what extent will people substitute coffee drinking for tea drinking? These concepts introduce the most basic tool in economic analysis—the *'law' of supply and demand*. As the price of a good or service increases there is a greater incentive for individuals to enter that particular market as a supplier. The quantity of goods supplied has a proportional relationship with the price of the good. On the other hand, consumers, in general, can be expected to consume more of a good or service, all things being equal, if its price falls. Demand is therefore inversely related to price. If the price of rice falls relative to the price of pasta, and rice is seen as a substitute for pasta, consumers will consume more rice and less pasta. The price of rice will not fall below the cost of supplying rice. If the greater price of pasta enables new suppliers to move into the pasta business, the quantity of pasta will increase relative to demand for pasta, driving down its price. And so on.

Similarly, if the costs of a particular activity or transaction increase, people will be increasingly reluctant to undertake the relevant activity and will switch their resources into other activities. In analysing the way in which individuals respond to changes in legal rules, Easterbrook[25] gives the example of changes in the rules of evidence to require the courts to exclude evidence obtained by illegal means. The rationale for this rule change is to deter the police from using illegal methods to gather evidence. A change in police methods for gathering evidence may, however, result in the police conducting fewer investigations and prosecutions, and would lower the conviction rate. Judges might well respond by increasing the level of fines imposed on those who are convicted, in order to deter potential criminals who may be encouraged to commit more crime because of the lower likelihood of being convicted. The net result could be that those who do get convicted suffer greater penalties than would have been the case without the new rule. Their rights are affected by an attempt to protect the rights of others.

Easterbrook's scenario is an example of *positive economic analysis*; it is also known as descriptive or predictive analysis. It can involve the analysis of the impact of legal policies on human behaviour (impact or behavioural analysis) or the analysis of the structure of legal doctrine.

Impact analysis involves the economist asking, if a certain legal policy is adopted, what predictions can be made about its likely economic impacts, both allocative and distributive. Allocative impacts have to do with the pattern of economic activities resulting from the legal policy; distributive impacts describe the individuals who will be advantaged or disadvantaged by the changes. This sort of analysis assumes that behaviour in the face of legal changes will be based on individualistic and subjective considerations. If, for example, laws are introduced to prohibit the sale of certain recreational drugs, what behavioural responses might be expected from those who supply drugs and those who demand them? If the supply is restricted, those drugs that are supplied might be more expensive, because of the greater costs and risks associated with their supply. If there are fewer drugs on the market, the prices might increase, and drug users might resort to desperate measures to buy the drugs they need. This is simply an application of the basic law of supply and demand.

Similarly, if the government legislates to keep the price of tractor roll bars as low as possible, more farmers will buy roll bars. The problem is, because the incentive for producing roll bars has decreased fewer manufacturers will make roll bars, and there will be a shortage of this important safety mechanism. This suggests that regulating tractor safety in this manner may not achieve the desired goal.

Structural analysis of legal doctrine revolves around the claim by some, but not all, law and economics scholars that the rules of common law that have survived best have done so because, at least implicitly, they obey economic logic. For example, economists such as Posner argue that rules governing commercial transactions have to reflect the parties' understandings of economic efficiency because if they did not the parties would arrange their transactions to accord with the norms of efficiency that they have chosen for themselves. Economists have also argued that the calculus used to determine the standard of care in negligence cases (where the probability and gravity of harm are weighed up against the burden of adequate precautions) is the rule most likely to achieve the optimum allocation of resources by minimising the sum of the parties' accident and avoidance costs.[26]

Normative analysis, or prescriptive economics, takes impact analysis one step further. It involves analysing the impact of alternative legal policies and rules and, all things being equal, adopting the one which is most efficient, regardless of who benefits or loses.

Neo-classical economists favour institutions which facilitate private relations and exchange between individuals, maintaining that goods gravitate to their most valuable use in a free market. This philosophy informs much of the contemporary economic libertarian thinking from the conservative side of Australian politics in relation to the regulation of the labour market. For example the Victorian *Employee Relations Act 1992* and the federal Liberal–National Party Coalition industrial relations policy favour individual employment contracts over the regulation of employment through the award system.[27] This preference is generally based on the proposition that two people will enter voluntarily into private exchange if both perceive that it will make them better off. It underpins the notion of freedom of contract. If you buy a newspaper from the newsagent, you have decided that you are better off having the newspaper in exchange for its price, and the newsagent feels she is better off having the price in exchange for the newspaper. Of course, this economic presumption that both parties benefit from private exchange depends on there being an efficient and properly functioning market—it may not be well founded where there are market failures such as monopolies (where one supplier supplies 100 per cent of the market), monopsonies (where a market contains only one or a small number of consumers) or externalities (discussed below).

From a political perspective, libertarians such as Hayek, Nozick and Milton Friedman argue that private ordering is important for individual autonomy.[28] Collective decisions are not the product of the voluntary agreement of all affected by the decision. Where collective decision making does occur, the central issue then becomes whether it will increase overall social welfare, made up of the aggregate of the increase or decrease in utility to each individual.

Welfare economics examines whether a particular transaction, policy or legal rule will make individuals affected by it better off in terms (as noted earlier) of how *they perceive their own welfare*. What is important, in this type of analysis, is how individuals think about what makes them better off, rather than speculation about their preferences. How is the aggregate welfare of all measured if a legal decision is taken which will increase the welfare of some and decrease the welfare of others? How do economists decide if the proposed transaction, policy or rule will result in people being generally better off? Welfare economists have developed two concepts of efficiency to assist with these judgments. *Pareto efficiency* holds that a transaction, policy or rule increases welfare if at least one person believes they are better off, while nobody believes they are worse off than before the change. This measure reflects the welfare arising from private exchange but is obviously less helpful in collective decision making, because it prevents an economist from offsetting the welfare of one individual against the welfare of another. Economists have therefore developed the concept of *Kaldor-Hicks efficiency*, also known as the potential Pareto improvement or hypothetical compensation test.[29]

Kaldor-Hicks efficiency accepts that a change in a legal rule is efficient if it results in sufficient gains for beneficiaries of the rule that they could, at least hypothetically, compensate those who are worse off for the introduction of the rule, until the latter are at least indifferent to the rule, but leaving the former with at least some benefits. The difference between Pareto and Kaldor-Hicks efficiency would disappear if the losers were actually compensated by the winners. Kaldor-Hicks efficiency requires only that the winners *could* compensate the losers, but not that they actually do so. Kaldor-Hicks efficiency is a form of cost-benefit analysis, and is favoured by most economists working in law and economics.

Limitations of the law and economics approach

It is clear that some of the assumptions of the economic way of thinking may not be realised in the real world. As the next chapter will argue, it may be that the essential assumptions of the voluntariness of human action do not exist in certain situations. Critics of the economic way of thinking often raise the economist's lack of concern for the existing maldistribution of income, which can lead poorer groups to value things like their own safety less highly than rich people do. The economist simply responds that it is not her job to decide whether the redistribution of income should be undertaken, but rather to spell out the implications on choices and efficiency of a change in the distribution of income.

Critics would maintain that, while law and economics offers apparently scientific ways of solving legal problems, it actually does what it claims to avoid; that is, it disguises important choices and obscures value judgments about how people should be treated. The approach gives no assistance in deciding *when* it is appropriate to seek an economic solution.

Likewise, complete information and the absence of externalities and transaction costs do not exist in many situations. Externalities arise where costs cannot be privatised, so that economic actors can make decisions without taking certain costs into account. For example, pollution costs may be externalised if the factory does not have to pay for the costs of cleaning up wastes which are siphoned into a nearby river, particularly if there are no immediate neighbours to lodge complaints. As the earlier example of the Coase theorem suggests, the role of law in this case might involve the internalisation of these costs, so that manufacturers are forced to take into account cleanup costs when making decisions to pollute.

Further, the economist's assumptions about preferences are subject to criticism from many quarters. Economists assume that all preferences are equally valid, whereas moral philosophers would argue that some preferences are morally unacceptable and should not be accorded the same importance as more noble preferences. Others would argue that preferences are socially constructed and should not be seen to be independent of the context (social, political, cultural, economic and legal) which shapes them.

The importance of individual autonomy in the economic way of thinking is challenged by those who prefer a communitarian conception of society. Communitarians emphasise the importance of participatory self-governance in which individuals exercise regard for the interests of others. They strongly dispute the notion that individuals are, or should be seen as, autonomous and self interested.[30]

Some writers have challenged the scientific nature of the economic analysis of law. For example, Leff[31] argues that the economic analysis of law is an oversimplification, and is not susceptible to any form of empirical support or falsification.[32] The notion of rationality itself is coming under attack. Increasingly, scholars in all disciplines are challenging the view that we can know the world and test our knowledge against it.[33] Economics, together with all rationality-based disciplines, is subject to these criticisms. The next chapter will examine the criticisms of rationality.

Durkheim, law and social solidarity

While the law and economics approach concentrates on the relationship between legal rules and economic efficiency, within the framework of liberal society and liberal values, other writers within the liberal tradition have assumed that the market was itself a chief cause of disorder and conflict in industrial societies. Writers such as Emile Durkheim rejected an abstract individualistic approach, and argued that a society in which individuals were simply left to pursue their own interests would disintegrate.[34] The market could co-ordinate economic activity, and satisfy human needs, only if social relations were governed by shared values other than those of self interest. Durkheim was opposed to individualism and was preoccupied with the problem of social order and the conditions under which social solidarity was possible.

In his work in the last decade of the nineteenth century and in the early twentieth, Durkheim sought to carve out sociology as a discrete social science. His interest in law was only tangential to his major sociological concerns. Sociology was the study of social collectivities and the products of collective life. Each individual made a contribution to social life, but the resulting product was greater than the sum of individual contributions. Society preceded and outlasted individuals. Collective life gave rise to a collective conscience, the only legitimate object for sociological study. Individuals had to be socialised into the collective conscience.

Durkheim championed a form of sociological positivism. He wanted to rescue sociology from speculative, armchair theorising. The sociologist was to use the same methods to study the facts of social life (social facts) as the scientist used to study the facts of the physical universe. Social facts were 'manners of acting, thinking and feeling external to the individual, which are invested with a coercive power by virtue of which they exercise control' over individual action, through physical force, custom and convention.[35] These constraints were for the good, because of their collective origins and nature, and because they preserved social order.

Durkheim assumed that consensual order and stability was the natural state of social systems. The basis of social order was moral and depended on social solidarity, or social cohesion. Society developed through a moral evolutionary process, with the function of law in society changing as society changed.

Legal rules, institutions and practices were, for Durkheim, social facts. He used the term 'law' to mean rules enforced by a threat of sanctions, rather than in the sense of formal and informal customary rules of behaviour. Law was distinguished from morality[36] because it was 'organised', rather than diffuse in character, and depended on specific institutions and persons (judges and the courts) to interpret it and apply sanctions following recognised procedures. Nevertheless, law derived from and expressed the collective morality or beliefs of society. Durkheim largely neglected to examine the relationship between law and politics, or even the impact of legislators, the courts or the police on the functioning of the law. The state was simply a special organ with the task of working out collective beliefs holding good for the whole community.[37]

Because of his definition of social facts in terms of constraint, Durkheim focused on certain aspects of law, principally its constraining or prohibitive aspects. From his very first work,[38] Durkheim espoused three major propositions about law.[39]

The first pertained to the way in which law should be conceived. In his study of social solidarity, or social cohesion, which he saw as entirely a moral phenomenon and not capable of precise observation and measurement, Durkheim conceived of law as an external index which symbolised the nature of social solidarity. Changes in the nature of morality could best be tracked by observing changes in the law, because law reproduced all the essential aspects of social solidarity.

Durkheim's second proposition concerned the evolution of law, which was part of the development of societies to more advanced forms. Durkheim identified two general types of law, which were defined according to the kinds of sanctions that enforced them. 'Repressive' laws, such as the criminal law, punished the offender by inflicting injury or disadvantage, such as deprivation of possessions, liberty, reputation or life. 'Restititutive' laws, on the other hand, contained sanctions aimed at restoring the state of affairs that existed before the unlawful conduct occurred. Tort, contract, and administrative law are examples of rules with restitutive sanctions.

Durkheim argued that simple or 'primitive' societies were closely integrated because they were collectivist in orientation and organisation, being comprised of a number of similar family units, performing similar activities, with common assumptions, and bound together by a common morality. These societies had few specialised institutions. Individual differences were virtually non-existent. Social solidarity was 'mechanical' and was founded on a structure of common beliefs (in which religion played a central role) and a collective conscience. The aberrant behaviour of a deviant minority was brutally dealt with through the law, to emphasise and symbolise the importance of the unifying norms. Law was essentially repressive law, or penal law with 'repressive organised sanctions'.

Within Durkheim's social evolutionary scheme, as societies became more socially differentiated, secular and individualistic, and individuals were emancipated from social and economic controls over their behaviour, this mechanical solidarity began to disintegrate. Individual rights and freedoms became more important, and individuals were distinguishable according to the different, highly specialised roles they played in the division of labour, which rested on individual specialisation and functional interdependence. Nevertheless, Durkheim argued that society would be based on consensus. Each individual had to rely on others to perform their functions if societal needs were to be performed. Social solidarity was now 'organic', and depended on the mutual interdependence of the division of labour rather than a collective consciousness. The collective consciousness became more general and abstract, setting down broad moral principles instead of strict rules for every aspect of human behaviour.[40] Durkheim assumed that human wants were insatiable and social controls were needed to keep those wants under control to prevent financial and commercial crises and struggles over the distribution of income. The regulation of social and economic life through stable institutions within a moral order, with individuals accepting their place within the division of labour, would keep expectations to a reasonable level and facilitate the achievement of individual autonomy and happiness.

The role of law changed as societies developed, to perform the function of restitution, playing its part in restoring a harmonious balance of interdependent interests. Restitutive law principally comprised civil law, procedural law, commercial law, constitutional law and administrative law.

Durkheim's third hypothesis related to the functioning of law, particularly criminal law. As societies evolved from mechanical to organic solidarity the nature of crime and punishment would change, and the balance would shift from repressive law to restitutive law and from brutal punishment to more humane alternatives. The punishment inflicted on deviants played the important integrating function of publicly repairing and reinforcing the law that had been contravened. The function of punishment was to 'maintain inviolate the cohesion of society by sustaining the common consciousness in all its vigour'.[41]

Durkheim's evolutionary social theory is typical of Enlightenment thinking about change and the perfection of progression.[42] To put it simply: as history unfolds, things get better. Part of this narrrative of progress is the negative construction of 'primitive' societies. The picture of these societies bears little resemblance to the empirical evidence of indigenous cultures.[43] Some 'primitive' societies were dependent on mediation and restitution; and repressive law was a characteristic of more complex societies.[44] Anthropologists have also disputed Durkheim's assertion that small-scale tribal societies lack a division of labour.[45]

Durkheim's positivism is now also unfashionable, due to the shift towards interpretive sociology. Social facts can never be the same as the facts of the physical universe, because they are at least partially created by the meaning and reasons people give to their own behaviour; and people's subjective interpretations of their own world are clearly part of the things to be studied by sociologists. This point will be developed in the analysis of Weber's sociology, and in the discussion of interactionism in chapter 6. Durkheim's consensus-based theories, too, have lost their influence since the late 1960s, when there has been a general drift in theoretical research perspectives away from consensualist approaches epitomised by Durkheim and Parsons (see below) to 'conflict' approaches. A number of conflict perspectives have been developed. These include Weberian, interactionist, marxist and feminist approaches. Weber is discussed in this chapter, and the remainder in chapters four and six.

Weber and the law as a framework for social action

Max Weber, whose major work also spanned the turn of the century, was a supporter of Western capitalism, but pointed out some of its contradictions and self-destructive tendencies. He favoured individualism, advocated freedom, but was suspicious of popular democracy, and leant towards authoritarian and despotic political leadership. His work was a reaction to the political and intellectual influence and implications of marxism.[46]

Weber was the first sociologist systematically to develop a sociology of law[47] as an integral part of his sociological theory. Weber defined law along positivist lines as an order externally guaranteed, in the sense of bringing about conformity or avenging violation, by the probability that physical or psychological coercion will be applied by 'a staff of people holding themselves specially ready for that purpose'.[48] Law was a system of rules within which the individual could orient her or his own conduct in the rational and purpose-directed manner so essential to capitalism. Unlike Durkheim's work, important largely for historical reasons, Weberian approaches feature prominently in contemporary debates in the sociology of law because of their focus on the unique development, characteristics and specific conditions of Western European capitalism. Particularly antipathetic to Durkheim's approach was Weber's interest in the legal profession, and in the relationships between law and domination and law and the economy.

In direct contrast to Durkheim, Weber's methodological starting point was subjectivism, which was central to his 'interpretive sociology'. While rejecting the positivist identification of the social sciences with the natural sciences, he asserted the possibility of scientific knowledge within the social sciences. Sociology should concern itself with the actions of individuals towards each other (i.e. social action) to achieve particular goals. Social action had to be understood by reference to the meanings, purposes or intentions which individuals ascribed to their action.[49] Weber separated 'means' from 'ends' and concentrated principally on the means chosen by individuals to achieve their ends. Means were rational in relation to the chosen end.[50] He took 'values' and 'ends' as given and not subject to scientific or rational assessment. In this sense Weber saw his sociology as 'value-free', a position since criticised as merely being a value-laden acceptance of the world as it is. His preference for rationality over irrationality is also value-laden. In short, his assertion of being value-free is effectively an acceptance of the logic of modern capitalism. It is also not clear as to what Weber meant by rationality—at times it referred to the internal logic of a system or set of ideas and at times it was used to describe efficiency or predictability. It is, however, clear that in his faith in rationality he adhered to the possibility of a logical, systematic and gapless system of legal rules which would cover all possible fact situations.[51] Consistent with his subjectivist methodology, which assumed that knowledge could only be gained through experience, Weber resorted to 'ideal types' as part of his sociological method. These were hypotheses developed by emphasising certain aspects of a phenomenon, and against which empirical evidence could be examined, so that order could be brought to experience.

For example, a key feature of Weber's sociology of law was his hypothetical typology of 'internal modes' of legal thinking. The types of legal thought refer to characteristics or procedures within legal processes (that is, the way in which legal rules were developed and applied), rather than to the content of legal thinking. First, Weber distinguished between 'formal' and 'substantive' systems. In 'formal' systems all the rules and procedures for decision making were available within the system. 'Substantive' systems drew on external criteria, such as political, ethical or religious values, and could represent reactions to individual cases ('empirical') or reactions based upon emotion or faith ('effectual'). He then distinguished between 'rational' and 'irrational' use of the rules and procedures of the system. Legal thinking therefore could be characterised in terms of formal rationality, substantive rationality, formal irrationality, and substantive irrationality. Weber favoured the realisation of formal rational law.

This is reflected in Weber's description of the process of legal development, which looked at the mode of creation of law, the formal qualities of that law and the types of justice it gave rise to. Law and procedure generally passed through a number of stages.

While Weber did not suggest that law was to be seen as an unfolding evolutionary process, he nevertheless described the development of law in terms of a process of negation of earlier forms—again bearing little resemblance to reality.[52] In his scheme primitive law (the first stage) was formal irrational law, involving charismatic revelation through 'law prophets' whose authority depended heavily on magic, which was inherently formalistic and irrational. This form of law gave rise to charismatic justice, lacking any consistent conception of substantive law.

Substantive irrational law (the second stage) resulted from the empirical creation of law by case-by-case jurisprudence, evaluated on an ethical, emotional or political basis. These systems gave rise to 'khadi' or 'Solomonian' justice, in which individuals submitted to the authority of an official who was free to make legal decisions without being bound by an extensive framework of legal rules. An example of substantive irrationality to Weber was the English common law system, based on precedent, where formal judgments were not given under rational concepts but by drawing on analogies and interpretations of concrete precedents.[53]

The third stage was the creation of law by secular or theocratic powers, through theocratic substantive rationality, giving rise to empirical justice. Here the legal system was based on non-legal principles, such as principles derived from religion or justice, and lacked the consistency of a system based on legal precedent.

The fourth stage was the systematised elaboration of law and the professionalised administration of justice by persons trained in law in a learned and formally logical manner, giving rise to rational justice.[54]

In contrast to Durkheim, Weber's concern was not to analyse the development of legal systems but rather to describe the factors contributing to the rationalisation of law through a transition from 'substantively rational law' to 'formally rational law'. The summit of rationality was the integration of all legal propositions in a logically clear, internally gapless system of abstract rules capable of dealing with all conceivable fact situations,[55] for example the European codes.

Consistent with his general sociological method, Weber favoured a multicausal, pluralistic explanation of the process of rationalisation, based on a parallel operation of his ideal types and detailed comparative and historical analysis. Rationalisation resulted from the confluence of developing bourgeois interest and the interests of absolute states or monarchical administration. Bureaucracies were developed to cope with the rapidly increasing administrative responsibilities of all collective enterprises in society (business firms, government departments, schools and so on), tended to produce rational means of administration, and consequently required rational law, in the form of codification.

Weber suggested that legal procedure and technique contributed to the rationalisation process because they determined the extent to which the system could respond to legal innovations, which themselves arose out of social and economic interests. He also recognised the causative impact of 'natural law', which he defined in terms of the norms which were valid independently of, and were superior to, any positive law, and which provided the very basis of legitimation of positive law.[56] Because they were appealed to by protagonists seeking legal change, theories of natural law were a means of legitimating legal change.

The most important factor in legal rationalisation was the legal profession.[57] Where the legal profession centred on apprenticeship-based training in law as a craft, it exhibited skills in the adaptation, use and innovation of substantive law and procedures in clients' interests. Weber thought that this form of the profession would prevent the development of a system of rational law. He argued that where professional skills and attitudes were developed through 'legal education' undertaken in universities or special schools away from the practice of law, and based on legal theory and science, this focused on the conceptual and abstract features of law and promoted the rational and logical characteristics of legal systems.[58]

Weber was concerned to explain the 'England problem', which arose because England was the first nation to experience the development of capitalism, despite the absence of a legal system typified by formal legal rationality. The 'irrational' English legal system developed through a craft-trained and pragmatically orientated legal profession concerned with case-by-case problem solving rather than the continental European system of university jurists stressing doctrinal systematisation.[59] The early common law was a 'magico-formalist' adversary system with irrational modes of proof, such as trial by ordeal or battle. As the common law developed, these irrational elements and feudal origins were incompletely overlaid by formal rationality but nevertheless proved durable enough to survive the great transformation to capitalism without formal change. The English legal system did not undergo the same systematic rationalisation process as occurred with continental law. To Weber this illustrated the multicausal and pluralistic nature of historical ocurrences—no particular legal development was essential to a particular economic development.[60] Weber believed that England achieved capitalist supremacy despite its judicial system, and that the powerful and monopolistic English legal profession had vested interests in maintaining an archaic and formalistic system and in resisting codification and rational legal education.

In his exploration of the characteristics of Western capitalist society Weber examined the relationship between 'law' and 'domination'. He examined the way in which one person's behaviour could be analysed as having been determined by another. Domination was a specific case of power, and power, for Weber, simply meant the fact of behaviour determination. While he recognised that the motivation to obey commands rested on factors varying from case to case, he described two sources of domination—by virtue of being in a monopoly position; and by virtue of authority ('legitimate domination'), that is, the power to command and the duty to obey.[61]

Weber introduced three ideal types of legitimate domination—traditional, charismatic and rational legal domination; each distinguished by the form of legitimacy upon which the system claimed to exercise domination. Traditional domination resulted from acceptance of long established authority. Charismatic domination arose where authority was accepted on an emotional basis, such as allegiance to a particularly revered leader. Both were based on personal authority and on a specific relationship between ruler and subject. Weber argued, however, that political legitimacy in Western societies was impersonal, and based principally on legal domination; with acceptance of the legitimacy of the actions of government because its authority was based on a legal order made up of an abstract and comprehensive set of rules. The state was granted legitimacy to the extent that political leaders were appointed to office and ruled according to specific legal procedures. Legal domination, therefore, envisaged a rule of law rather than the rule of individuals or other institutions.[62]

Weber tended to emphasise the similarity between legal domination and formal rational law. Despite its apparent value neutrality, Weber's theory of legal domination results in a fundamentally conservative legal order,[63] and one which incorporates and legitimises the domination of the market system.[64] This concept of legitimation is examined in chapter 4.

Weber suggested that legal domination took only one pure form, involving bureaucratic organisation following a formally rational decision making process. This involved a professional administration, with specialised and trained officials following rational rules when conducting official business. It also implied a high degree of separation of powers.[65] Consequently, bureaucratic administration was seen to stand outside the economic and political contests that permeate society. The concept of the state virtually disappeared from Weber's view of capitalist society and was replaced by the rationality of administration.[66]

Like Marx, Weber was heavily concerned with the relationship between the economic system and the wider social system. This was illustrated earlier in the discussion of the role of rational law in the development of capitalism. He investigated the extent to which economic factors contributed to the development of legal systems. Unlike Marx,[67] Weber rejected the notion that law was directly determined by economic forces or economic need. Rather, economic situations merely provided the opportunity for the spread of a newly invented legal technique.[68] Law was a relatively autonomous social phenomenon, both partially influenced by and partially influencing economic and other processes in society. The existence of formal rational law was a necessary, but not sufficient, condition for the emergence of capitalism.[69]

But what was the exact nature of the relationship between law and the economy? While capitalist interests were not the principal factor in the creation of the legal system, law was crucially related to economic forces and was directly at the service of economic interests. Rational economic activity, focused on the market and the operation of capitalist enterprises, was based on calculation, and required a legal and administrative system with internally logical processes and fixed general norms which maximised certainty, and whose functioning could be rationally predicted.[70] Law was a means of guaranteeing economic activity, by, for example, establishing legal rights and institutions (such as contract law) to guarantee certain types of exchange transactions. Weber recognised that, despite its abstract nature, law supported particular class and economic interests, and indeed contributed to the concentration of economic and social power. Contract law, for example, was available only to the owners of property, and so legitimised the unequal distribution of economic power.

Weber anchored his discussion of contract[71] in the development of market exchange relations and in the relationship between economic conditions and the recognition of legal rights. In societies where people were self-sufficient, and exchange was limited, the legal recognition of contractual freedom would be limited.[72] Not only did the development of the market quantitatively increase the number of exchange transactions, but interest groups emerged to assert their 'market interests' to influence the kinds of transactions the law should regulate. There was a change from 'status' contracts (governing, for example, landlord and tenant and family relations) to 'purposive' contracts, reflecting the move from barter to a money economy, which made transactions quantifiable, abstract and apparently neutral.

Like Marx, Weber recognised that a contractual form of law in the West was the product of a transition from feudal society (where rank, property, kinship and the like were recognised by the law) to a society based on capitalist institutions. With the development of the marketplace, the exchange process had to be liberated from religious, kinship and similar restrictions interfering with the mobility of persons, goods, property and prices. A fully rational market economy required both the freedom of individuals, regarded as equals, to contract with others on their own terms and the freedom of each individual to regulate relations with things—for example to dispose of property as she might wish.[73]

Weber did, however, recognise the problem of the inequality of bargaining power in the market. What determined freedom was the distribution of social and economic power, particularly the distribution of property. Contractual freedom, particularly in relation to the contract of employment, enabled parties to use their property in the market to achieve power over others without the same degree of proprietary power. Consequently, modern societies imposed limitations on contractual activity, in the interests of both the state and market-orientated groups themselves. For example, rules developed to govern consumer, employment and other relationships based upon power differentials.

Parsons and structural functionalism

Talcott Parsons sought to integrate the different streams of nineteenth and early twentieth century social thought. In particular, he tried to build on and synthesise the 'holistic' theories of social action associated with Durkheim and the 'individualistic' theories associated with Weber, while conveniently steering clear of the work of Marx. Parsons viewed social theory as a tool to organise logically and make sense of a confusing world, and to organise general ideas into a systematic framework of abstract concepts, or generalisations. He assumed that the social world was organised in a logical rational way, and set out to develop a logically coherent theory of social science. In contrast to Marx's critique of capitalism as a fundamentally contradictory system which would eventually collapse,[74] Parsons developed a theory to explain and understand the problems of capitalism in terms of an evolutionary process leading to greater stability and integration.[75] His heyday was the 1950s and 1960s and his work is now taken less seriously by sociologists, although his theories, like those of Durkheim, usefully describe the underlying assumptions and 'commonsense' thinking about law and society made by many lawyers.

Parsons assumed a consensus-based society, and a system of shared values, which stabilised the interaction between individuals. In a similar fashion to Durkheim he assumed that human beings were naturally self-centred, irrational, and in a state of metaphorical war with each other, and that social organisation had to mould and civilise individuals to ensure a stable and harmonious social order. Individuals then became the products of external society rather than actively creating their own lives. The link between the individual and society was through roles (as employers, employees, teachers, students, parents, children) which played a large part in determining behaviour. Disruption occurred when people did not properly fulfil their roles.

Parsons produced a systems analysis which attempted to demonstrate the existence of irreducible functional relations between components of the social system. The central metaphor in his theory was the biological organism or living system. A social system of action, like a biological organism, had needs which had to be met to ensure survival, and parts which functioned to meet the needs, hence the label *functionalist*. The different parts (the family, schools, hospitals, religion etc.) could be examined on their own, but the function of each part could only be understood in relation to the others, when the system was seen as a whole. Social life was a structure of different parts, hence the label *structuralist*.

Parsons tried to distil a basic model of social action from all existing social theory. The model involved actors, goals, means and an environment. What united most social theorists was a conception of human beings as being involved in a process of deciding between different goals and a number of means to achieve these goals. Choices were made within an environment of social and physical factors, including the physical and intellectual attributes of actors, the economic climate, other actors, and basic norms (including legal norms) and values of society. The social scientist had to make sense of the choices made within such constraints.[76] To maximise their own gratification from interactions with others, individuals tended to repeat gratifying transactions. As actors came to expect particular responses from other actors, so norms and generally accepted values developed, which then ensured the responses. Relationships stabilised and became institutionalised over time, resulting in a system of constant 'status roles' with rewards and sanctions.⁷⁷ Behaviour attached to each role remained constant, regardless of the occupant of the role. In short, behaviour in society was structured. Social relationships were patterned and recurrent. Values (people's belief in what the world should be like) provided general guidelines for behaviour, and were translated into more specific norms (socially accepted rules which people employed in deciding on their actions) and roles. The structure of society then became the sum total of social relationships governed by norms.

The functioning of the structure was discovered by examining the relationship between the different parts of the structure and society as a whole. In particular, the social scientist had to examine the contribution of the institution to the maintenance and survival of the social system. This in turn was generally discovered by investigating how the basic needs or requirements (functional prerequisites) of society were met in order for it to survive. The various parts had to have some degree of compatability and integration. Integration was based largely on 'value consensus', or agreement about values in that society.

Parsons identified a number of levels of systems and subsystems. The highest level was all living systems, the second level was the systems of action, and the third level (dealing with status roles) was the subsystems of action: the personality (the actor aiming for maximum gratification); the cultural system (a system of wider values giving coherence to the difference norms attached to the different status roles); the biological system (the physical environment to which society must adapt); and the social system. These four subsystems developed through a process of institutionalisation. At the fourth level were the subsystems of the social system, the political system, the socialisation system, the economy and the 'societal community'.

According to Parsons, any system or subsystem had to satisfy four requirements, needs or functional prerequisites if it were to survive; and in each instance a separate specialist subsystem had to be developed to meet each requirement.

Firstly, each system had to adapt to its environment (adaptation). Within the social system this function was performed by the economy. Secondly, each system had to have a means of mobilising its resources to attain its goals and to keep the system moving towards its goals (goal attainment). This function was performed by the political system. Thirdly, each system had to keep itself together, by maintaining internal co-ordination of its parts and dealing with deviance (integration). This function was concerned with citizenship and social solidarity and was performed by the societal community, the institutions of social control, which include the legal system, and informal rules of conduct. Finally, each system must, as far as possible, maintain itself in a state of equilibrium, by creating, preserving and replenishing the energies and values of members of the society (pattern maintenance). This function was performed by the socialisation process, which educated people into the cultural values and societal norms of the system. It ensured that the overall pattern of activities within the system was reproduced. The family and the education system were particularly important aspects of this process, and played an important part in shaping the attitudes and outlook of individuals so that they conformed to the established expectations and values of society.

Hence law and education both played a central role in functionalist thought in ensuring good role performance. People had to be educated to perform their roles as employees, spouses and so forth in order to ensure social harmony. Law and the legal system therefore played a part in satisfying one of the functional prerequisites in Parsons' conception of society.

Parsons also suggested that societies could be analysed by looking at their normative structure, which consisted of a hierarchy of elements with four levels.

At the top of this hierarchy were society's values, the commonly held conceptions of a desirable society.[78] These abstract values were the basis of social cohesion, and provided the justification for the system in the eyes of the citizenry. Whereas writers such as Durkheim had difficulty conceptualising the existence of these shared fundamental values, and other writers have disclaimed the existence of shared values,[79] Parsons simply assumed their existence.[80] At the next level down were more specific societal norms, including law, which applied these basic values to the special conditions of the different groups or subsystems within society. Values controlled these norms, in the sense that they strongly determined their content. At the third level were collectivities, such as businesses, hospitals and universities, which defined patterns of required action in specific situations. Just as values determined the content of norms, so norms controlled the activities of collectivities. At the most concrete level were individual roles, which specified the expectations governing the actions of individuals in relation to their membership of collectivities. Collectivities determined roles. Parsons argued that all of these levels of the hierarchy were strongly differentiated in Western society.

In Parsons' theory law was part of both the normative structure and the functional prerequisites. The autonomy of law in modern capitalist societies meant that it was strongly separated from other aspects of society. It was a distinct level of the normative structure, and played a functionally specialised role in integrating society. Parsons argued that the four functional subsystems corresponded with the four levels of the normative structure. Roles corresponded with the economy; collectivities, or institutions, with the polity; and values with pattern maintenance. Norms were linked with societal community. Cotterrell comments that 'it follows also that law ultimately reflects and depends on the society's shared values, but at the same time in western societies it normatively controls the *forms* of both economic and political action. The "rule of law" prevails'.[81]

Parsons argued that 'control' pushed its way down the normative structure, thereby stabilising the system and limiting change. If values changed this was reflected in changed norms which controlled collectivities which shaped roles. On the other hand, as environmental conditions (such as employment conditions) changed, those 'at the coal face' and involved in the economy (namely workers, managers and directors) found that their roles had changed

Figure 3.1 A summary of Parsons' theory

	Normative structure	Sub-systems	Functional requisites	
Stability ↓	values	family, education	pattern, maintenance	↑ Change
	norms	legal system	integration	
	collectivities	polity, institutions, organisations	goal attainment	
	roles	economy, environmental conditions	adaptation	

dramatically. This 'conditioning' exerted pressure on collectivities involved in the political system to change, so that firms made new plans and organised themselves differently, to reflect role changes. But the change was less dramatic at this level. Changes in collectivities would logically put pressure on norms, such as laws of employment or company law, to change but less so. At the top of the hierarchy there might be some pressure for basic values involved in pattern maintenance, for example concepts of workplace justice, to change but these were likely to be minimal.

Social change, in the Parsons schema, therefore involved conditioning moving up through the hierarchy, demanding changes to reflect pressures at the lowest level. Control, on the other hand, moved down, and stabilised the system by reasserting the basic values of society. Social change took place through this process of negotiation between the upward and downward moving pressures. Law, at the normative level, therefore changed to reflect the negotiated responses to these pressures, not only reinforcing fundamental values, but responding to basic changes in roles and collectivities.[82] Roles and the economy would change very quickly, but basic values would change slowly.

Like Weber and Marx, Parsons' theory (summarised in figure 3.1) explained the form of law in Western societies. Because of the clear distinction between levels of the normative structure, law was general in its application and secular. It was distinct from morality and religion, and rather than enforcing shared morality it had the role of fostering organic solidarity—to use Durkheim's term. Law was closely related to, but distinct from, politics. This relationship found expression through notions of judicial independence from the political process. In explaining this process of functional specialisation Parsons leant heavily on Durkheim's conceptualisation of the division of labour and organic solidarity. As functional differentiation increased so too did the level of interdependence. The 'general legal system' played an important role in this interdependence by providing a universal system of rights and duties for formally equal citizens who were members of the community. Law could only be autonomous if it was not too closely associated with moral or religious values or with a particular political regime. Law's role was to integrate the system, to hold together the different, interdependent subsystems by promoting those interdependent ties. As many commentators have pointed out, Parsons developed Durkheim's notion of law's part in social integration by articulating the role of law in systems integration. The legal profession, like all professions, epitomised for Parsons functional differentiation and interdependence. The legal profession had a specialisation in, and a monopoly of, legal knowledge, and correlatively had an obligation of public service. It had a crucial role in promoting the cohesion in society by integrating the legal system to ensure its autonomy and authority so that it could fufil its functions within the social system. It did this by ensuring that legal doctrine was coherent and consistent, that the rules were applied to fact situations, and that legislation met particular needs while remaining doctrinally coherent.[83]

The economic and sociological approaches discussed in this chapter share a number of common concerns and assumptions. Each theory is based on an acceptance of a capitalist social structure. Each seeks to explain human action in terms of the selection of means to achieve chosen goals. While the Weberian and economic approaches emphasise rationality and the importance of individual wants and preferences, Durkheim and Parsons were concerned with the integration of the individual into society. What most links the approaches outlined in this chapter is an acceptance of the fundamental tenets of liberalism and a belief that law is essentially benign. The next chapter looks at approaches to law and society which are based on more critical views.

Further reading

Law and economics

Hirsch, W. A. *Law and economics—an introductory analysis*, Academic Press, New York, 2nd edn, 1988
Ogus, A. I. and Veljanovski, C. G., eds *Readings in the economics of law and regulation*, Oxford University Press, Oxford, 1984

Durkheim

Clarke, M. 'Durkheim's sociology of law' (1976) 3 *British Journal of Law and Society* 249
Cotterrell, R. 'Durkheim on legal development and social solidarity' (1977) 4 *British Journal of Law and Society* 266
Parkin, F. *Durkheim*, Oxford University Press, Oxford, 1992

Weber

Albrow, M. 'Legal positivism and bourgeois materialism: Max Weber's view of the sociology of law' (175) *British Journal of Law and Society* 14

Bendix, R. *Max Weber: an intellectual portrait*, Heinemann, London, 1960

MacCrae, D. *Weber*, Fontana, London, 1974

Milanovic, D. 'Weber and Marx on law—demystifying ideology and law—toward an emancipatory political practice' (1983) 7 *Contemporary Crises* 353

Walton, P. 'Max Weber's sociology of law: a critique', in *The sociology of law*, ed. P. Carlen, Sociological Review Monograph 23, University of Keele, Keele, 1976

Parsons

Bredemeier, H. 'Law as an integrative mechanism', in *Law and sociology: exploratory essays*, ed. W. M. Evan, Free Press of Glencoe, New York, 1962

Mayhew, L. H. *Law and equal opportunity: a study of the Massachusetts Commission Against Discrimination*, Harvard University Press, Cambridge, Mass., 1968

Parsons, T. 'The law and social control', in *Law and sociology: exploratory essays*, ed. W. M. Evan, Free Press of Glencoe, New York, 1962

4

Objecting to objectivity: the radical challenge to legal liberalism

Gerry J. Simpson and Hilary Charlesworth

This chapter considers a number of critical theories[1] of law which provide alternative explanations of the function and position of law in (post)modern, (post)liberal states. These approaches can be distinguished from the models discussed in the previous chapter by their refusal to accept that law is essentially a benign, neutral and autonomous institution. The critical theorists discussed are particularly opposed to the conceptions of law considered in chapters 2 and 3 (favoured by liberal scholars and lawyers) which assume certainty and stability in legal doctrine and a degree of consensus within the society on which it acts. The approaches to law outlined here are reactions against the accepted, traditional mythology about the nature of law that is imbibed by law students, expounded by judges and legislators, assumed by practitioners and which comforts the general public. According to this mythology, the legal system can be differentiated from the political system or its cultural setting because, in contrast to activity in these spheres, law operates on the basis of abstract rationality and is thus universally applicable.[2] The durability and appeal of law can be accounted for within this mythology partly by its apolitical appearance. This account of the nature of law argues that law is above politics (or at least distinguishable from it) and merely resolves the competing claims of equal members of society. Accordingly, law involves the application of principles and rational argument. Logic and doctrine rather than power and influence are considered decisive.

The dominant liberal version of law as the expression of universal rationality is also dependent, to a degree, on the appearance or assumption of shared moral values and political ideals within the community. Law, then, is seen as a disinterested reflection of this value consensus.[3] A further assumption underlying the dominant legal discourse is that we can either gain access to objective truths or demonstrate the superiority of certain values. Indeed, the traditional strands of legal theory take for granted the existence of fundamental goods, whether these be material ideals (efficiency, utility),[4] social goals (equality, liberty),[5] or procedural entitlements (due process, natural justice, judicial rights).[6]

The critical schools discussed in this chapter attempt to demonstrate the highly contingent nature of these claims and the ideologies underlying them. The theories discussed below are diverse, contradictory and intricate. However, they each share, to varying degrees, a radical scepticism about liberal claims to objectivity and universalism.

The four critiques described in the chapter—marxism, critical legal studies, feminism and postmodernism—represent the major critical movements in legal theory over the past two decades (though marxism, of course, has a much longer heritage). Each term is something of an umbrella, covering a range of diverse and sometimes contradictory theoretical positions. Many of the individual theorists referred to defy these attempted categorisations. Others have travelled freely between the various schools. Carol Smart, for instance, has drawn on postmodernist thought to enrich feminist legal scholarship.[7] Alan Hunt has moved from an overtly marxist position to a more sceptical postmodern one. Most critical legal scholars maintain a foothold in another of the schools, for example Mark Tushnet's marxism,[8] and Patricia Williams' feminism and postmodernism.[9] The major themes and connections between the four schools are described here, before each critique is examined in detail.

The marxist approach to law remains significant despite the demise of marxist practices and the apparent retreat of left thinking in the political arena. The attempt to salvage marxist theory from Soviet practice continues unabated in law as in other disciplines where marxism has been influential.

The feminist legal scholar Catharine MacKinnon has drawn on marxist methodology to demonstrate the partial nature of law.[10] Feminist legal theory, throughout its various stages, has emphasised liberalism's failure to accord substantive justice to women as a class or gender. While early liberal feminism viewed law as an institution promoting and maintaining the unequal status of women by failing to include women in legislative schemes and law-making positions, more recent feminist treatments have emphasised the structural and material inequalities felt by women in their lived experience. Law is seen as acting upon these inequalities and maintaining and exacerbating them through the tenets of impartiality and neutrality.

The Critical Legal Studies (CLS) movement has drawn on legal realism (see below) and marxism to introduce new language and novel theories into the debate about law. CLS scholars confront the internal logic of law with insights derived from a wide array of other disciplines. Their project can be captured in the phrase 'law is politics'. CLS is a movement which seeks to demonstrate this claim in the face of opposing contentions that law is objective, neutral and free of ideology. In turn, North American CLS scholarship has been subject to critique by legal scholars of colour, who have developed their own 'critical race scholarship'.[11] While remaining sympathetic to many of CLS's claims, critical race theorists have been concerned to correct the white male perspective of some CLS arguments, which have the effect of disempowering minority groups.

Finally, postmodernism has approached law from the angle of a radical questioning of the certainties which have underpinned Western institutions since the Enlightenment. To the postmodern view, law's claims to objectivity, rationality and progress are unsustainable. These claims may function as legitimising narratives, but they can be deconstructed to reveal excluded perspectives and the power relations involved in their assertion. Postmodern challenges to law have drawn several critical responses. One reaction to postmodernism is what Alan Hunt has described as 'the Big Fear'.[12] This fear is premised on the belief that if rationality and objectivity are abandoned law will descend inevitably into total relativism. Can there be any ground from which to criticise legal institutions if there is no possibility of establishing a standard of justice against which they can be measured? Other critics of postmodernism suggest that if law is mere 'text' with no greater authority than a comic-book or a cornflakes packet, what possible reason could there be for complying with it and depending on it for social harmony?

Marx, marxism and law

In the 1960s Andy Warhol, the American pop artist, created a sequence of silkscreens with pictures of Mao Tse-tung tinted in slightly different shades. The message seemed to be that although there is only one Chairman Mao there are many Maos. Karl Marx, too, has been incarnated many times. The Karl Marx on whom legal theorists draw to support their marxist theories of law is an inconsistent and sometimes contradictory writer and as a consequence of this the definitive Marx has proved frustratingly elusive. Nevertheless, marxism remains a useful lens through which to view and explain the institutions of capitalist society. This section, therefore, explores a number of important versions of marxist legal thought, and considers their capacity to explain the phenomenon of law in the contemporary Western state.

Marxism remains one of the most influential critical political philosophies of the twentieth century. Its influence is felt everywhere in modern welfarist liberal democracies and yet is acknowledged hardly at all by those who govern them. Marxism is social theory *par excellence* and many of the social theorists discussed in the previous chapter are indebted to Marx for demonstrating the relationship between forms of law and types of social organisation. In law, as in most disciplines, marxism is a vital explanatory and critical tool. The demise of the Soviet Union has failed to divert the progress of marxist scholarship and theorising. As with previous generations of legal scholars, many critical roads continue to lead back to Karl Marx. Marxist scholarship has influenced many important strands of legal theory from the early schools of American and Scandinavian legal realism through to the more recent critical legal studies movement and various feminist approaches

Objecting to objectivity

to law. Indeed postmodernism, discussed later in this chapter, arguably represents the first attempt to construct an alternative approach to law that explicitly renounces the marxist method.

Marxist economics

Although he had studied law Marx himself wrote relatively little on the subject, concentrating his analysis instead on the economic and political manifestations of capitalism and class. Marx saw capitalism as a social and economic system in which the private ownership of property was central to the operation of all legal and political institutions. Private property remained in the control of a small capitalist class or *bourgeoisie*, who used its productive elements (machinery, factories, shops—i.e. capital) to produce profit and therefore entrench its class interests. According to Marx, however, the profits were produced not by capital but by labour; that is, by the industry of the *proletariat* or waged class. The difference between the labour costs (wages) and the price of goods was profit or surplus value. Capitalism's success was thus based on the exploitation of working class labour for the capitalist class's wealth and profit.

The marxist version of economics is, of course, markedly different from that of the economic analysis of law.[13] For marxists, economic value is expressed through a series of unequal, exploitative relationships between proletarian labour and capitalist power. The value of the work done by the proletarian is much greater than the amount she is paid for it. The surplus value is converted into profit for the capitalist. By contrast, classical liberals and 'law and economics' scholars assume that bargaining power is equal and employment transactions are entered into freely. The value of the work undertaken by the worker is exactly that which the employer is willing to pay for it (assuming no other employer is willing to pay any more and the worker herself is unable to convert her industry into a more fruitful end product). The revolutionary tendency in marxist thought is derived from the belief that the proletariat would become aware of its exploitation, attain consciousness of its historical and economic position as a class (class consciousness), and work to overthrow the capitalist system.

It is important to realise that Marx was describing and theorising about the social and economic relations he witnessed at a particular historical stage of capitalism. In the period of Marx's writings (the 1840s–1880s) capitalism in Western Europe was marked by the overt oppression and impoverishment of the vast majority of the working class, and a willingness on the part of the capitalist class to use repressive mechanisms of the state to discourage dissent. Initially, much of Marx and Engels' writing was merely descriptive of these conditions. Marx and Engels lived and worked during the grimmest period of the industrial revolution when the trade union movement had yet to organise effectively for an improvement in working conditions.[14] They witnessed the abject poverty of those who did not work and draconian labour supervision, coupled with oppressive terms of employment, for those who did.

From this historical position, however, Marx produced grand theory on the grandest possible scale.[15] His theory of historical materialism sought to explain the dynamics of historical change and hence to account for the entire course of human history, from beginning to end.

Historical materialism

The material or economic aspect of marxist theory begins from the premise that human beings need certain material goods in order to survive. To ensure the supply of these goods, societies are formed which are dedicated to economic production. The nature of production will define the type of society. This observation in turn leads to the insight that social change results from transformations in economic conditions and that major shifts in history come about when the means of producing wealth (the forces of production) change either through technological innovation or changing environmental conditions.[16] For example, the shift from feudalism to early capitalism coincided with the industrial revolution, which took place because the forces of production changed with the invention of steam-powered tools and machines, which in turn enabled mass production. Changes in the forces of production cause an alteration in the relations of production: for example, the shift from feudalism to capitalism has ultimately converted nations of rural workers into urban dwellers. Society is transformed and the individuals in it find themselves playing dramatically different roles. Thus economic relations ultimately determine the nature of cultural life and the constitution of political organisation.

Marx's historical materialism was a social evolutionary theory, envisaging the progress of human societies and their forms of government through a series of stages, some lasting thousands of years. Marx's notion that historical change was linear, progressive and inevitable situates him as a creature of the Enlightenment. Like the stories of social evolution discussed in the previous chapter,[17] Marx's version included the location of colonised societies at the bottom of the evolutionary scale. The four stages of society Marx identified were the clan society (hunting and gathering), the slave-owning society (pastoral), the feudal society and the modern capitalist society. These stages were the product of the economic impulses discussed above. In each stage there was a dominant idea (translated into the political system), known as the *thesis*, which was challenged by a competing or opposite idea, known as the *antithesis*. When the dominant idea or political system was destroyed by a change in the economic conditions and collapsed under the weight of its internal contradictions, a new system appeared which combined the surviving elements of the thesis and antithesis to produce a *synthesis*. This movement from thesis and antithesis to synthesis is known as a *dialectical process*.[18]

The transformation from feudalism to capitalism can again be used to illustrate how this dialectical process operated in practice. Under feudalism the monarchy was owed absolute unquestioning allegiance. Goods were distributed according to kinship, and status defined legal and economic relations. The thesis was monarchism, that is, the divine right of kings and queens; the antithesis was parliamentary sovereignty; and the synthesis of these ideas produced constitutional monarchy, with the separation of powers between executive and parliament.[19] However, the cycle continues with the struggle between the bourgeoisie, the class whose interests are paramount within a liberal democracy, and the proletariat who are the exploited class within this system. According to Marx and Engels, liberal ideas such as individual rights, freedom of contract, the rule of law and equality before the law played a role in maintaining capitalism. They were 'ruling ideas' which in reality worked only for the benefit of the capitalist class. Their presentation as universal, however, served to engender a false consciousness in the working class. They operated to obscure real inequalities and relations of exploitation, convincing workers that the capitalist economy was necessary and that their subordinate position was natural. The term 'ideology' refers to such ideas—those which present a false view of reality in the interests of one group in society. Eventually though, Marx predicted that the contradictions within capitalism would no longer be masked by the ideology of liberalism. The proletariat would discover the nature of its oppression by divesting itself of false consciousness and acquiring class consciousness. Capitalism would collapse under the weight of its internal contradictions and the antithesis, proletarian revolution, would be triumphant. This dialectic is millennial in its implications because the synthesis produced after a supposedly brief interregnum (the dictatorship of the proletariat) is the end-point of history itself: communism. Communist society would be free of the contradictions that doomed previous forms of social organisation and would harbour none of the conflicts that are catalysts for social change because wealth would come under collective ownership. There would be none of the class conflicts caused by the skewed distribution of private capital which marked previous political systems. The state, a capitalist institution designed to mask conflict, suppress dissent and protect the institutions of private property, would simply wither away. Law as an expression of state power would also be rendered unnecessary in this society.

The role of law

In anticipation of the disappearance of law marxists have been concerned to describe the role it plays in capitalist systems. In Marx's scheme society is founded on the infrastructure or base, defined as the economy, or the forms of production and the relations of production to which these give rise. What remains is superstructure. This includes law, culture, politics, aesthetics, education and religion, or what is sometimes collectively referred to as 'civil society'. The nature of social relations is determined by the economic infrastructure. Therefore, an understanding of the infrastructure is necessary to critique the institutions and phenomena in the superstructure where power *appears* to lie.

Taking the location of the legal system within the superstructure as a starting point, marxist theory has developed several distinct conceptions of the role of law in a capitalist state. Despite their differences these various marxist traditions share some common themes. Each is a response to the dominant liberal notions that law is either completely independent of political pressures and influences and so is ideologically neutral or, alternatively (on a pluralist approach), is subject to a multiplicity of pressures from a variety of social actors each competing for influence and eventually producing equilibrium or ideological balance.[20] Marxists reject the claims made by legal liberalism that law reflects value consensus, is value-neutral and is committed to equality.[21] They assert that law reflects class polarities, maintains economic subordination and entrenches social inequalities. However, there are a number of different explanations of how law manages this while maintaining a commitment to liberal values.

The first theoretical response discussed below, the law as social control model, devotes attention to law's function as a tool of class repression. This crude, mechanistic model offers law a negligible role in political philosophy. The second model sees law as relatively independent of powerful non-legal elites even though judges and politicians are largely drawn from these groups. Law, here, develops its own institutional autonomy and logic, and thus cannot be seen as an infinitely manipulable tool of the ruling elite. The third model, the commodity form model, is a variant of this approach. However, commodity form theorists de-emphasise the role of individuals and regard the independence of legal institutions from overt political control as irrelevant to the operation of law. Law is seen as the inevitable organisational form of capitalism. Finally, there is the model which suggests that the key to understanding law in modern capitalist societies lies in a study of its ideological dimension, its role in manufacturing consensus where there is conflict and in replacing reality with illusion. Each of these models is considered in turn.

The social control model: an instrumental view of law

The social control model derives its determinism from Marx and its revolutionary appeal from its simplicity. According to this view, law is an instrument of the ruling elite who use it to dominate the masses and repress dissidence. In a capitalist society the law is in the direct service of the masters of capital—the bourgeoisie. The class that controls the means of production also controls the legal system. In this way the legal system becomes a mere adjunct to the decisive relations played out in the economic infrastructure. The ruling class is monolithic and impervious to the independent ideal of professional neutrality in the law. The system's institutions are 'manned' exclusively by the bourgeoisie who, naturally, favour legal outcomes which maintain class hierarchies and capitalist efficiencies.[22]

Marx and Engels found numerous examples of law's transparently repressive function and documented them in their various writings. In *Capital*, Marx relates stories of farm labourers and rural dwellers being forced from their land by the authorities using court orders manufactured by fellow-bourgeois within the legal system.[23] Similarly, a century later, the British miners' strike of 1984 can be analysed from this perspective. In this case the Thatcher Government, the mining bosses and, finally and decisively, the police acted as a single class to crush a genuine workers' revolt. The actions of the police in using extremely violent force on the picket lines to end the strike was then sanctioned by a compliant judiciary. The bourgeois legal system was used simply as a weapon of direct class warfare. The Eureka Stockade and the great strikes of the 1890s[24] are historical examples of the use of law as a means of overt social control in Australia.

According to social control theorists, law is designed and implemented in its commercial form to maximise profit, in its civil form to protect property, and in its criminal form to distribute criminal sanctions. All this operates to the ultimate disadvantage of the proletariat. Law, on this view, is a highly discriminatory apparatus applied in accordance with the demands of class power and capitalist imperatives. At its most sceptical, this approach can lead to the suggestion that the realisation of social justice requires the abolition of law altogether.[25] The consequences for the use of law for progressive ends are obvious. In Alan Hunt's words, 'any such project leads to contamination'.[26]

The American legal realists, who flourished in the early 1930s, developed approaches which drew upon this instrumental view of law in a capitalist society. Writers such as Karl Llewellyn and Jerome Frank believed that law could not be understood simply by reference to statute or casebooks. Frank studied decisions at the initial trial court level[27] and concluded that, while the law at this level was well settled and relatively straightforward in its application, the facts of the case were always open to doubt and could not be scientifically proved. Therefore law, instead of being general, consistent and equally applied, was open to a number of informal and unscientific influences at the fact assessment stage. In contrast to fact sceptics like Frank, Karl Llewellyn was a rule sceptic. He believed that legal doctrine was also open-ended and that principles as well as facts were subject to the influence of judges.[28] The most notable Australian legal realist was Julius Stone, whose teaching at the Sydney University Law School influenced generations of lawyers, among them current High Court judges.[29]

For these realists, then, rules did not constrain judges and principles were not predictive of outcomes. Judicial discretion was the key to understanding adjudication and law could best be understood in relation to the behaviour of judges and officials. Llewellyn further argued that judicial behaviour depended on a number of personal, political or extra-legal factors.[30] In instrumentalist marxist terms, the behaviour of the judiciary both at the trial (fact finding and assessing) and appellate (doctrinal) level will reflect, uphold and favour dominant class interests. If judicial behaviour is decisive then these class interests will generally prevail.

Marxists are willing to admit two important qualifications to the notion that laws are an expression of class interest and economic relations. First, they accept that laws do not change automatically in accordance with historical developments, and second, they acknowledge that some statutes are designed to mitigate the worst effects of capitalism on the poor and even, in some cases, to cure the inequalities in relations between proletariat and bourgeoisie. Nevertheless, law continues to meet the requirements of the capitalist enterprise by virtue of the discretion employed within the system by judges, practitioners and law enforcement personnel. So, while individual laws or doctrines may undergo relatively little change between one historical period and another, the interpretation, application and enforcement of these laws can be radically transformed. Similarly, an apparently progressive piece of legislation can usually be undermined through the workings of the legal system, as the informal, social or discretionary elements of legal power are engaged in order to deprive individual statutes of effect. A typical informal element of legal power is the ability to pay for expert legal counsel. Marc Galanter has argued that, because of their ability to pay for better legal representation, and their general strategic position, those litigants with power, wealth and status will enjoy considerable advantages over less privileged adversaries, even in the enforcement of reformist laws such as consumer protection or equal opportunity legislation.[31] Galanter's argument and studies of the exercise of discretions by law enforcement personnel and legal practitioners are examined in more detail in chapter 6. Further arguments on how judges exercise discretions are considered in chapter 7.

Law as the logical form of capitalism: relative autonomy (I)

A rather more subtle, less reductive position than that of the social control model was favoured by E. P. Thompson, a marxist historian who found the idea of a crudely manipulated legal system insensitive to the complexities of actual historical experience. Thompson argued that although the legal system tends to reinforce the economic power of entrenched political interests it does not *always* do so. This is because the system develops its own internal logic and becomes relatively autonomous or independent of the capitalist system.[32] Lawyers take pride in the values of the legal order; judges, for example, cherish their independence. These values include neutrality and justice. In short, Thompson argued that the rule of law,[33] as a concept underpinning the legal system, was not simply a legitimating device of the ruling elite but a series of principles which demanded compliance from those working within the system, who might otherwise be disposed to ignore the law in coming to self-serving decisions. In the conclusion to his study of repressive penal legislation in eighteenth century England, Thompson noted that the legal system often delivered on its promises and offered support and protection to dissident and rebel groups and individuals within society.[34] Thompson offered a refinement of the marxist view of law as purely coercive and overtly biased. As a result, the form of law became critically important for marxist analysis.

Briefly, the argument runs, law in liberal societies can only function effectively if it is seen to be impartial. It cannot appear to be tyrannical and arbitrary if it is to be respected or at least obeyed by all groups within society. The standards of neutrality and generality to which the rule of law in liberal states subscribes cannot simply be disregarded when these conflict with the requirements of the ruling elite. Law's special position in society comes from its perceived independence and impartiality. Without this appearance of impartiality law would be revealed as an instrument of class power and would be resisted as such. This has two consequences. First, law cannot help but occasionally deliver justice in its liberal form. While the law is somewhat open to manipulation and tends to be the preserve of the moneyed classes, it is also obliged to make good on its promises of universality, impartiality and fairness. Failure to do so would endanger the law's mystique and result in its ineffectiveness. Thompson illustrated this view with some examples from the eighteenth century of cases where the ruling elites clearly wished subversives and rebels hanged or imprisoned, but where these individuals were freed by a legal system that afforded them basic natural justice and rights to a fair trial by a jury of their peers. The whims of the rulers were checked by the procedural requirements of a relatively autonomous legal system. In Thompson's words: 'The rulers were, in serious senses . . . the prisoners of their own rhetoric; they played the games of power according to the rules that suited them, but they could not break those rules or the whole game would be thrown away'.[35]

Thompson also demonstrated that law cannot be viewed simply as part of a superstructure taking its cue from the demands of economic forces. Instead, according to Thompson, law operates within the infrastructure itself. Economic practices do not merely give rise to legal doctrine. They are themselves defined by law. Thompson showed, for example, how longstanding agrarian practices became rights to quarry or to farm.[36] Even in modern contexts laws are often enacted simply to ensure predictability in behaviour that is already occurring. What people do within the infrastructure is accorded normative force by law.[37] The strict separation of superstructure and infrastructure or of law and economics, therefore, is no longer tenable.

Law as the commodity form of capitalism: relative autonomy (II)

> Skeeter says 'What is liberalism? Bringin' joy to the world, right? Puttin' enough sugar on dog-eat-dog so it tastes good all over, right?'[38]

Theorists such as Isaac Balbus and Evegeny Pashukanis take the idea of law's relative autonomy further. Again the argument is that law serves the capitalist economy and maintains the relations of production within it, but is institutionally entirely separate from that economy. There is, in other words, no overt political influence. Judicial personnel are independent of political parties and a strict separation of powers is maintained between the judiciary and the legislature and executive. Nevertheless law's liberal aspect facilitates the expansion of capitalism and the maintenance of economic hierarchy.

Law is autonomous because it functions independently of the will of particular groups or individuals. It is only relatively so because its form reflects and 'articulates' the form of capitalism itself. The law speaks the mind of capitalism. It is the written expression of capitalist practices. It is therefore far from ideologically neutral. However, its functional or instrumental impartiality is critical to its ability to perform its role in capitalist societies. It is because law does not respond directly to the perceived needs of the capitalist class that it is so successful in ensuring these needs are met. This occurs not because of the substance of particular laws, the make-up of the judiciary or the class biases of lawyers themselves. Instead it is inherent in the very form of the law—the commodity form.

In his article 'Commodity form and legal form'[39] Balbus draws a parallel between the way in which capitalist economies give all labour, products and talent an exchange value regardless of their real underlying value and the way in which the legal system assigns everyone an abstract, formally equal legal personality regardless of economic means, social status, education and so on. The adversary system is an expression of this 'commodification' because it professes to ignore the social background and economic position of individuals who come to court, on the basis of a commitment to formal equality. Individuals with varying degrees of eloquence, economic support and psychological capacity become simply plaintiffs and defendants for the period they are in court. Moreover, individuals are assigned a formally equal status with corporations, state instrumentalities and governments, via the device of considering these institutions as 'legal persons'. Another example of commodification is found in classical doctrines of contract, which assume that all parties to contracts are equally capable of assessing their own interests and freely choosing to enter contracts for their mutual benefit.

Thus the capitalist economy exchanges products and law exchanges people. Just as distinctive phenomena in the capitalist economy, whether they be McDonald's hamburgers or Tolstoy novels, become simply commodities, so too are diverse human beings and corporate entities given universal and commodified existence as legal persons in the legal system. Why does either system perpetuate capitalist inequalities and class dominance? The answer is that in order for capitalism and law to work effectively each must replace the reality of its outcomes with the ideology of its rhetoric. The rhetoric must in effect become reality. Capitalism is predicated on enormous gulfs in material and spiritual well-being. The law reinforces these gulfs. The legal principles of freedom of contract, equality of opportunity, equal pay for equal work and equality before the law represent the rhetoric, while the absence of equality in the workplace or in the exchange of labour is the reality. In Balbus's words, 'the systematic application of an equal scale to systemically unequal individuals necessarily tends to reinforce systemic inequalities'.[40]

Law as ideology

Perhaps the dominant current strain of marxist legal criticism locates law in the struggle over ideology. Theorists of this school[41] have drifted furthest from Marx's materialist concerns. They see ideas as equally important in creating the conditions for capitalism. Marx and Engels described the notion of 'ruling ideas', but gave them a relatively peripheral role. According to Marx and Engels, the ruling ideas were 'nothing more than the ideal expression of the dominant material relationships'.[42] Louis Althusser, the influential French marxist theorist, in effect reversed this equation, arguing that it was ideology that created and reproduced the conditions for capitalism.[43] Thus the various agencies of the ruling elite, such as the media, the law courts and the education system, are engaged in a continual process of manufacturing ideas and explanations which legitimise the practices of capitalism.

The Althusserian view of marxism is closely associated with and influenced by the concept of hegemony, first developed in the 1930s by the Italian communist Antonio Gramsci. Gramsci explained that in advanced capitalist states the repressive nature of the state and the law is minimised or disguised through the ideological apparatus of civil society.[44] The institutions of education, law, media and culture create a near monopoly on ideas, which are constantly presented and reinforced in order to reduce dissent to a minimum. Hegemony is thus a dynamic concept, involving the continual reproduction of assent to the dominant ideology. Assent will never be complete—the ideological project is ongoing because dissenting voices exist and must be countered. However, on the rare occasions when ideological hegemony is seriously threatened, the state has recourse to the use of force. Law is unique within civil society in operating within both the ideological and coercive domains. But law is more important as a tool of legitimation, ideologically justifying and naturalising the capitalist order, than as a source of coercive power.[45]

According to this marxist view, law in liberal societies is a structure of ideas with great political and psychological effects. It is politics empowered. Law unifies social formation, in effect inheriting that role from religion,[46] and has become the ideological mechanism most responsible for creating the myth of consensus in a deeply conflictual society. In modern capitalist societies law is employed directly in the interests of capital or class interests only very rarely, usually when the challenge to the state or commercial interests is particularly acute. More typically, the law will be used in a non-coercive manner to create a climate of consensus within society, in which disruptive events become infrequent. The use of state violence to destroy competing class formations is thought undesirable, since it reveals the true basis of class conflict and unmasks contradictions underlying capitalist society. Law is much more effective at the ideological level.

Thus, for example, law will not be used to suppress working class organisations such as trade unions. Rather, trade unions will either be co-opted into the capitalist process (through instruments such as the Prices and Incomes Accord entered by the Hawke Labor government and the ACTU[47]) or dissolved through ideological/legislative attempts to fragment the working class and individualise contractual bargaining (such as the *Victorian Employee Relations Act 1992*). This is highly persuasive because the effect produced by law is of workers dismantling their own institutions in their own interests, in pursuit of ideals such as liberty and equality.

The political advertising case[48] decided by the High Court in 1992 illustrates further how judicial reasoning performs both an overt ideological role, in suggesting that sectional political choices are collective assumptions, and a functional role, in creating the conditions for the dominance of private capital in the production of ideas. In this case the court found that there was an implied right to freedom of political speech in the Commonwealth Constitution, and declared invalid Commonwealth legislation intended to prohibit political advertising in the electronic media at election times.[49] The right to freedom of expression is a core liberal value, and the Court derived the right in this instance from the existence of representative government in Australia. For marxists, however, representative democracy in modern liberal states is a charade. Real power continues to reside in certain dominant elites and the manufacture of information and ideology is a bourgeois preserve. The influential marxist theorist Herbert Marcuse describes the right to freedom of expression as 'repressive tolerance'.[50] While all ideas are permitted expression, only a select number of dominant and acceptable ideas are circulated through the mass media. Alternative or radical ideas are effectively silenced, not by law but by the operation of the market. They are simply made invisible by the sheer mass of mainstream material. The means of production—the technology of mass marketing and media production and the networks of distribution and dissemination—are held by a tiny elite who seek to perpetuate the ideology of capitalism through these channels.

The decision in the political advertising case, then, can be viewed not as a victory for free speech but as means of ensuring continued access by powerful interests to the most influential electronic media. The right to free speech for all, idealised by the Court, is translated by marxists into a right to bought speech by an already dominant ruling class. One might ask why the government would attempt to restrict speech at all if this analysis is correct. The answer lies in the marxist analysis of power in the modern corporate state. Briefly, contemporary marxists argue that most power is now held not by repressive capitalist governments but by private corporate interests. Usually the interests of these two sectors coincide. The political advertising case can be seen, however, as an example of an occasion when there was a fissure within the ruling elite, and a court was called upon to resolve the dispute. In this case the ideology of choice, rights and liberty which underscores liberal legal discourse meant that a decision in favour of the continued ideological dominance of private interests was inevitable.

Objecting to objectivity

Summary

Latter-day marxists have grappled with the increasing complexity of Western capitalism. Class warfare and false consciousness are unwieldy theoretical tools with which to confront the modern liberal state. Classes are no longer easily identifiable and consciousness has become fragmented. Therefore, the key to explaining how capitalism reproduces itself, and the relations of production with which it is associated, lies in the ideological domain. Law retains an economic function, of course, but its ideological functions are paramount.

Firstly, law has a psychological–educative role. While functionalists[51] see this as integrative (producing social cohesion), marxists view it as repressive (reducing dissent). Law, according to marxists, circumscribes our capacity to re-envision the social order and re-imagine the world. It becomes increasingly difficult to comprehend social and economic relations beyond legal categories. Law therefore maintains the economic and social status quo by giving it the appearance of being natural and inevitable.

Secondly, law possesses a superstitious dimension, a mystique, which idealises out of existence the inequalities of distribution and the arbitrariness of authority.[52] The judiciary and the government derive their power and legitimacy not from democracy or reason but from law. Legal discourse, with its Latin and its wigs, frightens and mystifies. It operates at a deeply psychological level to render the absurd and oppressive natural and just.

Finally, and this insight draws heavily on the commodity form analysis, the law functions ideologically to create legal personality, define human relations and ultimately fix identity. Legal abstractions are made real and the reality of our social position and our lived experiences is obscured. This becomes critically important in preventing oppressed groups from attaining class consciousness and acting as a class.

Marxist legal theorists were the first to develop a systematic critique of liberalism in law. They have questioned and challenged the assumptions of a complacent legal system which is rhetorically committed to equality and liberty and yet fails to give these values substance. They have provided legal theorists with an array of progressive ideas from which to draw. However, marxist critiques have been accomplished through the use of an agenda in which ideas such as class, economic determinism and false consciousness are dominant. These terms have little purchase within the modern corporate state. Classes have become increasingly unstable or stratified, the state has functioned to provide welfare for the poor, and the workplace often appears as a site of agreement and co-operation rather than the terrain of class struggle. The apparent failures of marxism as a practice have compounded these theoretical difficulties and suggested the need for new radical approaches to law. The rest of this chapter is devoted to three of these perspectives.

Critical Legal Studies

Critical Legal Studies is an umbrella term applied to a range of ideas that challenge liberal legal and political philosophy. It is as much a mood as a formal movement. Some of the proponents of CLS draw on marxist critiques of law and many of the themes discussed in the previous section can be found in CLS writing: the rejection of the liberal legal claims that law is built on a consensus of values, that law is objective and neutral and essentially egalitarian. One distinction between marxist and CLS writers is that they have different starting points. As seen earlier, marxist analysis begins with the economy and class relations, and studies law from within that scheme. CLS analysis centres on legal rules and the process of adjudication, and is concerned with law's failure to live up to its own ideals.

Another intellectual precursor to CLS is legal realism, which was mentioned in the previous section.[53] The emphasis placed by legal realists on the malleability of the language of law and the inevitability of policy choice in judicial decisions has been further developed within CLS. The realists also argued that the judiciary should more explicitly state the basis for decisions, allowing their policy preferences to be scrutinised and criticised so that policy would ultimately rest on scientifically acceptable propositions. They assumed, therefore, that judicial activity and the law generally were perfectible and capable of operating as a totally rational and logical science. CLS, however, rejects the legal realists' confidence in the possibility of a legal science.

The beginnings of CLS

CLS has at least three distinct cultures: the British, American and German.[54] The focus here is on the American manifestation which was launched self-consciously at a small meeting in Madison, Wisconsin, in 1977. Its initiators came from a variety of backgrounds: legal academics who had been involved in the American civil rights movement and anti-Vietnam campaigns in the 1960s and 1970s; scholars interested in a more radical marxist critique of the social order; and lawyers practising in the area of public interest law in legal service centres and poverty law practices.[55] These groups had in common a dissatisfaction with the way they had been taught law because their legal education had offered little guidance for action in the political and social turmoil of the United States in the late '60s and early '70s. The notion of law as abstract, neutral and based on shared social values did not accord with the deep divisions on racial and political issues evident in American society in the civil rights and Vietnam eras. Experience of the legal system suggested that the apparent neutrality of legal rules in fact often operated to favour privileged groups and that ostensible advances in legal rules were always qualified to prevent real social change. For example, consumer protection laws could be thwarted by the disparity in resources between consumer and manufacturer. A manufacturer could fight every claim made against it while consumers might be deterred from pursuing legitimate claims because of the cost of such actions.[56] So, many young 'progressive' lawyers concerned with reform began to search for a more adequate explanation of the role of law in society.

Law as politics

The central tenet of CLS is its rejection of the notion that law is quite distinct from politics. For liberals, the rule of law is the central mechanism by which individual liberty is ensured. It contains and regulates the tendency of political power to encroach on individual freedom.[57] In this sense, law and politics are quite different phenomena: law, says Ronald Dworkin, is based on 'objective' decisions of principle, while politics depends on 'subjective' decisions of policy.[58] For CLS, by contrast, law is as negotiable, subjective and policy-dependent as politics. Indeed law *is* politics and the rule of law is a myth.[59] 'Legal reasoning' merely rationalises the political decisions that are actually made. The asserted autonomy of the discipline of law, some CLS writers suggest, is not just narrow professionalism but also a method of avoiding scrutiny of the motives and ideology of case law and legislation.[60]

However, critical legal scholars generally view the legal system as considerably more complex than simply a rationalisation for the arbitrary, subjective exercise of power. CLS generally rejects the proposition that law operates in a monolithic way to benefit one class and to oppress another. The argument rather is that, by asserting its neutrality and abstract nature, and offering occasional comfort to unprivileged groups, the law is accepted both by those who generally benefit from it and by those who generally do not. In this way law *legitimises* the social order, operating to make existing distributions of wealth and privilege appear natural. This CLS argument is similar to the 'law as ideology' version of marxist legal theory discussed in the previous section.

The anthropologist Clifford Geertz makes the same point when he observes that law 'is not a bounded set of norms . . . but part of a distinctive manner of imagining the real'.[61] Law is a belief system which constructs social realities rather than simply reflecting them. Its principles have independent authority and influence decision making because alternatives to them seem impossible or unimaginable. What becomes important for CLS scholars is, then, to examine how the legal imagination is constrained: the investigation of how and why particular elements and rules of a legal system are given a privileged status and the effect this has on the structure of society.[62] Some CLS scholars have used the techniques of structuralist philosophy and literary theory to 'deconstruct'[63] classical legal texts in order to discern how legal categories are created and how they have functioned to justify particular social practices. Duncan Kennedy's complex analysis of the work of the eighteenth century lawyer William Blackstone is an example of this genre.[64] Others have shown how legal doctrine can perpetuate inequality by providing justifications for it. For example, legislation prohibiting racial discrimination in particular contexts can imply its acceptability in other areas.[65]

Crucial to CLS theory is the notion of the 'false necessity' of legal concepts. Many CLS scholars have examined how legal rules achieve an image of necessity and have challenged that inevitability and naturalness. One example is the sanctity accorded to private property within the common law's system of beliefs. A right to private property is accepted as inevitable and assumed to be determined by economics or human nature. The perceived necessity of such a right means that its consequences, for example poverty and inequality, are not regarded as legal issues but as questions of economics or politics. In this sense the legal system reinforces poverty and inequality through inaction.

CLS scholars emphasise that legal beliefs and meanings, far from being inevitable and natural, are contingent and constructed. They argue that the contingency of legal structures should be observed and described in order to make clear the political choices inherent in every legal rule. If we appreciate that the support and protection afforded to private property through the legal system are not inevitable, but are the endorsement of particular economic arrangements, reform becomes easier. Exposing the contingency of existing legal rules allows the rethinking of many basic legal concepts and their replacement with more satisfactory, if just as contingent, principles.

Some CLS writers have focused on particular areas of law in order to establish that rules and principles do not necessarily entail a particular result. This 'indeterminacy' argument holds that legal doctrines cannot determine absolutely the outcome of a case. All doctrines are manipulable, and thus a number of outcomes could be justified in any particular case by reference to the relevant doctrine. In a torts case, for example, it is never certain whether application of the rules regarding duty of care, breach of duty and causation will result in a decision for the plaintiff or for the defendant. Once again, the choices that are made in arriving at a particular result are political. Other CLS scholars have gone further in arguing that liberal legal doctrines such the notion of rights (see below) or the public/private distinction[66] are contradictory or incoherent. The process of exposing the incoherence and indeterminacy of legal rules is referred to by some CLS writers as 'trashing'.[67]

Law in a post-liberal society

One critical legal theorist, Roberto Unger, has attempted to formulate a general theory of law and politics in what he identifies as post-liberal society.[68] Unger argues that there has been a shift from the classic liberal state of the late nineteenth century to the post-liberal or corporate state of the late twentieth century. The post-liberal state has emerged from the disillusionment of right-wing thinking and left theory. The left can no longer conceive of a totally socialised economy without a commensurate loss of political freedom, while the sophisticated right has abandoned its allegiance to the unmediated free market and resigned itself to intervention on behalf of the market.⁶⁹ The result of these compromises has been a shift in the nature of the state. Law no longer plays the same role in modern liberal democracies that it did in, say, the 1950s.

Firstly, there is much more law and many more lawyers.⁷⁰ The amount of legislation passed by Australian parliaments, for example, has increased exponentially in recent years.⁷¹ Secondly, the law itself is different. A great deal of law is what Unger describes as law-government,⁷² or what in Australia is called administrative law. In the classic liberal state, law was used to regulate private relations between citizens (e.g. contract law) or was part of the state's enforcement machinery (criminal law). In the post-liberal state, governments have become highly interventionist. There is a marked tendency to use law to regulate the economy, redistribute wealth and organise social relations. Law has, in the process, relinquished its apparent generality and impartiality in many spheres.

In addition, law is no longer merely applied by officials but is also made by those officials. Rather than laying down clear rules, legislation now tends to use open-ended standards, requiring officials to decide, for example, what is in the 'public interest' or what is 'reasonable in the circumstances'. Legislation also prescribes that officials 'may' take certain actions, and they must decide how to exercise that discretion.⁷³ The increasing resort to administrative discretion in preference to principled decision making has led to the bureaucratisation of law.⁷⁴

At the same time, judges are more willing to take a purposive rather than a formalistic approach to decision making. The *Australian Capital Television* case is a good example of the application of purposive rather than formal legal reasoning.⁷⁵ The majority judges based their decision on their view of the overall scheme of the Commonwealth Constitution rather than on its literal words (or absence of words) concerning freedom of expression. The Murray Islands case, which carved out a special right to native title for some Aboriginal groups, illustrates judicial rejection of formally equal treatment in favour of substantive justice.⁷⁶ Unger argues that the shift from formalism to procedural and substantive concerns and methods is a product of the welfare state, with its emphasis on procedural and distributive fairness.⁷⁷ Moreover:

> As purposive legal reasoning and concerns with substantive justice begin to prevail, the style of legal discourse approaches that of commonplace political or economic argument. Indeed, policy-oriented legal argument represents an unstable accommodation between the assertion and the abandonment of the autonomy of legal reasoning . . .
>
> Courts begin to resemble openly first administrative, then other, political institutions. Thus, the difference between lawyers and other bureaucrats or technicians starts to disappear.⁷⁸

Post-liberalism, then, effects the demise of the separation of powers and the rule of law;⁷⁹ law becomes indistinguishable from politics.

Ironically, if modern liberal theory has become anachronistic, as Unger seeks to demonstrate, much of the criticism of that theory also loses its bite. If liberalism is no longer the dominant political ideology it ceases to be a significant target for attack. Unger's thesis is not universally accepted, however, and many would continue to maintain the relevance of both liberalism and its critiques.

Critique of rights

A prominent strand in CLS writing is that of the critique of rights. This critique draws on the marxist tradition, but stops short of identifying rights as a product of capitalism alone or accepting Marx's prediction of the obsolescence of rights in a properly communal society.[80] The critique of rights rests on what Duncan Kennedy has called 'the fundamental contradiction' in liberal legal theory: 'relations with others are both necessary to and incompatible with our freedom'.[81] Individual freedom depends upon, and at the same time is threatened by, coercive action by the state. The rhetoric of rights provides a way for liberal theory to resolve this paradox: if the only rationale for collective coercion is deemed to be the protection of individual rights, the apparent tension between individual and state is sublimated.

The CLS attack on rights as the heartland of liberal legalism has several aspects. There is the charge that the content of the rights asserted to be universal and fundamental is in fact culturally relative; and that modest developments in technology or gentle shifts in public temperament could render particular freedoms redundant.[82] For example, women would not need the right to an abortion (i.e. to destroy an unwanted foetus) if technological advances enabled the foetus to be removed without being destroyed, and if society then guaranteed an alternative caretaker to all foetuses. Connected to this is the claim that statements of rights are indeterminate and thus highly manipulable in both a technical and a more basic sense. CLS analyses of United States Supreme Court decisions on constitutional rights stress a pattern of reinforcing privilege. The right to freedom of speech provided in the US Bill of Rights, for example, has been interpreted as privileging those with money to buy access for their speech.[83] Recourse to the language of rights may give a rhetorical flourish to an argument, but this provides only an ephemeral advantage and masks the fact that what is really needed is political and social change so that it is not just the privileged few who benefit in practice.[84]

To assert a legal right, some CLS scholars argue, is to mischaracterise social experience and to assume the inevitability of social antagonism by affirming that social power rests in the state and not in the people who compose it.[85] The state is called upon to solve problems when parties could find solutions for themselves. The individualism promoted by traditional understandings of rights is alienating and ignores 'the relational nature of social life'.[86] Talk of rights is said to make contingent social structures seem permanent and to undermine the possibility of their radical transformation:

the only consistent function of rights has been to protect the most advantaged groups in society. A parallel, but quite distinct, critique of rights has been made by some feminist scholars and this is discussed below in the section on feminist legal theories.

One of the strongest responses to the CLS critique of rights has come from scholars from minority groups within American society, for example African Americans and Hispanic Americans.[87] The founders and major theorists within CLS have all been white men and this has inevitably shaped their worldview.[88] 'Critical race theorists' have argued, by contrast, that the assertion of rights can have great symbolic force for oppressed groups within a society, offering a significant vocabulary to formulate political and social grievances which is recognised by the powerful. Thus Patricia Williams has pointed out that for African Americans talk of rights has been a constant source of hope. As slaves African Americans were simply the objects of whites' property rights. Having attained the status of subjects with rights of their own, they are reluctant to relinquish them for the sake of a radical theory.

> 'Rights' feels so new in the mouths of most black people. It is still so deliciously empowering to say. It is a sign for and a gift of selfhood that is very hard to contemplate restructuring . . . at this point in history. It is the magic wand of visibility and invisibility, of inclusion and exclusion, of power and no power . . .[89]

Martha Minow articulates well the problem of denying rights discourse to traditionally dominated groups:

> I worry about criticising rights and legal language just when they have become available to people who had previously lacked access to them. I worry about those who have, telling those who do not, 'you do not need it, you should not want it.'[90]

Minow suggests that the open-textured language of rights can allow debate on legal and political choices without assuming a settled social agenda. In this sense the language of rights can be interpreted as a communal rather than individualistic discourse, 'a brave and fragile assertion that the weak have rights against the strong'.[91] It affirms 'a community dedicated to invigorating words with a power to restrain, so that even the powerless can appeal to those words'.[92] Sandra Berns points out that the critics of the CLS critique of rights affirm the value of rights discourse rather than the truth of traditional understandings of rights. They seek to transform rights to be inclusive of minority needs and experiences. In this way rights discourse can become a method of upsetting, rather than confirming, existing distributions of power.[93]

Critical legal education?

CLS scholars have been very critical of current forms of legal education.[94] The denial of the inherent logic or inevitability of the legal system and the concern with the way it is constructed, characteristic of CLS jurisprudence, suggest radical changes in legal education. Traditional forms of legal education encourage a belief in the naturalness, efficiency and fairness of the structure of law, the legal profession and of society as a whole.

Critical legal scholars have argued that law schools provide a thoroughgoing ideological training for service in the hierarchical worlds of government and the corporate sector. The training involves provision of inadequate, truncated information about the law and how it works, and relies on impoverished notions of legal competence and possibilities of life as a lawyer.[95]

Both the substance and methods of traditional forms of legal education have been scrutinised and criticised by CLS writers. Most of these writers have been from North America. The experiences and observations they draw on, however, are paralleled in Australian law schools where, generally, the transmission of information about legal rules is regarded as the core of legal education and legal reasoning is presented as the chief skill a law student should hope to develop; where classes are conducted in a formal and hierarchical manner; and where three-hour final exams are relied on as the sole or chief method of testing students' learning.[96]

The content of traditional forms of legal education, CLS observers argue, is deficient because of its emphasis on learning a series of rules, divided arbitrarily into discrete subjects, as though they were logically ordained. The rules are either discovered or interpreted (or both) by the techniques of legal reasoning, which is taught and learned as a specialised method of analysis.[97] These techniques reinforce the idea that legal decisions emanate from a more pure and filtered source than political and ethical beliefs and choices. They are employed to explain and justify the basic legal rules while at the same time defusing contradictions within the scheme of rules by reconciling or distinguishing cases, or identifying decisions as anomalous or unsound. Matters not susceptible to legal reasoning are regarded as 'non-legal'; that is, matters of morality or politics which are qualitatively different from legal issues.

The notion of a distinct method of legal analysis is an attractive target for the CLS movement because it is so central to the claims of logic and objectivity of the legal status quo, to the claim that we live under a 'government of laws not of men'. 'Legal' reasoning assumes, firstly, that the law on a particular issue is clear and pre-existing, and can be identified through an objective process; secondly, that the facts relevant to the determination of a legal dispute can be settled by objective means (for example through the application of the rules of evidence); and thirdly, that a proper result in a particular case is achieved through the routine application of the objectively determined law to the equally objective facts.[98] Even though it is highly manipulable the doctrine of precedent, which aims to preserve consistency with prior decisions, reinforces the idea that legal decisions have a special claim to objectivity.[99]

CLS scholars acknowledge that the analysis of legislative and judicial policy plays some part in legal education, but argue that it has a marginalised and perfunctory role.[100] The policies called upon to explain legal rules, or to balance or tip the scales in hard cases, are presented as communal ones but in fact they are drawn from a very limited, vaguely defined group: for example 'progress', 'efficiency', 'the need for certainty', the 'need for flexibility', 'protecting the administration of justice', 'encouraging out-of-court settlements', 'promoting competition', 'protecting consumers', 'not opening the floodgates'. Invocation of these policy formulae does not disturb the idea of a detached and fair legal system because they suggest that there is an inexorable logic to developments in the law.[101] This type of 'policy analysis' stops short of examining the political dimension of the asserted policies and values: how they support particular patterns of domination.[102]

The second aspect of the attack on traditional legal education is concerned with its method. Typical law school teaching methods, CLS writers claim, encourage passivity. Law school classes revolve around the teacher as an authority figure, presenting determinate rules in fixed categories. Transmission of 'good notes' becomes the signal of a good teacher and a good course.[103] Because legal doctrine is not taught in conjunction with legal practice it can be pictured as a distinct and pure science unsullied by the compromises and political choice of the 'real' legal world.[104] The separation between theory and practice in legal education also has the effect of reducing students' confidence about entering the legal profession, confining their ambitions to that of apprenticeship in hierarchical legal practices rather than engagement in less traditional work.[105]

CLS scholars assert that both the substance and the process of legal education implicitly and explicitly present the law as a system of necessary rules ordained by logic operating within an hierarchical system. Duncan Kennedy, for example, writes:

> Legal education supports [legal hierarchy] by analogy, provides it with a general legitimating ideology by justifying the rules that underlie it, and provides it with a particular ideology by mystifying legal reasoning. Legal education structures the pool of prospective lawyers so that their hierarchical organisation seems inevitable, and trains them in detail to look and think and act just like all the other lawyers in the system.[106]

Students emerge from formal legal education with a belief that the legal system is basically alright and can imagine only tinkering at its edges to improve it.[107] This type of legal education also trains students to accept that lawyers deserve a privileged status because they are the neutral guardians of the social order.[108]

What forms could a Critical legal education take? An important aspect of such an education is the understanding that the legal order is a system of beliefs and choices, ultimately developed in the same ways that ethical and political positions are. Students should come to understand the law's contingency and controversiality and, at the same time the ways in which it operates as a real constraint in decision making—how its rules are made to appear necessary and natural.

Teaching students how and why contradictory arguments can be made about legal propositions is one way of achieving this.[109] Students should recognise that interpreting any text involves a series of choices and that a completely 'neutral' or 'objective' analysis is never available. But this method goes beyond simply making students argue both sides of a case, flexing clever technical muscles. It is possible to articulate contrary legal arguments about a particular case and yet remain confident that only one will ever be seriously considered. This confidence is based on particular policies or values which participants in the legal system are assumed to share.[110] One aim of a Critical legal education is to locate and then dissect these apparently shared, general, objective values, to study the ways in which they are assumed to operate together, and finally to examine how they constrain the legal imagination and commit us to a particular distribution of wealth and power. James Boyle and Gerald Frug have given examples of how this might be done, in the context of a torts class and a contracts class respectively.[111] As Feinman notes: 'The critical vision requires an explicit engagement with values. Legal education in particular ought to focus more freely on explaining the political nature of the law. What choices are made? What choices are not made? What choices are not offered?'[112]

Exposure of the optional and controversial nature of legal propositions and policy considerations that are presented as fixed, secure and general in traditional legal education allows students to understand the structures of the legal system and to identify the possibilities for change within it. This process also allows scrutiny of the traditional vision of the legal system moving inexorably from the 'old, bad law' to the 'modern, enlightened law'.[113]

A second feature of a Critical legal education is the method by which students will gain a knowledge of legal principles. Recognising the political dimensions of the legal system will be of limited utility in practice unless students also understand the accepted rules and principles of the law. This does not justify a traditional legal education involving the transmission of 'masses of ill digested rules'.[114] CLS scholars argue instead that law schools should teach the way to learn the law, emphasising skills such as research, advocacy, counselling and negotiation over 'correct' answers.[115]

The passivity developed in law school classrooms is reinforced by the methods of assessment typically employed: exercises dealing with problems within strict subject categories to which it is assumed that there is a 'correct' response. The type of examination or test that assesses a limited range of abilities and then ranks students in order of success does not necessarily reward or encourage the skills important in practice. The results of these exercises are presented as a single mark, usually without any other comment on the student's performance.[116] By accentuating the difference in student capabilities these marks produce a merit ordering of students which in turn underlines the necessity and fairness of hierarchy in the legal profession. Differentiating the capacity of law students through problem-oriented exams, argues Duncan Kennedy, has no bearing on the quality of legal services they later perform. Law schools should aim to even up differences in student capacity through systematic training in real and useful skills and the provision of constant detailed feedback on progress in learning those skills.[117]

A third aspect of a Critical legal education would be the incorporation of a clinical or practical component into it. Some observers have discerned a tendency in the CLS movement to be 'purely intellectual', 'concerned only with the search for a satisfactory social theory of law . . . lead[ing] legal scholarship into becoming, like economics, largely an ideological weapon'.[118] In fact, many CLS writers have championed the importance of clinical legal education, which is often the most marginal and vulnerable teaching activity in the law schools which offer it.[119] Integrating theory and practice in legal education would enable students to directly observe the manipulability of apparently neutral legal rules and the way in which they operate to privilege particular groups. It would also allow them to see that many 'legal' responses to problems are quite inadequate.[120] At the same time, clinical experience would promote students' confidence in their ability to cope in practice and to contemplate careers outside large corporate legal structures.

The vision of legal education presented in the CLS literature has provoked some strong responses. Some commentators have even questioned whether critical legal scholars are appropriate members of law faculties. Paul Carrington, when Dean of Duke University Law School in North Carolina, argued that the radical questioning of the legal order by the CLS movement, and its apparent loss of 'romantic innocence' and faith in the idea of law and its institutions, meant that its proponents had 'an ethical duty to depart the Law School'.[121] Dean Carrington even suggested that the 'cynicism' of CLS may result in students learning 'the skills of corruption: bribery and intimidation'.[122] In Australia, the Commonwealth Tertiary Education Commission's review of law schools ('the Pearce Report') described CLS as apparently 'attack[ing] law schools very fundamentally . . . [and] oppos[ing] strongly efforts to educate students for careers requiring full legal qualifications'.[123] It seemed to imply that CLS was beyond the bounds of appropriate theoretical and critical enquiry in law schools.[124]

The charge that the aims of CLS are fundamentally at odds with the education of students 'for careers requiring full legal qualifications' is based on a misunderstanding of the Critical project. CLS challenges traditional forms of legal education, but it does not question the importance of legal education in training legal practitioners. Indeed, the asserted incompatibility of the CLS movement and legal education can only be sustained if the proper role of legal education is seen as simply the transmission and absorption of packages of rules.[125]

Proponents of CLS insist that the training of students as lawyers should widen rather than reduce their skills and horizons: lawyers should not simply staff the legal system but be actively concerned with changing it to achieve real social justice. CLS rejects the study of law in a social and political vacuum and a form of training that encourages complacency about the legal system.

Critiques of the critics

Critics have charged that CLS's criticism and decoding of the legal status quo is not accompanied by any clear or realistic agenda for change.[126] While some writers sketch alternatives to existing legal institutions,[127] these options tend to be utopian and the means for achieving them unstated. Little empirical work is undertaken by CLS scholars and only vague guidance is offered on how the insights of CLS may be incorporated in the actual practice of law.

A more basic and recurring criticism of the CLS project is directed towards its perceived nihilism: its lesson is 'who decides is everything, and principle [is] nothing but cosmetic'.[128] Many readers find this message disturbing and demoralising, or irresponsible.[129] Owen Fiss is one who has been alarmed by the 'purity of [CLS's] negativism'. 'Critical legal scholars want to unmask the law, but not to make law into an effective instrument of good public policy or equality. The aim of their critique is critique.'[130] Fiss sees CLS (and law and economics) as a symptom of a wider malaise, the disintegration of social values. He calls for social regeneration and the articulation of new public values through law (perhaps the Murray Islands case is an example of such a move), warning that critique without visions of alternatives will lead finally to 'the death of the law'.[131]

Some CLS scholars do not deny the charge of nihilism, describing the continuing critique of existing society as their first task rather than achieving reform in the short run.[132] They claim that critique will ultimately allow transformation of the legal tradition. The nihilism charge is not so readily applicable to others in the CLS tradition, such as Roberto Unger, who have sought to articulate social and legal frameworks with richer ethical content than the traditional legal canon offers.[133]

Like any theory of law, CLS is incomplete and unsatisfactory in some respects. Its value lies in its radical questioning of legal orders accepted as natural and in its challenge to the comforting notions of legal neutrality and objectivity. Law loses its claim 'to guarantee civilisation or to provide procedural cures for the real world of conflict'.[134]

Feminist legal theories

The feminist project is to analyse the causes of women's oppression and to develop strategies for ending that oppression. Feminist legal theorists have been particularly concerned to expose the ways in which law contributes to and perpetuates women's oppression. The last fifteen years have seen the development of an extensive feminist legal literature. Feminist legal scholars have drawn on some of the existing critiques of law, such as marxism and CLS, but have refined and redirected them.[135] For feminist legal theorists the starting point is not the economy or legal doctrine but women's experiences. Rather than seeking to analyse legal institutions and legal doctrine on their own terms, feminists have examined the mismatch between institutions and doctrine and women's lives. They have shown how laws and legal institutions silence women and fail to include or respond to their experiences. For example, the very categories in which the law operates—torts, criminal law, contract—are based on male terms of reference which leave unrecognised most kinds of injuries women suffer.[136]

Central to this argument is the notion that women's experience is different from men's. As Catharine MacKinnon has written:

> Feminism is an approach to society from the standpoint of women, a standpoint defined by concrete reality in which all women participate to one degree or another. This is not to say that all women are the same or that all women in all cultures and across history have been in an identical position. Rather, it is to say that the experience of women is concrete, not abstract, and socially defines women as such and distinguishes them from men across time, space and culture.[137]

Certainly there is consistent evidence that, despite the egalitarian promises of liberal philosophies, women as a group are in a much worse economic, social, political and legal position than are men. For example, even in a wealthy developed country like Australia, households headed by women are likely to be living in poverty.[138] Australian women earn less than men in all areas;[139] they are significantly underrepresented in political and public life;[140] they suffer disproportionately from domestic violence, and from the failure of the legal system to offer adequate protection against it.[141]

Yet, just as the CLS movement has been criticised for its limited perspective by members of minority groups, white, Western feminist legal theorists have been challenged by other women for their assumption that all women are oppressed in the same way. For example Larissa Behrendt, an Aboriginal lawyer, argues: 'Feminist analysis which sees the world as a struggle between men and women fails to see the pervading effect that racial oppression has on black men and women . . . For white women, sexism is the enemy. For black women, racism is just as insidious'.[142] While Behrendt observes the oppression of Aboriginal women by Aboriginal men, she contends that this phenomenon was a product of the European invasion of Australia.[143] Feminist legal theorists have also tended to avoid a class analysis of law and to overlook the fact that men do not benefit equally from legal sexism.[144]

Nevertheless, in common with feminist work in other disciplines, the feminist project in law is diverse: it has many methods and many voices. Some feminist legal scholars have drawn on feminist writing in philosophy, literature and psychology to expose the hidden gender of the structure and vocabulary of the law, its privileging of the masculine at every point.[145] (As Catharine MacKinnon has argued, the law sees and treats women in the same way that men see and treat women.) Feminist approaches to law can be categorised in a variety of ways. None fully captures the overlap and intersections between feminist theories.

Liberal feminism

Liberal legal feminism accepts the language and aims of liberal legal theory, but argues that these will only be made good when women have equal access to the 'liberal promise'.[146] It is concerned to provide a 'level playing field' for women so that they can compete with men on the same basis. When women and men are in the same position, or are equally qualified for a particular position, there should be no discrimination between them on the basis of sex. Liberal feminists reject any notion that the law should tolerate or recognise intrinsic differences between women and men. Their strategy is to require the law to fulfil the liberal claims that it is objective and rests on a principled basis. These claims are compromised by discrimination between the sexes.

The liberal approach characterised the first years of feminist legal studies and has achieved a certain level of official acceptance. Liberal feminists have worked for reform of the law to remove legal and social barriers to women being treated like men in the public sphere. Federal and State equal opportunity laws are a product of this spirit. Their goal is to achieve equal treatment for men and women in the public areas of paid employment, the provision of goods and services, education and the housing market. Liberal feminism also informed attempts to remove 'protective' provisions,[147] such as weight-lifting restrictions which kept women out of certain industries,[148] the ban on women working in the lead industry because of its consequences for foetal health,[149] or the exclusion of women from combat duties in the military.

Not all liberal feminists adhere to a strict equal treatment or purely formal model of equality. As noted in chapter 2[150] some liberals are more concerned with substantive equality or equality of outcomes for all groups in society, and many liberal feminists see this as a more important goal for women than merely equal treatment. Thus liberal feminists have also promoted affirmative action legislation, which is designed to ameliorate the effects of past discrimination and to overcome historic barriers to women's participation. Special treatment for women is justified in this situation, because its aim is to promote an ultimately neutral outcome.[151] Apart from this limited acknowledgement of the need for structural change to achieve equality, liberal feminists do not regard the legal system itself as contributing to the inferior position of women. This approach adopts the vocabulary, political theory and epistemology of the law as it currently operates.

'Epistemology' refers to the basis for knowledge within a particular field. Liberalism as a theory tends to be allied with the epistemology of empiricism—a method which seeks to draw objective conclusions from direct observation of the world. Feminist empiricists have pointed out that knowledge in all areas has tended to be generated by men observing other men; thus empiricism has failed to live up to its claim of objectivity. The feminist empiricist argument is that true objectivity will only be attained when women are included as both the subjects and objects of knowledge. In other words, androcentrism is a methodological bias in all disciplines (including law) which, once identified, can be eradicated. As Sandra Harding notes, on this view the problem is 'bad science . . . not science-as-usual'.[152]

Adopting this epistemological stance, liberal feminism assumes that the law is ultimately rational, impartial and capable of achieving justice if it includes women and allows proper individual choice. The reluctance of some judges to give effect to equal opportunity legislation by interpeting it in a purposive way may be attributed by liberal feminists to the overwhelming maleness of the judiciary and the resultant male bias in legal decision making, which, they may argue, can be cured by appointing more women judges. Liberal feminism is less likely to take issue with discrimination that occurs in areas deemed 'private'—for example, the family, religious institutions or private clubs. Yet it is arguable that discrimination in these areas (such as the disproportionate burden of child care and domestic responsibilities borne by women) contributes a great deal to women's disadvantages in the 'public' sphere. Feminist concerns with the distinction between public and private are discussed further below.

More problematic still is the individualistic nature of the law designed to combat sex discrimination. In dealing with individual cases of discrimination rather than structural inequalities such as gender segregation and pay inequity across the workforce, law can at most solve a limited number of discrete problems and it fails to address the underlying causes of sex discrimination. The principle of equal opportunity, says Nicola Lacey, is 'inadequate to criticise and transform a world in which the distribution of goods is structured along gender lines'.[153] It assumes 'a world of autonomous individuals starting a race or making free choices [which] has no cutting edge against the fact that men and women are simply running different races'.[154]

Cultural feminism

Cultural feminists reject any notion that women should seek to assimilate their aspirations and opportunities with those of men. As Clare Dalton has observed, they see the language of equal rights and the work of litigation and lobbying as tacitly reinforcing the basic organisation of society and only giving women access to a world already constituted by men.[155] While liberal feminism argues that women and men have equal capacities and therefore should be treated the same, cultural feminism asserts the difference, and superiority, of women's understandings of social life. Epistemologically, it is a feminist standpoint theory. Standpoint theories emphasise the importance of knowledge based upon experience. They have been developed particularly by marxist theorists, who have focused on working class experience and argued that the view from the bottom of society, including the experience of oppression, is both more authentic and more complete than the view from the top. Feminist standpoint theorists have adapted this point to assert that women's subjugated position allows them to formulate more complete and accurate accounts of nature and society, 'morally and scientifically preferable' to those produced by men.[156]

The work of the American child psychologist Carol Gilligan has been particularly important in the development of this variety of feminist legal theory. In her book *In a different voice*[157] Gilligan identifies two ways of speaking about moral issues, which she terms the 'logic of justice' and the 'ethic of care'. The logic of justice deals with moral problems in an abstract way in terms of hierarchies of rights. The ethic of care, by contrast, deals with moral problems in terms of webs of connection. For example, in one study Gilligan confronted two eleven-year-olds with a dilemma involving the question of whether a man should steal a drug he could not afford to buy, in order to save his wife's life. The boy in the study adopted the logic of justice, arguing that the man should steal the drug, since life is more important than property. If he was then convicted of theft the judge would probably take the circumstances into account in sentencing. The girl in the study applied the ethic of care, emphasising the preservation of relationships and the importance of 'talking it through', so that a way could be found to let the wife have the drug and to keep the husband out of jail.

According to a widely accepted hypothesis of six universal stages of moral development in children, an ethic-of-care response ranks a full stage lower in maturity than one applying the logic of justice.[158] Gilligan notes a general disparity between women's experience and the representation of human development contained in the psychological literature. The usual interpretation of this phenomenon was that it indicated problems in women's psychological development. Gilligan points out, however, that most developmental theories have been based on research which has used male research subjects only. She turns the traditional analysis on its head by arguing that the failure of women to fit existing models of human growth suggests a limitation in the notion of the human condition contained in those models. She tries to avoid making generalisations about women or men, or about the origins of the differences in moral reasoning.

Although Carol Gilligan's conclusions have been criticised by some fellow psychologists,[159] her work has struck a strong chord with many legal feminists. The hypotheses drawn from Gilligan's research are that the logic of justice and the ethic of care correspond to masculine and feminine styles of reasoning, and that just as traditional psychological theories have privileged a male perspective and marginalised women's voices, so too law privileges a male view of the universe. Law's hierarchical organisation, its adversarial format and its aim of the abstract resolution of competing rights make it an intensely patriarchal institution. The language and imagery of the law underscore its maleness: it lays claim to rationality, objectivity and impartiality, characteristics traditionally associated with men; and it is defined in contrast to emotion, subjectivity and contextualised thinking, the province of women.[160] The reasonable man, the benchmark invoked in many legal decisions, may have been gender-neutralised into the reasonable *person*, but this change of language merely obscures the masculinity of the standard, which is maintained by the very requirement of reasonableness and the way in which that requirement is understood.[161] Christine Boyle has argued that law and legal scholarship that ignore issues of particular concern to women 'ought not to make a claim to universality. "Men and the Law" is tolerable as an area of intellectual activity, but not if it is masquerading as "People and the Law"'.[162]

Some feminist jurists have tried to devise methods of introducing a different, women's, voice into the legal process. They have questioned the adversarial model of justice which assumes that the right resolution of legal disputes emerges from a contest between two parties, judged by a neutral decision maker.[163] Some have proposed a model of feminist justice in which the decision maker goes beyond adjudicating on the cases presented by the parties and can act creatively to avoid a win/lose situation.[164] Mediation and conciliation have been explored as alternatives to litigation. Other feminist lawyers have advocated broader notions of who has a sufficient interest to pursue particular claims, or wider conceptions of the evidence deemed to be relevant in a particular case. Feminist constitutional rights have been described, based not on the traditional respect for individual autonomy but on communal values. For example, Susanna Sherry envisages a right to freedom of religion which could protect membership in a community rather than individual liberty.[165] It has been argued that women judges could bring a 'new humanity' to the decision making process.[166]

Celebrating the differences between feminine and masculine modes of reasoning in the legal system is not without problems; indeed Gilligan's work has been referred to as a potential 'Uncle Tom's Cabin' for feminist legal theory.[167] No challenge is offered to the mainstream legal system by a 'different voice' appearing in various isolated areas of the law. Indeed some feminist jurists have pointed to the risk that 'feminine' methods of dispute resolution such as mediation between parties in an unequal position with respect to skills, information and power can in fact perpetuate inequality.[168] Further, the strategy of introducing 'women's voices' into the legal system could support essentialist theories about women and men and relegate women to a caring, supportive, inferior sphere.[169] It also begs the question of the cause of the difference between gendered modes of reasoning. Catharine MacKinnon has questioned the authenticity of the feminine voice documented by Carol Gilligan. The 'feminine', she argues, is defined by a patriarchal culture: 'For women to affirm difference, when difference means dominance, as it does with gender, means to affirm the qualities and characteristics of powerlessness ... [W]hen you are powerless, you don't just speak differently. A lot, you don't speak.'[170] End the system of male dominance, MacKinnon says, 'then we will hear in what tongue women speak'.[171]

Radical legal feminism

Catharine MacKinnon's work is another manifestation of feminist standpoint theories in law, although MacKinnon defines women's standpoint in a quite different way from that of cultural feminists. Qualities such as caring and conciliation have been foisted on women, she contends, by the structure of patriarchal societies, and are premised on a male view of womanhood. MacKinnon argues that the common failing of liberal and cultural feminist theories is that they implicitly accept a male yardstick: women are viewed as either the same as or different from a male norm.[172] By contrast, she asserts that sex is not merely a difference but a hierarchy involving dominance and subordination. Social relations are based on the premise 'that men may dominate and women must submit'.[173] The law preserves the gender hierarchy by keeping women 'out and down'.[174] Her analysis thus centres on male power and its deployment against women.

In developing her analysis MacKinnon was influenced by several elements of marxism, such as the notion of dominant and oppressed classes, and the dominant class's capacity to engender false consciousness in the oppressed so that they are unable to recognise their oppression. But MacKinnon rejects marxism's emphasis on economic relations as the primary ordering principle of society. Rather, she argues that gender is the most fundamental social division. Hence she maintains that her feminism is not an adjunct to any other theory, such as liberal feminism ('liberalism applied to women') or socialist feminism ('marxism applied to women'), but constitutes 'pure' feminism, or 'feminism unmodified'.[175]

MacKinnon's epistemological argument is that in a system of male power the way that men see the world is projected as objective knowledge. The male 'point of view is the standard for point-of-viewlessness, its particularity the meaning of universality'. '[W]hat counts as truth is produced in the interest of those with power to shape reality'.[176] In particular, the male point of view defines, objectifies and dominates women. MacKinnon points out that the male perspective is a way of knowing (and hence a form of power) that is not necessarily shared by all men. However, men will tend to adhere to it because it makes sense to them. For example, some men accept that when a woman says 'no' to sex she means 'no'; but many men believe, in their own self-interest, that when a woman says 'no' she often means 'yes'. Moreover, women are pushed to see reality in the same terms, even though it may contradict their lived experience. Thus a woman who eventually submits to sex even though she didn't want to may categorise her experience as sex rather than rape.[177] Again, prior to the 1980s, women knew that they were supposed to laugh at, put up with or be flattered by sexual innuendo and attentions at work. Only in the past decade has this behaviour been named from the woman's point of view as sexual harassment.

MacKinnon has worked for an expansion of the ambit of the law to cover traditionally legally unrecognised harms of particular concern to women, such as sexual harassment[178] and pornography.[179] She argues that the feminist project in law is to legitimise the real injuries women suffer in order to make them unacceptable.[180] She has campaigned, for example, to have pornography legally recognised as a form of sex discrimination against women, and to enable women harmed by pornography to claim compensation. From the perspective of male dominance, pornography is either a form of speech that requires protection in the interests of individual freedom or is 'obscene' in the sense that it offends 'community standards'. These conceptualisations ignore its impact on women.

MacKinnon's focus on sexual harassment and pornography are consistent with her argument that male power is chiefly exercised through the sexual subordination of women. Radical feminists in general have been most concerned with women's sexuality and women's bodies. Radical legal feminists have worked on issues such as rape law reform and better protection for women against family violence.

Catharine MacKinnon has also turned her attention to equality doctrine and, as noted above, has rejected the traditional understanding of equality in terms of sameness or difference. She describes an alternative legal analysis of inequality for which the central question is whether a given policy or practice perpetuates women's subordination.[181] The law should support freedom from systematic subordination *because* of sex, rather than freedom being treated without regard to sex. If the issue of gender inequality is redescribed as one of domination and subordination, sex discrimination laws simply promising equal treatment are of limited utility. Following MacKinnon's analysis, Christine Littleton has proposed defining the goal of equality as 'acceptance', so that social institutions could be required to be restructured to fit women and their life patterns.[182]

Catharine MacKinnon's theories about law and inequality have been controversial both inside and outside the feminist community. Critics have wondered how MacKinnon can identify an authentic women's voice in a world she describes as utterly dominated by men and how she can work within a legal system she describes as unremittingly gendered.[183] MacKinnon's work has also been read as endorsing an essentialist position without regard to the influence of race, class or sexual preference.[184] In turn, MacKinnon has been vigorous in her own defence[185] and has engendered lively debates among feminist and non-feminist legal scholars alike.

Postmodernist and critical legal feminism

A final set of feminist approaches to law are those which draw on the insights of Critical Legal Studies and postmodernism. CLS was discussed in the previous section of this chapter, and postmodernism is discussed in the next section. While the foundational theorists of both CLS and postmodernism have been white men, feminists have found various aspects of their work useful. The feminist historian Joan Scott writes:

> Post-structuralism and contemporary feminism are late-twentieth-century movements that share a certain self-conscious critical relationship to established philosophical and political traditions. It thus seemed worthwhile for feminist scholars to exploit that relationship for their own ends.[186]

As explained in the next section, one of the themes of postmodernist scholarship has been the questioning of universal theoretical claims. Grand theories of society and/or history, such as those put forward by Durkheim, Weber and Parsons[187] and by Marx,[188] have been rejected in favour of the examination of particular exercises of power and sites of struggle. In a similar vein the British feminist legal theorist Carol Smart has questioned whether Catharine MacKinnon's construction of Grand Feminist Theory is useful in women's struggles. Such endeavours, she suggests, do not capture the contextualised and partial nature of women's knowledge and experience.[189] She points out, for example, that law is not a totalising, patriarchal institution; legal doctrine is not uniform, but is full of inconsistencies and contradictions[190]—a point made also by feminists allied with CLS. Thus the law does not operate in a monolithic way to oppress women and advantage men. It is important to realise that in saying this Smart is not articulating a more 'acceptable', middle-of-the-road version of feminism, but is insisting that feminists pay careful attention to the specific operations of law and positions of women.

Allied with a rejection of grand theory is a rejection of essentialism. Postmodernist feminists argue that there is no essential 'Woman', and no broad category of 'Women' whose uniform 'interests' can be pursued in law reform. In this, postmodernist feminists echo the voices of African American and Aboriginal feminists who insist that their experiences, perspectives and stories are different from those of the white, middle class feminists who have claimed to speak on their behalf.

Postmodernist feminists might go further, however, in embracing 'the fractured identities . . . [of] modern life'.[191] So just as there is no essential women's experience, neither is there an essential Black women's experience. Patricia Williams plays with the notion of multiple identities in her book *The alchemy of race and rights*. Although the book is subtitled 'Diary of a law professor', she makes it clear that being a law professor does not provide her with a unified or stable identity:

> I am a commercial lawyer as well as a teacher of contract and property law. I am also black and female, a status that one of my former employers described as being 'at oxymoronic odds' with that of commercial lawyer . . . [M]y attempts to write in my own voice have placed me in the center of a snarl of social tensions and crossed boundaries . . . [T]o speak as black, female, *and* commercial lawyer has rendered me simultaneously universal, trendy, and marginal.[192]

The dangers of exploring multiple subject positions are frankly articulated by Williams's down-to-earth sister, who dismisses her in medical and racial terms—just another 'schizophrenic black lady'.[193] Yet as Williams insists, 'subject position is everything in my analysis of the law'.[194]

Storytelling is one method that builds on the idea of different subject positions and that has been taken up by some feminist legal writers. Storytelling is a radically different method from traditional legal theoretical writing, since the writer foregrounds his or her individual experience rather than assuming a distanced, purportedly objective stance. Consequently, it has been attacked as an illegitimate form of legal scholarship.[195] Nevertheless, as Sandra Berns argues, storytelling has the unique ability to draw attention to the effects of law on particular lives, and to project alternative futures.[196]

Another postmodernist concern that has been taken up by feminist legal scholars is the notion that, contrary to empiricist claims, we can never have direct, unmediated access to 'reality'. Rather, all our experiences and understandings are filtered through language. Binary oppositions are a particular linguistic feature which structure thought in a wide range of areas. As noted earlier, for example, feminist arguments about equality for women have revolved around the question of whether women are the same as or different from men. While the sameness/difference dichotomy may appear inescapable, postmodernist feminist writers have sought to deconstruct the dichotomy and to arrive at new understandings of equality which might be more useful to women in a variety of contexts.[197]

Postmodernists further see language as organised into specific discourses, of which law is one. As such, law does not simply act upon pre-existing masculine and feminine identities, it actively helps to constitute those identities.[198] Thus postmodernist feminists have been interested to analyse legal texts in order to identify the ways in which gender is constructed in and through law. Gender identities are never constituted once and for all, however, but are constantly re-presented and re-made in discourse.[199] Consequently, legal discourse is one possible site for political struggle over the meanings of gender.[200] There is room for feminists to present arguments which confront traditional legal representations of women. For example, feminist lawyers have been vocal in challenging the ideas, taken for granted by many male judges and lawyers, that rape has a greater impact on 'chaste' women than on prostitutes, or that it is acceptable for a man to subject his wife to 'rougher than usual' handling in order to get her to consent to intercourse, or that when a woman says 'no' to sex she often means 'yes'. By resisting the stereotyping of women in these ways, feminist activism has changed the nature of public discourse about rape. This is a different use of law from the law reform strategies proposed by liberal or radical feminists.

Carol Smart argues, however, that feminists should think twice about engaging with law. She is particularly concerned that Catharine MacKinnon concedes too much authority to law: although MacKinnon urges changing the values of the law she nevertheless accords it considerable power, preserving its place in the hierarchy of male structures.[201] Smart is more concerned to de-centre law. On the one hand, she sees various areas of law as simply parts of wider discourses. Thus it is unhelpful to focus only on legal doctrine. For example, 'tackling family law means tackling constructions of fatherhood, masculine authority, and economic power'.[202] It is these constructions which are the underlying 'problems' for women within marriage and at its dissolution, and they are merely manifested in the legal rules. Moreover, Smart urges feminists to deny law's claims to make authoritative pronouncements about women. For example, if a woman says 'I was raped', and the law says 'you consented', feminists should not try to change the law on consent, but should refuse to believe the legal story and stop according to law the power to speak the 'truth'. In this respect it is better, Smart has said, to be a feminist journalist than to be a feminist lawyer.[203]

The public/private distinction

One explanation that feminist scholars of various persuasions offer for the dominance of men and the male voice in all areas of power and authority in the Western liberal tradition is the dichotomy drawn in liberal discourse between the public sphere and the private or domestic one.[204] Although the public/private distinction has been thoroughly attacked and exposed as a culturally constructed ideology it continues to have a strong grip upon legal thinking. The language of public and private is built into the language of the law itself: law lays claim to rationality, culture, power, objectivity—all terms associated with the public or male realm. It is defined in opposition to the attributes associated with the private, female sphere: emotion, nature, passivity, subjectivity.[205]

Moreover, according to liberal legalism, the operation of the law has always been primarily within the public domain. The workplace, the economy, the distribution of political power are all seen as appropriate for legal regulation, while the family, the home and what goes on within it have been long regarded as unsuitable for direct state intervention.[206] 'Domestic' violence, for example, has generally had a different legal significance from that of violence that takes place between non-family individuals and/or in public places. Women have difficulty convincing law enforcement officials that violent acts within the home are criminal.[207] Injuries recognised as legally compensable are those occurring outside the home. Damages in civil actions are typically assessed in terms of inability to participate in paid work.[208] In this way law also helps to construct the division between public and private. Placing an aspect of life inside or outside the law marks it as public or private.[209]

While the private world is characterised by an absence of law, that does not mean it is uncontrolled. Regulation of marriages, taxation, social security, education, health and welfare all have immediate effects upon the private sphere and construct a particular and often oppressive legal vision of the appropriate role of families and of women within them.[210] As Frances Olsen points out, the notion that the state does not intervene in the private realm is a myth which masks its control.[211] Olsen adopts some CLS themes in arguing that legal rules involve policy choices about the family, and that the concepts of state intervention or non-intervention in the family are incoherent. She notes that, far from simply acting upon pre-existing 'families', the state makes policy choices which define and redefine the family. For example, '[l]aws establish who is married to whom and who shall be considered the child of whom'.[212] Such laws affect the formation and functioning of families.[213]

In this context it is difficult to say what measures constitute intervention and what measures constitute non-intervention in the family. For example, is it intervention in the family to make divorce easy or to make divorce difficult? Is it intervention or non-intervention to grant divorce at all?[214] Moreover, different people may experience the same policy choice differently.

If the state decides to allow lesbian and gay marriages, lesbians and gay men who want to get married may see that as non-intervention in their private lives. On the other hand, people opposed to lesbian and gay marriage will see the decision as (an unwarranted) intervention in 'community values' concerning marriage. Some lesbians and gay men would also oppose such a step as an intervention in lesbian and gay relationships, aimed at making them conform more closely to the heterosexual norm. Ultimately, Olsen argues, intervention means no more than disturbing a current norm, while non-intervention means reinforcing the status quo.[215] Distinctions such as public/private and intervention/non-intervention provide the ideological underpinnings of the current system in which women and children are subordinate to men in family hierarchies.

Indeed, as Katherine O'Donovan notes, legal 'non-intervention' leaves the power of husbands and fathers in families unrestrained. Men have power in families because of their superior economic position, which places other family members in a position of dependence.[216] Economic independence is gained by work in the public sphere; work in the private sphere, which is mostly performed by women, is not considered work and is done for love rather than wages.[217]

Although liberals have been concerned with inequalities which are manifest in the public sphere, they have tended to ignore inequalities within families. Susan Moller Okin is one liberal feminist who has attempted to remedy this deficiency.[218] She urges liberal theorists to take private inequality seriously, on the ground that public equality will never be achieved so long as hierarchy and subordination persist within the family.

Critique of rights

Another feminist project in jurisprudence is a critique of rights: questioning whether the acquisition of legal rights advances women's equality. Some feminist scholars have argued that, although the search for formal legal equality through the formulation of rights may have been politically appropriate in the early stages of the feminist movement, a continuing focus on the acquisition of rights may not be beneficial to women.[219] To some extent, this debate echoes that generated by the CLS critique of rights.

Feminists have pointed out that the indeterminacy and incoherence of rights discourse works to the disadvantage of women: 'the meaning of . . . rights is determined by the perspective of the person who is the potential rights-bearer or rights-granter, and dependent on precisely who is defined as the rights-bearer'.[220] For example, a right to family privacy can be interpreted to support or undermine a law requiring medical workers to notify a young woman's parents that she is using contraception, depending on whose privacy is given priority. A related problem is that rights discourse reduces intricate power relations in an overly simple way.[221] The acquisition of formal rights, such as the right to equal treatment, is often assumed to have solved an imbalance of power. In practice, however, the promise of rights is thwarted by the structural inequalities of power: economic and social dependence of women on men may discourage invocation of legal rights which are premised on an adversarial relationship between the holder of a right and the infringer.[222] For example, although women who are the targets of violence in the home may have a legal right to obtain some form of intervention order, the nature of their relationship with the perpetrator of the violence may make it impossible in fact to invoke the right.

More problematic still are rights which are designed to apply to women only and which are not equally applicable to men, such as rights to reproductive freedom and to choose abortion. Assertion of such rights often produces considerable political controversy and invites unresolvable counter-claims which conflict with women-specific rights, such as the right to life of a foetus.[223] A related issue is that rights are cast in individual terms and promote individualism. Invocation of sexual equality rights therefore may occasionally solve a particular case of inequality for a particular woman but it will leave the position of women generally quite unchanged. Indeed, the position of women generally may not be visible within a rights-based framework.

A second major problem with the assumption that the formulation of rights inevitably spells progress for women is that of competing rights: a right for women and children not to be subjected to violence in the home may be balanced against a man's property rights in his home or his right to family life.[224] Or a rape victim's right not to be cross-examined on her prior sexual history may give way to the alleged rapist's right to life, liberty and security.[225] Moreover, particular rights may come to be appropriated by more powerful groups: Carol Smart gives the example of the use made of the provisions relating to family life in the European Convention on Human Rights, by fathers asserting their authority over ex-nuptial children.[226]

A third, related concern feminists may have with a rights approach to achieve equality is the way in which particular rights can operate to the detriment of women. The right to freedom of religion is an example of a 'human' right which can have a differing impact on women and men. Freedom to exercise all aspects of religious belief is not always of benefit to women as many accepted religious practices involve reduced social positions and status for women. Islamic law, for example, allows men much greater rights in divorce than it does women.[227] In Australia, Christian churches have relied on the right to freedom of religion to argue that they should not be subject to sex discrimination legislation, thereby conceding the incompatibility between Christian doctrine and equality for women.[228]

Not all feminist legal theorists are sceptical of rights discourse. For reasons similar to those advanced by critical race theorists, set out above, some feminists point to the mobilising and liberating aspects of the invocation of rights. The use of the rhetoric of rights can allow 'private' concerns to become part of the political and legal agenda.[229] Jenny Morgan has argued for the consideration of gendered rights—in other words, rights which 'explicitly address ... the inequalities of power between women and men'.[230]

Rights which acknowledge that the subordination of women is the central issue in gender inequality, and which are 'capable of promoting a transformation of patriarchal order and control',[231] could be a useful outcome of Australian constitutional reform.

Postmodernism comes to the law school

Postmodernism is, in one sense, simply a theoretical response to a particular moment in history, a reaction to the catastrophic failures of global political idealism in the Age of Reason. Firstly, there has been the failure of the most prominent Enlightenment theories to explain the present condition of humanity. Theories such as liberalism, Weberian rationalism and marxism have been subjected to devastating critiques by scholars from a wide disciplinary field. Their central premises have been rejected by a substantial number of political and legal critics.

Secondly, Enlightenment doctrines and philosophies have aspired to universal explanations but delivered, in reality, totalitarian governments (marxism) or empty consumerist ideologies (liberalism). Marxism offered the promise of equality but delivered the reality of Stalin and the gulag. Liberalism, even in its most successful manifestations, is often dogged by relative material deprivation and spiritual impoverishment. At its worst, during the Weimar experiment with representative democracy in the 1930s, it allowed Hitler to flourish and attain power. The Holocaust and the failure of late twentieth century politics to avoid its repetition has led to widespread scepticism about the possibilities of legitimate government or universal social progress.[232] Postmodernism is therefore antagonistic to the Enlightenment values that have informed liberal discourse since the eighteenth century and which include a commitment to individual rights and secular democracy and a belief in human progress, moral consensus and the possibility of discovering universal truths through the application of reason.[233] The experience of the twentieth century seems to demonstrate that attempts to organise communities around these ideas or goals leads inevitably to either terror or social paralysis. Accordingly, it is not merely philosophically desirable to question these foundational theories but politically necessary.[234]

Thirdly, and finally, postmodernism is a response to the human condition in the post-industrial age. Postmodernists have devoted themselves to the study of life in a period of technological and social transformation. In particular, some postmodernists have directed much of their attention to the surface manifestations of the homogeneous global culture (e.g. television, advertising, low art, fast food franchises), finding the meaning of contemporary life there as much as in the parliaments or academies that are the traditional focus of political philosophy.[235]

Postmodernism as a practice is even more difficult to define or locate than is CLS or marxist jurisprudence. Postmodernist approaches have become influential in a variety of disciplines over the past twenty years, but law has only recently confronted postmodernism for the first time.[236] This may be because while feminism, marxism and CLS openly embrace political agendas and are fuelled by a sense of social injustice, postmodernist thought originated in the aesthetic sphere. Architecture and literary theory[237] have been two of the most fruitful disciplines for postmodern theory. Indeed, postmodernism has been seen as a retreat from politics to the academy, following the failure of the Paris student riots to change the world in 1968.[238] Although the French postmodernist criminologist-historiographer Michel Foucault did develop a theory of power (see below), postmodernism is generally uneasy with the sphere of politics. In politics and law there is traditionally a demand for unity, explanation and coherence, while postmodernism entails the denial or subversion of these ideals. Nevertheless, postmodernist thought may have enormous implications for the way political and legal issues are characterised and approached. This section identifies some of the major themes of postmodern thought and sketches their potential impact on law.

The rejection of grand theory and the commitment to local knowledges

Postmodernism is marked most by a rejection of totalising or universalising theories and explanations; postmodernist writers are commonly sceptical about grand theory or foundational truths. Most political theory in the modern age has incorporated certain essential and objective beliefs about human nature, such as the primacy and autonomy of the individual and the division of humanity into male and female. These insights were thought to have universal significance and whole societies have been organised according to such principles. Liberals, for example, have been committed to the idea of the independent and rational self, marxists claim to be able to outline and predict the shape of history on the basis of an economic theory of human behaviour, and radical and cultural feminism are premised on the possibility of describing the essential and universal experience of 'Woman'. Postmodernists argue that there can be no grand theory upon which to ground a description of all human behaviour or prescriptions for good human communities. The diversity of human experience and the complexity of social arrangements doom such ventures. The avatar of postmodernism, Frederick Nietzsche, developed a theory of radical subjectivity which announced not just the death of God but the demise of all transcendental and rational normative grounding.[239] Postmodernism begins at the point where the search for such explanations ends.

Postmodernism therefore rejects theories of law which are built around a fundamental truth or norm, such as practical reasonableness (Finnis), the right to liberty (Nozick), the rule of recognition (Hart), representative democracy,[240] economic rationality (law and economics)[241] or the economic principle of history (Marx).[242] No foundation exists which provides the legal system with a meaning or authority external to itself. Law's empire,[243] according to those who follow Nietzsche, is built on nothing but imperial pretensions.

A corollary of the rejection of grand theory is the idea that only local, qualified solutions are tolerable or even possible. Richard Rorty has described this as the 'banality' of postmodern politics. In place of large-scale transformation there is the pursuit of a series of different, microcosmic changes. What is envisioned is not a new politics for the world but an improved scenario for the community.[244] One aspect of this localism is a commitment to hearing and theorising marginal concerns, individuals and groups. Another, closely associated, concern of postmodernists is to question the distinction between dominant or accepted discourses and voices and those that are represented as marginal and peripheral. The refusal to accept existing hierarchies as inevitable or natural has animated much postmodern thinking. In particular, writers such as Michel Foucault have addressed the forms and exercises of power which produce and entrench these divisions of experience (see below).

The postmodernist questioning of accepted foundations and hierarchies and concentration on particularities potentially results in total relativism. There is no ground for saying that any perspective is any more true or valid than any other, no standard by which any argument or program can be judged. In this sense, postmodernism is anti-political. Yet its inclination to study the margins and to challenge acts of marginalisation does give it a political dimension and utility as a critical tool. This in turn has made it useful to critiques such as feminism, CLS and critical race theory.[245]

Authority, power and knowledge

Law and liberal legal theory are heavily dependent on claims to objectivity. The classic, positivist account of law cherishes and upholds, above all else, law's autonomy from the political system and the social structures surrounding it. This autonomy in turn is thought to reinforce the authority of law. For example, legislation is regarded as authoritative by virtue of its positivistic source, the Crown in parliament, and judges are regarded as authoritative interpreters of that legislation by virtue of their independence from politics and their application of legal reasoning to arrive at correct legal answers.[246] Postmodernism's encounter with law has left these claims to truth and authority severely deflated.

Law involves the exercise of institutional power by one group of human beings over another. However, this essential characteristic of law is generally obscured by a series of mystifications designed to legitimise and domesticate the use of power. Power becomes 'authority' or 'government' in Western liberal political and legal theory, and in the process undergoes a transformation from might (force) to right (rules). This transformation has been the object of postmodern scrutiny, with the purpose of unravelling the operation and legitimation of law/power in its many guises. Much of Michel Foucault's writing was dedicated to an examination and critique of power. His work focused on the practices and institutions which consolidate and deploy power in society (what he termed the 'technologies' of power). Foucault challenged the rationality, inevitability and legitimacy of power as the means by which individuals are governed.[247] He argued that the apparently inexorable and predetermined power processes and hierarchies within Western society can be dislodged, undermined or reversed by calling them into question, tracing their histories and revealing them as chosen and arbitrary rather than external or natural.[248]

Foucault's analysis also presented power not as a commodity which is concentrated in institutions but as a diffuse force which circulates through society and can be appropriated for particular ends. According to postmodernists who draw on the writings of Foucault, then, the authority of law is derived from its appropriation of power rather than from nature, reason, legitimacy or democracy. And though power unquestionably resides in law, it is also found in a whole number of sites, ranging from those where power has been traditionally located, such as politics, administration and religion, to less obvious ones such as culture, the family, sport and psychology. Indeed, Foucault argued that the legal form of power (rules backed by force) would be replaced as the dominant form by the 'disciplinary' power of discourses such as medicine, psychology, education and industrial relations, which coerce behaviour more subtly but more completely. Carol Smart has questioned the prediction that legal power will decline in importance but, as noted earlier, she has also cautioned against directing too much attention to the study of law as the single repressive or dominant institution in society.[249] Margaret Davies has pointed out that law is interpenetrated by other systems of power, relationships and social meanings (for example the gender order, economic relations, 'current community standards' and 'expert' opinions), which prevent it from being understood in one-dimensional terms.[250]

Foucault also examined the relationship between power and knowledge. In the traditional Enlightenment account, knowledge was produced by reason, and consisted of objective, universal (that is, true) propositions about reality.[251] By contrast, postmodernists insist that knowers are compelled to interpret and represent the world through language, hence knowledge is socially constructed and context-dependent. Foucault's particular contribution was the observation that knowledge is an effect of power. Authorised knowledges or truths are versions of reality backed by power.[252] Law, for example, privileges a small number of experiences and understandings of the world, and dismisses other understandings (such as that of a losing party, or of someone for whom there is no established legal claim) as 'non-legal' or misguided. Legal knowledge, however, is no more than a product of law's appropriation of the power to define reality.

Poststructuralism, deconstruction and texts

The analytical methods of postmodernism are often described as poststructuralist or deconstructive; poststructural methods and the techniques of deconstruction are employed by some though not all postmodernists. 'Poststructuralism' refers to the body of theory which has developed from earlier, structuralist theories. The most renowned and influential structuralists were the linguist Ferdinand de Saussure and the anthropologist Claude Levi-Strauss. Talcott Parsons, whose functionalist account of the social system was examined in chapter 3, is another example of a structuralist theorist. Structuralism focused on the internal mechanisms that give meaning to a phenomenon—such as language, a religious ritual or a social system—rather than its source in history, its social context or the role of human agency in producing it. Saussure argued that meaning is generated by *differences* between concepts within a system. That is, meaning is relational not unitary, it is constructed negatively rather than positively.[253] For example, the concept of a 'table' gains meaning only in contrast to other concepts such as 'chair', 'desk', 'bench', 'floor' and so on. Saussure's insights were applied broadly to the understanding of societies, cultural phenomena, myths and literary texts as systems of signification (systems through which meaning is constructed), whose parts were interdependent and relationally defined. Thus, for example, Parsons described the social system as made up of interdependent subsystems, which were functionally differentiated and which produced different kinds of norms and meanings.

Poststructuralists adopt many of the insights of structuralism, although they renounce its belief in a single, discoverable pattern of structures capable of explaining social phenomena and organisation. They hold that any phenomenon (a human being, Madonna concert, city, comic strip, etc.) can be 'read' in the same way as a literary text to decipher its meanings. All texts are worthy of study and the privileging of some texts over others is a contingent and political activity. At its simplest this can mean that the distinction, say, between primary and secondary sources in a law course becomes untenable. On a deeper level, the contrast between texts styled as 'authoritative' (e.g. legal opinions) and those described as 'cultural' (e.g. the oral history of an Aboriginal group) is challenged and politicised. In reading a text poststructuralists are interested in its internal arrangement rather than the status of its writer.[254] Its social contexts are also relevant:

> Poststructuralists insist that words and texts have no fixed or intrinsic meanings, that there is no transparent or self-evident relationship between them and either ideas or things, no basic or ultimate correspondence between language and the world. The questions that must be answered in such an analysis, then, are how, in what specific contexts, among which specific communities of people, and by what textual and social processes has meaning been acquired?[255]

The technique of extremely close readings of texts in order to allow them to reveal their many meanings was first developed by Roland Barthes in his notorious interpretive study exercise *S/Z*.[256] Barthes applied poststructuralist method to a Balzac short story, resulting in a critique much longer than the story itself. It was Barthes, too, who celebrated the 'death of the author',[257] meaning the demise of any 'authoritative' version of a text based on the intentions of its writer. The author became merely one creator of the text, with readers also playing a creative role in interpreting it. While much conventional literary theory is concerned with imputing authorial intention or excavating the definitive author's voice through biographical exegesis, poststructuralists refuse to privilege the author's intended meanings over the reader's interpretation. This makes the meaning of a text multiple and fluid. Some critics object that such an approach might be fun to play with, but serves no useful purpose.

This denial of fixed meaning is significant for law because traditional accounts of judicial interpretation are predicated on the possibility of a single, definitive translation of legal material by a judicial body, often, in turn, based on the revealed intentions of previous 'authors', such as the framers of a constitution or the majority judges in a precedent case. In permitting texts to speak their various meanings, which have usually been obscured for political reasons, and in revealing the hidden dependencies of a legal text, postmodernists engage in a political exercise threatening to the dominant ideology of law.

'Deconstruction', as a method associated with poststructuralism, is one of modern scholarship's great buzzwords. In its loosest sense deconstruction refers to a method which subverts, challenges or even undermines conventional or dominant thinking. It is clear that everyone from Socrates through Galileo to John Pilger uses deconstructive techniques in this casual sense. The more precise rendering of the term, and the one most relevant to the postmodern project, is that of a method by which texts are taken apart to reveal the hidden assumptions and exclusions upon which they are founded and which they have sought to conceal. Often, the assumptions underlying a text are contradictory and are revealed only at its margins.

Poststructuralists have discovered that rational, Enlightenment thinking is premised on a series of dualisms which have the appearance of natural symmetry but are in fact human, political and historical constructions. Jacques Derrida has shown that the whole of the Western system of beliefs is based on a sequence of binary opposites, such as presence/absence, unity/diversity, culture/nature, civilised/primitive, science/superstition, reason/emotion, active/passive, written/oral, male/female, law/morality.[258] In each case the first term in the pair is accorded greater authority or is privileged over the other, subordinated, term. The terms are, however, interdependent. The first term only gains meaning as the negative of the other, and only arrives at its dominant position by the negation or repression of the other. Derrida has demonstrated that this interdependency of terms is rarely acknowledged, so that it appears that the primary term has a meaning independent of the other. More importantly, he has shown that the positioning of the terms is the culmination of an historical process involving the use of power.

Deconstruction is therefore the method of reading a text which highlights these points. It permits the text to 'speak' its textual ambiguities, its reliance on unstable foundations, its incoherent dualisms and its lack of unity; it looks for silences and gaps, and seeks to reveal what is suppressed. In showing how one particular understanding of the world has come to dominate and subsume others it also shows that there are alternative ways of being in and knowing the world,[259] and seeks to bring those alternatives from the margins to the centre.

The relevance of deconstruction for law is clear from the fact that law is a discourse which is heavily reliant on binary oppositions. As well as those listed above, one might add public/private, objective/subjective, individual/state, law/policy, commission/omission (the distinction which dictates that there is 'no duty to rescue' in tort law),[260] and physical harm/psychological harm (the distinction which denies recovery for pain and suffering in the absence of physical injury and which has led to the absurdities of the law regarding 'nervous shock'). Deconstruction questions the appropriateness of these oppositions as bases for organising meaning or legitimising power in legal discourse.

Maggie Troup, for example, presents a deconstructionist reading of *R v Hakopian*,[261] a rape case in which the court followed precedent in holding that the defendant should receive a lighter sentence because the woman he had raped was a prostitute. Troup shows how the 'facts' of the case were constructed through a series of oppositions, in which the court privileged the position or experience of some women while devaluing that of other women. For example, harm was divided into 'real', physical, assault-like harm versus mere psychological harm; women were categorised as either chaste/respectable/married women, and therefore worthy of full legal protection, or prostitutes incapable of suffering the same level of harm and therefore not warranting such protection.[262] Deconstruction thus demonstrates that legal reasoning and interpretation is not a deductive, scientific method applied to transparent material or 'reality'. Instead it is an artifice constructed on its own metaphors. Moreover, Troup argues that deconstruction raises the possibility of transformation (not merely evolution) of the law, through the effort to recuperate the subordinated 'other'. It allows us to contemplate that harms not currently recognised in the legal system, such as psychological harms and harms to prostitutes, may be recognised in future.[263]

Law and the subject

In liberal legal theory, the operation of the legal system is premised on the existence of free, autonomous and equal individuals acting in contractual relationships with each other (private law), providing a rational collective basis for legitimate public action (constitutional law) and accepting individual responsibility for their actions (criminal law). For postmodernist theorists, liberalism's dependence on the rational, definable and single self is problematic. The unified self has been exposed as an illusion. The subject is both relationally defined and multiple according to postmodernists: a person may occupy a host of subject positions at different times and in different relations. The nature of these selves is historically contingent and contextually dependent. This makes human agency or personal autonomy an unsatisfactory means on which to base action or the quest for legitimacy.

This aspect of postmodernist thinking has proved both dangerous and fruitful for those working in areas such as critical race theory, feminism, critical legal education and indigenous rights. These groups have observed the typical experience, perspective and position of the subject in liberal theory to be that of the white middle class male. On the one hand, then, while marginalised groups have sought the status of legal subjecthood for themselves, there is a danger that it may melt in their grasp. In Susan Williams' words, 'the rise of . . . postmodernism at precisely this moment may appear highly suspicious: just when previously silenced persons have begun to speak for themselves, the concept of the subject and the possibility of truth come under fire'.[264] Williams is also concerned that the subject may become so de-essentialised that concepts such as 'women' 'will become useless as the basis either for theory or for political organisation'.[265] On the other hand, the decentering of the traditional liberal subject creates space for the enrichment of theory with a multiplicity of previously unheard voices.

In a postmodern analysis of an Aboriginal land rights case, *Gerhardy v Brown*,[266] Geoff Airo-Farulla argues that the concept of the prior self as a holder of human rights against society, and as the source of truth and perception about reality, is a liberal assumption given the appearance of timelessness. In the case, the High Court held that the traditional Aboriginal owners of land were not entitled to bar other people from their land since such a prohibition would offend the *Racial Discrimination Act 1975* (Cwlth). According to Airo-Farulla, this decision resulted from the Court taking an essentialist position, claiming that all people were *a priori* equal and that the law was there to protect that already existing equality. He denies, however, that either the self or society are foundational or prior. Instead they are interdependent, each one reliant on the other. Thus there is no essential truth about any human being. They are neither essentially equal nor essentially different—indeed these terms also depend on each other for meaning. In the circumstances, however, the decision exacerbated substantive inequalities by interpreting the legislation as embodying only a single essence of equality; that is, formal, juridical equality.[267]

Perhaps the reason that law's encounter with postmodernism has been so fraught is that law and legal training are the antithesis of postmodernism's central precepts. Law and legal education represent the submersion of identity in the model of the anonymous lawyer-technician. In order to learn to be a lawyer and to think like a lawyer it is necessary for many law students to subjugate other aspects of themselves, such as their sex, race, ethnicity, sexuality. By contrast, postmodernism brings out the various identities sought to be concealed. This is the lesson of Patricia Williams's humane exercise in postmodern feminism, *The alchemy of race and rights*, discussed earlier in this chapter. Throughout the book Williams juggles with her various identities—as the great-great-granddaughter of a slave, as a black woman in contemporary American society, as a commercial law professor at an Ivy League School—and concludes that the law fails to accommodate certain identities and cannot hear the various voices in which they are spoken. Only in her role as law professor is she a (partially) free and equal citizen in her country.

While postmodernism brings to law a profound scepticism about law's foundational narratives and legitimising principles, it also brings the possibility of democratic replenishment. It returns authority to the local, the invisible and the marginalised. It calls for wider participation in social power while constantly challenging the legitimacy of authority and government. Associated with this project is the desire to continually postpone closure of readings and meanings. Texts may be democratised; new and previously effaced and powerless readings may be heard and incorporated into the challenge to the single, authorised interpretation of meaning. This means listening to and absorbing 'outsider' and 'non-legal' narratives into the story of what it means to be governed by law and how this law should develop. At this level, at least, postmodernism is profoundly political and has implications for law teaching and administration. If the meeting of postmodernism and law threatens nihilism and relativism in some versions, it promises rejuvenation and participation in others.

Further reading

Marxism

Collins, Hugh *Marxism and law*, Clarendon Press, Oxford, 1982
'Debate: marxism and the rule of law' (1990) 15 *Law and Social Inquiry*, 633–730
O'Malley, Pat *Law, capitalism and democracy*, Allen & Unwin, Sydney, 1983
Phillips, P. *Marx and Engels on law and laws*, Martin Robertson, Oxford, 1980
Tushnet, Mark 'Marxism and the law', in *The left academy*, eds B. Ollman and R. Vernoff, Praeger, New York, 1984

Critical legal studies

Davies, Margaret *Asking the law question*, Law Book Co., Sydney, 1994
Fraser, David 'What a long, strange trip it's been: deconstructing law from legal realism to critical legal studies' (1990) 5 *Australian Journal of Law and Society* 3
Hunt, Alan 'The theory of critical legal studies' (1986) 6 *Oxford Journal of Legal Studies* 1
Kelman, Mark *A guide to critical legal studies*, Harvard University Press, Cambridge, Mass., 1987
Kennedy, Duncan and Klare, Karl 'A bibliography of CLS' (1984) 94 *Yale Law Review* 461 (periodically updated)
Krygier, Martin 'Critical legal studies and social theory—a response to Alan Hunt' (1987) 7 *Oxford Journal of Legal Studies* 26

Feminist legal theories

Fineman, Martha A. and Thomadsen, Nancy S. eds *At the boundaries of law: feminism and legal theory*, Routledge, New York, 1991

MacKinnon, Catharine A. *Toward a feminist theory of the state*, Harvard University Press, Cambridge, Mass., 1989
Morgan, Jenny 'Feminist theory as legal theory' (1988) 16 *Melbourne University Law Review* 743
Scutt, Jocelynne A. *Women and the law*, Law Book Co., Sydney, 1990
Stang Dahl, Tove *Women's law: an introduction to feminist jurisprudence*, Norwegian University Press, 1987

Postmodernism

Carty, A. ed. *Postmodern law: enlightenment, revolution and the death of man*, Edinburgh University Press, Edinburgh, 1990
Cornell, Drucilla *Beyond accommodation: ethical feminism, deconstruction and the law*, Routledge, New York, 1991
Cornell, Drucilla, Rosenfeld, Michel and Carlson, David Gray eds *Deconstruction and the possibility of justice*, Routledge, New York, 1992
Douzinas, Costas, Warrington, Ronnie and McVeigh, Shaun *Postmodern jurisprudence: the law of the text in the texts of law*, Routledge, London, 1991
Kennedy, David 'Spring break' (1985) 63 *Texas Law Review* 1377
Schank, Peter 'Understanding postmodern thought and its implications for statutory interpretation' (1992) 65 *Southern California Law Review* 2505

Part three

5

Explaining law reform

Rosemary Hunter and Richard Johnstone

The last three chapters have examined competing theoretical perspectives on the role of law in society. In this chapter the emphasis shifts from introducing to applying those theories, by means of case studies. The case study method provides a contrast with the more abstract discussions of the previous chapters. It allows a more in-depth illustration and comparison of some of the theoretical approaches, although it cannot deal comprehensively with each one. The specific case studies used here are case studies of law reform. They allow an examination to be made of the ways in which different theories regard and explain law reform.

'Law reform' is a broad term which may refer to any effort to improve the law via the legislative process. (Judicial changes to the common law are not generally considered within the concept of 'law reform'; judicial decision making is discussed further in chapter 7.) Legislative change may encompass a wide range of actions, from the introduction of new equal opportunity legislation to the alteration of the current taxation or social security regime, a change in the structure of a statutory authority, the introduction of new enforcement procedures in an area, or the removal of statutory constraints on a particular activity. This chapter focuses on legislative innovations that purportedly respond to perceived social problems. Just as liberals, sociologists, marxists, feminists, critical legal scholars and postmodernists have different views on the role of law in society, it follows that they have different views on why particular legal rules might have been established. All explanations of the origins of legislation are grounded, however implicitly, in a particular theoretical perspective.

Traditional legal scholarship has tended to explain legal change in positivist terms. As noted in chapter 2, positivists see law as a closed and autonomous system of rules. A positivist's primary interest in legal change is how the new law came to meet the system's rules of recognition (that is, how it acquired its status as a *legal* rule).[1] Thus a positivist account of a particular law reform would focus on the formal stages of a Bill's passage through parliament—first, second and third reading in each House and royal assent. It would have little interest in where the idea for the new legislation originated or why that particular reform was pursued by the government at that particular time, since these issues are irrelevant to the fact of the law's existence.

Other theoretical approaches are interested in the processes which produce specific reforms at specific moments. The major debate in socio-legal studies is between pluralist and marxist accounts of law reform. 'Pluralism' is a liberal model of law reform which seeks to explain legal change by reference to the activities of various interest groups in society. The argument is that in a liberal society individuals are free to pursue their self interest; often they join together to promote common interests. A liberal society fosters and tolerates many different interest groups, which then compete, negotiate and/or form coalitions to have their concerns embodied in legislation. People in a neighbourhood, trade unions, parents of young children, developers, employers, feminists, consumers, churches and animal liberationists are examples of interest groups (some permanently organised, others formed around a particular issue) which have the capacity to influence political outcomes. Clearly, this model rejects the marxist notion that class is the main dividing line in society.

Contemporary law reform processes often reflect the pluralist model of legal change. Governments generally refer social questions or potentially controversial issues to a parliamentary committee or a statutory Law Reform Commission,[2] which will then consult widely in formulating legislative proposals. Examples of Law Reform Commission inquiries (mentioned in this book) include the Australian Law Reform Commission's references on the recognition of Aboriginal customary laws (chapter 1) and on equality before the law for women (chapter 4). Individuals and interest groups are given the opportunity to make submissions to a Law Reform Commission or parliamentary committee inquiry, and the committee or Commission generally claims to represent the preponderance of views in its report. The government may then engage in further consultations with particular interest groups in deciding whether and how to implement the report. The consultation process is utilitarian in the sense that it aims to identify which proposals will produce the greatest level of community satisfaction.[3]

Some pluralist models assume that power is more or less equally divided between different interest groups and that this diffusion and balance of power, as well as constitutional checks and balances, prevent a ruling elite from emerging. In this view, too, the state is seen as a neutral arbiter, providing a framework for the appeasement and resolution of competing interests. Empirically, however, it would appear that some groups are more powerful and better able to achieve their interests than others are. The uneven distribution of power in society is taken into account in other versions of pluralism to explain why certain groups can exercise disproportionate power to shape the law to their interests at the expense of the interests of less powerful groups. These powerful groups may also have strong links with the state, so that the state cannot so easily be seen to be neutral.[4] On this view, the state itself acts as a kind of interest group, responding to the demands of social groups with its own concerns and agendas, and favouring some groups or arguments over others. Nevertheless, pluralists maintain that the capacity to affect legislative outcomes is fairly widely dispersed in society, and they particularly 'reject the notion that the level of economic power possessed by an actor necessarily translates into an equivalent amount of political influence'.[5]

By contrast, marxist approaches to law reform do tend to focus on exercises of class power and to ascribe a definite set of interests to the state, namely those of the ruling class. Marxist theorists analyse legislative reforms in terms of their instrumental, formal or ideological contribution to the maintenance of capitalism and the promotion of capitalist interests.[6] Marxists would argue that the appearance of consultation with individuals and interests groups serves to legitimise measures which inevitably work for the benefit of the most powerful interest groups representing capital. Some marxist writers also seek to locate particular reforms within the 'big picture' of historical processes and structures. Rather than examining the immediate context of reform they anchor their explanations of legislation within the broader 'political economy', which accounts for the emergence and relative power of interest groups themselves, as well as particular legislative outcomes.[7]

While pluralist and marxist versions have dominated the discourse on law reform, other theoretical perspectives have their own views to contribute. The functionalist model of society outlined in chapter 3, for example, contains a particular account of law reform. Functionalists envisage legislators enacting legal rules to embody agreed social values, or in response to pressures to adapt to environmental/economic change.

The debate within the feminist movement as to the value of law reform as a political activity was mentioned in chapter 4. Feminists have been concerned to analyse law reform processes as a basis for action. Liberal feminists tend to adopt a pluralist model of law reform, seeing themselves as an interest group with a special claim on the state, while accepting that opposing interest groups should also have the right to be heard. Their general picture is of legal progress for women. Thus women need only display persistence and their demands will eventually be met. Radical feminists, on the other hand, see the state as patriarchal and tending to favour outcomes that sustain patriarchy. They have greater difficulty in explaining why some law reform efforts to alleviate women's oppression are actually enacted. As Catharine MacKinnon acknowledges, radical '[f]eminism criticises [the] male totality without an account of our capacity to do so'.[8] In this situation pragmatism may prevail over theoretical purity. Radical feminists have contributed to the reform of rape law, for example. Socialist feminists might refer to the state's tendency to co-opt feminist efforts and legitimise itself, so that women are silenced and apparently satisfied by having their reform proposals accepted, even though the resulting legislation might be watered down or entrusted to male judges and officials to enforce, or otherwise produce far from satisfactory outcomes.[9]

Critical Legal Studies, as noted in the previous chapter, has focused on legal doctrine and the role of judges in making law, and has paid comparatively little attention to legislative reforms. A critical approach might challenge pluralist models, however, by questioning matters such as which proposals are subject to community consultation processes and which are not. How do some issues come to be designated as potentially controversial and therefore subject to consultation? Why is it, for example, that measures which may produce genuine reform for disadvantaged groups (such as equality before the law for women, legislation to protect native title, questions of access to justice, or methods of property division following the breakdown of a marriage) are thrown open for public comment, allowing the expression of views opposed to reform and requiring that they be taken into account, when other matters (such as tax cuts or increases) are not put through the same consultation process?

Postmodernists might argue that the state is a collection of different and sometimes contradictory sites of power which does not operate monolithically to produce determinate outcomes. A government may consult in one situation to legitimise the result it wants, and in another situation because it does not have a clear position and wants a decision made for it. The state may sometimes be responsive to 'progressive' reforms and sometimes not. As well as eschewing global political explanations, postmodernists may emphasise the process rather than the outcome of reform efforts. Law reform can be seen as 'a site of cultural intervention',[10] enabling marginalised groups to articulate their concerns, to challenge popular and institutional discourses, and to dispute law's claims to speak the 'truth' about them.[11] The interest is not so much in reforming the law as in 'using law reform as a vehicle by which to make people think about their attitudes'.[12]

Postmodernists will also be concerned to analyse closely the discourses of reform. How is the notion of 'reform' constructed? What broader discourses intersect with particular reforms? What is revealed when the explanations offered by those involved in reform efforts are deconstructed? CLS and postmodernism therefore do not have specific theories of law reform, but they can offer useful insights into particular instances of reform.

The four case studies presented here concern nineteenth century divorce law reform, the introduction of industrial conciliation and arbitration in Australia, the advent of new occupational health and safety legislation in Victoria in the 1980s, and the Victorian government's legislative response to the Murray Islands case—the *Land Titles Validation Act 1993* (Vic.). Nineteenth century divorce law reform is examined from positivist and feminist perspectives; conciliation and arbitration and occupational health and safety are analysed in terms of different versions of pluralism and marxism; and the Land Titles Validation Act is studied by means of functionalist and critical approaches. The chapter concludes with Roger Cotterrell's argument about the kinds of reform that are considered feasible in particular political systems.

Nineteenth century divorce law reform

The second part of the nineteenth century saw the introduction and reform of divorce legislation in the Australian colonies. Divorce in the colonies was practically impossible before the 1860s. There was no legal provision for divorce until the colonial governments were permitted by the Colonial Office to enact copies of the English Divorce Act of 1857. The initial colonial legislation mirrored the English Act in embodying a double standard of morality. A husband could petition for divorce on the ground of his wife's adultery alone, whereas a wife could only petition on the ground of aggravated adultery on the part of her husband; that is, adultery coupled with either bigamy, rape, severe cruelty, or desertion for two years.[13] In 1881, after a lengthy campaign by reformers, New South Wales enacted equal divorce rights, allowing women as well as men to petition on the ground of simple adultery. Efforts to introduce equal divorce rights in Victoria were unsuccessful. A further campaign led to the extension of the grounds for divorce in both Victoria and New South Wales.[14] These reforms broke the traditional nexus between divorce and adultery by allowing either husband or wife to petition on a range of new grounds including: three years' desertion; habitual drunkenness plus cruelty, leaving the petitioner without support or neglecting domestic duties; conviction of the respondent for attempted murder or serious assault of the petitioner; or three years' imprisonment.

Nineteenth century divorce legislation has received attention from legal historians and feminist historians. In comparing the different accounts of the changes in divorce law produced by these historians, it becomes clear that their different preoccupations result in very different emphases and conclusions. The legal historian J. M. Bennett, for example, explains divorce reforms within a positivist and constitutionalist framework. By contrast, the feminist historians Margaret James, Hilary Golder and Bridget Brooklyn have been concerned to discover the meaning of divorce law and legal change in women's lives and to understand historical constructions of gender. Before examining their studies in detail it should be noted that, while the feminist historians are interested in the motivations of law reformers, the history of nineteenth century divorce reform is not a feminist success story. It is often assumed that advances in women's legal status must have been achieved by women, but this has not always been the case. Women's interests and needs have always been open to paternalistic definition, and sometimes women have been given things they did not ask for. In Australia the first wave feminist movement, active in the late nineteenth and early twentieth century, was concerned with issues such as temperance, services for women and children, and women's suffrage, but it had very little to do with divorce reform.

J. M. Bennett's article, 'The establishment of divorce laws in New South

Wales',[15] traces New South Wales divorce provisions from 1788 to 1892. Throughout, Bennett's gaze is fixed steadily on legal institutions—parliament and the courts. He begins his discussion of each piece of legislation with its introduction into parliament. As explained earlier, this is a typically positivist approach. Bennett's history of the various divorce Bills then charts their parliamentary progress—a tortuous succession of withdrawals, reintroductions, second readings, discharges, prorogations, losses in committee, and finally passage through both Houses and assent. It is only after each Act has successfully made its way through parliament that its provisions are explained. In positivist terms, it has become a legal rule and now merits consideration of its substance.

Bennett is far less interested in the social context for divorce reform. While divorce reform might be expected to have been a topic of public discussion prior to any legislative proposals, Bennett only notes public *responses* (notably those of the Church) to Bills that have been introduced into parliament. There is no explanation of how they got there. Law is presented as both separate from and prior to politics.

Perceptions of the need for divorce law in the colony are treated briefly and seen primarily through the eyes of lawyers—a Supreme Court judge and the Attorney General. Both of these officers are quoted as being concerned with the relief of mistreated or deserted wives, but the actual problem for wives is not elaborated. Nor is there any consideration of why this concern should have arisen in New South Wales or whether it was peculiar to the Australian colonies. While the passage of equal divorce rights is recorded, there is no comment on its significance.

The theme that Bennett does develop, particularly in relation to extension of the grounds for divorce, is the resistance of the British authorities to colonial parliaments enacting divorce legislation that went further than English divorce provisions. All divorce Bills that diverged from the English Divorce Act were obliged to be reserved for Royal assent, and the Colonial Office advised the Queen not to give her assent to several Bills, generating outrage in the colonies and insistence that their legislative power in this matter should not be fettered. Bennett sums up this struggle:

> When the laws were ultimately acquired, their legal and political implications were very great. The Colony's statesmen made it plain to their counterparts at Westminster that they would no longer tolerate a subordinate position but would insist upon being masters of their own destiny, at least in domestic matters.[16]

The history of divorce law is thus located as part of Australian *constitutional* history, with colonial legislatures gradually winning independence from British control. It is about the development of Australian legal institutions, not about the development of women's rights. Ironically, Bennett makes this point using the image of the colonies freeing themselves from 'domestic subordination'; in feminist analyses of divorce law it is women's efforts to break free from domestic subordination to their husbands that is a central concern.

Bennett's theme of colonial independence lacks an account of motivations. Did local legislatures seek legislative autonomy for its own sake or were they pragmatically concerned to be able to make laws suited to local conditions? If the latter was the case (to whatever extent), what *were* the local conditions that prompted the introduction of divorce Bills that diverged from the English model? Margaret James supplies an answer in her essay, 'Not bread but a stone: women and divorce in colonial Victoria'.[17] She notes that both parliamentarians and the public saw a need for divorce on the ground of desertion in colonies where there was a high rate of men deserting their wives. With the impetus of the 1850s goldrushes in Victoria and New South Wales the male population of the colonies was highly mobile, far more so than was the case in England in the same period. Deserted wives were thus a social problem of particular movement in the colonies and there was a concern (driven by a variety of altruistic and cost-saving motives) that women in this position should be able to divorce and remarry. The conclusion that their husbands' desertion was perceived by women to be a far greater problem than their husbands' adultery is supported by the significant increase in divorce petitions made by women after the divorce extension reforms of the 1890s, when it became possible to petition on the ground of desertion.[18]

Feminist historians have been interested in women's use of divorce law, not just its existence. On this approach, the passage of legislation through parliament, to which Bennett devotes so much attention, was merely a prelude to the (uncertain) operation of the legal regime. Margaret James's piece is based on a study of divorce cases filed in Victoria between 1870 and 1872. Over that period women were far less likely to be successful in obtaining a divorce than were men, but women's lack of success was often due to their petitions being withdrawn before hearing rather than being dismissed by the court. Close examination of files revealed some of the reasons why women might withdraw their petitions, or be reluctant to petition in the first place. A woman might fear for the fate of her children if she took divorce proceedings, or suffer threats or physical assault from her husband. She would certainly fear for her status in society, since divorce cases always received stigmatising publicity in the press, from which even innocent wives would emerge with their reputations tarnished.[19] And since married women could not own their own property under the law at the time, women were dependent on their husbands to pay their legal costs.

The existence of these pressures suggests that the possibility of divorce was meaningless for most women.[20] The legal provisions failed to cater for women's experience and did nothing to alleviate the social system of male dominance. Bridget Brooklyn takes a more particularised approach when she points out that the law did not uniformly oppress women; it could sometimes be used by women for their own benefit.[21] Some women petitioners *were* successful, but Brooklyn also stresses that wives' 'success' should not be judged solely in terms of their record as petitioners. Her examination of South Australian divorce records focused on the stories of women respondents as well as women petitioners, and she shows that women who were dissatisfied with their marriages might choose to escape by framing themselves as the guilty party, especially if they had alternative means of economic support.

Writing about the New South Wales *Matrimonial Causes Act Amendment Act 1881*, Hilary Golder tackles the issue, which Bennett failed to address, of the significance of equal divorce rights.[22] Golder discusses both the parliamentary campaign for the amendment and its impact. Her account of parliamentary proceedings focuses on the substance of the parliamentary debates rather than the formal progress of the various Bills. This was the late nineteenth century, when equality before the law for women was a novel concept. Those in favour of the double standard argued that there was a relevant difference between women and men which justified different treatment. A wife's adultery was far more serious than a husband's, since '[a] wife's fall could introduce "spurious issue" into the family and thus distort the orderly and just transmission of property'.[23] Those in favour of the reform drew on a range of arguments—the claim that a marriage could equally be destroyed by a husband's adultery as by a wife's; chivalrous concern for allegedly suffering wives whose husbands committed flagrant adultery without any aggravating factors; the claim that concerns about 'spurious issue' were only relevant in 'caste-ridden societies like Britain'; and a general appeal to colonial radicalism against British conservatism and injustice.[24]

Golder points out that the legislators themselves failed to connect their arguments with social reality. Proponents of reform referred vaguely to hardships suffered by women under the present law, but did not call upon specific experience in divorce cases. Opponents predicted a flood of new petitions brought by impulsive women. But the amendment had little practical effect. The problem of women's economic survival after divorce still remained. Golder observes that the majority of female petitioners in the 1870s and 1880s were financially independent from their husbands before commencing divorce proceedings, and that most cases still involved aggravating factors such as desertion or cruelty in addition to adultery—'a wife might well think twice before risking the loss of status and comfort for "adultery alone"'.[25]

Golder's article illustrates a perennial feature of law reform efforts. While legislators may express hopes, fears and expectations about the effects of legal changes, these may be highly speculative or based on partial information or unfounded assumptions. Historians are in a position to test the claims of law reformers against the historical record. Positivist legal histories ignore this challenge and also fail to question the actual impact of legal change. In doing so they perpetuate the assumption that legislation provides objective, technical and effective solutions to social problems. The studies of law reform examined in the rest of this chapter, and the studies of law enforcement in the next chapter, demonstrate that the interaction of law and society is more complicated than that.

The introduction of industrial conciliation and arbitration in Australia

The colonial divorce reforms of the 1890s occurred alongside the early development of conciliation and arbitration systems for the resolution of industrial disputes. Australia and New Zealand are distinguished by their adoption of compulsory conciliation and arbitration systems. The New Zealand system lasted from 1894 until 1984, when it was partially dismantled. Its remaining vestiges were swept away in 1991. The federal industrial relations system in Australia has existed since the passage of the *Conciliation and Arbitration Act 1904* (Cwlth). The system now contained in the *Industrial Relations Act 1988* (Cwlth) has arguably evolved so far away from the original as to constitute an entirely different model. Nevertheless, Australia's compulsory conciliation and arbitration system has not formally been abolished.

Under conciliation and arbitration legislation, federal and State tribunals were established to take charge of industrial disputes and to attempt to resolve them by conciliation or, if that failed, by arbitration resulting in a binding determination of the parties' future rights and obligations in employment. In general, the tribunals dealt with 'interest' disputes, concerning the future desires or demands of a collectivity (whether workers represented by a union or employers represented by an employers' association) as to the terms and conditions of employment in occupations and industries. Disputes about individual legal rights under employment contracts (for example whether an employee had been unfairly dismissed) also occurred, but were not the focus of the system.[26] The outcome of an interest dispute was an industrial agreement reached between the parties or an award issued by the tribunal, which set out wage rates and/or terms and conditions binding on the unions and employers who were parties to the dispute. The systems were compulsory in the sense that a dispute could be brought before the tribunal without the consent of either or both parties, and awards were binding on the parties and could be enforced. Unions were accorded a recognised representative role within conciliation and arbitration systems. In return they were subject to regulation of their rules, structures and activities, particularly to ensure that they functioned democratically.

A number of different approaches to the origins of arbitration are represented in *Foundations of arbitration*, a collection of essays edited by Stuart Macintyre and Richard Mitchell.[27] A picture of the foundations of arbitration is built up by historians working from a variety of perspectives although, as in the case of divorce law reform, feminist historians have been less concerned with the circumstances surrounding the advent of the system—an all-male affair—than with its effects on women workers.[28] *Foundations of arbitration* also canvasses some non-historical accounts of the introduction of arbitration, drawing on general theories of law reform.

Michael Quinlan takes a 'political economy' approach, tracing the historical relations between capital, labour and the state and the broad economic forces in the Australian colonies which led to arbitration.[29] He points out a number of distinguishing features of the colonies which predisposed them to some form of state intervention in industrial relations, and which established industrial regulation as a site of conflict between capital and labour. In the first place, there had always been a high level of state intervention to facilitate economic development in the colonies. The state distributed land to pastoralists, provided infrastructure (e.g. road, rail and port facilities which in other countries were developed by private enterprise), helped to suppress Aboriginal resistance, and supplied and disciplined both convict and free labour. As pastoral and associated industries expanded up to the 1890s, capitalists relied on colonial governments to maintain the supply of labour through state-sponsored immigration, and to assist in its control through master and servant legislation. Indeed the colonial parliaments were dominated by the capitalist elite, as was the magistracy responsible for enforcement of labour laws. This concentration of economic wealth and political power 'was initially conducive to a highly instrumental approach to labour regulation'.[30] That is, labour regulation fulfilled the instrumentalist marxist prediction that capitalists would use the law directly to serve their class interests.[31] This simplistic model is belied, however, by the fact that workers in the colonies were able to enjoy a high degree of mobility and demand high wages during periods of labour shortages; and they also gained the vote earlier than did their British counterparts. During periods of unemployment they too turned to the state for assistance. And they exerted pressure for the statutory guarantee of working conditions such as the eight-hour day.[32]

By contrast, in Britain the state was becoming less and less involved in labour regulation. Prior to 1800 magistrates had had power to deal with labour disputes and to set wages and prices in a particular area (along with many other powers relating to the control of labour). After 1800, however, industrial disputation was constructed as a private matter between the parties, with the state having no interest in the outcome of disputes.[33] Quinlan's account helps to explain both why the Australian colonies adopted an interventionist approach and why they did so against the British trend in labour law.

The immediate catalyst for the introduction of new industrial relations systems in the Australian colonies was the great strikes of the 1890s. The maritime and shearers' strikes of 1890 were followed by further strikes in the shearing, mining and maritime industries in the period 1891–1894. These strikes must be located within the history of Australian capitalism rather than seen in isolation. They were sparked by employers' attempts to reduce wages in the context of economic depression and by their refusal to recognise or negotiate with unions. The unions suffered a crushing defeat at the hands of the employers backed by state force. The police and army were called out against the strikers and strike leaders were tried and jailed. Once more, the law appears to have been used instrumentally to serve capitalist interests. One consequence was a realisation by the labour movement that it could no longer rely on either industrial action or pressure on governments to achieve its goals. It had to join the state and gain the opportunity to harness the power of the state for its own ends. Thus the Australian Labor Party (ALP) was formed to provide labour with a direct voice in the political arena.

Another consequence of the strikes of 1890 was the appointment in New South Wales of a Royal Commission on Strikes, with a brief to find a solution to industrial conflicts. In the words of R. J. Hawke, there was a 'reaction to the unnecessary sufferings of industrial warfare and a widespread conviction that unlimited recourse to force for the settlement of disputes in industry should not be tolerated again'.[34] The Royal Commission recommended a system of voluntary conciliation and arbitration, and voluntary systems were established in several colonies over the course of the decade. These systems proved to be totally ineffective and it is arguable that their failure led to the adoption of stronger measures, namely *compulsory* arbitration.[35]

One of the longstanding debates in Australian labour history is the question of whether compulsory conciliation and arbitration systems were introduced in the interests of capital or of labour. An early marxist argument was that arbitration was created by employers to confine and control the working class.[36] However, many employers in fact opposed compulsory arbitration,[37] while it had considerable support in the labour movement, particularly in parliamentary Labor parties.[38] Yet neither was Labor responsible for the introduction of compulsory arbitration systems. At the time the relevant legislation was introduced in the various colonies/States and at federal level, Labor was still a relatively new parliamentary force, holding neither parliamentary majorities nor, necessarily, the balance of power.[39] Instead, it appears that compulsory arbitration was initiated and carried by liberals, in the period before the crystallisation of the Labor/non-Labor divide in Australian politics.

Stuart Macintyre points out that liberalism had been the dominant force in colonial politics since the 1850s.[40] Divorce reform, for example, was clearly attributable to liberal concerns, seeking to recast marriage as a contract (almost) like any other, made between two equal and freely choosing individuals.[41] In the late nineteenth century the focus of liberal political philosophy shifted from negative to positive liberty, from individual to collective and societal interests.[42] The intellectual history of this strand of liberalism, and its connection to compulsory arbitration, has been traced by Andrew Frazer.[43]

Frazer identifies a small number of Australasian political radicals who advocated the benefits of collectivism and state action. These included Charles Kingston, who drew up the first Bill providing for compulsory arbitration in South Australia;[44] William Pember Reeves, the initiator of compulsory arbitration in New Zealand; B. R. Wise, who introduced legislation in New South Wales; and H. B. Higgins, who was primarily responsible for the inclusion of the conciliation and arbitration power in the Commonwealth

Constitution (s. 51(xxxv)) and who became the first judge of the Commonwealth Arbitration Court. The theory of positive liberty held by these politicians required state action to guarantee individual freedom. Laissez faire and 'freedom of contract' merely provided an opportunity for the exploitation and degradation of less powerful individuals by those with greater power. It was the duty of the state to protect against human degradation and thereby create true equality and freedom.[45] For the reasons outlined by Quinlan, Australasia provided fertile ground for this interventionist doctrine. Its influence can be seen, for example, in the factories legislation introduced in the 1880s, which sought to prevent abuses of the wage relationship (between employers and white male workers) by regulating 'sweating' and the use of juvenile, female and Chinese labour.[46]

Compulsory arbitration was the liberal response to the great strikes. The strikes had seen employers refusing to negotiate with unions and coercing individual workers to accept lower wages, and had produced much human misery. The system proposed by Kingston sought to redress the power imbalance between individual workers and employers, and hence to prevent exploitation, by giving unions a central role.

> Unionism was collective action to remedy the inequality of bargaining power between labour and capital, and it was therefore the duty of the state to protect and encourage it. Real freedom of contract could only be attained by organised labour, for trade unions enabled workers to refuse poorly-paid work.[47]

The liberals believed that a state system which promoted agreements between collectivities of capital and labour would lead to a more harmonious ordering of society and an end to most strikes. Where the industrial parties could not agree, the state should 'protect the non-combatant public by resolving the dispute'.[48] The enormous social cost of the 1890s strikes should not be incurred again. Under the conciliation and arbitration systems that were introduced, strikes and lockouts were prohibited once the tribunal assumed jurisdiction over a dispute. Thus, in place of disruptive industrial warfare, compulsory arbitration was designed to usher in 'a new province for law and order'.[49] In summary, compulsory conciliation and arbitration systems were introduced in Australia by liberals with the support of fledgling Labor parties. The opportunity for their introduction arose from the great strikes of the 1890s and the general receptiveness of the Australian colonies to state intervention in economic activities, which in turn were products of the historical development of Australian capitalism.

Given the foregoing historical information, David Brereton turns to the theoretical debates on law reform to consider whether pluralist or marxist accounts provide the better explanation of the introduction of arbitration.[50] As noted earlier, pluralist theory argues that legislative reforms arise out of conflict and negotiation between interest groups. Legislation is therefore always a product of compromise, hence legal change tends to be gradual rather than radical. It is only in response to major social disruptions (such as the great strikes of the 1890s) that broad alliances are formed which permit the achievement of major reforms. Brereton also argues that while interest groups are unequal no one group is able to dominate all the time on all issues. This is explained partly by the observation that different state institutions have their own interests and preferences, which vary among institutions and over time. The shifting interests of state institutions and shifting alliances between interest groups in turn explain why political outcomes are relatively unpredictable.[51]

Brereton's chief criticism of marxist accounts is their insistence that legislative change will always (one way or another) serve the interests of capital. In the case of compulsory arbitration, an instrumentalist marxist would be unable to explain either employer opposition to the legislation or the role of liberals in its introduction.[52] By contrast, a pluralist account can accommodate the existence of a grouping that was 'neither capital nor labour'. Other versions of marxism might argue that compulsory arbitration was a limited concession to working class demands, or that it has served the long-run interest of the capitalist class, but Brereton argues that neither of these claims is empirically sustainable. He finds that pluralism fits better with the historical facts of the introduction of arbitration, in terms of the coalitions between liberals, protectionists and Labor that formed, in response to the great strikes, to support compulsory arbitration and enshrine the role of unions. He concedes that this account does not explain why the great strikes occurred in the first place (a marxist explanation is available here), nor why compulsory arbitration in particular gained the support of majorities in Australian parliaments.[53]

Brereton's dismissal of marxism may be questioned by reference to the discussion of marxist theories in chapter 4. Although Brereton does consider several variants of marxist theory on law reform he does not include any versions which emphasise the ideological role of law. On this view, the introduction of conciliation and arbitration systems which gave unions an acknowledged place can be seen as a means of co-opting the working class into the system of capitalist production. Law was used to create a climate of consensus in the industrial relations system, by promoting industrial harmony, attempting to minimise disruptions, and preventing the working class from acting on a class-wide basis. While the liberal promoters of compulsory conciliation and arbitration could see the dangers of the exercise of naked class power, they were also concerned to ensure continued economic progress under capitalism. This explanation of the introduction of compulsory arbitration appears to be at least as plausible as the pluralist account favoured by Brereton.

A more general criticism of the application of an ahistorical pluralist theory in this context is that it is reliant on a set of given historical facts which can never be fixed. As shown in chapter 1, historical scholarship constantly produces new interpretations and understandings of the past. As interpretations change, the degree of theoretical fit may vary. It is only possible to draw a contingent conclusion based on the present historical view. Even then there must be some doubt about the validity of applying a theory that was developed in the context of modern democratic practice to the conditions of a different historical period. In this context marxism does have the advantage of having its own theory of history and historical change.

It might be useful, though, to turn to a contemporary case study in order to explore further the competing claims of pluralist and marxist accounts of law reform, without the complicating factor of history.

Occupational health and safety in the 1980s

In 1985 the Labor government in Victoria enacted a new *Occupational Health and Safety Act*. A pluralist analysis of the origins of this Act would focus on the policy debates over occupational health and safety within the Victorian community (and in particular the Labor Party) during the 1970s and 1980s, and on the process of negotiation, both inside and outside parliament, by a government committed to reformist policies.

Such an explanation might begin in positivist fashion with a discussion of the legal precursors of the occupational health and safety provisions in Victoria. The first Victorian legislation was the *Factories and Shops Act 1885* (Vic.) (part of the same liberal program as divorce reform and compulsory conciliation and arbitration), which was modelled on the English Factories Act of 1878. In 1953 the Factories and Shops Act became known as the Labour and Industry Act. The pluralist account would then refer to the publication in 1972 of the Robens Report,[54] which was the product of an influential British committee of inquiry set up to 'review the provision made for the safety and health of persons in the course of their employment'. After identifying the defects of the British factories legislation (and by implication the Victorian Labour and Industry Act) the report recommended the streamlining of state regulation into a more unified and integrated system of health and safety legislation and administration, and the creation of a 'more effectively self-regulating system', with joint involvement of employers and employees in the formulation and implementation of health and safety policy at the workplace.

The pluralist account would then note that, in the two decades following the report, all the Australian jurisdictions introduced Robens-type legislation. In relation to Victoria, Jenny Doran has outlined a process of intense policy negotiation following the election of the Labor government in 1982.[55] In 1981 the State Conference of the Victorian Branch of the ALP adopted an occupational health and safety policy based on, and at times extending, the Robens Report and the British *Health and Safety etc. at Work Act 1974*. In 1983 the newly elected Victorian Labor government engaged in consultations with the community and with specific interest groups on the policy. It first published a discussion paper based on the policy, which received over two hundred responses. It then published a modified policy and, after further negotiations with employers and unions, introduced the Occupational Health and Safety Bill 1983. The Bill met a hostile reception, particularly as to its provisions governing the appointment of union health and safety representatives, and the powers to be given to those representatives to enforce the health and safety standards set out in the Bill. After indications that the Opposition-dominated Upper House would not pass the Bill it was withdrawn by the government. There followed further negotiations with the different interest groups, resulting in an amended Bill in 1984. Even though the Bill reduced the powers of health and safety representatives it was not acceptable to employer organisations and the Opposition, and was deferred pending the next State election. Following further negotiations with interest groups, resulting in further modifications, the Bill was passed in 1985 when the government had a temporary majority in the Upper House.

While there is no doubting the accuracy of the details of this explanation of the origins of the *Occupational Health and Safety Act 1985* (Vic.), it takes the relevant interest groups as given and abstracts their actions from broader historical processes and structures. The approach may be contrasted with that of Carson and Henenberg,[56] who have analysed the origins of the Occupational Health and Safety Act 1985 within a 'political economy' framework.[57] That is, like Quinlan, they have sought to 'make broader sense of the Act by linking its enactment and import to the wider social and historical structures, processes and developments within which it is embedded'.[58]

Carson and Henenberg begin with a discussion of the dominant, taken-for-granted ideologies of occupational health and safety, seeking to explain how certain ways of dealing with occupational health and safety issues came to be accepted as natural. The first 150 years of factory legislation led to the ideological separation of occupational health and safety from the industrial relations process and to the acceptance that occupational health and safety issues were the near exclusive concern of management and the state. The state assumed regulatory responsibility for health and safety, appointing inspectors to visit factories, who built up working relationships with management. Trade union involvement in occupational health and safety was largely confined to the commodifying of risk in the form of workers' compensation and danger money. To some extent the brutality of working conditions was accepted by male workers and unions as part of the definition of masculinity.

Although breaches of occupational health and safety legislation were formally criminal offences, the practice of factory inspectors reinforced historically developed ideologies to the effect that contraventions were not to be regarded as truly criminal and were most appropriately dealt with through informal mechanisms such as advice, education and warnings, with prosecution used as a very last resort. Moreover, accident investigations tended to emphasise the possible contribution of victims to their own injury, perpetuating the notion that workplace hazards were due to careless workers rather than the process of production itself. The important point is that these ideas were perceived as natural and timeless. If left unchallenged they would severely constrain any interest group pressure for legislative change.

Carson and Henenberg then examine the institutional and structural factors which led to a loosening of this hegemonic grip. While acknowledging the impact of the Robens Report, the change in political leadership in Victoria and increased trade union interest in occupational health and safety, they focus on the influence of the Prices and Incomes Accord concluded in 1983 between the federal ALP and the Australian Council of Trade Unions.[59] The Accord incorporated concerns with aspects of the 'social wage' such as occupational health and safety, in a context in which unions realised they could no longer achieve continuing increases in real wages. Carson and Henenberg also stress the impact of broader economic issues such as the enormous cost to the economy of industrial injury and illness, and the drive to increase Victoria's trade competitiveness by reducing workers' compensation premiums. A major aim was to reduce the number of injuries or diseases generating claims by 10 per cent over ten years. This was to be achieved by strong occupational health and safety legislation, of the type set out in the Labor Party's policy. Carson and Henenberg conclude their article with a discussion of the effect of the new Occupational Health and Safety Act, in terms of its interaction with the old ideologies of health and safety regulation. As a study of law enforcement, this aspect of the article is examined further in the next chapter.

Carson and Henenberg's analysis of the advent of the Occupational Health and Safety Act shows how a 'political economy' approach changes the focus of explanations about the origins of legislation and social policy, by bringing historical processes and structural issues into the analysis. It puts interest groups themselves into context, rather than taking them as the starting point. The approach remains limited, however, by its focus on economic issues and class forces. Adapting it to incorporate issues of race and sex would raise difficult questions of primacy between capitalism, colonialism and patriarchy. The political economy approach is also open to the postmodernist critique of theory based on broad historical processes and structures. The final case study, which involves racial divisions in society, suggests that in some situations neither pluralism nor political economy may provide convincing explanations of legislative change.

Validation of land titles in Victoria

In July 1993 the Victorian government became the first Australian government to introduce a legislative response to the High Court's decision in the Murray Islands case (discussed in chapter 1). The Land Titles Validation Bill passed rapidly through parliament and received assent on 18 August 1993. The Act purports to validate all land titles issued in Victoria between 31 October 1975 (the date of the Commonwealth Racial Discrimination Act) and a date to be proclaimed. Aboriginal people may claim compensation for any interference with their 'customary title' resulting from the validation.

The passage of the Act involved a striking lack of consultation, particularly with one of the most readily identified interest groups affected by the legislation, the Victorian Koori community. The Victorian parliament's Scrutiny of Acts and Regulations Committee held a public hearing on the Bill following its second reading, to which a number of groups, including the Victorian Aboriginal Legal Service,[60] made submissions. The Committee's capacity to make recommendations following the hearing was constrained by its terms of reference—it could not, for example, recommend that the Bill be withdrawn. In any case, the Committee's conclusions were ignored and the Bill was pushed through unaltered.[61] This history provides little scope for a pluralist analysis.

One way that the legislation may be accounted for is in functionalist terms. As seen in chapter 3, in the functionalist model of society the role of law is to maintain social cohesion by effecting value integration. A new law may arise from the need to produce stability in the social system by enforcing shared social norms, or it may be a response to pressures for change arising ultimately from the economy. The Land Titles Validation Act arguably fulfils both of these functions. It responds to the economic fears and uncertainties generated by the Murray Islands decision by setting out clear rules regarding the status of non-Aboriginal titles in Victoria. Those rules, in turn, are based on and reaffirm fundamental social values.

This functionalist account is manifest in the premier's second reading speech on the Bill.[62] The premier first stressed that the Victorian government had found it necessary to introduce the legislation as the High Court decision had 'cast a cloud of doubt over the validity and effectiveness' of grants of interests in Crown land since 31 October 1975.[63] Up to 18,000 land titles had been granted in Victoria since that date.[64] The security of those titles was vital for economic recovery and development in Victoria, particularly to assure potential investors 'that this State welcomes and encourages economic growth in an investment climate which is secure'.[65] Hence the need for the government to act and to act quickly.

Rapid validation of titles was also necessary, according to the premier, in order to affirm a key social value: 'It would be a gross dereliction of duty for the Government through omission to compromise one of the basic tenets of a free society: the right to private property and the security of private property for those who hold legal title to land'.[66] The solution to the Murray Islands problem was required to conform to another basic tenet, that of equal treatment before the law. Thus, for example, the 'Keating approach' (recognition of native title combined with broader moves towards reconciliation with the Aboriginal community) was rejected as divisive. '[I]t establishes two categories of Australians—Aboriginal and non-Aboriginal—for all time, and in such a way that the non-Aboriginals are then positively discriminated against. This is obviously unacceptable.'[67] It seems that a society based on shared social values cannot afford to recognise the different positions of different racial groups. Rather, everyone should be regarded and treated equally.

The premier's speech contains many references to the importance of equality before the law for all Victorians and the dangers of different treatment for different groups.[68] The Land Titles Validation Act offers validation of titles to non-Koori people and compensation for the loss or impairment of titles to Koories. In this way Koories are treated the same as any other person whose interest in land is compulsorily acquired or affected in some way by government action. In determining the amount of compensation payable in the event of a dispute, the Supreme Court is to have regard to the manner in which compensation would be determined under the *Land Acquisition and Compensation Act 1986* (Vic.). This 'ensures that the holders of any proved customary title are treated no differently from the holders of other forms of interest in land in relation to compensation for that interest'.[69]

The stated aims of the Land Titles Validation Act thus seem to fit with a functionalist analysis of the law as ensuring social cohesion. A critical analysis of the Act, by contrast, would scrutinise the premier's claims, the terms of the Act and the surrounding social and economic conditions using insights drawn from marxism, CLS, deconstruction and the particular postmodern critique of the marginalisation of non-Western 'others' known as postcolonialism.

Taking such a critical approach, it may first be noted that, although 18,000 titles may have been issued in Victoria since October 1975, that does not mean that 18,000 titles were put 'at risk' by the Murray Islands decision. Indeed, given the history of dispossession of Koories in Victoria, it is possible that none of those titles operated to extinguish subsisting native title in contravention of the Racial Discrimination Act, and thus no question of invalidity would have arisen.[70] In many cases, too, the interests that were granted would, according to the High Court's principles, be capable of co-existing with any native title over the same land, and again no question of invalidity would have arisen.[71] Furthermore, there were no major investment projects proposed for Victoria that were endangered by 'uncertainty' over the Murray Islands case.[72] Taking these matters into account, there appears to have been no real urgency for the Victorian government to act to validate titles. Indeed, although the Act was rushed through parliament, its operative sections had still not been proclaimed by the end of the year.

In this light the Act appears less as a necessary measure and more as a piece of political opportunism. The government appeared to be acting decisively while in fact achieving nothing. But even though it had no material effects the Act can be seen as an important intervention in the *discourse* about native title. The Act and the second reading speech were statements by the Victorian government which contributed to the construction of meaning around the concept of 'native title', including its level of acceptance within the non-Aboriginal community.

The Act uses the term 'customary title' in preference to the term 'native title' employed in the High Court's decision. The professed reason for this was that the High Court had provided no clear definition of 'native title'.[73] 'Customary title' was claimed to be a more descriptive term than 'native title', although it is no more specific, being defined, inter alia, as 'a right of any nature to or to the occupation, use or enjoyment of land by Aboriginal persons in accordance with Aboriginal tradition'.[74] ('Aboriginal tradition' is further defined.) The definition appears to be considerably broader than the High Court's concept of native title, despite the premier's assertion that the legislation in no way acknowledges or accepts the concept of native title beyond the Murray Islands decision.[75] Notably, the definition of 'customary title' does not require continuous occupation of the land, as required by the doctrine of native title laid down by the High Court. Thus it seems that customary title could be established through cultural/spiritual connection with the land even in the absence of physical connection. It follows that the effect of validation on 'customary title' might be different from its effect on native title. If the object of the Land Titles Validation Act was to reintroduce certainty in Victorian land management, the substitution of the term 'customary title' for native title was contrary to that object.

In fact, the change of terminology makes little sense except as a statement of denial of the Murray Islands decision. The Victorian government's refusal to use the term 'native title' echoed its refusal to use the Aboriginal name 'Gariwerd' for the mountainous region in north-west Victoria. One of the Kennett government's first acts when it came to power in 1992 was to reverse the previous government's efforts to recognise local indigenous culture, by reinstating the European name for the area: 'the Grampians'.

In justifying the Land Titles Validation Act the premier spoke of the need to uphold 'the right to private property and the security of private property for those who hold legal title to land'.[76] The premier's statement ignored the fact that, under the Murray Islands decision, native title holders also hold legal title to land, which should also be entitled to protection. Implicit in the statement was a contrast between 'private' property, which must be protected by the state, and native/customary title, which is not (except for the operation of the Racial Discrimination Act) the subject of rights or protection. Paradoxically, while libertarian governments generally consider state interference with 'private' property to be inappropriate,[77] in this instance state intervention to uphold the value of 'private' property was considered quite legitimate. The fact that such property is created and guaranteed by the liberal state would seem to place it in the category of 'public' rather than 'private'. Indeed, on this analysis, native title has more claim to be categorised as 'private', as in theory native title really did exist prior to the state. In practice, though, native title is also a creation of the state, as it exists and has force only by virtue of the judicial pronouncements in the Murray Islands case and the provisions of the *Native Title Act 1993* (Cwlth).[78] Ultimately, then, the public/private distinction is incoherent in this context. There is no principled basis for distinguishing between Aboriginal and non-Aboriginal titles by claiming that the latter are 'private' property rights. The language of public and private obscures the racially based political choice to privilege non-Aboriginal titles.

Apart from the sanctity of 'private' property, the other liberal tenet invoked in the premier's second reading speech, as noted earlier, was that of equality before the law. The model of equality adopted is strict identical treatment according to the prevailing norms of land management in Victoria. Thus, for example, Aboriginal people have fifteen years after the commencement of the Land Titles Validation Act to claim compensation for loss of native title, as that is the period of time allowed by the *Limitation of Actions Act 1958* (Vic.) for anyone else to bring an action to recover land.[79] Compensation is to be calculated by reference to the legislation governing compulsory acquisition of any other land, the Land Acquisition and Compensation Act 1986.

The strict identical treatment model of equality fails to recognise and accommodate differences from the norm it adopts for the purposes of comparison. Consequently, it has the effect of perpetuating substantive inequalities. In this case, it cannot account for the ways in which native title is different from other interests in land, and native title holders are disadvantaged to the extent that native title is not analogous to non-Aboriginal titles. For example, the compensation principles contained in the Land Acquisition and Compensation Act are based on the notion of land as a commodity and the assumption of individual landholding. Compensation is calculated by reference to the market value of the land, and any special *pecuniary* value it may have to the claimant. In addition, a small percentage of the market value may be added by way of *solatium* for intangible, non-pecuniary disadvantages. When applied to native title, these principles fail to account for the communal nature of the title, the cultural and spiritual significance of the land and particular sites, and the fact that land is understood as part of the self rather than as commodity—it cannot simply be exchanged for money or other land. In Derridaean terms,[80] this is a classic example of the Western privileging of presence over absence, physical over spiritual. Koori understandings of land are banished to the margins of consideration. A closer analogy in the Anglo-Australian compensation field for loss of land held under native title might be general damages in tort for severe and permanent personal injury.[81] But this analysis would still encounter the general problems that the Anglo-Australian damages system has in dealing with non-pecuniary harm: it is inadequately valued, and it should probably not be commodified the first place. An alternative management regime, which would centralise rather than marginalise Koori concerns, would leave 'customary titles' undisturbed and offer compensation to those for whom it would be meaningful—the non-Aboriginal title holders who might suffer some financial loss from having their titles invalidated.

In the scheme established by the Land Titles Validation Act, however, the rhetoric of 'equality before the law' operates to the benefit of those who define the norms against which equality is measured. Like property rights, the invocation of equality is ideological in that it appears to be universal and fair, and thus diverts attention from the marked partiality of its operation. In this context it has been argued that the real inequalities produced by the Land Titles Validation Act may be challenged under the Racial Discrimination Act. That is, the fact that the compensation principles in the Victorian Act deprive one racial group of adequate compensation by ignoring the nature of their interest in land may amount to unlawful racial discrimination.[82] Yet the Racial Discrimination Act is a somewhat uncertain refuge, as its application would depend upon High Court interpretation.[83] The Victorian government was clearly of the opinion that the Land Titles Validation Act did not conflict with the Racial Discrimination Act. These opposing opinions on the effect of the Racial Discrimination Act reflect that fact that its standards of equality and discrimination are manipulable and indeterminate.

The above analysis suggests that in Australia capitalism and its supporting liberal ideologies take a specifically colonialist form. While it may no longer be accurate to speak of the uniform oppression of the working class in Australia, it remains the case that Aboriginal people are oppressed as a group in a particularly stark way. The criminal law and property law still function as forms of repressive social control, ensuring the subjugation of the indigenous population as well as access to their land for economic purposes. This helps to explain why the Murray Islands case, while offering a strictly limited amount of land to some Aboriginal groups, was perceived as so disruptive.[84] The Land Titles Validation Act can be seen as a reassertion of the racial and economic hegemony of Anglo-Australian colonial capitalism. The concept of native title is transformed beyond recognition by its commodified assimilation into the capitalist land management system.

Conclusion

The functionalist and critical analyses of the Land Titles Validation Act proceed from very different assumptions and theoretical frameworks. It seems, however, that they capture the particular subject matter and history of the legislation more adequately than either side of the traditional debate between pluralist and marxist theories of law reform. The case studies in this chapter warn against the acceptance of either simple pluralist or simple marxist explanations of reform. They show that the theoretical approaches outlined in previous chapters provide a variety of tools for analysing particular instances of reform along with the broader historical forces, structures or discourses in which reforms are located. And they suggest that no one theory is adequate to explain the phenomenon of 'law reform' in its entirety. The difficulty of arriving at global explanations is illustrated by a comparison between the Victorian Land Titles Validation Act and the federal Native Title Act. The 'big picture' in each case was the same, and it is necessary to direct attention to the specific political positions of the respective governments in order to understand the different legislative results they achieved.

One element of a government's political position is the view that it takes of the appropriate role of legislation. Roger Cotterrell has drawn attention to the 'dominant ideology of law's functions'[85] held by libertarian governments such as the Thatcher government in Britain and the Liberal government in Victoria. Within this ideology the 'extensive positive and directive use of law to recreate a climate of free enterprise' is accepted as natural, but the 'use of law to plan a more egalitarian economic welfare, or to direct economic or other activity in the communal interest . . . is often seen as illegitimate, pointless, and even disastrous'.[86] That is, law may be used to influence people's behaviour and attitudes towards free market outcomes but it may not, and indeed cannot successfully, be used to promote, for example, public altruism or collective participation in social life and decision making.[87] Cotterrell shows that these beliefs about the legitimate role of law are based partly on empirical evidence about the effects of law reform,[88] but mostly on the supporting ideologies of liberalism: the right to private property, liberty, the minimal state and the rule of law.[89] Given the pervasiveness of these ideologies in liberal democratic societies, they will operate as constraints on the kinds of legislative outcomes any government in those societies is prepared to contemplate. This is one other factor to be considered in explanations of law reform.

Empirical evidence that legislative reforms do not always have the desired effect applies as much to the regulation of free enterprise as it does to the regulation of social welfare. The next chapter examines a range of studies of the law in action, as well as some of the methods by which legal outcomes may be measured.

Further reading

Bottomley, Stephen, Gunningham, Neil and Parker, Stephen *Law in context*, Federation Press, Sydney, 1991, ch. 12

Connell, R. W. and Irving, T. H. *Class structure in Australian history: documents, narrative and argument*, Longman Cheshire, Melbourne, 1980

De Angelis, R. and Parkin, A. 'Interest groups and power: pluralism and its critics', in *Government, politics and power in Australia*, eds D. Woodward, A. Parkin and J. Summers, Longman Cheshire, Melbourne, 3rd edn, 1985

Hay, Douglas 'Property, authority and the criminal law', in *Albion's fatal tree*, ed. Douglas Hay et al., Allen Lane, London, 1975

Tomasic, Roman ed. *Legislation and society in Australia*, Allen & Unwin, Sydney, 1980

6

Invocation and enforcement of legal rules

Richard Ingleby and Richard Johnstone

The previous chapter looked at different ways of explaining the origins of legislation. This chapter explores the 'gap' between legal rules ('the law in books') and their implementation ('the law in action'). Legal rules may appear to require, allow or proscribe certain activities. But the invocation or enforcement of the rules may reshape them into a form that bears little resemblance to the 'law in books'.

For example, a range of rules purports to protect workers from workplace illness and injury: common law negligence actions for compensation; statutory workers' compensation schemes; statutory rehabilitation schemes; the preventative provisions of occupational health and safety legislation. But how are such rules invoked by injured workers and enforced by the state? Do all workers suffering occupational illness or injury initiate actions for compensation? Does the occupational health and safety inspectorate prosecute all employers who have provided unsafe workplaces? Do workers exercise their individual and collective rights to refuse to work in hazardous conditions? Similarly, in the context of family and criminal law, both the common law and statutory provisions have formally provided the means for an abused partner to seek personal protection or sole occupation of the family home. Yet studies of family violence repeatedly reveal that individuals who suffer such violence do not resort to the legal system for protection. More characteristically they will either 'lump it' or leave the relationship. Even in the minority of cases where legal remedies *are* sought this often occurs only after all other avenues have been explored and long after the first acts which would have warranted legal intervention.

In looking at the ways in which legal rules are transformed in the course of their implementation, this chapter argues that one explanation for the 'gap' between the 'law in books' and the 'law in action' is the manner in which legal actors make legal decisions. Discretion is dispersed throughout the legal system, hence there are a great many legal decisions to be made and a great many legal actors who must make them. In order to make sense of the 'law in action' the concepts of 'legal actors' and 'legal decisions' must be defined broadly.

The chapter outlines methods by which to research the 'law in action' and considers the relationship between these research methods and the theoretical perspectives introduced in earlier chapters. There is then a discussion of empirical studies which have been carried out in various contexts, followed by consideration of the role of the legal profession as a particular set of legal actors and by some concluding comments on the relationship between the courts and out-of-court activity.

One of the most influential frameworks for the analysis of out-of-court activity is provided by the American socio-legal theorist Marc Galanter,[1] who uses the concepts of 'repeat players' and 'one-shotters' to explain why the 'haves' come out ahead, even in the case of laws which appear to empower socially disadvantaged groups. Galanter describes a repeat player as a party engaged repeatedly in similar litigation (such as governmental or large corporate bodies) and a one-shotter as a party who has only occasional recourse to the courts. For example, most workers' compensation claimants would only make one claim for compensation in their lifetime, but workers' compensation insurers are likely to be respondents to many claims in theirs.

Drawing on a range of studies of litigation and the criminal justice process, Galanter shows how repeat players are advantaged in the legal process because, among other things, they can structure transactions in the light of their experience in previous litigation, establish informal relationships with court staff, follow a long-term strategy in conducting their litigation, and choose which cases to run in order to establish favourable precedents and which cases to settle to avoid the creation of unfavourable precedents. Consequently, rules might develop to favour repeat players. Galanter argues that, while one-shotters can make use of the services of lawyers (themselves repeat players) to reduce repeat players' advantages, most specialist lawyers tend to cater for the special needs of repeat players. Lawyers who service one-shotters tend to make up the lower ranks of the legal profession and they find it difficult to 'mobilise' a clientele because of restrictions on advertising and so forth. And they cannot use the tactical options open to repeat players because it is unethical to trade off one one-shotter's gain against another's loss. Courts are essentially passive institutions and repeat players, who tend to be wealthy and well organised, are more knowledgeable about initiating legal action and better resourced to conduct it.

Galanter's article is a 'meta study', in that he draws on the empirical research of others in speculating on the limits of legal change. Such speculations can provide avenues for future empirical research, which might support the validity of earlier hypotheses or compel their rejection or reformulation. To understand the process by which a dynamic body of data

Invocation and enforcement of legal rules

and theory might develop it is necessary to consider the various empirical methods by which the 'law in action' might be examined.

Empirical research methods

Empirical legal research aims to observe, describe and interpret legal activity and people's experience of law. As defined in chapter 4[2] empiricism is a method which seeks to draw objective conclusions from direct observation of the world. While jurisprudential methods involve theorising about how law works, empirical methods try to find out what is 'really' happening 'on the ground'. Socio-legal researchers utilise a variety of empirical research methods, which may conveniently be categorised as 'positivist', 'interactionist' or 'critical'. These categories relate to the theoretical approaches considered in earlier chapters.

A positivist approach assumes that the world is capable of being understood in terms of objectively observable external data (facts).[3] Such an approach favours the production of quantitative data. For example, a positivist researcher who wanted to examine the workings of equal opportunity legislation might construct a multiple choice questionnaire and survey parties and members of potential client groups for their perceptions of the legislation. The project might count the number of complaints made under the legislation and the proportion of this number which were withdrawn, settled before a hearing upheld at a hearing, or dismissed. Positivist research produces figures, graphs and statistics to reveal trends and patterns of legal activity. Of course, such 'hard facts' are not beyond question. The researcher has selected categories and tabulated data in order to answer a particular inquiry, but there may be scope for disagreement on the research process, the interpretation of results and the relationship between the results obtained and the activity being examined.

Interactionism,[4] also known as 'social action theory', developed partly as a reaction against sociological positivism. The theoretical approaches underpinning interactionism include the micro-sociological work of Weber,[5] the focus of functionalism on action theory and roles,[6] the philosophy of pragmatism, and anthropological research methods such as participant observation.[7] Interactionists focus on the way in which individual social actors make choices.[8] They argue that people do not act in accordance with external constraints but have considerable room for manoeuvre, negotiation and creative action in their interactions with other individuals as they actively make sense of themselves, others and social situations. Rather than there being any reality in an absolute sense, people construct their own reality through the internal processes by which they ascribe meanings to things within the dynamic process of interaction.[9] The role of the researcher is to understand the interactionist processes by which definitions of self and situation are constructed and to interpret the meanings which actors give to their activities. How do some individuals come to be defined as 'criminals', for example? And how do the police respond to that label? Interactionists answer this question by examining the meanings generated in the interaction between police and individuals, in order to see how the police interpret the appearance, manner and behaviour of groups they frequently encounter.

Interactionism does not concern itself with analysis at the macro-sociological level. It places emphasis on social roles, but assumes that, for example, gender roles within the family are not fixed by the social structure—as functionalists and some feminists and marxists would argue. It assumes a diversity of values rather than the common values central to functionalism. Interactionism bears some resemblance to postmodernism,[10] in that both approaches look at the local, the concrete and the situated, and maintain that reality is socially constructed. Further, both interactionism and postmodernism could be described as a method or set of methods without a politics. Interactionism, however, developed long before postmodernism, in the early twentieth century, and it participates in that period's continued faith in the possibility of social science. While rejecting positivist methods in favour of ethnographic methods, it still assumes that truth is accessible through the application of those methods. By contrast, postmodern perspectives are deeply sceptical about the notion of any absolute truth to be discovered.

The third empirical research method examined here, which might be called 'critical interactionism', concentrates on the need to make some connections between the micro-level focus of interactionism and the structural context of interactions. C. Wright Mills[11] emphasised the need for social theorists to connect the detail of people's lives and everyday issues and problems to the 'big ups and downs'—the processes of historical change, the institutional contradictions and the structural forces of the society in which people live. This research method has affinities with the 'political economy' approach to law reform discussed in the previous chapter.

The following sections of the present chapter give examples of how the various research methods have been used by socio-legal researchers in different contexts.

Public regulation

Studies of the 'law in action' have consistently revealed that regulatory regimes (legal rules backed by criminal sanctions) are not always enforced against those who contravene them. This section examines this socio-legal phenomenon. It looks first at studies of crime in the traditional sense, involving police as the enforcing agents, and then at studies of what is often labelled 'white collar' crime, where the enforcement agency may be a factories inspectorate or other statutory 'watchdog'.

Policing

In an exemplary utilisation of interactionist methodology Aaron Cicourel[12] analysed the way in which a police officer in a large American city investigated a theft of money from a house in the block in which the suspect, a juvenile

Invocation and enforcement of legal rules

named Mark, lived. Using principally participant observation, Cicourel accompanied the officer in his dealings with Mark, and examined police records of extensive past contact between the police and Mark and his family. The contacts included neighbours' complaints about Mark's sister stealing mail, neighbours' concerns about Mark's mother's neglect of her children, police descriptions of the family's ill-kept home, and so on. As Cicourel commented, both the officer and Mark 'shared a system of relevances or meaning structures that could be described as "normal" for both'.[13] The exchange in which the officer got Mark to confess to the theft was 'part of a larger game that they participate in periodically and may expect to continue' while Mark was within the jurisdiction of the officer. Cicourel observed:

> ... subsequent trouble in the neighbourhood always led the police to Mark, and future encounters with the police must be negotiated within the context of the police characterisation of the home as 'bad'. I want to stress that Mark and his family fit the police conception of 'normal' causes of delinquency, and officers will therefore 'expect' Mark to be in trouble.[14]

Cicourel is not saying that the police invented Mark's delinquency, or that Mark was innocent. Rather he argues that juvenile activities that would otherwise have gone unnoticed were, in Mark's case, viewed as delinquent because he fitted the officers' conception of delinquency, and they would seek him out whenever there was trouble in the neighbourhood. The definition of Mark as a delinquent was constructed by the officers over a period of time from a series of interactions. The job of the researcher, in the context of an examination of police behaviour, was to unravel the meanings, expectations and understandings attached to the situation by the officer. In this case the meanings derived from previous actions—encounters with Mark and his family—came to direct the officer's actions in accusing Mark of the theft.

Greta Bird's study of the relationship between Aboriginal people and the police in South Australia[15] linked interactionist methods with the critical approach considered at the end of the previous section. Bird's statistical data suggested that Aborigines, particularly those in rural towns, were the subject of special police attention. She showed how, in exercising their discretion to arrest, police were subject to pressure from the local white community to maintain the appearance of order and to 'deal with the "Aboriginal problem"'. Some Aboriginal people were antagonistic to police authority, either because of past contacts or because of increased political assertiveness. Consequently, the police were forced to assert their authority by constructing disrespectful behaviour towards white authority as crime. They used minor offences, such as theft of a bunch of grapes, or public drunkenness, to control 'marginal' people who appeared to threaten public order. Bird shows the relationship between the specific situations of policing and the broader societal backdrop: 'the police do not just assert their authority in situations of specific challenge, but resort to it frequently once a group of people has acquired an identity as objects of policing'.[16] She argues that encounters between the police and Aboriginal people are routine expressions of underlying racist social relations.

Inspecting

Researchers such as Kit Carson[17] and Keith Hawkins[18] conducted studies on the way strict liability environmental and occupational health and safety offences have been enforced by the relevant inspectorates. Most criminal offences require proof of both a criminal act (*actus reus*) and guilty intent (*mens rea*) on the part of the accused. By contrast, strict liability offences require the prosecution to prove only that the relevant criminal act has been committed by the defendant; there is no need to prove *mens rea*. Carson and Hawkins showed how, despite the strict liability provisions of the environmental protection and occupational health and safety legislation, the decision whether to prosecute for a breach of the law was determined by the investigator's assessment of the 'moral fault' of the perpetrator.

Hawkins' primary research method was participant observation of pollution control officers in their field work. He states:

> I chose participant observation . . . in observance of the interactionist injunction to respect and reflect the nature of the empirical world. Observation provides the raw material which permits the activities of enforcement agents and their discretionary behaviour to be understood in the context of their routine work. It allows the researcher 'to attain a grasp of the meaning . . . of rules as common-sense constructs from the perspective of those . . . who promulgate and live with them'.[19]

One problem with participant observation as a method is that the presence of the researcher inevitably changes the environment that is sought to be observed. Hawkins attempted to deal with this problem by being 'careful not to interrupt the officers' daily routine and . . . [trying] to impress upon them that I wanted them to carry out their sampling, inspections and negotiations exactly as they would in my absence'.[20] This, plus his adoption of various strategies to blend into the background, left him ultimately satisfied that his presence had had a minimal impact on his research subject.[21] His espousal of interactionist methods and rejection of positivist methods is further indicated by the fact that he chose not to study any of the pollution legislation before doing his field work, so that he could 'learn the law as the field officers knew it' and avoid 'the distortion arising from a particular sense of relevance which thorough prior knowledge of the formal structure of rules may have conferred on what I was actually observing'.[22]

In making sense of his observations of field officers in action, Hawkins used the concept of a 'decision frame' to refer to the 'structure of knowledge, experience, values and meanings that the decision maker shares with others and brings to a choice'.[23] The decision frame informs and shapes the character of choices, by determining the information sought and used and the meaning, relevance and significance it is given. Different decision frames will produce different outcomes from the same basic information. Decision frames may change over time, as resources, priorities and other contextual factors change. A researcher of legal decision making therefore needs to examine the decision frame, rather than merely looking for the articulated factors given by decision makers to justify their decisions.

However, a researcher's understanding of decision frames will depend upon the researcher's own disciplinary perspective. For example, a researcher looking at the decision making processes of occupational health and safety inspectors from a psychological perspective will examine the cognitive strategies used by inspectors to facilitate rapid and repetitive decision making, and will evaluate the extent to which these strategies produce enforcement decisions consonant with the goals of the enforcement agency.[24] Psychologists studying routine decision making have used the concept of categorisation to describe how prior knowledge and experience inform subsequent decisions. Because decisions are repetitive the decision maker can develop mental categories of cases to which new cases can be allocated.[25] These categories can embrace not just the features of each case but also the parameters and context of the decision. Inspectors, for example, simplify their decision making along established lines, talking in terms of typical accidents and salient accident features, and categorising common types of accident automatically.[26] If decisions can fall into increasingly fixed patterns the new and unusual tend to be missed. As a consequence certain types of injuries on certain types of machines tend to become the norm for enforcement and prosecution strategies, often reflecting the legal categories in the relevant regulations. There may be little by way of development of new regulations, new patterns of inspection or new ways of inspecting hazards.

Empirical research on legal decision making has tended, however, to take a sociological rather than a psychological approach. The work of Kit Carson provides an illustration of the sociologist's and historian's method of explaining decision making in terms of a broader political economy—a contrast to the narrower focus of the psychologist or researcher preoccupied with microstudies. As noted earlier, Carson's study of the way in which inspectors made enforcement decisions in relation to strict liability factory legislation showed that, even though the notion of 'moral fault' was legally irrelevant, in fact 'moral fault' played a significant part in shaping the action taken against offenders. In research into the history of factory legislation Carson later showed that, this enforcement culture had an ideological longevity, and played a role in creating and recreating the conditions under which industrialisation and laissez faire capitalism could thrive.[27] The enforcement culture was traced back to the political economy underlying the enactment of the British *Factories Regulation Act* of 1833. A number of large, urban manufacturers had, with various motives, already voluntarily introduced improved conditions of employment in their factories and sought compulsory and effective regulation of working conditions in order to reduce long-term competition from smaller, less scrupulous manufacturers and from rural manufacturers. The Act also played a role in creating and maintaining a healthy and disciplined workforce.[28] Protective legislation would ensure that the state received the support of the British worker, but only if the legislation was seen to be effective and not a 'sham'.[29]

Carson argued that the Factories Regulation Act and subsequent Factory Acts manifested the contradictory tendencies of their own development and institutionalised the 'ambiguity' of factory crime. While factory offences have been statutorily described as crime and proscribed by law, they have been frequently committed and substantially tolerated in practice. Factory offences have been dealt with by administrative agencies that have different origins and are far removed from the normal machinery of criminal justice, so that the community views factory contraventions as being 'not really criminal'; and they have rarely been prosecuted.

Carson found that, historically, the prevailing structure, organisation and ideology of production was something in which contravention of the legislation was widespread, and practised even by 'respectable' employers[30] as a calculated short-term response to the economic circumstances they faced. Widespread use of prosecution would have entailed 'collective criminalisation' of employers 'of considerable status, social respectability and growing political influence'.[31] To try to resolve these contradictions, and in response to the low penalties imposed by magistrates, inspectors prosecuted only when satisfied that the offence stemmed from a concrete element of intention on the part of the employer and they developed conciliatory approaches to enforcement, based on informal advice, persuasion and warnings, with prosecution the last resort. Carson concluded that by the late 1840s the 'pattern of factory law enforcement had been set, and the ambiguity [and conventionalisation] of factory crime established'.[32]

Carson and Henenberg[33] argued that this prevailing ideology concerning factory crime would influence the implementation of the new Victorian *Occupational Health and Safety Act 1985* (discussed in the previous chapter), despite its attempt to take a different approach to occupational health and safety. They showed that since 1985 little had happened to counter either the ideologies of the ambiguity of occupational health and safety crime or the depoliticisation of occupational health and safety issues. They also suggested that structural changes such as the decentralisation of industrial relations practices generally would result in trade union resources being consumed by workplace bargaining over wages and conditions, at the expense of workplace health and safety.

Bridget Hutter used Carson's and other studies and her own empirical data as the basis for an analysis of the strategies used to enforce environmental health and occupational health and safety legislation in Britain.[34] Her study shows how the gathering and interpretation of empirical data can involve a two-way relationship between participant observation and broader theoretical perspectives. She describes how enforcement agencies generally followed 'accommodative' or 'compliance' strategies in which securing compliance with the legislation was the main objective, both through the remedying of existing problems and the prevention of others. Persuasion, negotiation and education were the principal enforcement methods used in this general approach. Agencies typically did not use 'deterrence' or 'sanctioning' enforcement strategies, in which prosecution was given an important role. Instead, Hutter noted, prosecution was used as a method of last resort, when all other means had failed. She nevertheless identified two distinct enforcement methods within the broad accommodative approach: the persuasive and the insistent. The persuasive method utilised informal tactics in which enforcement officers coaxed or cajoled offenders into complying with the law. The insistent technique was less benevolent and flexible; officers would spend less time negotiating and persuading before escalating their enforcement response to warnings and prosecution. Yet still their objective was compliance, not punishment for breaches of the law.

Hutter analysed the factors accounting for the variations in enforcement style. She argued that resources, peer group pressure, organisational hierarchies, recruitment practices and the wider political context all played some part in influencing the enforcement strategy adopted by a particular agency. The persuasive approach required large resources; where there were scarce opportunities for negotiation there was pressure to resort to formal legal procedures such as prosecution. Yet the cost of conducting prosecutions would restrict the number of offenders against whom prosecutions could be brought. Another important explanatory factor was the relational distance between the regulator and the regulated and their frequency of interaction. The smaller and more closely knit the community in which the parties operated the less likely that formal legal methods would be used. Likewise, the more frequent the interaction between the parties the less the inclination to resort to formal enforcement methods. Hutter's analysis in turn provides a possible framework for future research on regulatory activity.

Community attitudes

Carson's argument, outlined above, regarding the conventionalisation and ambiguity of factory crime, may apply specifically to the attitudes of factory inspectors or it may apply to community attitudes more generally. On the basis of their empirical research Grabosky, Braithwaite and Wilson[35] argued that the community as a whole does take 'white collar' crimes such as occupational health and safety offences seriously. The Australian Institute of Criminology in 1986 undertook a national survey of attitudes to crime. Just over 2500 respondents rated the seriousness of 13 hypothetical incidents. The results suggested that an incident in which a worker lost a leg in an unguarded machine 'because the employer knowingly failed to provide safety measures' was ranked fourth on the scale, ahead of armed robbery, child and wife bashing, and tax, social security and Medibank fraud. This rating suggests that factory crime is not viewed in the community as either conventional or ambiguous. Yet, on closer examination, the survey question sought community opinion on a particularly egregious workplace injury, which conformed to inspectors' conceptions of blameworthiness because of the employer's 'knowing' behaviour. Moreover, the event-focused nature of the question could not hope to capture the complex historical processes that might have led to the practical decriminalisation of occupational health and safety offences. While this example illustrates some of the limitations of survey research, surveys can often be the most appropriate means of gauging broad community attitudes to law or to socio-legal problems. In other words, determining community attitudes might call for different research methods from those that would be used to investigate legal decision making by individual actors.

Evidently, too, the scope, methods and even the subjects of empirical research are limited by the accessibility of the research subject to the researcher. Most empirical research in law focuses on litigation and public regulation, such as the work of the police and other enforcement agencies, because it is relatively easy for the researcher to observe the agency in action, count its activities and read its files. Research in the 'private' domain is more difficult, because the researcher has no easy access to, for example, couples facing marital breakdown or women experiencing domestic violence or sexual harassment. It would be difficult to conceive a study which used interactionist methodologies to investigate the impact of mandatory reporting of child abuse. This manifestation of the public/private distinction perpetuates the effects of the distinction identified by feminist legal theorists.[36] The research emphasis on the 'public' sphere means that activities in this sphere, in which men figure prominently if not exclusively, are carefully scrutinised and appear to be worthy of study. Conversely, activities in the 'private' sphere, where women are overrepresented, appear less worthy of study and become even more devalued and hidden.

The individual invocation of law

Criminal law, in which the state takes a role in enforcement, may be contrasted with areas of civil law such as torts, contracts, discrimination and family law, where it is left up to aggrieved individuals to take action on their own behalf. While studies of public regulation focus on the activities and decision making patterns of enforcement officials, studies of the civil law in action focus on the factors that affect individual decisions as to whether and how far to seek a legal remedy. To return to Galanter's terminology, discussed earlier, in criminal cases the regulators (police, inspectors) and often the objects of regulation (employers/factory owners) are repeat players. In civil cases, those expected to invoke the law are often one shotters, facing all of the problems Galanter identified.

Transformation of social phenomena into legal issues

A study conducted by members of the Oxford Centre for Socio-Legal Studies in 1984 showed that only 26 per cent of all accident victims surveyed even considered claiming compensation, that 23 per cent thought a claim might

Invocation and enforcement of legal rules

Table 6.1 Naming, blaming and claiming framework (Felstiner, Abel and Sarat)

1 Unperceived injurious experience
2 Perceived injurious experience (*naming*)
3 Attribution of perceived injurious experience to the fault of another individual or social entity (*blaming*)
4 Voicing of grievance to person or entity believed responsible with demand for remedy (*claiming*)
5 Rejection of claim in whole or in part = dispute

be possible, and only 14 per cent consulted a lawyer.[37] Consequently only 12 per cent of victims received any damages. Even road accident and work accident victims failed to initiate claims in 66 per cent and 76 per cent of cases respectively.[38] The researchers observed: 'Most potential claims are defeated at the outset: the accident victim does not realize that a legal remedy might be available or, even if he [sic] does, other constraining factors prevent him from consulting a solicitor about bringing a claim'.[39]

The legal system is only one of a range of options open to people who are unhappy with their situation. To understand how people use law the reasons why legal remedies are not invoked must be examined. A useful framework for such a discussion is the 'naming, blaming, claiming . . .' analysis developed by Felstiner, Abel and Sarat.[40] They consider the various processes which have to take place before a dispute exists. These are set out in Table 6.1.

This analysis shows that there are a number of 'transformations' which an experience must undergo before it can become a dispute. First, it must be perceived, and perceived as injurious. It must then be attributed to the fault of another, and that other person must be asked for a remedy. Only if that claim is rejected does a dispute come into existence. It follows that there are many things that may prevent the experience from being transformed into a dispute. And, by extension, there are many factors which may determine that the claim and dispute are not constructed in legal terms.

Examination of disputes within this framework involves examination of the various contexts which determine whether and if so how the various transformations take place. One relevant context is the location in which the injury occurred. A work injury, for example, might be more likely to be the subject of a legal claim than an injury incurred at home, since there is more likely to be some ready source of blame, as well as information available about compensation entitlements. The size of the injury might also be relevant in this context. Another important factor is who the injured person consults about the possibilities of claiming and blaming. Union officials, friends, relatives, doctors and lawyers all have different influences on the transformation process. The role of lawyers, in particular, is considered further below. A further context relevant to transformation has been argued to be the community's general level of 'litigation consciousness' at the time.

Consideration of the factors affecting transformation suggests that the law itself (the law in books) is only one source of normative order. To give a further example, workers in many Australian jurisdictions are given rights to elect health and safety representatives, to stop work in the face of immediate threats to their health and safety, to require hazards to be remedied, and to be involved in occupational health and safety committees. Yet whether workers exercise these rights, and the manner in which they are exercised, depends to a large extent on broader structural issues. For example, the unequal workplace power relations and the dominant workplace ideologies of managerial prerogative, production imperative and acceptance of work-related illness and injury as a necessary by-product of industrialisation mean that workers underutilise their rights. Even when these rights are invoked, they are exercised subject to the accepted workplace hierarchies which subordinate workers' interests to those of management. In addition, the established gender hierarchy means that health and safety representatives can often fail to recognise health and safety issues of concern to women. In other words, the operation of the legal order is modified by a complex combination of economic, political and social orders which reassert unequal gender and class relations.[41]

Informal resolution of disputes

The Oxford study of the use of the torts system for compensation for personal injuries showed that a minute proportion of cases (0.4 per cent) actually reached the stage of a court hearing.[42] The remainder received damages payments determined by a protracted settlement process. There were many pressures which induced plaintiffs to compromise out of court on levels of compensation much lower than might have been received if the case had gone to judgment. These factors included the risk that the plaintiff may not have been able to produce sufficient evidence of the defendant's fault in court; the expense and hardship to the plaintiff caused by delays in the matter reaching the court; the risk of damages being reduced for contributory negligence; and the skill of insurance companies (repeat players) in using their bargaining position to induce settlements to their advantage.[43] Financial resources enable parties to withstand transaction costs by not being 'starved out' during negotiations. They also enable parties to engage in extensive pre-trial preparation, for example by ensuring that there is full disclosure of financial details in negotiations towards a property settlement in a divorce case.

Mnookin and Kornhauser developed a framework for understanding informal settlement processes, which they refer to as 'bargaining in the shadow of the law'.[44] This framework posits five determinants of out-of-court activity: (1) the preferences of the parties; (2) the bargaining endowments created by the formal legal rules; (3) the uncertainty in court and parties' attitudes towards risk; (4) transaction costs and the parties' respective abilities to bear them; (5) lawyers' strategic behaviour. It is easier to set out the relevant factors than it is to compute their relative importance vis-a-vis each other. Nevertheless, the analysis makes the important point that the legal rules are not irrelevant to what goes on out of court. Indeed, they help to structure the informal bargaining process and the relative positions of the parties, by letting both parties know what is likely to happen if they do not settle the dispute themselves. Thus potential court proceedings have an impact on cases not actually heard in court.

Other writers have also pointed out that formal and informal processes are not two separate worlds but are interconnected. Barbara Yngvesson's analysis[45] of the way that legal remedies are used in continuing relationships demonstrates that the obtaining of an intervention order in a situation of family violence, for example, does not necessarily lead to the termination of the relationship between the parties. Rather, the use of the formal ('public') remedy may lead to a restructuring of the informal ('private') relationship; there is a 'permeability' between the formal and the informal.[46] This point can also be illustrated by references to criminal law. In the regulatory field, Carson's research into the enforcement of the British Factories Act during the late 1960s[47] showed that only 1.5 per cent of detected contraventions were prosecuted, while the remainder were dealt with informally. Over 85 per cent of cases were dealt with by notifying the employer or occupier of matters requiring attention. Later legislation in Britain and Australia institutionalised this approach by introducing legally sanctioned enforcement responses called improvement and prohibition notices. These required hazards to be removed or reduced, failing which prosecutions might be taken for failing to comply with the notice. The line between formal enforcement through criminal sanctions and informal advice and persuasion was effectively blurred by the use of these notices.

The role of lawyers

Theoretical accounts of the role of the legal profession have been considered in the discussion of Weber and Parsons in chapter 3 and in the discussion of critical legal education in chapter 4. Socio-legal scholars' interest in the legal profession stems from the observation that lawyers play a crucial role in the way that law is invoked and enforced. For members of the public whose contact with the legal system is mediated by legal representation the lawyer acts as 'gatekeeper' and 'translator' of the law.[48] The centrality of the legal profession to the presentation and representation of law has led to various research enterprises concerning, for example, the organisation and regulation of the profession[49] and its constitution in terms of gender, race, educational history and social background.[50] These issues affect the meanings that are given to law 'in practice'.

Maureen Cain has explored the question of who determines the content of the lawyer–client relationship.[51] Cain argued that lawyers are 'conceptive ideologists', translating client demands into the language and forms of the legal system. Her empirical study of lawyer–client relations suggested that the level of control exercised by the client was related to the extent to which the solicitor depended on the client for patronage. If the client was a repeat player, the solicitor was anxious to protect the ongoing source of work by following instructions as closely as possible. Where the client was a one-shotter, the other constraints on solicitors' activity, such as the need for quick turnover and the maintenance of relationships with professional colleagues, meant that the client's instructions would not be as prominent in the solicitor's decision frame. More recently, Sarat and Felstiner's use of tape-recorded lawyer–client interviews in the divorce context has presented a complex picture in which lawyers exercise a number of techniques in an attempt to secure control over their clients.[52] The way in which courts are presented to clients as mysterious and dangerous, in order to 'sell' a settlement which has been negotiated with the other spouse's lawyer, has obvious implications for the meaning of law. Law is what the lawyer represents the law to be—or what the client interprets the lawyer's representation of the law to be.

Richard Ingleby's study of divorce cases suggested that determinants of out-of-court activity include solicitors' need to attract and retain clients while they maintain relationships with other people such as their partners, their colleagues, the Legal Aid Commission, professional associations and court officials.[53] In other words, the meaning of law is determined by both the interactional considerations examined in the questions of 'who's in charge?' and 'bargaining in the shadow of the law' and the broader structural issues regarding professional organisation, regulation and constitution addressed in the studies referred to at the beginning of this section.

Pre-trial construction of disputes: preparing for litigation

The final section of this chapter looks at the transformative effects that impending litigation may have upon a civil dispute or a criminal case. Most of the socio-legal research in this area has focused on criminal cases, but some of the conclusions are equally applicable to civil cases.

The event-focused nature of the legal process

In the large majority of cases the legal process is concerned with an examination of events. If, for example, a driver suffers property damage as a result of a collision with another driver, and invokes the legal process to claim damages, both parties will focus their attention on the exact details of the event in their negotiations, pleadings and any resulting litigation over their liability for the damage. Similarly, if a person attacks another outside a pub late at night and is prosecuted for assault and battery, the police investigation, the construction of the charges, the plea bargaining, the ensuing trial if the defendant pleads not guilty and the sentencing decision will involve a close examination of the details of the assault itself.

Even where the phenomenon attracting the legal process is an ongoing or systemic practice the legal system tends to transform it into a series of isolated events. Sexual harassment litigation, for example, tends to ignore the ongoing gender relations in society and in the workplace itself and to be concerned primarily with a 'snapshot' of a particularly outrageous event or succession of incidents. Similarly, where employers are prosecuted for failing to provide and maintain a safe system of work the investigation and prosecution process will tend to focus on an event, usually an injury, resulting from the unsafe system.

There are many possible reasons for this event-focused nature of the legal process—for example, the convenience for the plaintiff or prosecutors in confining their investigation and preparation to specific events, and the requirements of the rules of procedure and evidence clearly to specify claims and charges and to confine evidence to them. But focusing the legal process on an event or incident has the 'effect of abstracting the legally relevant "facts" from their complex social reality, thereby depoliticising the issue before the court'.[54] The case 'takes on its own logic within the framework of the "facts of the case", and any other issues mentioned, hinted at or unknown, lose any relevancy to the meaning of the case that they may have to the meaning of the incident'.[55]

Not only is the law event focused but its focus is partial. Catharine MacKinnon describes how the law is unable to 'capture the dynamic' of a complex situation, interaction or process but instead 'gives us linear statics face to face'.[56] The case is depoliticised, so that the parties are unable to show the social or political issues underlying the act in question. In theft, for example, the accused cannot show how underlying economic and social conditions motivated her act, or argue that property is theft. Law, as Hunt observes, plays an important ideological role in individualising and decontextualising the experience of social relations under capitalism.[57] Issues are removed from their context and reconstituted 'in terms recognisable to the legal gaze, into the form of individual moral actor'.[58]

The construction of guilt and innocence

The studies of occupational health and safety enforcement discussed earlier in this chapter emphasised the way in which employers and occupiers were constituted as 'individual moral actors' for the purposes of prosecution, and were likely to be prosecuted only if they exhibited 'moral fault' in relation to a particular event which caused the injury or death of an employee. Richard Johnstone has further shown that the resources, organisation and investigation procedures of the Victorian occupational health and safety inspectors severely limited the information gathered by them prior to court proceedings. The prosecutor's shortage of information enabled defence counsel, at the sentencing stage, effectively to take control of the proceedings and to raise issues reducing the defendant's culpability which could only be challenged with great difficulty by the prosecutor.[59] In this instance, pre-trial activity had an important effect on the penalties imposed for occupational health and safety offences. As noted earlier, low penalties contribute to the construction of these offences as not really criminal.

By contrast, Doreen McBarnet's examination of the processes by which guilt was determined in Scottish magistrates' courts[60] showed how the prosecutor enjoyed a great advantage over the accused in the collection of evidence and in the presentation of their case. The police and public prosecutors were full-time players in the system who routinely worked to establish a case in law and in fact. The accused, usually a private citizen, could not match the power, resources or know-how of the agents of the state. McBarnet showed how the procedures in relation to police questioning left the suspect vulnerable,[61] despite the privilege against self-incrimination. The locality of the processing of the suspect—in the police station—created an atmosphere of guilt. As McBarnet notes, 'the power to define the situation is very much on one side'.[62] The accused was alone with the police, with limited access to legal advice and, accordingly, was 'exposed to only one version of how the law interprets the behaviour he [sic] has allegedly or actually committed, how the evidence looks against him, what chance he has of establishing his innocence and what the outcome is likely to be'.[63]

Pre-trial practices and procedures thus limit the information available to the accused and, subject to the advice given by the accused's legal representative, shape her or his perception of the case. Carlen's, Blumberg's and Baldwin and McConville's studies of the criminal jurisdiction have shown how plea bargaining has been the archetypical mode of disposition in relation to the minor offences which form the majority of the lower courts' turnover.[64] The most common form of this bargaining involves the prosecutor's withdrawing some of the charge, in exchange for a plea of guilty to the remainder by the accused. Without the prior determination of guilt and the consequent predominance of plea bargaining the courts would be unable to cope.

McBarnet's conclusion, however, was not that legal players simply failed to follow legal rules. Indeed, she specifically rejected the narrow focus of many studies that have concentrated solely on the minutiae of particular interactions, arguing that sociologists need to take the legal rules seriously in their analysis of the legal process. The researcher needs to examine formal procedures and rules of law which institutionalise deviation from the rhetoric of legality and justice. The gap McBarnet identified was not between law in books and law in action, but between the rhetoric of law, which embodied the ideals of due process, and the content of the legal rules which, she argued, institutionalised practices undermining the presumption of innocence. Her close examination of the legal rules and procedures in the Scottish criminal justice system indicated that the rules and procedures actually institutionalised and lent support to practices which were biased heavily in favour of the prosecution.[65] Such a finding should lead the researcher into an exploration of the underlying social, political and economic forces that underpinned the development of the law in this area.

The studies examined in this chapter demonstrate that legal decisions cannot be understood solely by reference to the content of statutes and precedents. The gap that exists between the law in books and the law in action opens up because the invocation and enforcement of legal rules involve discretions, which are exercised in contexts in which many other norms are operating.

Legal rules may thus be used to justify decisions which have already been made by reference to other criteria. The impact of formal law is not so much in determining the content of decisions as in confirming the validity of some ideas and invalidating others.[66] Legal rules are best understood not so much in the way they resolve disputes as in the way they provide frameworks for, or ratify decisions by, prosecutors, defendants, legal practitioners and civil litigants.

Further reading

Griffiths, J. 'Is law important?' (1979) 53 *New York University Law Review* 339

Public regulation

Carson, W. G. *The other price of Britain's oil: safety and control in the North Sea*, Martin Robertson, Oxford, 1981
Cranston, Ross *Regulating business: law and consumer agencies*, Macmillan, London, 1979
Deeves, Donald N. ed. *The regulation of quality: products, services, marketplaces and the environment*, Butterworths, Toronto, 1983
Piciotto, S. 'The theory of the state, class struggle and the rule of law', in *Capitalism and the rule of law*, eds B. Fine et al., Hutchinson, London, 1979

Individual invocation

Galanter, M. 'Reading the landscape of disputes: what we know and don't know (and think we know) about our allegedly contentious society' (1983) 31 *UCLA Law Review* 4
Genn, H. G. *Hard bargaining: out of court settlement in personal injury actions*, Oxford University Press, Oxford, 1987
Ingleby, R. 'Out-of-court settlement: policy, principle, practice, procedure' (1986) 11 *Mediation Quarterly* 57

Lawyers

Disney, J. et al. *Lawyers*, Law Book Co., Sydney, 2nd edn, 1986
Ellmann, S. 'Lawyers and clients' (1987) 34 *UCLA Law Review* 717
Hyman, J. M. 'Trial advocacy and methods of negotiation: can good trial advocates be wise negotiators?' (1987) 34 *UCLA Law Review* 863
Ingleby, R. 'Translation and the divorce lawyer: simulating the law and society interface' (1989) 1 *Legal Education Review* 237
Wiesbrot, D. *Australian lawyers*, Longman Cheshire, Sydney, 1989

7

Judicial decision making

Richard Ingleby and Richard Johnstone

This chapter explores the nature and implications of judicial activity. Whereas the previous one focused on the various processes which take place before a case reaches a hearing, this chapter is directed to the courtroom itself. It first considers questions about the nature of judicial activity, and the attempts which have been made to create an understanding of the exercise of judicial discretion. Much of this analysis has been theoretical and has concentrated on decision making by appellate courts. The chapter then goes on to discuss some of the ways in which judges and magistrates at first instance exercise discretions. The activities of first instance courts have generally been the subject of empirical research rather than theoretical speculation.

Practices and theories of judicial decision making

The High Court's decision in the Murray Islands case[1] illustrates several issues to be considered in an analysis of judicial decision making. This first section sets out some of the processes of reasoning that were involved in answering one particular question in the case: whether the common law recognises native title. The main concern is not a description of the different conclusions or their implications. Rather, what might the various approaches adopted by their Honours reveal about the nature of judicial discretion? The Murray Islands case was not the first in which questions of native title had ever been considered by a court. The High Court's treatment of earlier decisions warrants attention as the variations of approach within the High Court can be seen to relate to the differing treatments of these decisions.

The judgment of Blackburn J in the Gove case[2] was outlined in chapter 1. Briefly, Blackburn J held that the doctrine of native title did not form part of the common law received in the Australian colonies. In the Murray

Judicial decision making

Islands case, Dawson J referred to Blackburn J's 'full and scholarly examination' of the authorities and agreed with Blackburn J's view that the failure of the colonial authorities to take steps to compensate for the dispossession of Aboriginal people was an indication that the Crown did not recognise a concept of native title.[3] In the majority, Deane and Gaudron JJ stated their disagreement with the 'conclusions of general principle reached by Blackburn J'.[4] Brennan J held that the *Gove* decision did not apply to the facts of the Murray Islands case. This was because the holding in *Gove* was that 'individual members of the community . . . enjoy only usufructury rights' to their land. According to Brennan J, however, the holding that individuals did not have individual proprietary rights was not inconsistent with a communal proprietary title.[5] The *Gove* 'decision' therefore had different meanings for the various members of the High Court in the Murray Islands case. Dawson J's invocation of *Gove* in rejecting the concept of native title at common law was not matched by the rest of the court. Brennan and Toohey JJ held that *Gove* was not applicable to the facts of the Murray Islands case. Deane and Gaudron JJ held that *Gove* was based on a false premise.

The members of the High Court took similarly disparate approaches to earlier Privy Council decisions. In *Cooper v Stuart*[6] the Privy Council said that the colony of New South Wales had no 'established system of law', but 'consisted of a tract of territory practically unoccupied' at the time of British settlement. Consequently, 'the law of England must . . . become from the outset the law of the Colony'.[7] Brennan J distinguished *Cooper v Stuart* on the basis that 'The facts as we know them today do not fit the "absence of law" or "barbarian" theory underpinning the colonial reception of the common law of England'.[8] In other words, the decision was not followed because it was based on a false assumption. As stated in the judgment of Deane and Gaudron JJ 'the reasoning [in *Cooper v Stuart*] . . . consists of little more than bare assertion'.[9] By contrast, Dawson J hardly needed to refer to *Cooper v Stuart*. It was consistent with what his Honour considered to be the effect of other decisions.

Likewise, Brennan J,[10] Deane and Gaudron JJ[11] and Toohey J[12] considered that the Privy Council's statements in *Amodu Tijani v The Secretary, Southern Nigeria*[13] revealed the principle that native title was a burden on the radical title which the Crown acquired when Southern Nigeria was ceded in 1861. Dawson J, however, treated *Amodu Tijani* as a situation where the Crown explicitly recognised rights which existed prior to the assumption of its sovereignty.[14] The facts were therefore distinguishable from those in the Murray Islands case, where there was no express recognition of the Murray Islanders' rights to land when the islands were annexed by Queensland.

The preceding discussion illustrates various techniques for the High Court to deal with decisions whose authority stands in the way of a particular decision. Although the decision making processes of lower courts have a further constraint in the form of their obligation to follow the precedents laid down by higher courts, for all courts the scope of what was actually decided in a previous case, the extent to which the case can be distinguished on its facts, whether the case was 'correctly' decided and whether the earlier decision has been overruled or overtaken by subsequent developments are all issues capable of giving rise to disagreement.

Such disagreements are not limited to the use of previous legal decisions. The different judgments in the Murray Islands case can also be distinguished in terms of how they used the writings of historians. Just as their Honours interpreted earlier decisions in different ways, Henry Reynolds' *The law of the land*[15] was interpreted in different ways by the various judges who referred to it.[16] This suggests that there might be some relationship between judicial interpretation of legal texts and interpretation in other fields, a theme returned to later in this chapter.

Why is judicial discretion important?

The question of what judges do has long been a central concern of jurisprudence. In Australia judges are not elected but appointed, usually from the ranks of senior barristers. They are appointed by elected officials (Attorneys-General), after consultations with the Chief Justice of the relevant court, senior lawyers and government officials.[17] Judges make decisions about the application of legislation and about the common law in areas which have not been the subject of legislation. There are two related fears which are often expressed about judicial decision making power. One is that if judges were free to make whatever decisions they pleased, this would pose a threat to the doctrine of parliamentary sovereignty, whereby ultimate law-making power is vested in a democratically elected legislature.[18] The other is that the rule of law demands that there be predictability to judicial decision making.[19] These concerns are particularly powerful in jurisdictions such as Australia and the United States, where the judiciary has the power to declare legislation invalid if it violates certain constitutional requirements.[20]

Interest in what judges do when they decide cases derives from pragmatic as well as political considerations. Given the indeterminacy of language and the incapacity of legislatures to foresee the entire range of possible future fact situations, an understanding of how judges interpret legislation and other authorities is necessary even for the most descriptive understanding of law.[21] Judicial activity has to be explained so that predictions can be made about future behaviour, this being what many lawyers would describe as one of the defining characteristics of their profession. A second purpose in analysis of judicial activity is to reveal the 'real' processes of reasoning. A third purpose is to justify the activity of judges as consistent with particular political theories.[22]

The Murray Islands case can be used to illustrate these three possibilities. First, a theory of judicial adjudication might attempt to predict what the High Court will do in relation to future native title claims, although such predictions would be contingent on the impossible condition of the composition of the High Court remaining unchanged.[23] Second, the aim might be to demystify the reasoning of the judges in order to explain how the decision was really determined by considerations other than those explicitly stated by the court, for example the desire to maintain social cohesion or to maximise economic efficiency.[24] Third, the aim of the analysis might be to explain why the decision of the majority was more consistent with the existing precedents than that of the minority.[25]

Outlining just these three possible aims of a theory of adjudication shows how difficult it is to theorise on a purely predictive or descriptive basis. Conclusions about the predictability of a decision, or the factors relevant to a decision, necessarily involve evaluative and prescriptive considerations. For example, the discussion about the scope and validity of the Murray Islands case necessarily involves discussion of what the role of the High Court should be in this area. An explanation of the process by which a decision was reached in any particular case will not of itself be enough to predict the result in a future case. Lawyers would rarely consider themselves able to predict the outcome of any case with certainty, but they would not ascribe their lack of predictive capacity to a defect in their knowledge of previous decisions. Although there will be differences of degree in the predictability of any particular decision, one constant feature tending to unpredictability is that no two cases can ever be the same. Even if the facts, arguments and other forms of pre-trial construction are identical the decision in the earlier case is a feature of the later one which was not present in the earlier one.

Can judicial discretion be value-free?

The controversy over the Murray Islands case of whether judges should 'make' or 'declare' law has resurrected an old jurisprudential chestnut which many thought to have been long buried by the recognition that the 'reality of creative legal development'[26] does not sit easily within either paradigm. As Chief Justice Mason has stated in an extra-curial interview:

> The formulation of legal principle is, and always has been, undertaken in the light of policy considerations . . . [T]he fact that in *Mabo* . . . the Court had regard to policy considerations does not indicate that the Court is trespassing beyond its judicial function or going beyond what courts have traditionally done in the past . . . [F]ar from being an adventure on the part of the High Court, the decision reflects what's happened in the great common law jurisdictions of the world and in the International Court.[27]

Once it is accepted, for whatever reasons, that judges make decisions by taking into account considerations other than the strictest literal meaning of the words of statutes and *rationes decidendi*,[28] the idea that judicial decisions are made by way of syllogism must be rejected.[29] There is no single result which is determinable by the application of the laws of logic. The question is not so much whether interpretation is value-laden but what sort of values are and should be taken into account by the judiciary.

Sir Anthony Mason has argued that, because 'it is impossible to interpret any instrument . . . by reference to words alone, without any regard to fundamental values', judges should do two things. First, they should openly acknowledge the value-laden nature of their interpretive task. Second, the values they adopt should be the current values of the community.[30] David Wood points out that the second recommendation does not follow inevitably from the first. Sir Ninian Stephen's suggestion was that judges should 'lag a cautious distance behind' current values, whereas Justice Murphy would have seen the role of the judiciary in terms of changing community standards by being ahead of current values.[31] The choices posed by these three approaches are deceptively simple, for the question of what constitutes 'community values' or indeed 'community' is, as the Murray Islands decision has revealed, less than self-evident.

As the critiques of liberal legal theory discussed in chapter 4 all point out, the denial that values enter judicial decision making is itself ridden with values. This point is revealed with particular force by the recent discussions of gender bias in the judiciary. Judges have defended themselves against allegations of gender bias by asserting their judicial neutrality, while at the same time expressing 'commonsense' attitudes about, for example, women's sexuality or veracity which are regarded as offensive by large proportions of the rest of society.[32] Nevertheless, some 'commonsense' discriminatory attitudes towards women have in the past and may still constitute general community values. Is a 'current community values' test appropriate if those values are sexist, racist or homophobic?[33]

Adams and Brownsword provide an example of the way in which different values influence judicial decision making in the realm of contract law.[34] They note that judges may adopt a range of positions between two contractual ideologies, market-individualism and consumer-welfarism. The market-individualism approach envisages the function of contract as being to facilitate and establish the ground rules for competitive exchange. This approach requires that contract rules be clear, to ensure that parties are held to their bargains, to accommodate commercial practice, to promote freedom of contract and to impose minimal restraints on contractors. Consumer-welfarism, on the other hand, favours greater regulation to ensure consumer protection and application of the principles of fairness and reasonableness in contract. Parties may be relieved of their contractual obligations where it would be unfair or unreasonable to hold them to their bargain. Remedies should be proportional to the breach, parties should not be unjustly enriched, nor should they exploit the weak bargaining position of others, and so on.

Besides different ideologies of contract, judges also adhere to different ideologies of judicial decision making. At one extreme is formalism, where judges are to apply legal rules to the facts before them, irrespective of the result. The rule book is seen as a closed logical system and its purity is to be preserved. This approach is doctrinally conservative and eschews sympathy and politics in decision making. The courts are to avoid making rules which give them broad discretions, and are not to concern themselves with reforming out of date or unjust rules. In contrast, the other extreme of realism requires judges to hand down decisions in accordance with a particular political ideology, such as the maximisation of economic efficiency, irrespective of the requirements of the rules. The rules are not sacred and are not to be applied mechanically regardless of the fairness of the result. As Adams and Brownsword note, 'not only do realist judges put results before rules, they put pragmatism ahead of conceptual purity'.[35] They are willing to innovate and improvise with rules, and will take into account sympathy and politics in reaching decisions. A judicial decision in contract law would thus depend not only on the facts of the case, and the established rules, but also on the judge's preferred judicial and contractual ideologies. Whether a judge follows a previous case, distinguishes it or overrules or ignores it will depend on the judge's predispositions to values in contract law and in judicial decision making.

What is judicial about judicial discretion?

Liberal and formalist views of law rest on the assertion that there is a distinctively 'legal' body of reasoning completely distinguishable from other forms of reasoning. On the other hand, many critics of liberalism and formalism have argued that there is no formal constraint on judicial decision making whatsoever, that judges can do whatever they want to do rather than being bound to reach a particular decision in a particular case. For example, as discussed in chapter 4, a central theme of the Critical Legal Studies (CLS) movement is that there is no 'possibility of a method of legal justification that can be clearly contrasted to open-ended disputes about the basic terms of social life, disputes that people call ideological, philosophical or visionary . . . Because everything can be defended, nothing can; the analogy-mongering must be brought to a halt'.[36] In other words, the rule of law is a myth, and the open-ended nature of legal discourse makes it as irrational as other discourses against which it is compared.

The question of whether there is a definably 'legal' form of reasoning is a central jurisprudential question, one clearly related to the question of what is meant by 'law'. H. L. A. Hart argued that there is a definably 'legal' characteristic of legal reasoning, in the application by a category of 'legal' officials of a body of rules identifiable by reference to the rule of recognition in the relevant system.[37] Hart maintained that there would be a large 'core' area where rules could be applied mechanically, but conceded that, due to the indeterminacy of language and the incapacity of humans to foresee all future circumstances, there would also be situations in the 'penumbra' where it was not clear whether a particular consequence followed from a rule. For example, does 'No vehicles in the park' cover roller skates or bicycles?[38] Here, according to Hart, if 'such doubts are to be resolved, something in the nature of a choice between open alternatives must be made by whoever is to resolve them'.[39] Thus Hart saw judicial discretion coming into play in penumbral cases. As there was no applicable law in these cases judges were compelled to choose their own standards to apply, and there was no single 'right answer'.

Ronald Dworkin offered an alternative model for dealing with this situation. In cases not governed by clear legal rules, Dworkin argued, judges obviously have discretion in the 'weak sense' of a choice which demands the use of judgment. But they do not and should not have discretion in the 'strong sense' of being 'simply not bound by standards'.[40] An early version of Dworkin's emerging theory[41] argued that judges were constrained in cases where the outcome was not clearly determined by the application of a legal rule. The constraint was (roughly speaking) the requirement that the decision fit with the political theory which best justified the existing body of rules and principles in the area. So in regard to the Murray Islands case Dworkin might have argued that the High Court's task was to analyse the totality of judicial precedents and statutes on indigenous land rights,[42] develop a political theory which justified that entirety, and make the decision which best fitted with that theory. Dworkin argued that this concept of judicial adjudication, where the process of reasoning reveals what is already in some sense 'there', means that parties cannot complain about retrospective law-making by judges.

To give another example, in *Jaensch v Coffey*[43] the High Court had to decide for the first time whether a plaintiff who was not present at the scene of a road accident could recover against a negligent driver for nervous shock suffered when she saw her husband, the victim of the accident, at a later stage in hospital. The judgment of Deane J in *Jaensch v Coffey* could be seen as fulfilling Dworkin's requirement to construct a theory which best explained the body of existing precedent on duty of care. The theory he constructed included the concept of 'proximity' as an element in establishing whether a duty of care was owed by the defendant to the plaintiff. This theory was then applied to the facts of the case and resulted in a finding for the plaintiff. For Dworkin, there was an important sense in which the decision did not *make* law. The 'right' of the plaintiff was already there and the driver (or more precisely perhaps the driver's insurance company) could not legitimately complain about retrospective judicial legislation.

Dworkin has produced a refinement of his theory which is influenced by developments in literary theory.[44] This later version concentrates more on the process by which decisions are derived from existing authorities and argues that the 'text' of those authorities provides the essential constraint on judicial decision making. Dworkin identifies three stages by which a judge interprets the text of the pre-existing law. The first is 'a "preinterpretive" stage in which the rules and standards taken to provide the tentative content of the practice are identified'. The second is 'an interpretive stage at which the interpreter settles on some general justification for the main elements of the practice identified at the preinterpretive stage'. The third is 'a postinterpretive or reforming stage, at which [the judge] adjusts his [sic] sense of what the practice "really" requires so as better to serve the justification he accepts at the interpretive stage'.[45] A literary device which Dworkin invents to illustrate this theory is the idea of a chain novel. The example he uses is Dickens's *A Christmas carol*. Dworkin imagines that a series of writers is commissioned to write the novel. He compares the situation of a writer 'with only the very end to be written' with someone given 'only the first few sections'. He argues that the writer whose input was required toward the end of the novel could not portray Scrooge as either 'inherently and irredeemably evil' or 'inherently good but progressively corrupted by ... capitalist society'.[46] But the writer working at the earlier stage could plausibly develop the text in either of these directions if she or he thought that either was the 'best' interpretation of the material so far presented. This requirement of 'integrity', to develop the text in accordance with the best interpretation of the previous tradition, is according to Dworkin the key to understanding the process of judicial adjudication. The constraint constituted by 'integrity' allows Dworkin's liberal conscience to tolerate non-elected judicial officials' making of decisions in relation to the output of democratically elected legislatures.

It is important to note at this stage that the demand for 'integrity' in legal decision making is an essentially conservative one. Peoples and groups whose claims have historically been ignored or denied by the law will continue to have difficulty establishing their claims. Moreover, Dworkin's theory leaves no room for arguments about a more representative judiciary. If every judge is constrained in decision making by a requirement to remain faithful to the existing text of the law the gender or ethnicity of the individual judge is irrelevant. Lynne Hansen, a Canadian feminist theorist, argues that Dworkin underestimates the degree of controversy over the practice of law as a whole. Hansen suggests that the requirement of integrity imposes a political agenda on the interpreter and concludes that feminist jurisprudence ultimately falls outside the scope of Dworkin's interpretive enterprise.[47]

Another group of responses to the CLS challenge that there is no definably legal form of reasoning is to delineate positions between the descriptive implausibilities of Dworkin on the one hand and, on the other, the notion that there are no constraints whatsoever on judicial decision making. Jim Harris and Neil MacCormick are theorists who present related theories of judicial adjudication which contain some constraints on what judges can do without portraying the decision making process in determinist terms. Harris, for example, suggests a judge who:

> ... believes that there are sometimes sufficient reasons to be found in a body of received legal materials for disposing of controverted questions about the present law ... Even when such reasons are not sufficient to dispose of a case, they operate to restrict the rulings between which a choice must be made, and in that way distance his [sic] judgment from open-ended ideological controversy. His experience falsifies [Unger's] assumption that 'everything can be proved'.[48]

MacCormick's theory of judicial reasoning, which examines the requirements of consequences, coherence and consistency, reveals that there are limits to how free judges are to 'make it up as they go along', although there is also a certain degree of interpretive freedom.[49]

Another English legal theorist, Peter Goodrich, argues that, while legal language and legal categories are particularly open to interpretation, judges employ established interpretive methods which value adherence to tradition and historical meanings above other possible approaches.[50]

Goodrich has much in common with Stanley Fish, a deconstructionist[51] literary scholar, who presents a further response to Dworkin. Fish argues that there is a constraint on judicial and other forms of legal decision making but it is not the constraint argued by Dworkin. As explained in chapter 4, postmodernists reject the idea of a constraining text: reading the text of the law is always an interpretive act on the part of the reader. Thus there is no distinction between the interpretive stages that Dworkin purports to identify. According to Fish, '[e]xplaining and changing cannot be opposed activities . . . because they are the same activities'.[52]

Fish therefore rejects the notion that the 'text' dictates any particular meaning, but he also rejects the notion that interpreters 'are free to read into a text whatever they like'.[53] That is, Fish sees interpretation as neither the subjective 'nightmare' of judges 'making it up as they go along' nor the objective 'noble dream' of an answer being inevitably 'there' and waiting to be revealed.[54] Rather, '[i]nterpreters are constrained by their tacit awareness of what is possible and not possible to do, what is and is not a reasonable thing to say, what will and will not be heard as evidence in a given enterprise'.[55] The source of this tacit awareness is the relevant interpretive community. In the legal context, judges give reasons for their decisions in order to satisfy the legal community that they have decided the case according to law. They seek to persuade the community that they have decided correctly. The constraint on interpretation, then, is the persuasiveness of any particular interpretation to the legal interpretive community. Judges are unlikely to interpret the law to hold that property is theft, for example, as such an interpretation would be understood by the interpretive community to be a 'non-legal' argument, well outside the currently undisputed contexts of property and criminal law.

Fish's explanation of the constraints on legal interpretation accounts for both stability and change in legal rules.[56] Stability is ensured by interpretations generally remaining within the undisputed contexts held by the interpretive community. Change occurs where previously disputed contexts become undisputed, or undisputed contexts become disputed.[57] For example, the question of whether the common law recognised native title was an undisputed context before the Murray Islands case (it was widely accepted that native title was not recognised), but became disputed thereafter (the High Court's decision shook up the legal community and generated considerable controversy on the issue). In *Jaensch v Coffey*, Deane J can be seen to have made a persuasive argument for a reconceptualisation of duty of care, which was subsequently accepted by most of the other judges on the High Court to become an undisputed context. By contrast, when magistrate Pat O'Shane dismissed charges of malicious damage against women who had defaced a billboard depicting a lingerie-clad woman being sawn in half, and stated that 'The crime in this situation is the erection of those billboards depicting violence towards women',[58] she provoked an outcry which indicated that her argument did not persuade the interpretive community to accept a change to the undisputed contexts within which it perceived the case. This example also illustrates that the politics of law are revealed by an examination of currently undisputed contexts and the power relations they express.

The importance of interpretations being persuasive makes the question of who constitutes the legal interpretive community crucial. Possible contenders for inclusion are parliament, judges, barristers and solicitors, legal academics, law students, litigants and potential litigants.[59] There are striking differences in the gendered nature of these various communities. The underrepresentation of women in federal and State parliaments is a matter of public notoriety, but it pales into insignificance when compared with the absence of women from the higher courts and the upper echelons of the bar. The importance of the concept of the interpretive community to the question of what constitutes the law is one reason for the demands for women to be represented in greater numbers in the judiciary. It is only when admitted to this interpretive community that women have the opportunity to make arguments that may persuade their judicial brethren to a different way of seeing.[60] Moreover, the selection of lawyers to be judges is only one of the filtering steps by which the nature of the legal interpretive community is determined. It is also necessary to consider the admissions policies of university law schools, the content of legal education, and the processes by which law students are selected for their compulsory periods of professional training and employment,[61] as these too have an impact on the gender, racial, ethnic and class composition of the community, and hence on the nature of its undisputed contexts.

The concept of persuasiveness provides a key to unlocking the current debate about gender bias in the judiciary. Judges do not need to explicitly state, for example, that 'women lie about whether they consent to sexual relations' in order to be biased. It is enough if they are more easily persuaded to that conclusion than its opposite. The contested nature of the meaning of much human activity makes the persuasiveness of particular interpretations crucial. This analysis also sheds light on the debate about continuing judicial education. If judges are given the opportunity to learn about perspectives to which they would otherwise not be exposed, and are encouraged to examine the assumptions which they take for granted in their day-to-day decision making, then this is a form of education which is hardly a threat to the independence of the judiciary.

Judges as first instance decision makers

The jurisprudential debate about adjudication outlined above treats judicial activity as primarily the activity of higher appellate courts. But most judges are not Court of Appeal or High Court judges and most judicial activity concerns the routine of lower court business. When lower courts are examined new questions, issues and insights arise. The violent aspects of adjudication, the way that decisions are enforced on bodies, are revealed more directly here than in the more refined arena of the High Court.[62]

In her study of the routine business of a lower English civil court Maureen Cain found that, contrary to the rhetoric espoused by judges and court officials, the court's role was not to settle disputes or to enforce the law but rather continually to restate the law of property in cases brought against recalcitrant debtors. Cain's study involved participant observation, examination of court files, interviews and statistical analysis of the court. The great majority of the cases in her sample concerned an acknowledged debt. The plaintiffs were state agencies or private companies providing services and commodities, a substantial proportion being repeat players in the system. Defendants, who owed money to the plaintiffs as the result of a consumer transaction, were generally private citizens and one-shotters.[63] In judging these cases, the court was led continually to 'affirm the legal constitution of those relationships which are presented to them *by a particular set of users*' so as to reaffirm 'the approved relations of consumption'.[64]

> According to the plaintiffs, failure to have these repeated legal pronouncements would (or could) be interpreted as licence not to pay. Such a licence would amount to a *de facto* change in the rules which constitute use rights (property) in our society.[65]

To this extent, Cain found that the activities of the court conformed to the functionalist view that civil courts perform a socially integrative role by reinforcing social values or (in Cain's view) ideologies.[66]

Cain does note, however, that her sample was skewed by the fact that she was refused permission by the Lord Chancellor's Department to research proceedings pertaining to 'domestic matters' (family violence). Consequently, 'most of the disputes involving two active and qualitatively identical parties in contention over a mutually acknowledged issue'[67] were excluded from her study. This both limits the value of her results on the question of what courts do and perpetuates the invisibility of the 'private' domain in empirical research, as noted in the previous chapter.[68]

As well as studying the turnover of business in various courts, socio-legal scholars have been interested in the way judges exercise discretions. Judges have various types of discretion in interpreting legal rules and precedents. One type, discussed in the first section of this chapter, is the interpretive questions which arise out of the comparative weight of analogous cases. Another is the discretions conferred by statutes which authorise judges to weigh up a list of factors without giving strict guidance as to the process by which such factors should be weighed, as in criminal law sentencing guidelines or the distribution of matrimonial property under the *Family Law Act 1975* (Cwlth). A third is the use of words such as 'reasonable' or 'practicable' in statutes. These words have no self-evident meaning, and this necessarily devolves a decision making responsibility to the judges who have to apply them in particular cases. Discretion can be analysed jurisprudentially, as seen in the previous section, or empirically, as seen in the following case studies—though as noted in the previous chapter empirical research inevitably takes place within a particular theoretical framework.

Richard Ingleby studied section 55A(1) of the Family Law Act,[69] which provides that, where there are minor children of a marriage, a *decree nisi* of dissolution of marriage cannot become absolute unless 'proper' arrangements have been made for the children or there are circumstances by reason of which the decree should become absolute even though such arrangements have not been made.[70] What does the word 'proper' mean in this context? The initial reported judicial interpretations of this provision discussed the morality of the children's parents' relationships with third parties, in addition to matters of access, finance and the level of agreement about the arrangements.[71] More recent reported cases show the financial aspects receiving especial attention from the court.[72]

Although the reported cases reveal different possible interpretations of 'proper' they do not of themselves reveal anything about the thousands of unreported cases. To find out how this provision operated in practice, Ingleby and his research assistant observed dissolution proceedings in the Melbourne Registry of the Family Court of Australia from January to October 1990. The judges were not notified that the study was taking place, which was possible because the court is open to the public. The lack of notification was also necessary to ensure that the data reflected what judges normally did, rather than what happened when they knew they were the subject of a research project. The data analysed below were taken from 1875 dissolution hearings before nine judges and two judicial registrars.[73] In 781 of these cases the discussion in court revealed that there were children.[74]

The Family Law Rules required the parties to put certain aspects of the child care arrangements before the court. For each of the observed judges it was possible to calculate (1) a 'check rate' of the proportion of hearings in which a given issue was raised, and (2) a 'disapproval rate' where the inadequacy of the arrangements in a particular direction was a reason for the refusal to hold that the arrangements were proper. In relation to access there were wide disparities among judges in both check rates (from 15 per cent to 66 per cent) and disapproval rates (from 1 per cent to 11 per cent). On financial matters the check rates varied from 26 per cent to 95 per cent and the disapproval rates from zero to 30 per cent. One possible hypothesis is that the disparities relate solely to the fact situations; but differences of judicial approach would seem a more likely explanation, given the random nature of the way in which cases were allocated to judges.

The total proportion of cases involving children where the arrangements were held to be proper varied as between the judges from 57 per cent to 97 per cent. But the total proportion of cases in which a *decree nisi* became absolute varied only between 82 per cent and 99 per cent. This was because the judges who found that the arrangements were *not* proper were generally more likely to hold that the decree should become absolute in any event. This meant that the result of a *decree nisi* becoming absolute could be reached by different routes: no check on the child care arrangements at all; a check which held that the arrangements were proper; a check which disapproved of the arrangements but still held that they were proper; and a check which held that the arrangements were not proper but there were circumstances by reason of which the decree should become absolute in any event. The discretion in the statute permits judges to adopt their own approach to the requirement of supervision. A judge can ignore the provision by not taking it seriously, pay lip service to the provision, give the appearance of scrutiny or even actually scrutinise.

The study also prompts questions relating to the costs of regulation. The provision in section 55A was introduced to protect children on their parents' divorce. But there have been longstanding concerns about the extent to which this can be done by a court-based regulatory technique, which takes place at least a year after the separation of the parents and which contains no practical method for future supervision. A philosophical approach to the section, which examined questions such as the purpose of regulation, could not ignore the realities revealed by empirical study. Calculation of the economic efficiency of the provision would also rely on empirical analysis. A detailed economic analysis would demand data on the time spent in court, the frequency of legal representation, the matters questioned in court, and so on.

The use of a range of methodologies is also illustrated by Richard Johnstone's examination of the prosecution of occupational health and safety offences in Victoria from 1983 until 1991.[75] Research methods used in the study included interviews with magistrates and occupational health and safety inspectors, observation of a sample of 160 magistrates' court prosecutions, an examination of departmental files and documents, a statistical analysis of prosecution outcomes and an analysis of the relevant substantive and procedural rules. The study showed that the Victorian enforcement authorities were heirs to an enforcement culture, noted in chapter 6, that relied on persuasion and advice rather than formal resort to the criminal law by way of prosecution. And, despite its enactment in criminal form, the occupational health and safety legislation was regarded as 'quasi criminal', not really crime at all.

When prosecutions *were* taken the fines imposed on occupational health and safety offenders were on the low side, expressed as a percentage of the statutory maximum fine, even though only the most egregious cases were prosecuted. The study showed that the ambiguity of occupational health and safety crime was deeply entrenched within the Victorian magistracy itself. The statistical data showed that good behaviour bonds (where proceedings were adjourned without conviction on condition that the defendant be of good behaviour for a specified period) were, at least until the late 1980s, a disproportionately favoured form of disposition by magistrates. And this even in the face of judicial authority that this sentencing option was inappropriate for the vast majority of occupational health and safety cases, which involve serious injury.

The standards contained in the occupational health and safety statutes and their regulations from the outset decontextualised the offences. As Geertz has noted, a defining feature of law is 'the skeletonisation of fact so as to narrow moral issues to the point where determinate rules can be employed to decide them'.[76] For example, in machinery-guarding offences, under which the majority of prosecutions in the study were taken, the court was simply required to examine the standard of guarding on the relevant machine, and was not required to look into the way work was organised or the general occupational health and safety procedures practised at the workplace. The study also found that magistrates themselves were decontextualised in relation to occupational health and safety crime. They had very little experience of the organisation of industrial work and, because of their social and career backgrounds, they identified more closely with management than with workers.

A third form of decontextualisation resulted from the nature of the trial itself, which had the 'effect of abstracting the legally relevant "facts" from their complex social reality, thereby depoliticising the issue before the court'.[77] This characteristic of abstracting 'the facts of the case' from the social, economic and political context is basic to the form of the criminal law used in contemporary Victoria. Abstracted issues are then recontextualised 'in terms recognisable to the legal gaze'. For example, the defendant employer is cast into the form of individual moral actor for the purpose of fitting the corporate persona into the discourse of criminal law conceptions of responsibility and sanctioning.[78]

The study showed that, at least until 1991, most of the inspectorate's inspection activities, most of their accident investigations and hence most prosecutions were concerned with 'events', in that they generally focused on the circumstances resulting in the death or injury of a worker. A study of the legal rules comprising the substantive offences showed that gradually the courts closed off defences which enabled employers and occupiers to avoid liability—defences based principally on the alleged inadvertence or disobedience of the injured or deceased worker, the unforeseeability of the danger, the inspectorate's previous endorsement of the hazardous practice, or the fact that the allegedly hazardous practice was common to the industry. These 'commonsense' arguments, however, continued to flourish in the *sentencing* process. What might have been a defence in a case involving *mens rea* became a factor in mitigation of sentence.

An analysis of sentencing processes in these cases showed how issues were further transformed and individualised. Defence counsel used a number of 'isolation techniques' to transform the issues from being about systems of work, supervision, training and instruction to being about technical aspects of a completely disembodied event. These techniques involved painting the defendant as a 'good corporate citizen' with a good attitude to safety and a good safety record, submitting that the 'accident' was an unusual 'one-off' event—or at least the result of a confluence of unusual circumstances—and focusing the plea on the steps taken by the defendant occupier or employer after the event so that the event could be sealed off from the defendant's current practice. In most cases a number of these techniques were used, so that invariably the case was never deserving of a penalty at the top of the scale. This process of neutralising moral blame has been noted in other studies of the prosecution of regulatory offences.[79]

These two studies illustrate the difficulties inherent in using individualistic legal institutions and processes to regulate units of social organisation such as the family or the corporation. These units may be legal individuals for the purpose of legal doctrine under the rule of law, but the most straightforward examination of the effects of their treatment as individual legal units reveals its artificiality and abstraction. It is a further example, like many others explored in this book, of the unresolved tension between the assumptions of the liberal legal system and the realities of post(?)liberal, post(?)modern and post(?)colonial society.

Further reading

Theories of adjudication

Dworkin, Ronald 'Law as interpretation' (1982) 60 *Texas Law Review* 527

Fish, Stanley 'Working on the chain gang: interpretation in law and literature' (1982) 60 *Texas Law Review* 550

Fiss, Owen 'Objectivity and interpretation' (1982) 34 *Stanford Law Review* 739

Graff, G. '"Keep off the grass", "drop dead", and other indeterminacies' (1982) 60 *Texas Law Review* 405

White, G. Edward 'The text, interpretation and critical standards' (1982) 60 *Texas Law Review* 569

Wikler, Norma J. 'Identifying and correcting judicial gender bias', in *Equality and judicial neutrality*, eds Sheilah L. Martin and Kathleen E. Mahoney, Carswell, Toronto, 1987

Lower courts

Baldwin, J. and McConville, M. *Courts, prosecution and conviction*, Clarendon Press, Oxford, 1981

Bottoms, A. and McLean, J. *Defendants in the criminal process*, Routledge & Kegan Paul, London, 1976

Legal Studies Department, La Trobe University, *Guilty Your Worship: a study of Victoria's magistrates courts*, La Trobe University, Bundoora, Vic., 1980

Notes

Mention of a chapter, not forming part of a citation, refers to a chapter in the present book.

Introduction

1 See M. Chesterman and D. Weisbrot, 'Legal scholarship in Australia' (1987) 50 *Modern Law Review* 709.
2 Perhaps our 'major' omission is any explicit discussion of comparative law and comparative legal methods. Chapter 1, however, is an exercise in comparative law; and the rest of the book provides foundations for the essential task of understanding 'foreign' legal rules in their historical, political, social and economic contexts.
3 For an account of legal formalism, see Margaret Davies, *Asking the law question*, Law Book Co., Sydney, 1994, 115–20. See also the discussion of positivism in chapter 2.
4 Law Institute of Victoria, *Career patterns of law graduates*, Law Institute, Melbourne, 1990; 'Women in law—the statistical picture' (1992) *Law Institute Journal* 161; D. Weisbrot, *Australian lawyers*, Longman Professional, 1990, 83–90.
5 In 1993 Justice Bollen of the South Australian Supreme Court made headlines with his statement that a husband might attempt to persuade his wife 'in an acceptable' way to consent to intercourse, and that such persuasion might include 'rougher than usual handling'.
6 Suzanne Hatty, *Male violence and the police: an Australian experience*, School of Social Work, University of New South Wales, Kensington, 1988; 'System makes it difficult to find support: studies', the *Age*, 7 June 1993.

Chapter 1 Law and history in black and white

1. Alex C. Castles, *An Australian legal history*, Law Book Co., Sydney, 1982, 2. W. J. V. Windeyer in fact begins his textbook *Before the Norman Conquest in England in the year 600: Lectures on legal history*, Law Book Co., Sydney, 2nd edn (rev.), 1957.
2. 'The word "aborigine" is a noun which refers to an indigenous group of ANY country . . . As a name of a group of people it is non-descriptive, placing us into a hodge-podge of peoples, without giving us a named identity . . . In response to Koorie demands, some attempt was made to make us a little more distinctive by spelling "aborigine" with a capital A . . . The worst thing about the use of "Aboriginal" is that it places us into the category of being a non-existent people, thus sustaining (as is no doubt intended), the "legality" of the TERRA NULLIUS annexation of our land.' Eve Mungwa D. Fesl, 'How the English language is used to put Koories down, deny us rights, or is employed as a political tool against us', Monash University, 1989. See also the discussion of 'labelling' by law enforcement agencies in chapter 6.
3. Chris Healy, '"We know your mob now": histories and their cultures', *Meanjin*, (1990) 49, 512. See also Bain Attwood, 'Introduction', in *Power, knowledge and Aborigines*, eds Bain Attwood and John Arnold, La Trobe University Press in association with the National Centre for Australian Studies, Monash University, Melbourne, 1992, ix–x.
4. The dominant Western philosophical conceptions of law are discussed in the second section of this chapter, and in chapter 2. One of the aims of the book is to question the ways in which 'law' may be defined: see especially the rest of this chapter and chapters 6 and 7.
5. *Mabo v Queensland (No. 2)* (1992) 175 CLR 1.
6. The term 'the Murray Islands case' is used throughout this book, in deference to the family of the first-named plaintiff who died, and to the contribution to the case of other Murray Islanders.
7. Aboriginal people have sought to reassert their identity by requesting the use of their own names for themselves. 'Koori' (sometimes spelt Koorie) refers to indigenous people from Victoria, New South Wales or Tasmania. The word 'Murri' is used in Queensland and parts of New South Wales; 'Nunga' is used in parts of South Australia and 'Nyungar' (pronounced noongar) is used in parts of Western Australia. Other terms may be used for particular clans, language groups and communities, for example Kurnai, Yorta Yorta (Victoria), Bandjalang, Wiradjuri (New South Wales), Pitjantjatjara (central Australia—the Pitjantjatjara name for themselves is Anangu), Yolngu (Arnhem Land), Tiwi (Melville and Bathurst Islands). Adapted from 'Guidelines for the use of non-racist language at The University of Melbourne', 1993.
8. Gary Foley, 'Teaching whites a lesson', in *A people's history of Australia since 1788, vol. 4: staining the wattle*, eds Verity Burgmann and Jenny Lee, McPhee Gribble/Penguin, Melbourne, 1988, 200–1. For further discussion of the materialist and individualist bases of European society see chapter 2.
9. Peter Fitzpatrick, *The mythology of modern law*, Routledge, London, 1992. See further the discussion of social evolutionary theories in chapters 3 (Durkheim) and 4 (Marx).
10. Reassertions of the backwardness of Aboriginal societies have been prominent in the debate following the Murray Islands decision; for example comments

Notes

by Hugh Morgan, Tim Fischer, Marshall Perron, Henry Bosch, John Gorton and Geoffrey Blainey, reported in the *Age* (Melbourne), 1 July 1993, 7 July 1993, 28 July 1993; the *Australian* 1 November 1993; the *Age Saturday Extra*, 18 December 1993.

11 *Australians to 1788*, eds D. J. Mulvaney and J. Peter White, Fairfax, Syme & Weldon, Sydney, 1987, 3.
12 Healy, 'We know your mob now', 515.
13 ibid.
14 ibid. 514.
15 By contrast, according to one Aboriginal history, the law of the British invaders was immoral since it could be manipulated to suit human needs. Hobbles Danaiyairi (Yarralin people, Victoria River District, NT), quoted in ibid. 517. Cf. natural law theory, discussed in chapter 2.
16 In this sense Aboriginal law is like Jewish law. There is no 'private' sphere of life that is unregulated by law. By contrast, in liberal societies the distinction between the 'public' (legal) and 'private' (unregulated) realms is fundamental—see chapter 2.
17 Pat Dodson, 'Policy statement', in *International law and Aboriginal human rights*, ed Barbara Hocking, Law Book Co., Sydney, 1988, 140.
18 For example, the staff of the Koori Oral History Unit, based at the Victorian State Library, have been responsible for gathering oral histories with the aim of establishing a durable resource centre for Aboriginal people and non-Aboriginal researchers.
19 Barry Morris, 'Frontier colonialism as a culture of terror', in *Power, knowledge and Aborigines*, 73.
20 Healy, 'We know your mob now', 520.
21 Protectors were appointed, following a House of Commons Select Committee report in 1837, 'to protect Aborigines from abuses and to provide the remnant populations around towns with some rations, blankets and medicine'. Australian Law Reform Commission, *Report No. 31: the recognition of Aboriginal customary law*, AGPS, Canberra, 1986, para. 25.
22 See e.g. M. F. Christie, *Aborigines in colonial Victoria 1835–86*, Sydney University Press, Sydney, 1979.
23 ibid. 13–14.
24 See further the discussion of empirical research methods in chapters 6 and 7.
25 Foley, 'Teaching whites a lesson', 200.
26 Cf. Batman's treaty with the Aborigines—see the next section of this chapter.
27 See also the discussion in chapter 6 of interactionism as a research method.
28 *Australians to 1788*, 87.
29 Tim Murray, 'Aboriginal (pre)history and Australian archaeology: the discourse of Australian prehistoric archaeology', in *Power, knowledge and Aborigines*, 16.
30 ibid.
31 Foley, 'Teaching whites a lesson', 199.
32 Murray, 'Aboriginal (pre)history and Australian archaeology', 18–19.
33 See, for example, Ann McGrath, 'History and land rights', *Law and history in Australia, vol. 3*, ed. Diane Kirkby, La Trobe University, Bundoora, 1987, 14–26. Cf. Diane Bell, 'In the case of the lawyers and anthropologists' (1986) 11 *Legal Service Bulletin* 202. See also Native Title Act 1993 (Cwlth), s. 108(3): for the purpose of performing its functions, the National Native Title

Tribunal may carry out research into the history of dealings with particular land, linguistics, and anthropology. (The functions of the National Native Title Tribunal are outlined later in this chapter.)

34 See further the discussion of participant observation as a socio-legal research method in chapters 6 and 7.

35 Gillian Cowlishaw, 'Studying Aborigines: changing canons in anthropology and history', in *Power, knowledge and Aborigines*, 23. Eve Fesl observes:

> Many anthropological and other works refer to 'traditional' societies when referring to our people living different lifestyles from urban dwellers. Just what is meant by 'traditional'? Maintenance of the term perpetuates a belief held by many non-Koories that our society was fossilized in some undefined reference point in the past. Our society has always been changing and adapting to meet the differing needs created by environment and in the last 200 years, the changes caused by invasion of our lands . . . If you are writing about Koorie culture, say so—drop the useless, non-descriptive term 'traditional'! (Fesl, 'How the English language is used to put Koories down', 2)

36 This bias is reflected in the Murray Islands decision, which will benefit remote/'traditional' Aborigines but not urban Aborigines—see the third section of this chapter.

37 Phillip Toyne and Daniel Vachon, *Growing up the country: the Pitjantjatjara struggle for their land*, McPhee Gribble/Penguin, Melbourne, 1984, 5. Note that Phillip Toyne is a lawyer rather than an anthropologist.

38 See e.g. Jan Pettman, 'Gendered knowledges: Aboriginal women and the politics of feminism', in *Power, knowledge and Aborigines*, 123.

39 Diane Bell, 'Women's business is hard work: Central Australian Aboriginal women's love rituals', in *Religion in Aboriginal Australia: an anthology*, eds Max Charlesworth, Howard Morphy, Diane Bell and Kenneth Maddock, University of Queensland Press, St. Lucia, 1984, 347–51. For some of the 'recuperative' work of women anthropologists see e.g. Catherine H. Berndt, 'Women and the "secret life"', in *Aboriginal man in Australia*, eds Catherine H. and Ronald M. Berndt, Angus & Robertson, Sydney, 1960; *Women's role in Aboriginal society*, ed. Fay Gale, Australian Institute of Aboriginal Studies, Canberra, 1970; *We are bosses ourselves: the status and role of Aboriginal women today*, ed. Fay Gale, Australian Institute of Aboriginal Studies, Canberra, 1983; Diane Bell, *Daughters of the dreaming*, Allen & Unwin, Sydney, 1983. For comments on Diane Bell's work, see Francesca Merlan, 'Review of D. Bell, "Daughters of the dreaming"' (1984–85) 55 (3) *Oceania* 225–9; 'Gender in Aboriginal social life: a review', in *Social anthropology in Australian Aboriginal studies: a contemporary overview*, eds R. M. Berndt and R. Tonkinson, Aboriginal Studies Press, Canberra, 1988, 15–76. See further the discussion of feminism in chapter 4.

40 See e.g. Gillian Cowlishaw, 'Studying Aborigines'.

41 It may not be wholly useful in the West, either, as demonstrated by the studies of the invocation of law outlined in chapter 6.

42 Kenneth Maddock, 'Aboriginal customary law', in *Aborigines and the law: essays in honour of Elizabeth Eggleston* eds Peter Hanks and Bryan Keon-Cohen, Allen & Unwin, Sydney, 1984, 221.

43 See e.g. the discussion of 'Is Aboriginal "law" law?', in ibid.; and R. D. Lumb,

'The Mabo case—public law aspects', in *Mabo: a judicial revolution: the Aboriginal land rights decision and its impact on Australian law*, eds M. A. Stephenson and Suri Ratnapala, University of Queensland Press, St. Lucia, 1993, 13.
44 See further the discussion of the translation and transformation of legal claims in chapter 6.
45 Natural law and positivism are discussed in more detail in chapter 2.
46 'Additional instructions for Lieutenant James Cook' in *A source book of Australian legal history: source materials from the eighteenth to the twentieth centuries*, eds J. M. Bennett and Alex C. Castles, Law Book Co., Sydney, 1979, 253–4.
47 This was later overtaken by the requirement of possession asserted by the Protestant colonisers. For an account of the change in emphasis from discovery to possession, see D. W. Greig, 'Sovereignty, territory and the international lawyer's dilemma' (1988) 26 *Osgoode Hall Law Journal* 127.
48 See, for example, M. F. Lindley, *The acquisition and government of backward territory in international law: being a treatise on the law and practice relating to colonial expansion*, Negro University Press, New York, 1969. Lindley notes that the term 'backward' was not an international legal term of art, iii.
49 L. C. Green and O. P. Dickason, *The law of nations and the New World*, University of Alberta Press, Alberta, 1989, gives a detailed treatment of the trend of founding colonies in inhabited territories pursuant to the doctrine of *terra nullius*.
50 'Sovereignty' at international law is an ill-defined term. It has evolved from the notion of the absolute power of princes over their subjects to include the notions of territorial integrity and equality of states. It overlaps with the notions of statehood and membership of the international community. In the colonial period, even where the terminology of conquest and cession was used, indigenous sovereignty was rarely acknowledged by the colonial powers and treaties between the colonisers and the colonised were given little or no effect.
51 Green and Dickason, *The law of nations and the New World*.
52 See Castles, *An Australian legal history*, 16.
53 The principle of self-determination has developed over time through several United Nations General Assembly resolutions which build on references to self-determination in the United Nations Charter. It is now included in the International Covenant on Civil and Political Rights, 16 December 1966, 999 UNTS 171 (entered into force 13 March 1976) and the International Covenant on Economic, Social and Cultural Rights, 16 December 1966, 999 UNTS 3 (entered into force 3 January 1976).
54 Advisory Opinion on Western Sahara, ICJ Reports 1975, 12.
55 Sir William Blackstone, *Commentaries on the laws of England: book 1*, Garland, New York, facs. repr. 1978; first publ. 1765; 9th edn 1783, 107–8.
56 'Additional instructions for Lieutenant James Cook', 253–4.
57 'Cook takes possession of New South Wales', in *Select documents in Australian history vol. 1: 1788–1850*, ed. Manning Clark, Angus & Robertson, Sydney, 1950, 25–6.
58 Henry Reynolds, *The law of the land*, Penguin, Ringwood, 1987, 31 (2nd edn 1992).
59 ibid. *passim* and especially 32.
60 ibid. 1.

61 Australian Courts Act 1828 (Imp.). This cut-off date applied also to Van Dieman's Land (Tasmania), and to Victoria and Queensland which were still part of New South Wales at that time. English laws were received as of the date of settlement in Western Australia (18 June 1829) and South Australia (28 December 1836).
62 See, for example, the discussion of nineteenth century divorce law reform in chapter 5. For a detailed account of the constitutional history of the Australian colonies see Castles, *An Australian legal history*.
63 See, for example, *Attorney-General v Brown* (1847) 2 SCR(NSW)(App) 30. See further discussion of these cases in chapter 6.
64 *Cooper v Stuart* (1889) 14 App. Cas. 286 at 292.
65 See the discussion in Castles, *An Australian legal history*, 515.
66 Australian Law Reform Commission, *Report No. 31*, 18. In 1991 the Australian Census listed 265,459 Aborigines and Torres Strait Islanders in Australia, representing 1.6 per cent of the total population.
67 See Henry Reynolds, *The other side of the frontier*, Penguin, Ringwood, 1982.
68 Phillip Pepper, *You are what you make yourself to be: the story of a Victorian Aboriginal family 1842–1980*, Hyland House, Melbourne, 1980, 30–2; Heather McRae, Garth Nettheim and Laura Beacroft, *Aboriginal legal issues*, Law Book Co., Sydney, 1991, 19.
69 ibid. 22–3.
70 ibid. 20.
71 See, for example, Peter Read, *The stolen generations: the removal of Aboriginal children in N.S.W. 1883–1969*, NSW Ministry of Aboriginal Affairs, Sydney, 1982.
72 The problems of obtaining accurate and comprehensive statistical information about Australia's indigenous populations are discussed in J. C. Altman, 'Statistics about indigenous Australians: needs, problems, options and implications', in *A national survey of indigenous Australians: options and implications*, ed. J. C. Altman, Centre for Aboriginal Economic Policy Research, ANU, Canberra, 1992. Since 1987 there has been an overall decline in the collection of identifiable statistical information on Aborigines and Torres Strait Islanders: ibid. 3.
73 Human Rights and Equal Opportunity Commission, *Report of the national inquiry into racist violence*, AGPS, Canberra, 1991, 119–22.
74 Australian Bureau of Statistics, *1991 census: Australian Aboriginal and Torres Strait Islander population*, AGPS, Canberra, 1993.
75 ibid.
76 Australian Bureau of Statistics, *Aboriginal child survival: an analysis of results from the 1986 census of population and housing*, Cat. No. 4126.0, 2–5.
77 McRae, Nettheim and Beacroft, *Aboriginal legal issues*, 34.
78 Royal Commission into Aboriginal Deaths in Custody, *Final report, vol. 1*, AGPS, Canberra, 1991, 224.
79 ibid. *vol. 4*, 1–3.
80 *Milirrpum and Others v Nabalco Pty Ltd and the Commonwealth of Australia* (1970) 17 FLR 141.
81 *Coe v Commonwealth of Australia and Another* (1979) 24 ALR 118.
82 *Gove*, 266.
83 ibid. For further discussion of the definition of law see chapter 2 (natural law/positivism) and chapters 6 and 7.

84 ibid. 266, 268.
85 ibid. 202.
86 ibid. 242, 244.
87 The other grounds for his decision were: that if there was a doctrine of native title it did not include the plaintiffs' interest as they could not be said to own the land in the European sense (ibid. 272–3); and in any event all interests would have been extinguished by the ordinance which allowed mining by Nabalco (ibid. 292).
88 ibid. 201–41.
89 ibid. 255.
90 ibid. 252–62.
91 ibid. 255–62.
92 ibid. 255.
93 For an account of the treatment of Aboriginal people on reserves see Pepper, *You are what you make yourself to be.*
94 Reynolds, *The law of the land,* 60, 131–3.
95 Proclamation published in *N.S.W. Government Gazette,* 2 September 1835, reproduced in *Select documents in Australian history,* 93.
96 *Gove,* 256–7.
97 ibid. 256.
98 Some of the arguments, such as the claim of interference with Aboriginal rights to freedom of religion, are not considered here.
99 *Coe,* 132.
100 ibid. 130.
101 ibid. per Jacobs J, 132, Murphy J, 137.
102 ibid. 130.
103 For an account of Malo's Law and Meriam myth see Nonie Sharp, 'No ordinary case: reflections upon Mabo (No. 2)' (1993) 15 *Sydney Law Review* 143–58.
104 See e.g. Noel Pearson, 'The deed of grant in trust and Hope Vale Aboriginal community, North Queensland' (1989) 2/38 *Aboriginal Law Bulletin* 12–13. By the time the High Court handed down its decision in the Murray Islands case, the Queensland government no longer proposed to bring the Islands under the DOGIT system.
105 *Milirrpum v Nabalco* (1971) 17 FLR, 153–6; Ron Castan QC, 'The Mabo case', paper delivered to the Labor Lawyers' Conference, Melbourne, May 1992, 17; B. A. Keon-Cohen, 'Some problems of proof: the admissibility of traditional evidence', in *Mabo: a judicial revolution,* 185–205.
106 *Mabo v Queensland: Determination of Facts,* Supreme Court of Queensland, Moynihan J, unreported, 16 November 1990.
107 Brennan J (with whom Mason CJ and McHugh J agreed), Deane and Gaudron JJ and Toohey J. Dawson J dissented.
108 *Mabo v Queensland (No. 2)* (1992) 175 CLR 1, per Brennan J, 29.
109 ibid.
110 Some of the legal theorists discussed in chapters 4 and 7 would deny that there is any such thing as skeletal principles in law.
111 *Murray Islands,* 30. For further discussion of the relationship between morality and law see chapter 2.
112 ibid. 139–42.
113 ibid. 145.
114 ibid. per Deane and Gaudron JJ, 93–4. Their Honours' view is consonant with

the idea that judges 'find' law which is already in existence. Similarly, Richard Bartlett argues that the High Court has not changed the law but merely offered the first explicit statement of native title: '*Mabo*: another triumph for the common law' (1993) 15 *Sydney Law Review* 185.
115 ibid. per Brennan J, 48–50, 55–7; Deane and Gaudron JJ, 82–5; Toohey J, 183–4.
116 ibid. per Brennan J, 58; Deane and Gaudron JJ, 87–8; Toohey J, 187.
117 Brennan and Toohey JJ were careful not to comment on the status of native title vis-a-vis Anglo-Australian forms of property: see e.g. Toohey J, ibid. 194–5. Deane and Gaudron JJ do insist that native title is only a personal right to occupy or use the land, rather than a full legal estate or equitable interest in the land: ibid. 88, 89–90, 92, 93, 110. However, they were prepared to require compensation for extinguishment of native title, despite its 'lower' status; see below.
118 *Gove*, 272–3.
119 *Murray Islands*, per Brennan J, 40.
120 According to Brennan and McHugh JJ and Mason CJ, native title will remain so long as the people remain as an identifiable and self-identified community, living on the land under their own laws and customs as they currently exist: ibid. 59–60, 70. Deane, Gaudron and Toohey JJ go further in holding that the essential item for the survival of native title is the continued occupation and use of the land since before white settlement. So long as this relationship between the group and the land is maintained, they suggest that native title will subsist despite even a total loss of traditional law and customs: ibid. 110, 188–93.
121 ibid. per Brennan J, 70.
122 See discussion in section 1, above.
123 Michael Mansell, 'The court gives an inch but takes another mile' (1992) 2/57 *Aboriginal Law Bulletin* 4, 6: only 50,000 of the 300,000 Aboriginal people counted in the 1986 census might benefit.
124 G. McGinley, 'Indigenous peoples rights: *Mabo and others v State of Queensland*: the Australian High Court addresses 200 years of oppression' (1993) 21 *Denver Journal of International Law and Policy* 311, 330.
125 *Murray Islands*, per Brennan J, 68, 69–70; Deane and Gaudron JJ, 89–90, 110.
126 ibid. per Brennan J, 64; Deane and Gaudron JJ, 111; Toohey J, 195–6.
127 ibid. per Brennan J, 69; Deane and Gaudron JJ, 110.
128 ibid. per Brennan J, 70.
129 ibid. 64–5, 66–7.
130 ibid. per Brennan J, 68, 70; Deane and Gaudron JJ, 110.
131 ibid. per Brennan J, 71, 72–3; Deane and Gaudron JJ, 116–17; Toohey J, 197. Toohey J did suggest that the lease of two acres on Mer to the London Missionary Society, if it was valid, probably would have extinguished native title. Deane and Gaudron JJ suggested that the lease over Dauer and Waier would not have extinguished native title, due to conditions in the lease protecting traditional gardening and fishing activities. Brennan J's view of this lease is criticised by Noel Pearson in '204 years of invisible title', in *Mabo: A judicial revolution*, 87.
132 *Murray Islands*, per Deane and Gaudron JJ, 111; Toohey J, 195. However, their Honours also considered that any claim for compensation would be

subject to ordinary limitation periods: per Deane and Gaudron JJ, 112; Toohey J, 196. This qualification would greatly restrict the capacity of Aboriginal groups to claim compensation for any extinguishment before the 1980s.
133 ibid. 63, 64, 69.
134 *Mabo v Queensland (No. 1)* (1988) 166 CLR 186.
135 *Murray Islands*, 69.
136 Geoffrey Blainey, 'Land rights for all', the *Age*, 10 November 1993.
137 P. P. McGuinness, 'High court's role now irrevocably politicised', the *Australian*, 13–14 November 1993.
138 For example, opinion polls and talkback radio responses reported in the *Age*, 18 June 1993, 22 July 1993, 3 November 1993; Hugh Morgan, *News Weekly*, 29 August 1992; Tim Fischer, the *Age*, 24 September 1993; Rob Borbidge, the *Australian*, 1 November 1993; Geoffrey Blainey, the *Age*, 10 November 1993; Malcolm Fraser, the *Age*, 1 December 1993; Western Australian government advertisement, the *Australian*, 6–7 November 1993.
139 See further the discussion of 'equality' in the next chapter.
140 Such concerns have been expressed by miners: the *Age*, 24 May 1993, 22 July 1993, 20 October 1993, 26 October 1993, 5 November 1993, the *Australian*, 3–4 July 1993, 10 December 1993; farmers: the *Age*, 24 May 1993, the *Australian*, 16–17 October 1993; banks: the *Age*, 20 July 1993, the *Australian*, 28 July 1993; politicians: the *Age*, 16 October 1993, 18 November 1993, the *Australian*, 17 November 1993; business leaders: the *Australian*, 19 October 1993; and others: the *Age*, 4 June 1993, 14 June 1993, 19 June 1993, 28 June 1993, 30 July 1993, the *Australian*, 9 August 1993, 11 August 1993, 17 November 1993.
141 Another source of doubt is Toohey J's opinion in *Murray Islands* that dealings with native title land could constitute a breach of fiduciary duty towards Aboriginal people by State and/or federal governments. The Wik people of western Cape York Peninsula have brought an action against the Queensland government alleging breaches of fiduciary duty in the granting of mining leases over their land. If their claim succeeds it could have far-reaching implications; however a High Court decision on the claim is many years away.
142 The principles set out in the Murray Islands decision provide sufficient guidance on the status of pastoral and mining titles vis-a-vis native titles. See also Henry Reynolds, 'Native title and pastoral leases', in *Mabo: a judicial revolution*, 119–31; 'Mabo and pastoral leases' (1992) 2/59 *Aboriginal Law Bulletin* 8–9. In relation to land titles issued since the date of the Racial Discrimination Act, many have been issued but few would relate to land on which Aborigines have been in continuous occupation. Thus the extent of unlawful extinguishment could be identified and remedied.
143 Richard Bartlett, 'The Aboriginal land which may be claimed at common law: implications of *Mabo*' (1992) 22 *University of Western Australia Law Review* 272, 295; 'The primacy of the Commonwealth: the rejection of the WA and NT legislation' (1993) 3/62 *Aboriginal Law Bulletin* 14, 14–15.
144 Native Title Act 1993 (Cwlth), ss. 14 and 19, providing for validation of 'past acts', which are defined in ss. 228–232.
145 ibid. ss. 15(1)(a), 19.
146 ibid. ss. 16, 19.
147 ibid. ss. 15(1)(d), 19, 238.
148 ibid.

149 ibid. ss. 17, 18, 20, 51.
150 ibid. s. 223, which imports the common law notion of native title into the Act.
151 ibid. ss. 13, 61, 251.
152 ibid. s. 74.
153 ibid. ss. 11, 21–25, 233–236. 'Future acts' are legislative acts occurring on or after 1 July 1993 or non-legislative acts occurring on or after 1 January 1994: s. 233.
154 ibid. s. 23(3).
155 ibid. ss. 23(4)(a), 235, 238.
156 ibid. s. 26.
157 ibid. ss. 27, 43.
158 ibid. s. 42.
159 ibid. s. 51(6).
160 For example, Geoffrey Blainey, 'Land rights for all'.
161 Native Title Act, s. 201.
162 Islamic and customary laws are recognised in judicial decisions and by state and federal statutes. See e.g. Wu Min Aun, *The Malaysian legal system*, Longman, Selangor Darul Ehsan, 1990, ch. 5.
163 According to Hooker, this form of pluralism is the one most commonly adopted. M. B. Hooker, *Legal pluralism: an introduction to colonial and neo-colonial laws*, Clarendon Press, Oxford, 1975.
164 (1883) 4 LR (NSW) 355, 356.
165 See, for example, Constitutional Commission, *Report of the individual rights committee*, AGPS, Canberra, 1987, 70; cf. *Final report of the Constitutional Commission*, AGPS, Canberra, 1988, 109–10. The Constitutional Convention held in Sydney in 1991 accepted the principle of a reference to the unique position of Australia's indigenous peoples in the preamble to the Constitution, but was unable to agree on an appropriate wording.
166 The proposed preamble to the Aboriginal and Torres Strait Islander Commission Act 1989 was removed from the Bill to ensure its passage, and was finally passed in the form of a Senate resolution on 17 October 1989 over the protest of the Opposition. For a discussion of this and other preambles see Frank Brennan and James Crawford, 'Aboriginality, recognition and Australian law: where to from here?' (1990) 1 *Public Law Review* 53.
167 See Frank Brennan SJ, 'Waiting for the resolution' (1989) 61 *Australian Quarterly* 242–3.
168 Reprinted in (1993) 3/61 *Aboriginal Law Bulletin* 4.
169 Council for Aboriginal Reconciliation Act 1991 (Cwlth), ss. 5, 6.
170 For example, the *Aboriginal and Torres Strait Islander Heritage Protection Act 1984 (Cwlth)*. On the history and operation of cultural heritage laws see Graeme Neate, 'Power, policy, politics and persuasion' (1989) 6 *Environment and Planning Law Journal* 214; C. Warren, 'Aboriginal power over cultural heritage' (1991) 16 *Legal Service Bulletin* 6.
171 James Crawford, Peter Hennessy and Mary Fisher, 'Aboriginal customary law: proposals for recognition', in *Ivory scales: black Australians and the law*, ed. Kayleen M. Hazlehurst, New South Wales University Press, Kensington, 1987, 198. See also John McCorquodale, 'Judicial racism in Australia? Aboriginals in civil and criminal cases', in the same volume, 30.
172 Australian Law Reform Commission, *Report no. 31*, paras 208–9.

173 ibid. paras 257–7, 505–17, 978.
174 Aboriginal Land Rights Commission, *Second report*, AGPS, Canberra, 1974, para. 568. The Northern Territory government began a campaign in late 1993 to have the mining veto removed from the Land Rights Act, to bring it into line with the Native Title Act: the *Australian*, 22 November 1993, 20 December 1993, 23 February 1994.
175 For a description of these laws see Richard Johnstone, 'Aboriginal land rights', in A. Bradbrook, S. MacCallum and A. Moore, *Australian real property law*, Law Book Co., Sydney, 1991, 31–3; McRae, Nettheim and Beacroft, *Aboriginal legal issues*, 148–60. These summaries were written before the introduction of the Aboriginal Land Act 1991 (Qld), which allows for ongoing claims to land on the basis of traditional and historical affiliation.
176 Christine Jennett, 'Aboriginal affairs policy', in *Hawke and Australian public policy: consensus and restructuring*, eds C. Jennett and R. G. Stewart, Macmillan, Sydney, 1990, 255–7.
177 See Gerry Hand, *Foundations for the future*, AGPS, Canberra, 1987.
178 ibid. See also Jennett, 'Aboriginal affairs policy', 261–4.
179 On the early workings of ATSIC see Tim Rowse, 'Top-down tensions', *Modern Times*, no. 4, June 1992, 22. See also the *Weekend Australian*, 27–28 November 1993, 24. The Royal Commission into Aboriginal Deaths in Custody recommended that ATSIC be established as a separate entity outside the Public Service in order to make it more independent (Recommendation 189). This recommendation has not been endorsed by the federal government.
180 David Ross, Central Land Council, addressing the United Nations Working Group on Indigenous Populations in 1991: Department of Foreign Affairs and Trade, *Backgrounder*, vol. 3, no. 9, 22 May 1992, 5–6.
181 McRae, Nettheim and Beacroft, *Aboriginal legal issues*, 32.
182 Frank Brennan, 'ATSIC: seeking a national mouthpiece for local voices' (1990) 2/43 *Aboriginal Law Bulletin* 4.
183 See, for example, Australian Law Reform Commission, *Report No. 31*; Geoff Airo-Farulla, 'Community policing and self-determination' (1992) 2/54 *Aboriginal Law Bulletin* 8–9; Paul Ban, 'The quest for legal recognition of Torres Strait Islander customary adoption practice' (1993) 3/60 *Aboriginal Law Bulletin* 4–5; Richard Bradshaw, 'Community representation in criminal proceedings' (1986) 11 *Legal Service Bulletin* 111.
184 See 'Implementation of Commonwealth Government Responses to the Recommendations of the Royal Commission into Aboriginal Deaths in Custody', *First annual report 1992–93*, AGPS, Canberra, 1994.
185 Royal Commission into Aboriginal Deaths in Custody, *Final report*, vol. 2, 542–63, *vol. 4*, 31–8; G. Crough, 'Funding Aboriginal programs and services' (1992) 2/57 *Aboriginal Law Bulletin* 9; G. Crough, 'Aboriginal Australia and the "new federalism" initiative', Discussion Paper No. 2, ANU North Australia Research Unit, 1991.
186 M. Mowbray and K. Shain, 'Self-management: one Northern Territory experience' (1986) 11 *Legal Service Bulletin* 106.
187 C. Fletcher, *Aboriginal politics: intergovernmental relations*, Melbourne University Press, Melbourne, 1991, 67–145.
188 Sylvia de Rose, addressing the 'Aboriginal peoples, federalism and self-determination' conference, Townsville, August 1993.
189 Canadian Constitution s. 35.1. See Doug Sanders, 'Towards Aboriginal self-

government: an update on Canadian constitutional reform' (1992) 2/58 *Aboriginal Law Bulletin* 12; R. Gerritsen, 'Cause for hope? Self-management and local government in Australia', discussion paper for the Royal Commission into Aboriginal Deaths in Custody, October 1990.
190 See Michael Mansell, 'Treaty proposal: Aboriginal sovereignty' (1989) 2/37 *Aboriginal Law Bulletin* 4.
191 Frank Brennan SJ, '*Mabo* and its implications for Aborigines and Islanders', in *Mabo: a judicial revolution*, 26–7.
192 Noel Pearson, 'Reconciliation: to be or not to be' (1993) 3/61 *Aboriginal Law Bulletin* 14.
193 ibid. 15.
194 See H. C. Coombs, 'The case for a treaty', in *Black Australians: the prospects for change*, ed. E. Olbrei, James Cook University Union, Townsville, 1982, 57; Symposium on the Makarrata (1982) *Aboriginal Law Bulletin* 5, 5; G. J. L. Coles, 'The international significance of an Aboriginal treaty' (1982) 21 *World Review* 42.
195 Barunga Statement, reprinted in McRae, Nettheim and Beacroft, *Aboriginal legal issues*, 317–8.
196 R. J. Hawke, quoted in Frank Brennan SJ, 'Is a bipartisan approach possible?' (1989) 14 *Legal Service Bulletin* 66.
197 G. Nettheim and T. Simpson, 'Aboriginal peoples and treaties' (1989) 12 *Current Affairs Bulletin* 22–3, extracted in McRae, Nettheim and Beacroft, *Aboriginal legal issues*, 318–9. See also James Crawford, 'The Aboriginal legal heritage: Aboriginal public law and the treaty proposal' (1989) 63 *Australian Law Journal* 392.
198 *Council for Aboriginal Reconciliation Act 1991 (Cwlth)*, s. 6(1)(g) and (h).
199 For useful overviews of this area see *International law and Aboriginal human rights*, ed. Barbara Hocking, Law Book Co., Sydney, 1988; *The rights of peoples*, ed. James Crawford, Oxford University Press, Oxford, 1988. See also H. Hannum, 'New developments in indigenous rights' (1988) 28 *Virginia Journal of International Law* 649; Garth Nettheim, 'Indigenous rights, human rights and Australia' (1987) 61 *Australian Law Journal* 291; Sarah Pritchard, 'The right of indigenous peoples to self-determination under international law' (1992) 2/55 *Aboriginal Law Bulletin* 4–7; Royal Commission into Aboriginal Deaths in Custody, *Final report, vol. 5*, chapter 36.
200 See Hilary Charlesworth, 'New rights of international redress for human rights violations in Australia', University of Adelaide Law School Continuing Legal Education Papers, 1993.
201 Statute of the International Court of Justice, art. 34. The Court has the power to give advisory opinions on questions referred to it by certain United Nations bodies: art. 65.
202 The application and response are reprinted in (1978–80) 8 *Australian Year Book of International Law* 420.
203 Communication No. 167/1984, Bernard Ominayak, Chief of the Lubicon Lake Band v Canada, United Nations, *Report of the Human Rights Committee, vol. II*, General Assembly (45th Sess.) (Supplement No. 40 A/45/40), 1–30.
204 ibid.
205 ibid.
206 Sixth Boyer Lecture, ABC Radio, 28 November 1993. See also Garth Nettheim,

'"The consent of the natives": Mabo and indigenous political rights' (1993) 15 *Sydney Law Review* 237.
207 See P. Thornberry, *International law and the rights of minorities*, Oxford University Press, Oxford, 1991, 334–68.
208 See Russell L. Barsh, 'An advocate's guide to the Convention on Indigenous and Tribal Peoples' (1990) 15 *Oklahoma City University Law Review* 209.
209 Art. 1(3) of the Convention stipulates that the use of the term 'peoples' is not to be construed as having any international legal implications.
210 For a discussion of the work of the UNWGIP in drafting the Declaration see Catherine J. Iorns, 'Indigenous peoples and self determination' (1992) 24 *Case Western Reserve Journal of International Law* 199.
211 UN Doc. E/CN.4/Sub.2/1992/33.
212 See Iorns, 'Indigenous peoples and self determination', 271–7.
213 Frank Brennan SJ, 'Self-determination: the limits of allowing Aboriginal communities to be a law unto themselves' (1993) 16(1) *University of New South Wales Law Journal* 262–3.
214 For example, feminist scholars have raised concerns regarding the exclusion of women's voices in the exercise of self-determination. See Hilary Charlesworth, Christine Chinkin and Shelley Wright, 'Feminist approaches to international law' (1991) 85 *American Journal of International Law* 613.
215 Royal Commission into Aboriginal Deaths in Custody, *Final report*, vol. 5, chapter 36.

Chapter 2 Themes in liberal legal and constitutional theory

1 The postmodernist critique of Enlightenment thinking is considered in chapter 4.
2 On the transition from laissez faire to welfare liberalism, see P. Selznick, 'Dworkin's unfinished task' (1989) 77 *California Law Review* 505.
3 Of course, it was only propertied, white, male, adult individuals who were sought to be protected at first. Feminists and critical race theorists have argued that the exclusion of women and non-white racial groups was not merely an oversight but central to the whole liberal project. See chapter 4.
4 See, for example, Robert Nozick, *Anarchy, the state and utopia*, Blackwell, Oxford, 1974, 9.
5 Peter Singer argues that the notion of rights to private property is also necessary to sustain the underlying assumption of liberal society that acquisitiveness is desirable: *How are we to live?*, Text Publishing, Melbourne, 1993, 55–6, 73–4.
6 Utilitarianism was specifically constructed in opposition to natural law theory (see section 2 of chapter 1 and the discussion in this chapter of the relationship between law and morality). Bentham described the notion of the 'rights of man' as 'nonsense on stilts'. Utilitarianism has some affinities with law and economics, especially public choice theory and welfare economics—see chapter 3.
7 See further the discussion of pluralist accounts of law reform in chapter 5.
8 John Rawls, *A theory of justice*, Oxford University Press, Oxford, 1973, 60. On the relationship between the two principles see 61. See also John Rawls, *Political liberalism*, Columbia University Press, New York, 1993.
9 Rawls, *A theory of justice*, 61.
10 Rawls develops this principle further so that, in its final form, redistributive

measures are required to be to 'the *greatest* benefit of the least advantaged'; ibid. 302–3.
11 See also the discussion of Roberto Unger's arguments about the post-liberal state, in the section on critical legal studies in chapter 4.
12 (1992) 177 CLR 106.
13 ibid. 140.
14 ibid. per Brennan J, 149, Deane and Toohey JJ, 169, Gaudron J, 213, McHugh J, 227.
15 ibid. 186.
16 See, for instance, Charles Sampford, 'Law, institutions and the public/private divide' (1991) 20 *Federal Law Review* 185, and references therein.
17 Recent work on the concept of the rule of law includes: T. R. S. Allen, 'Legislative supremacy and the rule of law: democracy and constitutionalism' (1985) 44 *Cambridge Law Journal* 111; David Feldman, 'Democracy, the rule of law, and judicial review' (1990) 19 *Federal Law Review* 1; Bob Fine, *Democracy and the rule of law: liberal ideals and marxist critiques*, Pluto Press, London, 1984; Kenneth Henley, 'Abstract principles, mid-level principles, and the rule of law' (1993) 12 *Law and Philosophy* 121; Joseph Raz, 'The politics of the rule of law' (1990) 3 *Ratio Juris* 331; Geoffrey de Q. Walker, *The rule of law: foundation of constitutional democracy*, Melbourne University Press, Melbourne, 1988.
18 Cf. Walker, *The rule of law*, 3–5; see also Feldman, 'Democracy, the rule of law, and judicial review', 11–18.
19 See, for example, W. Sadurski, 'Equality before the law: a conceptual analysis' (1986) 60 *Australian Law Journal* 131.
20 Walker, *The rule of law*, 3.
21 See further the discussions of Durkheim and Parsons in chapter 3.
22 Lon L. Fuller, *The morality of law*, Yale University Press, New Haven, rev. edn, 1969, 46–81.
23 ibid. 42.
24 See the discussion of Dworkin in chapter 7.
25 Note that Fuller admits that retroactivity may sometimes be justified in order to correct other failings, for instance where a law was not properly publicised or could not in practice have been obeyed. See J. W. Harris, *Legal philosophies*, Butterworths, London, 1980, 131.
26 See further the discussion of the relationship between law and morality, below.
27 Fuller, *Morality of law*, 5–6. The examples of the morality of duty given by Fuller were the morality of the Old Testament and the Ten Commandments. See also the requirements of natural law, below.
28 ibid. 5.
29 H. L. A. Hart, *Essays in jurisprudence and philosophy*, Oxford University Press, Oxford, 1983, 350.
30 John Finnis, *Natural law and natural rights*, Oxford University Press, Oxford, 1980, 273–4.
31 Allan Hutchinson, *Dwelling on the threshold*, Carswell, Toronto, 1988, 23.
32 See Dworkin's distinction between equal treatment and treatment as an equal, *Taking rights seriously*, Duckworth, London, 1978, 227.
33 Walker, *The rule of law*, 5.
34 See further the section on marxism in chapter 4.
35 John Austin, 'The province of jurisprudence determined', reprinted in *The*

province of jurisprudence determined and the uses of the study of jurisprudence, Weidenfeld & Nicolson, London, 1955, 363–93; quoted in Roger Cotterrell, *The politics of jurisprudence*, Butterworths, London, 1989, 119.
36 *Family Law Act 1975 (Cwlth)*, ss. 75(2)(o), 79(4)(e). As an extreme example of this point, E. Philip Soper has posited a hypothetical legal system with only one law: 'All disputes are to be settled as justice requires: Legal theory and the obligation of a judge: the Hart/Dworkin dispute' (1976) 75 *Michigan Law Review* 512.
37 Hart, *Essays in jurisprudence and philosophy*, 12.
38 H. L. A. Hart, 'The minimum content of natural law', in *The concept of law*, Oxford University Press, Oxford, 1961, ch. 9.2.
39 See also Joseph Raz, *The authority of law*, Oxford University Press, Oxford, 1979, 219–20, 260.
40 For a more detailed account of that history see J. W. Harris, *Legal philosophies*, 6–21.
41 Cicero, *De Republica* III, xxii, 33, quoted in ibid. 8.
42 Finnis, *Natural law and natural rights*.
43 ibid. 276.
44 There are further arguments for a presumption that law should be obeyed, based on consent and/or fairness, which are not considered here.
45 Finnis, *Natural law and natural rights*, 360.
46 See Geoffrey Marshall, *Constitutional theory*, Oxford University Press, Oxford, 1971, 97, 124.
47 As Locke noted, it may be 'too great a temptation to human frailty, apt to grasp at power, for the same persons who have the power of making laws to have also in their hands the power to execute them, whereby they may exempt themselves from obedience to the laws they make'; *Second treatise of civil government*, ch. xii, para. 143. See Marshall, *Constitutional theory*, 101.
48 See further the discussion in chapter 7.
49 Commonwealth Constitution, s. 128.
50 For example, s. 61 of the Commonwealth Constitution.
51 *New South Wales v Commonwealth* (1975) 135 CLR 337, per Barwick CJ, 364–5.
52 Sir John Kerr, *Matters for judgment: an autobiography*, Macmillan, Melbourne, 1978, 334–5, 360–4.
53 Gough Whitlam, *The truth of the matter*, Allen Lane, Ringwood, 1979, 177–9.
54 Ian Duncanson, 'Lawyers' stories and the possibilities of reconstruction', paper delivered at the Law and Society Conference, Macquarie University, December 1993, 6.
55 This is another feature of the post-liberal state identified by Roberto Unger and discussed in the section on critical legal studies in chapter 4.
56 See e.g. *Administration Decisions (Judicial Review) Act 1977 (Cwlth); Administrative Law Act 1978 (Vic)*.
57 An argument could be made for an alternative system of appeal to an external court, on the model of the International Court of Justice.
58 Commonwealth Constitution, s. 7. Strictly, this is only required of *original* States.
59 See C. J. G. Sampford, 'Reconciling responsible government and federalism', in *The emergence of Australian law*, eds M. P. Ellinghaus, A. J. Bradbrook and A. J. Duggan, Butterworths, Sydney, 1989, 355.

Chapter 3   Economic and sociological approaches to law

1. R. L. Heilbroner, *The making of economic society*, Prentice-Hall, Englewood Cliffs, NJ, 9th edn, 1993, 1.
2. ibid. 5.
3. F. Easterbrook, 'The inevitability of law and economics' (1989) 1 *Legal Education Review* 3.
4. See C. Veljanovski, *The economics of law: an introductory text*, Institute of Economic Affairs, London, 1990, 16ff; W. Letwin, *The origins of scientific economics: English economic thought, 1660–1776*, Methuen, London, 1963.
5. See the introduction to chapter 2 and the section on postmodernism in chapter 4.
6. Beccaria's *An essay in crime and punishment* (1764) applied utilitarian principles to penology. See the section 'What is a liberal?' in chapter 2 for a brief outline of utilitarianism.
7. Smith's major work in political economy was *The wealth of nations* (1776).
8. See 'What is a liberal?' in chapter 2.
9. For a more detailed outline of Public Choice theory see S. Bottomley, N. Gunningham and S. Parker, *Law in context*, Federation Press, Sydney, 1991, ch. 8. See also the discussion of 'interest group' theories of law reform in chapter 5.
10. See, for example, R. Posner, *Economic analysis of law*, Little, Brown & Co, Boston, 4th edn, 1992.
11. See A. Duggan, 'Law and economics in Australia' (1989) 1 *Legal Education Review* 37.
12. See, for example, *Todorovic v Waller* (1981) 150 CLR 402.
13. Bottomley, Gunningham and Parker, *Law in context*, 156–8. See also A. K. Klevorick, 'Law and economic theory: an economist's view' (1975) 65 *American Economic Review* 237.
14. G. Calabresi, *The costs of accidents*, Yale University Press, New Haven, 1970.
15. See further chapter 6.
16. See chapter 7.
17. See Veljanovski, *The economics of law*, 33–4.
18. Easterbrook, 'The inevitability of law and economics', 5.
19. Veljanovski, *The economics of law*, 38.
20. ibid. 42.
21. See R. Coase, 'The problem of social costs' (1960) 3 *Journal of Law and Economics* 1.
22. For a more detailed treatment of a similar example see A. Polinsky, *An introduction to law and economics*, Little, Brown & Co, Boston, 2nd edn, 1989, ch. 3.
23. The validity of the Coase Theorem has been challenged by the empirical research of R. Ellickson, *Order without law*, Harvard University Press, Cambridge, 1991.
24. See T. C. Schelling, *Choice and consequences: perspectives of an errant economist*, Harvard University Press, Cambridge, Mass., 1984, ch. 1.
25. Easterbrook, 'The inevitability of law and economics', 18–19.
26. See Posner, *Economic analysis of law*, ch. 6; Polinsky, *An introduction to law and economics*, ch. 6. For a summary of the critiques of this argument see Bottomley, Gunningham and Parker, *Law in context*, 188–92.

Notes

27 For an attempt to provide a theoretical underpinning to this approach see P. Brook, *Freedom at work*, Oxford University Press, Oxford, 1990. For a discussion of the history of the award system, see chapter 5.
28 See the discussion of liberalism in chapter 2.
29 See C. Veljanovski, *The new law and economics*, Oxford University Press, Oxford, 1982, 21–2.
30 See generally M. Sandel, *Liberalism and its critics*, New York University Press, New York, 1984.
31 A. Leff, 'Economic analysis of law; some realism about nominalism' (1974) 60 *Virginia Law Review* 451.
32 Proponents of law and economics assert that in recent times economics has made greater use of mathematical models, and that this form of economic modelling is infiltrating law and economics scholarship: see R. Cooter and T. Ulen, *Law and economics*, Scott Foresman, Glenview, Ill., 1988, 9.
33 See, for example, M. Minow, 'Partial justice: law and minorities', in The fate of law, eds A. Sarat and T. Kerns, University of Michigan Press, Ann Arbor, 1991, 40.
34 See A. Gamble, *An introduction to modern social and political thought*, Macmillan, London, 1981, 176.
35 E. Durkheim, *The rules of sociological method*, trans. W. D. Halls, Macmillan, London, 2nd edn, 1982, 52. For example, human and group motives were not social facts, and therefore not the subject of sociological study.
36 See chapter 2.
37 Durkheim indicated in his later writings that if the state takes on an absolutist form the transition from repressive to restitutory laws can be retarded. See E. Durkheim, 'Two laws of penal evolution' (1973) 2 *Economy and Society* 285.
38 E. Durkheim, *The division of labour in society*, trans. W. D. Halls, Macmillan, London, 1984, 40.
39 See generally S. Lukes and A. Scull, *Durkheim and the law*, Martin Robinson & Co., Oxford, 1983, introduction.
40 See again the discussion of morality and law in chapter 2.
41 Durkheim, *The division of labour in society*, ch. 3.
42 Karl Marx (see chapter 4) and Charles Darwin were other nineteenth century thinkers who adopted evolutionary schemes. See generally Fitzpatrick, *The mythology of modern law*, Routledge, London, 1992, ch. 4.
43 See, for example, chapter 1. The evidence about Aboriginal law contradicts Durkheim's evolutionary theory.
44 See P. O'Malley, *Law, capitalism and democracy*, Allen & Unwin, Sydney, 1983, 149; Lord Lloyd of Hampstead and M. D. A. Freeman, *Lloyd's introduction to jurisprudence*, Stevens, London, 5th edn, 1985, 558, citing J. A. Barnes, 'Durkheim's division of labour in society' (1966) 2 *Man* 158; B. Malinowski, *Crime and custom in savage society*, Routledge & Kegan Paul, London, 1926; B. Lenman and G. Parker, 'The state, the community and the criminal law in early modern Europe', in *Crime and the law: the social history of crime in western Europe since 1500*, eds V. A. C. Gatrell, B. Lenman and G. Parker, Europa Publications, London, 1980; R. Schwartz and J. C. Miller, 'Legal evolution and societal complexity' (1964) 70 *American Journal of Sociology* 159; S. Sheleff, 'From restitutive law to repressive law: Durkheim's *The division of labour in society* revisited' (1975) XVI *European Journal of Sociology* 29; S. Spitzer, 'Punishment and social organisation: a study of Durkheim's theory of penal evolution' (1975) 9 *Law and Society Review* 613.

45 See Lord Lloyd of Hampstead and Freeman, ibid. 558; A. Hunt, *The sociological movement in law*, Macmillan, London, 1978, 141.
46 See Hunt, ibid. 95–6.
47 M. Weber, *On law and economy in society*, trans E. Shils and M. Rheinstein, Harvard University Press, Cambridge, Mass., 1954.
48 ibid. 5.
49 See T. Parsons, 'Introduction', in M. Weber, *The methodology of the social sciences*, trans E. A. Shils and H. A. Finch, Free Press of Glencoe, New York, 1949, 10; quoted in Hunt, *The sociological movement in law*, 100.
50 See also the approach taken by economists, discussed earlier in this chapter.
51 Hunt, *The sociological movement in law*, 100–1, 105–6.
52 Fitzpatrick, *The mythology of modern law*, 106.
53 Weber recognised a rationalisation of the common law through a change in the precedent system from relying on analogies drawn from fact situations to being based on principles of law and their relevance to the particular case, as a result of rational grounds being demanded for decisions. The need to give rational grounds accelerated the development of abstract general rules and principles. But it cannot be said that the English common law system has developed into a fully rational system.
54 Weber, *Law and economy*, 303.
55 ibid. 62, 226.
56 ibid. 287–8. Cf. chapter 2.
57 See chapters 6 and 7.
58 Cf. the view of legal education taken by critical legal scholars—see chapter 4.
59 R. Cotterrell, *The sociology of law: an introduction*, Butterworths, London, 2nd edn, 1992, 154.
60 Cf. Marx's view of history—see chapter 4.
61 Weber, *Law and economy*, 943.
62 See again the discussion of the rule of law in chapter 2.
63 O'Malley, *Law, capitalism and democracy*, 25.
64 Hunt, *The sociological movement in law*, 115–16.
65 See again the discussion of the separation of powers in chapter 2.
66 Hunt, *The sociological movement in law*, 116.
67 See chapter 4.
68 Weber, *Law and economy*, 131.
69 Hunt, *The sociological movement in law*, 120, 122. But see the discussion of the 'England problem' earlier in this section.
70 M. Weber, *Economy and society: an outline of interpretive sociology*, ed. G. Roth and C. Wittich, Bedminster Press, Totowa, NJ, 1968, 1394.
71 Weber, *Law and economy*, ch. 6.
72 Cf. M. P. Ellinghaus, 'Towards an Australian contract law', in *The emergence of Australian law*, eds M. P. Ellinghaus, A. J. Bradbrook and A. J. Duggan, Butterworths, Sydney, 1989, 54–62.
73 O'Malley, *Law, capitalism and democracy*, 35. See chapter 2.
74 See the section on marxism in chapter 4.
75 See I. Craib, *Modern social theory: from Parsons to Habermas*, Wheatsheaf Books, London, 1984, 37.
76 Compare this approach with that of economists to the analysis of law.
77 Craib, *Modern social theory*, 41.
78 See again the discussion of law and morality in chapter 2.

Notes

79 See chapter 4.
80 At first Parsons assumed a consensus of values. He later conceded that it was a problem, but never solved it.
81 Cotterrell, *The sociology of law*, 84.
82 See the discussion of the origins of legislation in chapter 5.
83 Cf. the critique of this legal professional role by critical legal scholars. See the discussion of 'critical legal education' in chapter 4.

Chapter 4 Objecting to objectivity

1 The collective reference to 'critical theories' for the purposes of this chapter is not to be confused with Critical Theory associated with the Frankfurt School, incorporating theorists such as Theodor Adorno, Walter Benjamin and Jürgen Habermas.
2 See chapter 3, especially the section on Weber.
3 See chapter 3, particularly the discussion of Parsons.
4 See chapter 3 on the economic analysis of the law.
5 See chapter 2 on liberal social and legal values.
6 See chapter 2 on the rule of law.
7 Carol Smart, *Feminism and the power of law*, Routledge, London, 1989.
8 Mark Tushnet, 'A marxist analysis of American law', *Marxist Perspectives*, Spring 1978, 96.
9 Patricia J. Williams, *The alchemy of race and rights: diary of a law professor*, Harvard University Press, Cambridge, Mass., 1991.
10 Catharine MacKinnon, 'Feminism, marxism, method and the state: toward feminist jurisprudence' (1983) 8 *Signs* 635.
11 See, for example, Mari J. Matsuda, Charles R. Lawrence III, Richard Delgado and Kimberle Williams Crenshaw, *Words that wound: critical race theory, assaultive speech and the First Amendment*, Westview Press, Boulder, 1993.
12 Alan Hunt, 'The big fear: law confronts postmodernism' (1990) 35 *McGill Law Journal* 507.
13 See chapter 3.
14 Friedrich Engels, 'The condition of the working class in England', in *Marx and Engels on law*, eds Maureen Cain and Alan Hunt, Academic Press, New York, 1979, 101–4.
15 Marx's major contribution to political economy (he virtually invented the term) is *Capital*, 1894, repr. Lawrence & Wishart, London, 1970.
16 Contrast this with Weber's multicausal approach to the process of rationalisation, outlined in chapter 3.
17 See particularly the discussions of Durkheim and Weber.
18 Marx drew the dialectical elements of his theory from Hegel, but substituted his material view of change for Hegel's idealism. Idealism and materialism have been seen as the two possible sources of historical change. Materialists believe that physical conditions and sensed experiences produce change, while idealists believe that the mind generates ideas which are converted into political behaviour relatively independent of environmental conditions. See, for example, Hegel, *Philosophy of history*, 1840. For a critique of apparently encompassing dichotomies such as materialism/idealism see the discussion of deconstruction in the section on postmodernism, below.
19 See the discussion of separation of powers in chapter 2.

20 See the description of pluralism in chapter 5.
21 W. Chambliss, 'Functional and conflict theories of crime', in *Whose law, what order? A conflict approach to criminology*, eds W. Chambliss and M. Mankoff, John Wiley, New York, 1976, 4.
22 Hunt describes a variant of this model as a 'content of law' perspective. See Alan Hunt, 'Marxism and the analysis of law', in *Sociological approaches to law*, eds A. Podgorecki and C. J. Whelan, Croom Helm, London, 1981, 96. See also, for example, J. Griffith, *The politics of the judiciary*, Fontana, London, 4th edn, 1991.
23 Marx, *Capital*, Penguin, Harmondsworth, 1976, 877–904.
24 The great strikes are discussed in the section on conciliation and arbitration in chapter 5.
25 This was the position adopted by the Spanish anarchists and was also favoured by their intellectual mentor, the Russian theorist Bakunin.
26 Hunt, 'Marxism and the analysis of law', 96.
27 Jerome Frank, *Law and the modern mind*, Anchor, New York, 1963; *Courts on trial: myth and reality in American justice*, Princeton University Press, Princeton, 1949. For discussion of recent analyses of trial court decision making see chapter 7.
28 Karl Llewellyn, *The bramble bush: or our law and its study*, Oceana Publications, New York, 1951; *Jurisprudence: realism in theory and practice*, University of Chicago Press, Chicago, 1962. See further the discussions of CLS and postmodernism in this chapter and of judicial decision making in chapter 7.
29 See, for example, Julius Stone, *Province and function of law*, Maitland, Sydney, 1950, 415; *Legal system and lawyers' reasonings*, Maitland, Sydney, 1964, 321. See further the discussion of judicial decision making in chapter 7.
30 Llewellyn, *Jurisprudence*.
31 Marc Galanter, 'Why the "haves" come out ahead: speculations on the limits of legal change' (1974) 9 *Law and Society Review* 95.
32 E. P. Thompson, *Whigs and hunters: the origins of the Black Act*, Penguin, Harmondsworth, 1977, 259.
33 Refer to the discussion of the rule of law in chapter 2.
34 Thompson, *Whigs and hunters*.
35 ibid. 263.
36 ibid. 261.
37 For an example of this see the discussion of the Land Titles Validation Act (Vic.) in chapter 5.
38 John Updike, *Rabbit redux*, in *A rabbit omnibus*, Penguin, London, 1981, 332.
39 Isaac Balbus, 'Commodity form and legal form: an essay on the relative autonomy of law' (1977) 11 *Law and Society Review* 571.
40 ibid. 577.
41 See generally Louis Althusser, *For Marx*, Allen Lane, London, 1969; Antonio Gramsci, *Selections from the prison notebooks*, Lawrence & Wishart, London, 1971. For an application of this model to law, see Colin Sumner, *Reading ideologies: an investigation into the marxist theory of ideology and law*, Academic Press, London, 1979.
42 Karl Marx and Friedrich Engels, 'The German ideology', in Karl Marx, *The essential writings*, ed. F. L. Bender, Harper & Row, New York, 1972, 183.
43 Althusser, *For Marx*; *Lenin and philosophy and other essays*, Left Books, New York, 1971.

Notes

44 Gramsci, *Prison notebooks*, 12–14, 245, and generally 206–77.
45 According to Professor Reisner, 'a Marxist can study law only as a sub-category of the species Ideology'. Quoted in Evegeny Pashukanis, *Law and marxism*, Ink Links, London, 1978, 72.
46 N. Poulantzas, *Political power and social class*, Humanities Press, Atlantic Fields, New Jersey, 1973; *State, power and socialism*, New Left Books, London, 1978.
47 See further the discussions of compulsory conciliation and arbitration systems and occupational health and safety legislation in chapter 5.
48 *Australian Capital Television Pty Ltd v Commonwealth* (1992) 177 CLR 106, discussed previously in chapter 2.
49 *The Political Broadcasts and Political Disclosures Act 1991 (Cwlth)* introduced into the *Broadcasting Act 1942 (Cwlth)* a Part IIID which purported to prohibit broadcast of election material in relation to Commonwealth, State or Territory elections (ss. 95B, 95C, 95D). The Act also required broadcasters to make free time available to certain qualifying political parties.
50 Herbert Marcuse, 'Repressive tolerance', in *A critique of pure tolerance*, eds Herbert Marcuse, Barrington Moore Jr and Robert Paul Wolff, Cape, London, 1965, 93–139.
51 See the discussion of Parsons in chapter 3.
52 See D. Wolff, *In defence of anarchism*, Pantheon, New York, 1978, 3–19.
53 See the discussion of instrumental marxism and the work of Jerome Frank and Karl Llewellyn.
54 On the English movement see P. Goodrich, 'Critical legal studies in England: prospective histories' (1992) 12 *Oxford Journal of Legal Studies* 195.
55 See R. W. Gordon, 'New developments in legal theory', in *The politics of law*, ed. D. Kairys, Pantheon Books, New York, 1982, 281.
56 See, for example, Galanter, 'Why the "haves" come out ahead'; G. Binder, 'On critical legal studies as guerrilla warfare' (1987) 76 *Georgetown Law Journal* 1, 27–8.
57 See the discussion of the rule of law in chapter 2.
58 Ronald Dworkin, *A matter of principle*, Harvard University Press, Cambridge, 1985.
59 See A. Altman, *Critical legal studies: a liberal critique*, Princeton University Press, Princeton, 1990, 22–7.
60 C. Norris, 'Law, deconstruction, and the resistance to theory' (1988) 15 *Journal of Law and Society* 166.
61 Clifford Geertz, *Local knowledge*, Basic Books, New York, 1983, 173.
62 Gerald Frug, 'A critical theory of law' (1989) 1 *Legal Education Review* 43; Gordon, 'New developments in legal theory', 291–2.
63 See the section on postmodernism, below, for an explanation of deconstruction.
64 Duncan Kennedy, 'The structure of Blackstone's Commentaries' (1979) 28 *Buffalo Law Review* 205. Blackstone's exposition of the English common law principles relating to colonisation was discussed in chapter 1.
65 See A. Freeman, 'Legitimizing racial discrimination through antidiscrimination law' (1978) 62 *Minnesota Law Review* 1049. See also Duncan Kennedy, 'Legal formality' (1973) 2 *Journal of Legal Studies* 351; Karl Klare, 'Judicial deradicalization of the Wagner Act and the origins of modern legal consciousness, 1937–1941' (1978) 62 *Minnesota Law Review* 265.
66 See e.g. Frances Olsen, 'The myth of state intervention in the family' (1985)

18 *University of Michigan Journal of Law Reform* 835. This article is discussed in the section on feminism, below.
67 See e.g. Mark Kelman, 'Trashing' (1984) 36 *Stanford Law Review* 293.
68 Roberto M. Unger, *Politics: a work in constructive social theory*, Cambridge University Press, Cambridge, 1987.
69 See e.g. Roger Cotterrell, 'Feasible regulation for democracy and social justice' (1988) 15 *Journal of Law and Society* 5, 6.
70 In 1960 there were just over 6500 lawyers in Australia. At the end of 1992 there were 27,762 lawyers, with a further 19,481 students in law schools: John Birmingham, 'The long tentacles of the law', *Independent Monthly*, August 1993, 16.
71 The Commonwealth parliament passed around 1000 Acts totalling 7500 pages in the 1960s, compared to nearly 1700 Acts totalling 30,000 pages in the 1980s: ibid.
72 Roberto M. Unger, *Law in modern society: towards a criticism of social theory*, Free Press, New York, 1975. See also Cotterrell, 'Feasible regulation for democracy and social justice'.
73 See e.g. D. J. Galligan, *Discretionary powers: a legal study of official discretion*, Clarendon Press, Oxford, 1986.
74 Mechanisms for the review of administrative decision making in Australia include administrative appeals tribunals, ombudsmen, the *Administrative Law Act 1978 (Vic.)* and the *Administrative Decisions (Judicial Review) Act 1977 (Cwlth)*. See also the discussion of Weber in chapter 3.
75 This case was discussed in chapter 2 (see What is a liberal?) and in a previous section of this chapter (Law as ideology).
76 This aspect of the Murray Islands case is discussed in chapter 1.
77 Unger, *Law in modern society*, 194–200.
78 ibid. 200.
79 Refer back to chapter 2.
80 S. Lukes, 'Can a marxist believe in human rights?' (1982) 1 *Praxis International* 344.
81 Kennedy, 'The structure of Blackstone's Commentaries', 213.
82 Mark Tushnet, 'An essay on rights' (1984) 62 *Texas Law Review* 1363, 1364–71. See also Mark Tushnet, 'Rights: an essay in informal political theory' (1989) 17 *Politics and Society* 403.
83 See e.g. *Buckley v Valeo* 424 US 1 (1976). See D. Kairys, 'Freedom of speech', in *The politics of law*, ed. Kairys, 140, 141.
84 Tushnet, 'An essay on rights', 1371–2.
85 P. Gabel and P. Harris, 'Building power and breaking images: critical legal theory and the practice of law' (1982–83) 11 *New York Review of Law and Social Change* 369, 375–6.
86 Tushnet, 'An essay on rights', 410.
87 Liberals have also sought to defend liberalism from the attacks of CLS. See e.g. Ronald Dworkin, *Law's empire*, Harvard University Press, Cambridge, Mass., 1986, 440–4.
88 See Richard Delgado, 'The ethereal scholar: does critical legal studies have what minorities want?' (1987) 22 *Harvard Civil Rights–Civil Liberties Law Review* 304; Richard Delgado, 'Critical legal studies and the realities of race—does the fundamental contradiction have a corollary?' (1988) 23 *Harvard Civil Rights–Civil Liberties Law Review* 407; Mari J. Matsuda, 'Looking to

the bottom: critical legal studies and reparations' (1987) 22 *Harvard Civil Rights–Civil Liberties Law Review* 323.
89 Patricia J. Williams, 'Alchemical notes: reconstructing ideals from deconstructed rights' (1987) 22 *Harvard Civil Rights–Civil Liberties Law Review* 401, 431. See also Williams, *The alchemy of race and rights*, 147–159.
90 Martha Minow, 'Interpreting rights: an essay for Robert Cover' (1987) 96 *Yale Law Journal* 1860, 1910.
91 S. Sedley, 'Freedom of speech for Rupert Murdoch?', *London Review of Books*, vol. 13, no. 24, 19 December 1991, 5.
92 Minow, 'Interpreting rights', 1881.
93 Sandra Berns, *Concise jurisprudence*, Federation Press, Sydney, 1993, 18. See also Mari J. Matsuda, 'Voices of America: accent, antidiscrimination law, and a jurisprudence for the last reconstruction' (1990) 100 *Yale Law Journal* 1329.
94 This section draws on H. Charlesworth, 'Critical legal education' (1990) 5 *Australian Journal of Law and Society* 27.
95 Duncan Kennedy, 'Legal education as training for hierarchy', in *The politics of law*, ed. Kairys, 40.
96 John Goldring suggests that the lack of a tradition in Australia of full-time teachers of law may be one reason why this is so. Until recently Australian law teachers were drawn from the ranks of practitioners and since then 'law teachers have felt a need to continue to provide courses which are largely descriptive, and which neither challenge basic assumptions nor seek to relate what is described to a wider social environment': John Goldring, 'Babies and bathwater: tradition or progress in legal scholarship and legal education' (1987) 17 *University of Western Australia Law Review* 216, 244. See also M. Chesterman and D. Weisbrot, 'Legal scholarship in Australia' (1987) 50 *Modern Law Review* 709, 710–13.
97 D. Kairys, 'Introduction', in *The politics of law*, ed. Kairys, 3.
98 ibid. 1–2. See also the discussion of judicial decision making in chapter 7.
99 D. Kairys, 'Legal reasoning', in *The politics of law*, ed. Kairys.
100 Kennedy, 'Legal education as training for hierarchy', 45.
101 Gordon, 'New developments in legal theory'.
102 See, for example, the 'policy' arguments invoked by the High Court in *Giannarelli v Wraith* (1988) 165 CLR 543 and by the House of Lords in *Hill v Chief Constable of West Yorkshire* [1989] AC 53.
103 See Marlene Le Brun and Richard Johnstone, *The quiet (r)evolution. Improving student learning in law*, Law Book Co., Sydney, 1994, chs 1, 3, 5–7, 9.
104 For a commentary on this point see Alex M. Johnson Jr, 'Think like a lawyer, work like a machine: the dissonance between law school and law practice' (1991) 64 *Southern California Law Review* 1231.
105 Kennedy, 'Legal education as training for hierarchy', 53–61.
106 ibid. 59.
107 See e.g. Ian Duncanson, 'Legal education and the possibility of critique: an Australian perspective' (1993) 8 *Canadian Journal of Law and Society* 59.
108 Functionalists make a similar argument (see the discussion of Parsons in chapter 3), but they see this as a good thing rather than a bad thing.
109 Frug, 'A critical theory of law', 49; R. W. Gordon, 'Critical legal studies as a teaching method' (1989) 1 *Legal Education Review* 59, 77.

110 Gordon, ibid. 68. Note that functionalists assert that participants in the legal system *do* share a set of values. See the discussion of Parsons in chapter 3.
111 J. Boyle, 'Anatomy of a torts class' (1985) 34 *American University Law Review* 1003, 1020–4; Frug, 'A critical theory of law', 44–51.
112 J. Feinman, 'Priests and prophets' (1986) 35 *St Louis University Law Journal* 53, 59.
113 R. W. Gordon, 'Historicism in legal scholarship' (1981) *Yale Law Journal* 1017, 1018–24.
114 Kennedy, 'Legal education as training for hierarchy', 52.
115 On the objectives of legal education (and appropriate methods of assessment to meet those objectives) see Le Brun and Johnstone, *The quiet (r)evolution*, ch. 4.
116 On assessment generally, see Derek Rowntree, *Assessing students: how shall we know them?*, Kogan Page, London, 1977.
117 Kennedy, 'Legal education as training for hierarchy', 51–2.
118 Goldring, 'Babies and bathwater', 217.
119 Mark Tushnet, 'Scenes from the metropolitan underground: a critical perspective on the status of clinical legal education' (1984) 52 *George Washington Law Review* 272, 273–5.
120 See A. J. Goldsmith, 'An unruly conjunction? Social thought and legal action in clinical legal education' (1993) 43 *Journal of Legal Education* 415.
121 Paul Carrington, 'Of law and the river' (1984) 34 *Journal of Legal Education* 222, 226–7.
122 ibid. 227.
123 D. C. Pearce, *Australian law schools: a discipline assessment for the Commonwealth Tertiary Education Commission*, AGPS, Canberra, 1987, para. 1.118.
124 The report's strong criticism of Macquarie Law School, leading to a recommendation for its radical restructuring or closure, was linked to the identification of that institution's staff with the CLS movement. See paras 1.119, 22.56–71. The Pearce Report's concern about the effect of CLS, particularly at Macquarie, was taken up and amplified in the Australian press. Thus the columnist P. P. McGuinness wrote in the *Financial Review* that proponents of CLS should not be allowed to teach in law schools because 'it is their avowed intention not to teach law in a way that will be useful to practitioners in the actual legal system': 'Legal creation science', *Australian Financial Review*, 1 February 1989. See also editorial, 'The trouble with a law school', *Sydney Morning Herald*, 10 January 1989.
125 This was clearly not the Pearce committee's view. One of its conclusions was that 'all law schools should examine the adequacy of their attention to theoretical and critical perspectives, the study of law in operation and of the relations generally between the law and other social forces and considerations': paras 1.143, 1.149.
126 See e.g. A. Hutchinson and Monahan, 'Law, politics, and the critical legal scholars: the unfolding drama of American legal thought' (1984) 36 *Stanford Law Review* 199, 238; D. Brosnan, 'Serious but not critical' (1986) 60 *Southern California Law Review* 259, 262–8.
127 See e.g. Gerald Frug, 'The city as a legal concept' (1980) 93 *Harvard Law Review* 1057; Roberto Unger, 'The critical legal studies movement' (1983) 96 *Harvard Law Review* 561.
128 Carrington, 'Of law and the river', 227.

Notes

129 Owen Fiss, 'The death of the law?' (1986–87) 72 *Cornell Law Review* 1, 10–13.
130 ibid. 10.
131 ibid. 16.
132 Mark Tushnet, 'Critical legal studies: an introduction to its origins and underpinnings' (1986) 36 *Journal of Legal Education* 505, 510.
133 Unger, *Law in modern society*, 238–41.
134 Hunt, 'The big fear', 540.
135 For a discussion of the relationship between CLS and feminist legal thought see Deborah L. Rhode, 'Feminist critical theories' (1990) 42 *Stanford Law Review* 617 and Robin West, 'Jurisprudence and gender' (1988) 55 *University of Chicago Law Review* 1.
136 Lucinda M. Finley, 'Breaking women's silence in law: the dilemma of the gendered nature of legal reasoning' (1989) 64 *Notre Dame Law Review* 886, 898; quoted in Regina Graycar and Jenny Morgan, *The hidden gender of law*, Federation Press, Sydney, 1990, 3.
137 Catharine A. MacKinnon, 'Feminism in legal education' (1989) 1 *Legal Education Review* 85.
138 For example, in 1985, 89 per cent of female sole parents received social security payments compared with 9 per cent of all married couples with dependent children: Graycar and Morgan, *The hidden gender of law*, 69.
139 National Women's Consultative Council and Labour Research Centre, *Pay equity for women in Australia*, AGPS, Canberra, 1990.
140 For example, in December 1993 women made up 8.84 per cent of the (federal) House of Representatives and 21.1 per cent of the Senate, while 14.2 per cent of all State and Territory politicians were women: Australian Law Reform Commission, *Discussion paper no. 54: equality before the law*, AGPS, Canberra, 1993, 59–60.
141 Australian Law Reform Commission, *Report no. 67: interim report on equality before the law*, AGPS, Canberra, 1994.
142 Larissa Behrendt, 'Aboriginal women and the white lies of the feminist movement: implications for Aboriginal women in rights discourse' (1993) 1 *Australian Feminist Law Journal* 27, 32, 34. See also Angela P. Harris, 'Categorical discourse and dominance theory' (1989–90) 4 *Berkeley Women's Law Journal* 181, 182.
143 Behrendt, ibid. 33.
144 Ngaire Naffine, *Law and the sexes*, Allen & Unwin, Sydney, 1990, 21.
145 A very useful overview of feminist legal theory is contained in Graycar and Morgan, *The hidden gender of law*.
146 The term 'liberal promise' was used by Margaret Thornton in the title of her book about equal opportunity legislation: *The liberal promise: anti-discrimination legislation in Australia*, Oxford University Press, Melbourne, 1990.
147 For a discussion of historical arguments for and against protective provisions see Carol Lee Bacchi, *Same difference: feminism and sexual difference*, Allen & Unwin, Sydney, 1990.
148 See *Najdovska v Australian Iron & Steel Pty Ltd* (1985) EOC 92–140.
149 See *Discrimination against women in the lead industry*, Occasional Papers from the Sex Discrimination Commissioner, No. 5, Human Rights and Equal Opportunity Commission, Sydney, 1990; *Human Rights and Equal Opportunity Commission v Mount Isa Mines*, digested at (1993) EOC 92–548.

150 See the section on the rule of law and the concept of equality.
151 Frances E. Olsen, 'Feminism and critical legal theory: an American perspective' (1990) 18 *International Journal of the Sociology of Law* 199, 203. See also s. 33 of the Sex Discrimination Act (Cwlth), which allows special measures to be taken for persons of a particular sex or marital status, or for pregnant women, so long as they have 'a purpose of . . . ensur[ing] that persons of a particular sex or marital status, or persons who are pregnant, have *equal opportunities* with other persons'.
152 Sandra Harding, *The science question in feminism*, Cornell University Press, Ithaca, 1986, 25.
153 Nicola Lacey, 'Legislation against sex discrimination: questions from a feminist perspective' (1987) 14 *Journal of Law and Society* 411, 415.
154 ibid. 420.
155 Clare Dalton, 'Where we stand: observations on the situation of feminist legal thought' (1987–88) 3 *Berkeley Women's Law Journal* 1, 5.
156 Harding, *The science question in feminism*, 26.
157 Carol Gilligan, *In a different voice*, Harvard University Press, Cambridge, Mass., 1982.
158 Lawrence Kohlberg, *The philosophy of moral development: moral stages and the idea of justice*, Harper & Row, San Francisco, 1981.
159 See e.g. D. Nails, 'Social scientific sexism: Gilligan's mismeasure of man' (1983) 50 *Social Research* 643; M. T. Mednick, 'On the politics of psychological constructs' (1989) 44 *American Psychologist* 1118.
160 Olsen, 'Feminism and critical legal theory'. Katharine Bartlett has argued that there is no sharp dichotomy between abstract and contextualised reasoning in either legal or feminist method: 'Feminist legal methods' (1990) 103 *Harvard Law Review* 829, 856–8.
161 Leslie Bender, 'A lawyer's primer on feminist theory and tort' (1988) 38 *Journal of Legal Education* 3, 20–5; Lucinda M. Finley, 'A break in the silence: including women's issues in a torts course' (1989) 1 *Yale Journal of Law and Feminism* 41, 57–65.
162 Christine Boyle, 'Book review' (1985) 63 *Canadian Bar Review* 427, 430–1.
163 L. Henderson, 'Legality and empathy' (1987) 85 *Michigan Law Review* 1574.
164 Carrie Menkel-Meadow, 'Portia in a different voice: speculations on a women's lawyering process' (1985) 1 *Berkeley Women's Law Journal* 39.
165 Susanna Sherry, 'Civic virtue and the feminine voice in constitutional adjudication' (1986) 72 *Virginia Law Review* 543, 594–5. See also K. Karst, 'Woman's constitution' (1984) *Duke Law Journal* 447; Catherine Iorns, 'A sexed bill of rights for New Zealand?' (1987) 17 *Victoria University of Wellington Law Review* 215.
166 Madame Justice Bertha Wilson, 'Will women judges really make a difference?' (1990) 28 *Osgoode Hall Law Journal* 507. See also Judith Resnick, 'On the bias: feminist reconsideration of the aspirations for our judges' (1988) 61 *Southern California Law Review* 1877; Sean Cooney, 'Gender and judicial selection: should there be more women on the courts?' (1993) 19 *Melbourne University Law Review* 31.
167 Ann Scales, 'The emergence of feminist jurisprudence: an essay' (1986) 95 *Yale Law Journal* 1373, 1381. *Uncle Tom's Cabin* was an anti-slavery novel by Harriet Beecher Stowe, first published in serial form in 1851–52. Although a liberal text at the time, the novel's image of the Christian slave Uncle Tom

Notes

stoically accepting his fate and forgiving his masters has since been recognised as antithetical to the civil rights cause.

168 Renata Alexander, 'Practising feminism: painting pictures of lives in law' (1994) 2 *Australian Feminist Law Journal* 150, 159–60; Hilary Astor and Christine M. Chinkin, *Dispute resolution in Australia*, Butterworths, Sydney, 1992, 109–12; Anne Bottomley, 'Resolving family disputes: a critical view', in *The state, the law and the family*, ed. M. D. A. Freeman, Tavistock, London, 1984, 293–303; Lisa Lerman, 'Mediation of wife abuse cases: the adverse impact of informal dispute resolution on women' (1984) 7 *Harvard Women's Law Journal* 57; Janet Rifkin, 'Mediation from a feminist perspective: promises and problems' (1984) 2 *Law and Inequality* 21.
169 Mary Joe Frug, 'Progressive feminist legal scholarship: can we claim "a different voice"?' (1992) 15 *Harvard Women's Law Journal* 37.
170 Catharine A. MacKinnon, *Feminism unmodified: discourses on life and law*, Harvard University Press, Cambridge, Mass., 1987, 39.
171 ibid. 45.
172 ibid. 34. See also Lacey, 'Legislation against sex discrimination', 417.
173 MacKinnon, *Feminism unmodified*, 3.
174 ibid. 205.
175 MacKinnon, 'Feminism, marxism, method and the state', 639.
176 ibid. 635–40.
177 See further the discussion of persuasive arguments and interpretive communities in chapter 7.
178 Catharine A. MacKinnon, *Sexual harassment of working women*, Yale University Press, New Haven, 1979.
179 MacKinnon, *Feminism unmodified*, 127–213.
180 ibid. 104.
181 MacKinnon, 'Difference and dominance: on sex discrimination', in *Feminism unmodified*, 32–45.
182 Christine Littleton, 'Equality and feminist legal theory' (1987) 48 *University of Pittsburgh Law Review* 1043, 1052. Similarly, Riki Holtmaat describes a feminist 'other law' which systematically takes women's needs into account: 'The power of legal concepts: the development of a feminist theory of law' (1989) 17 *International Journal of the Sociology of Law* 481, 492–4.
183 Carol Smart, *Feminism and the power of law*, Routledge, London, 1989, 75–7.
184 Rhode, 'Feminist critical theories', 624–5; Patricia A. Cain, 'Feminist jurisprudence: grounding the theories' (1989–90) 4 *Berkeley Women's Law Journal* 191, 197–205; Angela P. Harris, 'Race and essentialism in feminist legal theory' (1990) 42 *Stanford Law Review* 580, 590–601.
185 See e.g. Catharine A. MacKinnon, 'From practice to theory, or what is a white woman anyway?' (1991) 4 *Yale Journal of Law and Feminism* 13.
186 Joan W. Scott, 'Deconstructing equality-versus-difference: or, the uses of post-structuralist theory for feminism' (1988) 14 *Feminist Studies* 33, 34. See also D. Currie, 'Feminist encounters with postmodernism: exploring the impasse of debates on patriarchy and law' (1992) 5 *Canadian Journal of Women and the Law* 63; 'For Mary Joe Frug: a symposium on feminist critical legal studies and postmodernism' (1992) 26 *New England Law Review* 639.
187 These three theorists are discussed in chapter 3.
188 See the first section of this chapter.
189 ibid. 70–2; Bartlett, 'Feminist legal methods', 872–7. In a review of MacKinnon's

Feminism unmodified Frances Olsen defends MacKinnon's 'grand theory' as analytically useful and politically mobilising, even if oversimplified: 'Feminist theory in grand style' (1989) 89 *Columbia Law Review* 1147.
190 Smart, *Feminism and the power of law*, 68–9.
191 Harding, *The science question in feminism*, 28. See also D. Patterson, 'Postmodernism/feminism/law' (1992) 77 *Cornell Law Review* 254.
192 Williams, *The alchemy of race and rights*, 6–7.
193 ibid. 7.
194 ibid. 3.
195 See, for example, Daniel A. Farber and Suzanna Sherry, 'Telling stories out of school: an essay on legal narratives' (1993) 45 *Stanford Law Review* 807.
196 Berns, *Concise jurisprudence*, ch. 6.
197 Scott, 'Deconstructing equality-versus-difference'; Mary Joe Frug, *Postmodern legal feminism*, Routledge, New York, 1992, 3–29.
198 Judith G. Greenberg, 'Introduction', in Frug, ibid. xxiii.
199 ibid. xxix.
200 Frug, *Postmodern legal feminism*, 126.
201 Smart, *Feminism and the power of law*, 81, 88–9.
202 ibid. 87.
203 Carol Smart, 'Feminist jurisprudence', seminar at La Trobe University, December 1987.
204 See e.g. M. Z. Rosaldo, 'Women, culture, and society: a theoretical overview', in *Women, culture and society*, eds M. Z. Rosaldo and L. Lamphere, Stanford University Press, Stanford, 1974, 17; Carole Pateman, 'Feminist critiques of the public/private dichotomy', in *Public and private in social life*, eds S. I. Benn and G. F. Gaus, Croom Helm, Canberra, 1983, 281. The public/private distinction as a liberal tenet was introduced in chapter 2.
205 Olsen, 'Feminism and critical legal theory'; Margaret Thornton, 'Feminist jurisprudence: illusion or reality?' (1986) 3 *Australian Journal of Law and Society* 5, 6–7.
206 Katherine O'Donovan, *Sexual divisions in law*, Weidenfeld & Nicolson, London, 1985; Tove Stang Dahl and A. Snare, 'The coercion of privacy', in *Women, sexuality and social control*, eds Carol Smart and Barry Smart, Routledge, London, 1978, 8.
207 See *Crimes against women: proceedings of the international tribunal*, eds D. Russell and N. Van de Wen, Frog in the Well, East Palo Alto, 1984, 58–67, 110–175.
208 See e.g. Regina Graycar, 'Hoovering as a hobby: the common law's approach to work in the home' (1985) 28 *Refractory Girl*, 22; 'Women's work: who cares?' (1992) 14 *Sydney Law Review* 86.
209 O'Donovan, *Sexual divisions in law*, 3, 6.
210 ibid. 7–8.
211 Olsen, 'The myth of state intervention in the family'.
212 ibid. 846.
213 ibid. 837.
214 ibid. 842.
215 ibid. 843.
216 O'Donovan, *Sexual divisions in law*, 7–8.
217 ibid. 8. See also Rosemary Hunter, 'The representation of gender in legal

analysis: a case/book study of labour law' (1991) 18 *Melbourne University Law Review* 305.
218 Susan Moller Okin, *Justice, gender and the family*, Basic Books, New York, 1989.
219 Elizabeth Gross, 'What is feminist theory?', in *Feminist challenges: social and political theory*, eds Carole Pateman and Elizabeth Gross, Allen & Unwin, Sydney, 1986, 192; Smart, *Feminism and the power of law*, 138–9.
220 Jenny Morgan, 'Equality rights in the Australian context: a feminist assessment', in *Towards an Australian Bill of Rights*, ed. Philip Alston, Oxford University Press, Sydney, forthcoming 1994, 1 of MS.
221 Smart, *Feminism and the power of law*, 144.
222 ibid.
223 ibid. 146–57. For a discussion of the feminist ambivalence towards 'gendered' laws such as statutory rape laws see Frances E. Olsen, 'Statutory rape: a critique of rights analysis' (1984) 63 *Texas Law Review* 387.
224 Smart, *Feminism and the power of law*, 145.
225 See *R v Seaboyer; R v Gayme* [1991] 2 SCR 577, discussed in Elizabeth Sheehy, 'Feminist argumentation before the Supreme Court of Canada in *R v Seaboyer; R v Gayme*: the sound of one hand clapping' (1991) 18 *Melbourne University Law Review* 450.
226 Smart, *Feminism and the power of law*, 145. For a similar argument in the Canadian context see Joel Bakan, 'Constitutional interpretation and social change: you can't always get what you want (nor what you need)' (1991) 70 *Canadian Bar Review* 307.
227 See D. Arzt, 'The application of international human rights law in Islamic states' (1990) 12 *Human Rights Quarterly* 202, 203.
228 See House of Representatives Standing Committee on Legal and Constitutional Affairs, *Half way to equal: report of the inquiry into equal opportunity and equal status for women in Australia*, AGPS, Canberra, 1992, paras 10.1.92–101; Kirsty Magarey, 'Discrimination and the church' (1991) *Reform* no. 62, 101; Archbishop Frank Little, 'Religion and discrimination: the archbishop responds', the *Age*, 14 June 1993.
229 Morgan, 'Equality rights in the Australian context', 8.
230 ibid. 23.
231 Dianne Otto, 'Violence against women—something *other* than a violation of human rights?' (1993) 1 *Australian Feminist Law Journal* 159, 162.
232 See e.g. Jacques Derrida, 'Force of law: the mystical foundation of authority' (1990) 11 *Cardozo Law Review* 919.
233 See chapter 2.
234 See e.g. Jean-Francois Lyotard, *The postmodern condition: a report on knowledge*, Manchester University Press, Manchester, 1984; Derrida, 'Force of law'.
235 See e.g. Jean Baudrillard, *America*, trans. Chris Turner, Verso Books, London, 1988; *Selected writings*, ed. M. Poster, Polity Press, Cambridge, 1988.
236 See e.g. Alan Hunt 'The big fear: law confronts postmodernism' (1990) 35 *McGill Law Journal* 522.
237 See e.g. Roland Barthes, *Mythologies*, trans. A. Lavers, Paladin Grafton, London, 1973; Frederic Jameson, *Postmodernism, or, the cultural logic of late capitalism*, Duke University Press, Durham, 1991; Stanley Fish, *Doing what comes naturally: change, rhetoric and the practice of theory in literary and legal studies*, Clarendon Press, Oxford, 1989.

238 C. Norris, *What's wrong with postmodernism: critical theory and the ends of philosophy*, Johns Hopkins University Press, Baltimore, 1990.
239 See e.g. Frederick Nietzsche, *A Nietzsche reader*, ed. R. Hollingdale, Penguin, Harmondsworth, 1977.
240 See chapter 2, discussions of liberalism (Nozick), the relationship between law and morality (Hart, Finnis), and constitutional theory.
241 See chapter 3.
242 See the first section of this chapter.
243 This phrase is Ronald Dworkin's: see the discussion of judicial decision making in chapter 7.
244 Richard Rorty, 'The intellectuals at the end of socialism', *Harper's Magazine*, May 1992, 16–19.
245 See e.g. Williams, *The alchemy of race and rights*; *Race-ing justice, en-gendering power: essays on Anita Hill, Clarence Thomas and the construction of social reality*, ed. Toni Morrison, Chatto & Windus, London, 1993.
246 See further the discussion of judicial decision making in chapter 7.
247 Michel Foucault, *Madness and civilisation*, Tavistock, London, 1961; *The archeology of knowledge*, Harper & Row, New York, 1972; *The birth of the clinic*, Tavistock, London, 1973; *The order of things: an archeology of the human sciences*, Vintage Books, New York, 1973; *Discipline and punish; the birth of the prison*, Penguin, Harmondsworth, 1977; *Power/knowledge*, Harvester Press, Brighton, 1980; *Remarks on Marx*, Semiotext, Columbia University Press, New York, 1988.
248 Michel Foucault, *The history of sexuality: an introduction*, Tavistock, London, 1979.
249 Smart, *Feminism and the power of law*. See the discussion of postmodernist feminism, above.
250 Margaret Davies, *Asking the law question*, Law Book Co., Sydney, 1994, 253–4.
251 See e.g. Susan H. Williams, 'Feminist legal epistemology' (1993) 8 *Berkeley Women's Law Journal* 63, 64–6.
252 This is similar to Catharine MacKinnon's epistemological argument about the system of male power operating to represent the male perspective as objective truth. Foucault, however, would disagree as to the existence of a totalising system of male power. Likewise, the marxist argument that law is ideological in that it projects a version of reality in the interests of the capitalist class differs from Foucault's argument in its understanding of power and of who may use it.
253 For a detailed account of Saussurian linguistics and structuralism see Davies, *Asking the law question*, 229–36.
254 David Kennedy, 'Critical theory, structuralism and contemporary legal scholarship' (1985–86) 21 *New England Law Review* 209.
255 Scott, 'Deconstructing equality-versus-difference', 35.
256 Roland Barthes, *S/Z*, trans. R. Miller, Hill & Wang, New York, 1974. See also Roland Barthes, *The pleasure of the text*, trans. R. Miller, Hill & Wang, New York, 1975.
257 Roland Barthes, *Image music text*, Fontana, London, 1977, 145–6.
258 Consider all of the ideas presented in the previous chapters in these terms.
259 Magdalen Troup, 'Rupturing the veil: feminism, deconstruction and the law' (1993) 1 *Australian Feminist Law Journal* 63, 66.

260 See e.g. Alan Hutchinson, *Dwelling on the threshold: critical essays on modern legal thought*, Carswell, Toronto, 1988, 23.
261 Unreported, 8 August 1991, County Court of Victoria; Troup, 'Rupturing the veil'.
262 ibid.
263 ibid. 81, 88.
264 Williams, 'Feminist legal epistemology', 91.
265 ibid. 83.
266 (1985) 159 CLR 71.
267 Geoff Airo-Farulla, '"Dirty deeds done dirt cheap": deconstruction, Derrida, discrimination and difference/ance in (the High) court' (1991) 9 *Law in Context* 102.

Chapter 5 Explaining law reform

1 See the discussion of H. L. A. Hart in the section on the relationship between law and morality in chapter 2.
2 Law Reform Commissions exist at federal level and in most States; in Victoria the Law Reform Commission was abolished by the Kennett government soon after it came to power in 1992.
3 See the discussion of utilitarianism in the section 'What is a liberal?' in chapter 2.
4 See W. Chambliss and R. Seidman, *Law, order and power*, Addison-Wesley, Reading, Mass., 2nd edn, 1982; Stephen Bottomley, Neil Gunningham and Stephen Parker, *Law in context*, Federation Press, Sydney, 1991, 314–5; Pat O'Malley, *Law, capitalism and democracy*, Allen & Unwin, Sydney, 1983, 19–20.
5 David Brereton, 'Theoretical perspectives on legislative innovation: the case of compulsory arbitration', in *Foundations of arbitration: the origins and effects of state compulsory arbitration 1890–1914*, eds Stuart Macintyre and Richard Mitchell, Oxford University Press, Melbourne, 1989, 296.
6 See the discussion of different versions of marxist legal thought in chapter 4.
7 See O'Malley, *Law, capitalism and democracy*, 19.
8 Catharine MacKinnon, 'Feminism, marxism, method, and the state: toward feminist jurisprudence' (1983) 8 *Signs* 635.
9 This is Nicola Lacey's argument in 'Legislation against sex discrimination: questions from a feminist perspective' (1987) 14 *Journal of Law and Society* 411.
10 Wayne Morgan, 'Identifying evil for what it is: Tasmania, sexual perversity and the United Nations' (1994) 19 *Melbourne University Law Review* 741.
11 ibid. 756–7.
12 ibid. 757.
13 See e.g. *Matrimonial Causes Act 1858 (SA)*; *Divorce and Matrimonial Causes Act 1861 (Vic.)*; *Matrimonial Causes Act 1873 (NSW)*.
14 *Divorce Law Amendment Act 1890 (Vic.)*; *Divorce Extension Act 1892 (NSW)*.
15 (1963) 4 *Sydney Law Review* 241.
16 Bennett, ibid. 243.
17 Margaret James, 'Not bread but a stone: women and divorce in colonial Victoria', in *Families in colonial Australia*, eds P. Grimshaw, C. McConville and E. McEwen, Allen & Unwin, Sydney, 1985, 42–56.

18 Hilary Golder, 'An exercise in unnecessary chivalry: the New South Wales Matrimonial Causes Act Amendment Act of 1881', in *In pursuit of justice: Australian women and the law 1788–1979* eds J. Mackinolty and H. Radi, Hale & Iremonger, Sydney, 1979, 46.
19 This consideration probably accounts for the fact that the majority of nineteenth century divorce litigants came from the middling and lower ranks of society, where a divorce would not be considered such a social disaster: ibid. 51, 53.
20 See further chapter 6—the invocation of law and the difference between the law in books and the law in action.
21 'Nothing to lose: women and divorce in South Australia 1859–1918', in *Feminism, law and society* ed. Judith Grbich, La Trobe University Press, Melbourne, 1990 (special issue of *Law in Context*, vol. 8 (2)), 70–91.
22 Golder, 'An exercise in unnecessary chivalry'.
23 ibid. 43.
24 ibid. 42–6.
25 ibid. 54.
26 There were constitutional restrictions on the powers of the Australian federal tribunal to deal with individual rights, but even State tribunals focused on interest disputes.
27 *Foundations of arbitration: the origins and effects of state compulsory arbitration 1890–1914*, Oxford University Press, Melbourne, 1989.
28 Diane Kirkby, 'Arbitration and the fight for economic justice', in ibid. 334–51; and references cited therein.
29 Michael Quinlan, '"Pre-arbitral" labour legislation in Australia: its implications for the introduction of compulsory arbitration', in ibid. 25–49.
30 ibid. 28.
31 See chapter 4—marxism.
32 Quinlan, '"Pre-arbitral" labour legislation', 27–9.
33 Richard Mitchell, 'State systems of conciliation and arbitration: the legal origins of the Australasian model', in *Foundations of arbitration*, eds Macintyre and Mitchell, 80.
34 R. J. Hawke, 'The Commonwealth arbitration court—legal tribunal or economic legislature?' (1956) 3 *University of Western Australia Annual Law Review* 422, 423. It should be noted that there had been earlier inquiries on the subject, predating the great strikes; for example, the 1884 Victorian Royal Commission and the 1889 Canadian Royal Commission on the Relations of Labour and Capital.
35 David Plowman, 'Forced march: the employers and arbitration', in *Foundations of arbitration*, eds Macintyre and Mitchell, 135–55.
36 See Ray Markey, 'Trade unions, the Labor party and the introduction of arbitration in New South Wales and the Commonwealth', in ibid. 157; Jack Hutson, *penal colony to Penal powers*, Amalgamated Engineering Union, Sydney, 1966.
37 Plowman, 'Forced march', 135–55. Employer opposition was manifested after the passage of federal conciliation and arbitration legislation in frequent High Court challenges to the constitutionality of various aspects of the system: David Plowman and Graham Smith, 'Moulding federal arbitration: the employers and the High Court, 1903–1935' (1986) 2 *Australian Journal of Management* 203.

38 Markey, 'Trade unions, the Labor party and the introduction of arbitration', 156–77.
39 Stuart Macintyre, 'Neither capital nor labour: the politics of the establishment of arbitration', in *Foundations of arbitration*, eds Macintyre and Mitchell, 178–200.
40 ibid. 185.
41 A. V. Dicey, *Lectures on the relation between law and public opinion in England during the nineteenth century*, Macmillan, London, 1963 (1st edn, 1905), 190–1, 347; Stuart Macintyre, *A colonial liberalism: the lost world of three Victorian visionaries*, Oxford University Press, Melbourne, 1991, 201–2, 206 (regarding divorce reform in Victoria).
42 J. H. Baker, *An introduction to English legal history*, Butterworths, London, 2nd edn, 1979, 187; Macintyre, ibid. 196. See the distinction in chapter 2 between laissez faire and welfare liberalism.
43 Andrew Frazer, 'Conceptions of law and industrial arbitration in New South Wales, 1880–1901', in *Law and history in Australia, Vol. IV*, ed. Diane Kirkby, La Trobe University, Bundoora, 1987, 111–33.
44 Mitchell, 'State systems of conciliation and arbitration', 85–7.
45 Frazer, 'Conceptions of law and industrial arbitration', 122–5.
46 Macintyre, 'Neither capital nor labour', 187.
47 Frazer, 'Conceptions of law and industrial arbitration', 125 and n. 66.
48 ibid. 125.
49 See H. B. Higgins, 'A new province for law and order' (1915) 29 *Harvard Law Review* 13.
50 Brereton, 'Theoretical perspectives on legislative innovation', 293–312.
51 ibid. 296–9.
52 ibid. 300–9.
53 ibid. 296–9.
54 *Report of the Committee on Safety and Health at Work 1970–72*, London, HMSO, 1972.
55 Jenny Doran, 'Implementing the Victorian government's policy on occupational health and safety—1982–1984', in *The industrial relations of occupational health and safety*, eds W. B. Creighton and N. Gunningham, Croom Helm, Sydney, 1985, ch. 8. See also W. B. Creighton, *Understanding occupational health and safety law in Victoria*, CCH, Melbourne, 1986, 11–13.
56 W. G. Carson and C. Henenberg, 'The political economy of legislative change: making sense of Victoria's new occupational health and safety legislation' (1988) 6 *Law in Context* 1.
57 For similar overseas studies see R. Elling, *The struggle for workers health*, Baywood Publishing Co., New York, 1986; V. Navarro, 'The determinants of social policy. A case study: regulating health and safety at the workplace in Sweden' (1983) 14 *International Journal of Health Services* 517; E. Tucker, 'Worker participation in health and safety regulation: lessons from Sweden' (1992) 37 *Studies in Political Economy* 95, 96–7. Tucker uses a model developed by W. Korpi in *The working class in welfare capitalism*, Routledge & Kegan Paul, London, 1978, 32–54. See also W. G. Carson, 'Occupational health and safety: a political economy perspective' (1989) 2 *Labour and Industry* 301.
58 Carson and Henenberg, 'The political economy of legislative change', 1.
59 The Accord re-established a centralised wage fixing system and initially was

aimed at controlling wages and prices. The Accord also referred to a number of 'supportive policies', which included appropriate action on occupational health and safety.

60 For a summary of the VALS submission see Mark Harris, 'Jeff Kennett, *Mabo* and the *Land Titles Validation Bill*' (1993) 3/64 *Aboriginal Law Bulletin* 22, 23.
61 The Committee's role was to consider the impact of proposed legislation on existing rights. It found that the provisions of the Land Titles Validation Bill on compensation for loss of 'customary title' could lead to a reduction in Aboriginal rights; the *Australian*, 11 August 1993.
62 *Victorian parliamentary debates*, Legislative Assembly, 20–22 July 1993, 82–8.
63 ibid. 83.
64 ibid. 87.
65 ibid. 83.
66 ibid. 88. See chapter 2 for the source of this 'basic tenet', and chapter 4 for the marxist critique thereof.
67 ibid. 84.
68 ibid. 84, 86, 87, 88.
69 ibid. 86.
70 See Garth Nettheim, 'Little evidence of uncertainty to justify Kennett's Mabo Bill', the *Australian*, 28 July 1993.
71 ibid.
72 ibid.
73 *Victorian parliamentary debates*, 20–22 July 1993, 86.
74 *Land Titles Validation Act 1993 (Vic.)*, s. 3.
75 *Victorian parliamentary debates*, 20–22 July 1993, 86.
76 ibid. 88.
77 See the discussion of liberalism in chapter 2, especially Nozick.
78 The Native Title Act is discussed in the section on the Murray Islands case in chapter 1.
79 *Victorian parliamentary debates*, 20–22 July 1993, 86.
80 See the discussion of deconstruction in the section in postmodernism in chapter 4.
81 This analogy was suggested by the Victorian Aboriginal Legal Service in an analysis of the Land Titles Validation Bill.
82 See e.g. Nettheim, 'Little evidence of uncertainty'.
83 See, for example, Geoff Airo-Farulla's analysis of *Gerhardy v Brown*, discussed towards the end of the section on postmodernism in chapter 4.
84 See the discussion at the end of the section on the Murray Islands case in chapter 1.
85 Roger Cotterrell, 'Feasible regulation for democracy and social justice' (1988) 15 *Journal of Law and Society* 5, 5.
86 ibid. 8.
87 ibid. 9.
88 ibid. 14–15.
89 ibid. 8–13.

Notes

Chapter 6 Invocation and enforcement of legal rules

1. Marc Galanter, 'Why the "haves" come out ahead: speculations on the limits of legal change' (1974) 9 *Law and Society Review* 95.
2. See the discussion of liberal feminism in that chapter.
3. See the discussion of legal positivism in chapter 2 and of Durkheim in chapter 3.
4. See generally H. Blumer, *Symbolic interactionism: perspectives and method*, Prentice Hall, New Jersey, 1969, ch. 1; I. Craib, *Modern social theory: from Parsons to Habermas*, Wheatsheaf Books, London, 1984, 72–4; G. H. Mead, *Mind, self and society*, University of Chicago Press, Chicago, 1934; E. Willis, *The sociological quest: an introduction to the study of social life*, Allen & Unwin, Sydney, 1993, 99–100.
5. See the discussion of Weber in chapter 3.
6. See the discussion of the functionalist theory of Talcott Parsons in chapter 3.
7. See the discussion of anthropological research methods in the first section of chapter 1.
8. Unlike economists, interactionists do not assume that individuals are rational maximisers of their own self interest. See chapter 3 on 'law and economics'.
9. M. Haralambros, *Sociology: themes and perspectives*, University Tutorial, Slough, 1st edn, 1980, 15–18, 543–52.
10. See the last section of chapter 4.
11. C. Wright Mills, *The sociological imagination*, Oxford University Press, Oxford, 1959, ch. 1.
12. Aaron Cicourel, *The social organisation of juvenile justice*, Wiley, New York, 1968, 183–90.
13. ibid. 185.
14. ibid. 190.
15. Greta Bird, *The 'civilising mission': race and the construction of crime*, Contemporary Legal Issues No. 4, Faculty of Law, Monash University, Melbourne, 1987, 29–31.
16. ibid. 30.
17. W. G. Carson, 'Some sociological aspects of strict liability and the enforcement of factory legislation' (1970) 33 *Modern Law Review* 896. See also La Trobe/Melbourne Occupational Health and Safety Project, *Victorian occupational health and safety—an assessment of law in transition*, National Centre for Socio-Legal Studies, La Trobe University, Bundoora, 1989, 45–8.
18. Keith Hawkins, *Environment and enforcement: regulation and the social definition of pollution*, Oxford University Press, Oxford, 1984.
19. ibid. 229.
20. ibid.
21. ibid. 231.
22. ibid. 229.
23. Keith Hawkins, 'On legal decision-making' (1986) 43 *Washington and Lee Law Review* 1161, 1191.
24. See e.g. Sally Lloyd-Bostock, 'The psychology of routine discretion: accident screening by British factory inspectors' (1992) 14 *Law and Policy* 45, 46.
25. ibid. 47.
26. ibid. 67.
27. W. G. Carson, 'The institutionalisation of ambiguity: early British Factory

Acts', in *White-collar crime: theory and research*, eds G. Gess and E. Scotland, Sage Publications, Beverly Hills, 1980; W. G. Carson, 'The conventionalisation of early factory crime' (1979) 7 *International Journal of the Sociology of Law* 37.
28 Carson, 'Some sociological aspects of strict liability', 45; Carson, 'The conventionalisation of early factory crime', 150–51.
29 Carson, 'The conventionalisation of early factory crime', 46; Carson, 'The institutionalisation of ambiguity', 152.
30 Carson, 'The conventionalisation of early factory crime', 48.
31 Carson, 'The institutionalisation of ambiguity', 167.
32 ibid. 169.
33 W. G. Carson and C. Henenberg, 'The political economy of legislative change: making sense of Victoria's new occupational health and safety legislation' (1988) 6 *Law in Context* 1. See the discussion of occupational health and safety, and of this article in particular, in chapter 5.
34 Bridget M. Hutter, 'Variations in regulatory enforcement styles' (1989) 11 *Law and Policy* 153.
35 Peter Grabosky, John Braithwaite and Paul Wilson, 'The myth of community tolerance of white collar crime' (1987) 20 *Australia and New Zealand Journal of Criminology* 33.
36 See the discussion of the public/private distinction in the section on feminism legal theories in chapter 4.
37 D. W. Harris et al., *Compensation and support for illness and injury*, Clarendon Press, Oxford, 1984, 46.
38 ibid. 46.
39 ibid. 47.
40 William L. F. Felstiner, Richard L. Abel, and Austin Sarat, 'The emergence and transformation of disputes: naming, blaming, claiming . . .' (1981) 15 *Law and Society Review* 631.
41 Carson and Henenberg, 'The political economy of legislative change'; S. Henry, *Private justice: towards integrated theorising in the sociology of law*, Routledge & Kegan Paul, London, 1983.
42 Harris et al., *Compensation and support for illness and injury*, 46.
43 See further the discussion of cost-benefit analysis in the section on 'law and economics' in chapter 3.
44 Robert H. Mnookin and Lewis Kornhauser, 'Bargaining in the shadow of the law: the case of divorce' (1979) 88 *Yale Law Journal* 950, 966.
45 Barbara Yngvesson, 'Re-examining continuing relations and the law' (1985) *Wisconsin Law Review* 623.
46 ibid. See also Marc Galanter, 'Vision and revision: a comment on Yngvesson' (1985) *Wisconsin Law Review* 647, 653.
47 Carson, 'Some sociological aspects of strict liability'.
48 See Carol Smart, *The ties that bind: law, marriage and the reproduction of patriarchal relations*, Routledge & Kegan Paul, London, 1984, ch. 8; Maureen E. Cain, 'The general practice lawyer and the client: towards a radical conception', (1979) 7 *International Journal of the Sociology of Law* 331.
49 See J. Disney, J. Basten, P. Redmond and S. Reis, *Lawyers*, Law Book Co., Sydney, 2nd edn, 1986; David Weisbrot, *Australian lawyers*, Longman Cheshire, Melbourne, 1990; *Understanding lawyers: perspectives on the legal profession in Australia*, ed. Roman Tomasic, Law Foundation of New South Wales,

Sydney, 1978; *Lawyers and the community*, ed. Roman Tomasic, Law Foundation of New South Wales, Sydney, 1978.
50 See e.g. Michael King and Mark Israel, 'The pursuit of excellence, or how solicitors maintain racial inequality?' (1989) 16 *New Community* 107; Law Institute of Victoria, *Career patterns of law graduates*, Law Institute, Melbourne, 1990.
51 Cain, 'The general practice lawyer and the client'.
52 Austin Sarat and William L. F. Felstiner, 'Law and strategy in the divorce lawyer's office' (1986) 20 *Law and Society Review* 93.
53 Richard Ingleby, *Solicitors and divorce*, Oxford University Press, Oxford, 1992, 175–8.
54 N. Sargent, 'Law, ideology and corporate crime: a critique of instrumentalism' (1989) 4 *Canadian Journal of Law and Society* 39, 50.
55 Doreen J. McBarnet, *Conviction: law, the state, and the construction of justice*, Clarendon Press, Oxford, 1981, 23.
56 Catharine A. MacKinnon, 'Feminism, marxism, method, and the state: toward feminist jurisprudence' (1983) 8 *Signs* 635, 652.
57 Alan Hunt, 'The ideology of law: advances and problems in recent applications of the concept of ideology to the analysis of law' (1985) 19 *Law and Society Review* 11.
58 N. Sargent, 'Law, ideology, and social change: an analysis of the role of law in the construction of corporate crime' (1990) 1 *The Journal of Human Justice* 97, 106.
59 Richard Johnstone, *The court and the factory: the legal construction of occupational health and safety offences in Victoria*, unpublished PhD thesis, University of Melbourne, Melbourne, 1994.
60 Doreen J. McBarnet, *Conviction*; also 'Pre-trial procedures and the construction of conviction', in *Sociology of law*, ed. Pat Carlen, Sociological Review Monograph, Keele, 1976.
61 Most Australian states have police questioning procedures which ameliorate the accused's vulnerability to some extent. In this respect, McBarnet's argument is not directly transferable to the Australian context.
62 McBarnet, 'Pre-trial procedures and the construction of conviction', 183.
63 ibid.
64 Pat Carlen, *Magistrates' justice*, Martin Robertson, London, 1976; A. S. Blumberg, *Criminal justice*, Quadrangle Books, Chicago, 1970; J. Baldwin and M. McConville, *Negotiated justice*, Martin Robertson, London, 1977.
65 McBarnet, *Conviction*, ch. 8.
66 Roger Cotterrell, 'Feasible regulation for democracy and social justice' (1988) 15 *Journal of Law and Society* 5, 18–19; D. Trubek, 'The handmaiden's revenge: on reading and using the newer sociology of civil procedure' (1988) 51 *Law and Contemporary Problems* 111.

Chapter 7 Judicial decision making

1 *Mabo v Queensland (No. 2)* (1992) 175 CLR 1. See chapter 1.
2 *Milirrpum v Nabalco* (1971) 17 FLR 141.
3 *Murray Islands*, 149.
4 ibid. 102.
5 ibid. 51; see also Toohey J, 179, 186.
6 (1889) 14 App. Cas. 286.

7   ibid. 291.
8   *Murray Islands*, 39.
9   ibid. 103–4. See also Toohey J, 181.
10 ibid. 52, 56.
11 ibid. 82, 92.
12 ibid. 183.
13 [1921] 2 AC 399.
14 *Murrary Islands*, 124. Julius Stone, *Precedent and law: dynamics of common law growth*, Butterworths, Sydney, 1985, 124–7 might see this dispute as revealing the 'indeterminacy of the material facts'.
15 Henry Reynolds, *The law of the land*, Penguin, Ringwood, 2nd edn, 1992.
16 *Murray Islands*, per Deane and Gaudron JJ, 107, 120; Dawson J, 142, 144, 150; Toohey J, 178.
17 See Sean Cooney, 'Gender and judicial selection: should there be more women on the courts?' (1993) 19 *Melbourne University Law Review* 31; George Winterton, 'Appointment of federal judges in Australia' (1987) 16 *Melbourne University Law Review* 185.
18 See the discussion of the separation of powers in chapter 2.
19 See the discussion of the rule of law in chapter 2.
20 See the discussion of federalism in chapter 2. See also Mark Tushnet, 'Following the rules laid down: a critique of interpretivism and neutral principles' (1983) 96 *Harvard Law Review* 781, 785; Sir Anthony Mason, 'Putting *Mabo* in perspective', *Australian Lawyer*, July 1993, 23.
21 Roger Cotterrell, *The politics of jurisprudence: a critical introduction to legal philosophy*, Butterworths, London, 1989, 153–4.
22 Obviously, these three purposes are not the only possibilities.
23 Note, for example, with only one personnel change, the difference between *Mallet v Mallet* (1984) 156 CLR 605 (Gibbs CJ, Mason, Wilson, Deane and Dawson JJ) and *Norbis v Norbis* (1986) 161 CLR 513 (Mason, Wilson, Brennan, Deane and Dawson JJ) on the extent to which the Full Court of the Family Court of Australia was entitled to lay down guidelines for the exercise of discretion by trial judges.
24 Cotterrell, *The politics of jurisprudence*, 209.
25 ibid. 156.
26 ibid. 150.
27 Mason, 'Putting *Mabo* in perspective', 23.
28 The notion of a 'literal' meaning of a word is seen by many as unsustainable: see the discussions of legal realism and postmodernism in chapter 4. See also e.g. Stone, *Precedent and law*, 51.
29 ibid. 2. A syllogism is a form of argument in which a conclusion (the right answer to a legal problem) is logically drawn from a major premise (the statute or precedent) and a minor premise (the facts of the case). Thus, for example: it is an offence to carry a knife; the defendant was carrying a knife; therefore the defendant has committed an offence.
30 See David Wood, 'Adjudication and community values: Sir Anthony Mason's recommendations', in *The emergence of Australian law*, eds M. P. Ellinghaus, A. J. Bradbrook and A. J. Duggan, Butterworths, Sydney, 1989, 89–90.
31 ibid. 91.
32 See e.g. the discussion of judicial defences in 'Sit down girlie' (1994) 19 *Alternative Law Journal* 86, 86.

Notes

33 See further the discussion of the objections to utilitarianism in chapter 2.
34 J. N. Adams and R. Brownsword, 'The ideologies of contract' (1987) 7 *Legal Studies* 205; J. N. Adams and R. Brownsword, *Understanding contract law*, Fontana-Collins, London, 1987.
35 Adams and Brownsword, 'The ideologies of contract', 217.
36 Roberto M. Unger, 'The critical legal studies movement' (1983) 96 *Harvard Law Review* 563, 564, 570.
37 H. L. A. Hart, *The concept of law*, 92. See the discussion of positivism in chapter 2. See also J. M. Finnis, 'On "the critical legal studies movement"' (1985) 30 *American Journal of Jurisprudence* 21; D. Tucker, 'Unger on liberalism' (1986) 11 *Bulletin of the Australian Society of Legal Philosophy* 174, 184; M. Krygier, 'Humdrum, hero and legal doctrine: a comment' (1986) 11 *Bulletin of the Australian Society of Legal Philosophy* 220.
38 Hart, ibid. 123.
39 ibid. 124. See also Cotterrell, *The politics of jurisprudence*, 151.
40 Ronald Dworkin, *Taking rights seriously*, Duckworth, London, 1978, 31–2. In fairness to Hart it should be stated that his concept of law was not so different from Dworkin's as Dworkin would have us believe. See Hart, *The concept of law*, 124.
41 A later version was elaborated in Ronald Dworkin, *Law's empire*, Fontana, London, 1986; discussed further below.
42 The example raises the obvious problem of the definition of the 'relevant' area in relation to a particular case.
43 (1984) 155 CLR 549. See also *McLoughlin v O'Brian* [1983] 1 AC 410, discussed in Dworkin, *Law's empire*, 26–9, 38–9, 238–50.
44 Dworkin, *Law's empire*.
45 ibid. 65–6.
46 ibid. 232–8.
47 Lynne Hansen, 'Feminist jurisprudence in a conventional context: is there room for feminism in Dworkin's theory of interpretive concepts?' (1992) 30 *Osgoode Hall Law Journal* 355.
48 J. W. Harris, 'Unger's critique of formalism in legal reasoning: hero, Hercules and humdrum' (1986) 11 *Bulletin of the Australian Society of Legal Philosophy* 199, 213. See also J. W. Harris, *Law and legal science*, Clarendon Press, Oxford, 1979.
49 Neil MacCormick, *Legal reasoning and legal theory*, Oxford University Press, Oxford, 1978.
50 Peter Goodrich, *Reading the law: a critical introduction to legal method and techniques*, Blackwell, Oxford, 1986, 141–4. Goodrich identifies this interpretive method as 'hermeneutics'. In his chapter 6 he also draws attention to the rhetorical aspects of judicial decision making.
51 See the discussion of deconstruction in the section on postmodernism in chapter 4.
52 Stanley Fish, *Doing what comes naturally: change, rhetoric, and the practice of theory in literary and legal studies*, Duke University Press, Durham, 1989, 98.
53 ibid. 97.
54 This opposition is derived from H. L. A. Hart, 'American jurisprudence through English eyes: the nightmare and the noble dream', in *Essays in jurisprudence and philosophy*, Oxford University Press, Oxford, 1983.

55 Fish, *Doing what comes naturally*, 98.
56 See Maureen E. Cain, 'Necessarily out of touch: thoughts on the organisation of the English bar', in *The sociology of law*, ed. Pat Carlen, Sociological Review Monograph No. 23, University of Keele, Keele, 1976.
57 Martin F. Katz, 'After the deconstruction: law in the age of post-structuralism' (1986) 24 *University of Western Ontario Law Review* 51, 55-9.
58 Pat O'Shane, 'Launch of the Australian Feminist Law Journal, August 29 1993, The University of Melbourne' (1994) 2 *Australian Feminist Law Journal* 3, 5.
59 Cotterrell, *The politics of jurisprudence*, 179.
60 See e.g. Madame Justice Bertha Wilson, 'Will women judges really make a difference?' (1990) 28 *Osgoode Hall Law Journal* 507.
61 See e.g. Sharyn Roach Anleu, 'Women in the legal profession' (1992) 66 *Law Institute Journal* 162; Michael King and Mark Israel, 'The pursuit of excellence, or how solicitors maintain racial inequality?' (1989) 16 *New Community* 107.
62 Sandra Berns, *Concise jurisprudence*, Federation Press, Sydney, 1993, 68.
63 The concepts of 'repeat players' and 'one-shotters' are explained early in chapter 6.
64 Maureen E. Cain, 'Where are the disputes? A study of a first instance court in the U.K.', in *Disputes and the law*, eds M. E. Cain and K. Kulcsar, Akademai Kiado, Budapest, 1983, 132.
65 ibid. 131.
66 See the discussion of functionalism in chapter 3.
67 ibid. 122.
68 See the discussion of public regulation in chapter 6, as well as discussions of the private/public distinction in chapters 2 (What is a liberal?) and 4 (feminism).
69 See Richard Ingleby, *Family law and society*, Butterworths, Sydney, 1993, chs 2 and 6.
70 A *decree nisi* is effectively a declaration that the grounds for divorce have been established, even though the marital status of the parties is not terminated until a *decree absolute* issues from the court. See Ingleby, ibid.
71 See e.g. *Howe v Howe* [1961] ALR 425; *Baker v Baker* (1961) 2 FLR 285; *Turk v Turk* [1961] ALR 436; *Bass v Bass* (1963) 5 FLR 466; *Mann v Mann* [1964] ALR 47; *Viney v Viney* (1965) 6 FLR 417. See also S. Burbury, 'Family law: some extra-judicial reflections upon two years' judicial experience of the Commonwealth Matrimonial Causes Act 1959' (1963) 36 *Australian Law Journal* 283.
72 In particular, *In the Marriage of RJ and L Evans* (1990) 14 Fam LR 136.
73 Three judges and one judicial registrar were observed conducting fewer than 25 hearings each. This was not considered sufficient evidence to warrant these observations being analysed.
74 There may have been children in other cases which were adjourned for reasons unrelated to children, such as the documents not being served properly.
75 Richard Johnstone, *The court and the factory: the legal construction of occupational health and safety offences in Victoria*, unpublished PhD thesis, University of Melbourne, Melbourne, 1994.
76 Clifford Geertz, *Local knowledge: further essays in interpretive anthropology*, Basic Books, New York, 1983, 170. See also the discussion of the event-focused nature of law enforcement in the section on pre-trial construction in chapter 6.

Notes

77 N. Sargent, 'Law, ideology and corporate crime: a critique of instrumentalism' (1989) 4 *Canadian Journal of Law and Society* 39, 50.
78 N. Sargent, 'Law, ideology, and social change: an analysis of the role of law in the construction of corporate crime' (1990) 1 *The Journal of Human Justice* 97, 106.
79 See H. Croall, 'Mistakes, accidents, and someone else's fault: the trading offender in court' (1988) 15 *Journal of Law and Society* 293; K. Mann, *Defending white collar crime: a portrait of attorneys at work*, Yale University Press, New Haven, 1985. In the arena of more traditional crime, see R. M. Emerson, *Judging delinquents*, Aldine, Chicago, 1969; J. Shapland, *Between conviction and sentence*, Routledge & Kegan Paul, London, 1981; D. Nelken, *The limits of the legal process: a study of landlords, law and crime*, Academic Press, London, 1983, ch. 6.

Bibliography

Aboriginal Land Rights Commission, *Second report*, AGPS, Canberra, 1974
Adams, J. N. and Brownsword, R. 'The ideologies of contract' (1987) 7 *Legal Studies* 205
——*Understanding contract law*, Fontana-Collins, London, 1987
Airo-Farulla, Geoff 'Community policing and self-determination' (1992) 2/54 *Aboriginal Law Bulletin* 8
——'"Dirty deeds done dirt cheap": deconstruction, Derrida, discrimination and difference/ance in (the High) court' (1991) 9 *Law in Context* 102
Alexander, Renata 'Practising feminism: painting pictures of lives in law' (1994) 2 *Australian Feminist Law Journal* 150
Allen, T. R. S. 'Legislative supremacy and the rule of law: democracy and constitutionalism' (1985) 44 *Cambridge Law Journal* 111
Althusser, Louis *For Marx*, Allen Lane, London, 1969
——*Lenin and philosophy and other essays*, Left Books, New York, 1971
Altman, A. *Critical legal studies: a liberal critique*, Princeton University Press, Princeton, 1990
Altman, J. C. 'Statistics about indigenous Australians: needs, problems, options and implications', in *A national survey of indigenous Australians: options and implications*, ed. J. C. Altman, Centre for Aboriginal Economic Policy Research, ANU, Canberra, 1992
Arzt, D. 'The application of international human rights law in Islamic states' (1990) 12 *Human Rights Quarterly* 202
Astor, Hilary and Chinkin, Christine M. *Dispute resolution in Australia*, Butterworths, Sydney, 1992
Attwood, Bain and Arnold, John eds *Power, knowledge and Aborigines*, La Trobe University Press in association with the National Centre for Australian Studies, Monash University, Melbourne, 1992
Aun, Wu Min *The Malaysian Legal System*, Longman, Selangor Darul Ehsan, 1990
Austin, John 'The province of jurisprudence determined', reprinted in *The province of*

Bibliography

jurisprudence determined and the uses of the study of jurisprudence, Weidenfeld & Nicolson, London, 1955

Australian Bureau of Statistics, *Aboriginal child survival: an analysis of results from the 1986 census of population and housing*, Cat. No. 4126.0

——, *1991 Census: Australian Aboriginal and Torres Strait Islander Population*, AGPS, Canberra, 1993

Australian Law Reform Commission *Discussion paper no. 54: equality before the law*, AGPS, Canberra, 1993

——*Interim report no. 67: equality before the law*, AGPS, Canberra, 1994

——*Report no. 31: the recognition of Aboriginal customary laws*, AGPS, Canberra, 1986

Bacchi, Carol Lee *Same difference: feminism and sexual difference*, Allen & Unwin, Sydney, 1990

Bakan, Joel 'Constitutional interpretation and social change: you can't always get what you want (nor what you need)' (1991) 70 *Canadian Bar Review* 307

Baker, J. H. *An introduction to English legal history*, Butterworths, London, 2nd edn, 1979

Balbus, Isaac 'Commodity form and legal form: an essay on the relative autonomy of law' (1977) 11 *Law and Society Review* 571

Baldwin, J. and McConville, M. *Negotiated justice*, Martin Robertson, London, 1989

Ban, Paul 'The quest for legal recognition of Torres Strait Islander customary adoption practice' (1993) 3/60 *Aboriginal Law Bulletin* 4

Barsh, Russell L. 'An advocate's guide to the Convention on Indigenous and Tribal Peoples' (1990) 15 *Oklahoma City University Law Review* 209

Barthes, Roland *Image music text*, Fontana, London, 1977

——*Mythologies*, trans. A. Lavers, Paladin Grafton, London, 1973

——*S/Z*, trans. R. Miller, Hill & Wang, New York, 1974

——*The pleasure of the text*, trans. R. Miller, Hill & Wang, New York, 1975

Bartlett, Katharine 'Feminist legal methods' (1990) 103 *Harvard Law Review* 829

Bartlett, Richard '*Mabo*: another triumph for the common law' (1993) 15 *Sydney Law Review* 185

——'The Aboriginal land which may be claimed at common law: implications of *Mabo*' (1992) 22 *University of Western Australia Law Review* 272

——'The primacy of the Commonwealth: the rejection of the WA and NT legislation' (1993) 3/62 *Aboriginal Law Bulletin* 14

Baudrillard, Jean *America*, trans. Chris Turner, Verso Books, London, 1988

——*Selected writings*, ed. M. Poster, Polity Press, Cambridge, 1988

Beccaria, Cesare *An essay in crime and punishment*, 1764

Behrendt, Larissa 'Aboriginal women and the white lies of the feminist movement: implications for Aboriginal women in rights discourse' (1993) 1 *Australian Feminist Law Journal* 27

Bell, Diane *Daughters of the Dreaming*, Allen & Unwin, Sydney, 1983

——'In the case of the lawyers and anthropologists' (1986) 11 *Legal Service Bulletin* 202

——'Women's business is hard work: central Australian Aboriginal women's love rituals', in *Religion in Aboriginal Australia: an anthology*, eds Max Charlesworth, Howard Morphy, Diane Bell and Kenneth Maddock, University of Queensland Press, St. Lucia, 1984

Bender, Leslie, 'A lawyer's primer on feminist theory and tort' (1988) 38 *Journal of Legal Education* 3

Bennett, J. M. 'The establishment of divorce laws in New South Wales' (1963) 4 *Sydney Law Review* 241

Bennett, J. M. and Castles, Alex C. eds *A source book of Australian legal history: source materials from the eighteenth to the twentieth centuries*, Law Book Company, Sydney, 1979

Berndt, Catherine H. 'Women and the "secret life"', in *Aboriginal man in Australia*, eds Catherine H. and Ronald M. Berndt, Angus & Robertson, Sydney, 1960

Berns, Sandra *Concise jurisprudence*, Federation Press, Sydney, 1993

Binder, G. 'On critical legal studies as guerrilla warfare' (1987) 76 *Georgetown Law Journal* 1

Bird, Greta *The 'civilising mission': race and the construction of crime*, Contemporary Legal Issues No. 4, Faculty of Law, Monash University, Clayton, 1987

Birmingham, John 'The long tentacles of the law' *Independent Monthly*, August 1993

Blackstone, Sir William *Commentaries on the laws of England: book 1*, Garland, New York, facs. repr. 1978; 1st publ. 1765; 9th edn 1783

Blainey, Geoffrey 'Land rights for all', the *Age*, 10 November 1993

Blumberg, A. S. *Criminal justice*, Quadrangle Books, Chicago, 1970

Blumer, H. *Symbolic interactionism: perspectives and method*, Prentice Hall, Englewood Cliffs, 1969

Bottomley, Anne 'Resolving family disputes: a critical view', in *The state, the law and the family*, ed. M. D. A. Freeman, Tavistock, London, 1984

Bottomley, Stephen, Gunningham, Neil and Parker, Stephen *Law in context*, Federation Press, Sydney, 1991

Boyle, Christine 'Book review' (1985) 63 *Canadian Bar Review* 427

Boyle, J. 'Anatomy of a torts class' (1985) 34 *American University Law Review* 1003

Bradshaw, Richard 'Community representation in criminal proceedings' (1986) 11 *Legal Service Bulletin* 111

Brennan, Frank 'ATSIC: seeking a national mouthpiece for local voices' (1990) 2/43 *Aboriginal Law Bulletin* 4

——'Is a bipartisan approach possible?' (1989) 14 *Legal Service Bulletin* 66

——'*Mabo* and its implications for Aborigines and Islanders', in *Mabo: a judicial revolution*, eds M. A. Stephenson and Suri Ratnapala, University of Queensland Press, St. Lucia, 1993

——'Self-determination: the limits of allowing Aboriginal communities to be a law unto themselves' (1993) 16(1) *University of New South Wales Law Journal* 245

——'Waiting for the resolution' (1989) 61 *Australian Quarterly* 242

Brennan, Frank and Crawford, James 'Aboriginality, recognition and Australian law: where to from here?' (1990) 1 *Public Law Review* 53

Brereton, David 'Theoretical perspectives on legislative innovation: the case of compulsory arbitration', in *Foundations of arbitration*, eds Stuart Macintyre and Richard Mitchell, Oxford University Press, Melbourne, 1989

Brook, P. *Freedom at work*, Oxford University Press, Oxford, 1990

Brooklyn, Bridget 'Nothing to lose: women and divorce in South Australia, 1859–1918', in *Feminism, law and society*, ed. Judith Grbich, La Trobe University Press, Melbourne, 1990

Brosnan, D. 'Serious but not critical' (1986) 60 *Southern California Law Review* 259

Burbury, S. 'Family law: some extra-judicial reflections upon two years' judicial experience of the Commonwealth Matrimonial Causes Act 1959' (1963) 36 *Australian Law Journal* 283

Cain, Maureen E. 'Necessarily out of touch: thoughts on the social organisation of the

bar', in *The sociology of law*, ed. Pat Carlen, Sociological Review Monograph no. 23, University of Keele, Keele, 1976
——'The general practice lawyer and the client: towards a radical conception' (1979) 7 *International Journal of the Sociology of Law* 331
——'Where are the disputes? A study of a first instance court in the U.K.', in *Disputes and the law*, eds M. E. Cain and K. Kulscar, Akademai Kiado, Budapest, 1983
Cain, Patricia A. 'Feminist jurisprudence: grounding the theories' (1989–90) 4 *Berkeley Women's Law Journal* 191
Calabresi, Guido *The costs of accidents*, Yale University Press, New Haven, 1970
Carlen, Pat *Magistrates' justice*, Martin Robertson, London, 1976
Carrington, Paul 'Of law and the river' (1984) 34 *Journal of Legal Education* 222
Carson, W. G. 'Occupational health and safety: a political economy perspective' (1989) 2 *Labour and Industry* 301
——'Some sociological aspects of strict liability and the enforcement of factory legislation' (1970) 33 *Modern Law Review* 896
——'The conventionalisation of early factory crime' (1979) 7 *International Journal of the Sociology of Law* 37
——'The institutionalisation of ambiguity: early British Factory Acts', in *White collar crime: theory and research*, eds G. Gess and E. Scotland, Sage Publications, Beverly Hills, 1980
Carson, W. G. and Henenberg, C. 'The political economy of legislative change: making sense of Victoria's new occupational health and safety legislation' (1988) 6 *Law in Context* 1
Castan, Ron QC 'The Mabo case', Labor Lawyers' Conference, Melbourne, May 1992
Castles, Alex C. *An Australian legal history*, Law Book Co., Sydney, 1982
Chambliss, W. 'Functional and conflict theories of crime', in *Whose law, what order? A conflict approach to criminology*, eds W. Chambliss and M. Mankoff, John Wiley, New York, 1976
Chambliss, W. and Seidman, R. *Law, order and power*, Addison-Wesley, Reading, Mass., 2nd edn, 1982
Charlesworth, Hilary 'Critical legal education' (1990) 5 *Australian Journal of Law and Society* 27
——'New rights of international redress for human rights violations in Australia', University of Adelaide Law School Continuing Legal Education Papers, 1993
Charlesworth, Hilary, Chinkin, Christine and Wright, Shelley 'Feminist approaches to international law' (1991) 85 *American Journal of International Law* 613
Chesterman, M. and Weisbrot, D. 'Legal scholarship in Australia' (1987) 50 *Modern Law Review* 709
Christie, M. F. *Aborigines in colonial Victoria 1835–86*, Sydney University Press, Sydney, 1979
Cicourel, Aaron *The social organisation of juvenile justice*, Wiley, New York, 1968
Clark, Manning ed. *Select documents in Australian history vol. 1: 1788–1850*, Angus & Robertson, Sydney, 1950
Coase, R. 'The problem of social costs' (1960) 3 *Journal of Law and Economics* 1
Coles, G. J. L. 'The international significance of an Aboriginal treaty' (1982) 21 *World Review* 42
Constitutional Commission *Final report of the Constitutional Commission*, AGPS, Canberra, 1988
——*Report of the individual rights committee*, AGPS, Canberra, 1987

Coombs, H. C. 'The case for a treaty', in *Black Australians: the prospects for change*, ed. E. Olbrei, James Cook University Union, Townsville, 1982

Cooney, Sean 'Gender and judicial selection: should there be more women on the courts?' (1993) 19 *Melbourne University Law Review* 31

Cooter, R. and Ulen, T. *Law and economics*, Scott Foresman, Glenview, Ill., 1988

Corbett, Helen, Sixth Boyer Lecture, Radio National, 28 November 1993

Cotterrell, Roger 'Feasible regulation for democracy and social justice' (1988) 15 *Journal of Law and Society* 5

——*The politics of jurisprudence: a critical introduction to legal philosophy*, Butterworths, London, 1989

——*The sociology of law: an introduction*, Butterworths, London, 2nd edn, 1992

Cowlishaw, Gillian 'Studying Aborigines: changing canons in anthropology and history', in *Power, knowledge and Aborigines*, eds Bain Attwood and John Arnold, La Trobe University Press, Melbourne, 1992

Craib, Ian *Modern social theory: from Parsons to Habermas*, Wheatsheaf Books, London, 1984

Crawford, James 'The Aboriginal legal heritage: Aboriginal public law and the treaty proposal' (1989) 63 *Australian Law Journal* 392

Crawford, James ed. *The rights of peoples*, Oxford University Press, Oxford, 1988

Crawford, James, Hennessy, Peter and Fisher, Mary 'Aboriginal customary law: proposals for recognition', in *Ivory scales: black Australians and the law*, ed. Kayleen M. Hazlehurst, New South Wales University Press, Kensington, 1987

Creighton, W. B. *Understanding occupational health and safety law in Victoria*, CCH, Melbourne, 1986

Croall, H. 'Mistakes, accidents, and someone else's fault: the trading offender in court' (1988) 15 *Journal of Law and Society* 293

Crough, G. 'Aboriginal Australia and the "new federalism" initiative', Discussion paper no. 2, North Australia Research Unit, ANU, Canberra, 1991

——'Funding Aboriginal programs and services' (1992) 2/57 *Aboriginal Law Bulletin* 9

Currie, D. 'Feminist encounters with postmodernism: exploring the impasse of debates on patriarchy and law' (1992) 5 *Canadian Journal of Women and the Law* 63

Dalton, Clare, 'Where we stand: observations on the situation of feminist legal thought' (1987–88) 3 *Berkeley Women's Law Journal* 1

Davies, Margaret *Asking the law question*, Law Book Co., Sydney, 1994

Delgado, R. 'Critical legal studies and the realities of race–does the fundamental contradiction have a corollary?' (1988) 23 *Harvard Civil Rights–Civil Liberties Law Review* 407

——'The ethereal scholar: does critical legal studies have what minorities want?' (1987) 22 *Harvard Civil Rights–Civil Liberties Law Review* 304

Department of Foreign Affairs and Trade, *Backgrounder*, vol. 3, no. 9, 22 May 1992

de Rose, Sylvie, Paper given at 'Aboriginal peoples, federalism and self-determination conference', Townsville, August 1993

Derrida, Jacques 'Force of law: the mystical foundation of authority' (1990) 11 *Cardozo Law Review* 919

Dicey, A. V. *Lectures on the relation between law and public opinion in England during the nineteenth century*, Macmillan, London, 1963, 1st edn 1905

Discrimination against women in the lead industry, Occasional papers from the Sex Discrimination Commissioner, No. 5, Human Rights and Equal Opportunity Commission, Sydney, 1990

Bibliography

Disney, J., Basten, J., Redmond, P. and Reis, S. *Lawyers*, Law Book Co., Sydney, 2nd edn, 1986
Dodson, Pat 'Policy statement', in *International law and Aboriginal human rights*, ed. Barbara Hocking, Law Book Co., Sydney, 1988
Doran, Jenny 'Implementing the Victorian government's policy on occupational health and safety—1982–84', in *The industrial relations of occupational health and safety*, eds W. B. Creighton and N. Gunningham, Croom Helm, Sydney, 1985
Duggan, A. J. 'Law and economics in Australia' (1989) 1 *Legal Education Review* 37
Duncanson, Ian 'Lawyers' stories and the possibilities of reconstruction', paper delivered at the Law and Society Conference, Macquarie University, December 1993
——'Legal education and the possibility of critique: an Australian perspective' (1993) 8 *Canadian Journal of Law and Society* 59
Durkheim, E. *The division of labour in society*, trans. W. D. Halls, Macmillan, London, 1984
——*The rules of sociological method*, trans. W. D. Halls, Macmillan, London, 2nd edn, 1982
——'Two laws of penal evolution' (1973) 2 *Economy and Society* 285
Dworkin, Ronald *A matter of principle*, Harvard University Press, Cambridge, Mass., 1985
——*Law's empire*, Fontana, London/Harvard University Press, Harvard, Mass., 1986
——*Taking rights seriously*, Duckworth, London, 1978
Easterbrook, Frank 'The inevitability of law and economics' (1989) 1 *Legal Education Review* 3
Ellickson, R. *Order without law*, Harvard University Press, Cambridge, 1991
Elling, R. *The struggle for workers health*, Baywood Publishing Co., New York, 1986
Ellinghaus, M. P. 'Towards an Australian contract law', in *The emergence of Australian law*, eds M. P. Ellinghaus, A. J. Bradbrook and A. J. Duggan, Butterworths, Sydney, 1989
Emerson, R. M. *Judging delinquents*, Aldine, Chicago, 1969
Engels, Friedrich 'The condition of the working class in England', in *Marx and Engels on law*, eds Maureen Cain and Alan Hunt, Academic Press, New York, 1979
Farber, Daniel A. and Sherry, Suzanna 'Telling stories out of school: an essay on legal narratives' (1993) 45 *Stanford Law Review* 807
Feinman, J. 'Priests and prophets' (1986) 35 *St Louis University Law Journal* 53
Feldman, David 'Democracy, the rule of law, and judicial review' (1990) 19 *Federal Law Review* 1
Felstiner, William L. F., Abel, Richard L. and Sarat, Austin 'The emergence and transformation of disputes: naming, blaming and claiming . . .' (1981) 15 *Law and Society Review* 631
Fesl, Eve Mungwa D. 'How the English language is used to put Koories down, deny us rights, or is employed as a political tool against us', Monash University, Clayton, 1989
Fine, Bob *Democracy and the rule of law: liberal ideals and marxist critiques*, Pluto Press, London, 1984
Finley, Lucinda M. 'A break in the silence: including women's issues in a torts course' (1989) 1 *Yale Journal of Law and Feminism* 41
——'Breaking women's silence in law: the dilemma of the gendered nature of legal reasoning' (1989) 64 *Notre Dame Law Review* 886
Finnis, J. M. *Natural law and natural rights*, Oxford University Press, Oxford, 1980

——'On "the critical legal studies movement"' (1985) 30 *American Journal of Jurisprudence* 21
Fish, Stanley *Doing what comes naturally: change, rhetoric and the practice of theory in literary and legal studies*, Clarendon Press, Oxford, 1989
Fiss, Owen 'The death of the law?' (1986–87) 72 *Cornell Law Review* 1
Fitzpatrick, Peter *The mythology of modern law*, Routledge, London, 1992
Fletcher, C. *Aboriginal politics: intergovernmental relations*, Melbourne University Press, Melbourne, 1991
Foley, Gary 'Teaching whites a lesson', in *A people's history of Australia since 1788, vol. 4: staining the wattle*, eds Verity Burgmann and Jenny Lee, McPhee Gribble/Penguin, Melbourne, 1988
'For Mary Joe Frug: a symposium on feminist critical legal studies and postmodernism' (1992) 26 *New England Law Review* 639
Foucault, Michel *Discipline and punish: the birth of the prison*, Penguin, Harmondsworth, 1977
——*Madness and civilisation*, Tavistock, London, 1961
——*Power/knowledge*, Harvester Press, Brighton, 1980
——*Remarks on Marx*, Semiotext, Columbia University Press, New York, 1988
——*The archeology of knowledge*, Harper & Row, New York, 1972
——*The birth of the clinic*, Tavistock, London, 1973
——*The history of sexuality: an introduction*, Tavistock, London, 1979
——*The order of things: an archeology of the human sciences*, Vintage Books, New York, 1973
Frank, Jerome *Courts on trial: myth and reality in American justice*, Princeton University Press, Princeton, 1949
——*Law and the modern mind*, Anchor, New York, 1963
Frazer, Andrew 'Conceptions of law and industrial arbitration in New South Wales, 1880–1901', in *Law and history in Australia, vol. IV*, ed. Diane Kirkby, La Trobe University Press, Bundoora, 1987
Freeman, Alan 'Legitimising racial discrimination through antidiscrimination law' (1978) 62 *Minnesota Law Review* 1049
Frug, Gerald 'A critical theory of law' (1989) 1 *Legal Education Review* 43
——'The city as a legal concept' (1980) 93 *Harvard Law Review* 1057
Frug, Mary Joe *Postmodern legal feminism*, Routledge, New York, 1992
——'Progressive feminist legal scholarship: can we claim "a different voice"?' (1992) 15 *Harvard Women's Law Journal* 37
Fuller, Lon L. *The morality of law*, Yale University Press, New Haven, rev. edn, 1969
Gabel, P. and Harris, P. 'Building power and breaking images: critical legal theory and the practice of law' (1982–83) 11 *New York Review of Law and Social Change* 369
Galanter, Marc 'Vision and revision: a comment on Yngvesson' (1985) *Wisconsin Law Review* 647
——'Why the "haves"'come out ahead: speculations on the limits of legal change' (1974) 9 *Law and Society Review* 95
Gale, Fay ed. *We are bosses ourselves: the status and role of Aboriginal women today*, Australian Institute of Aboriginal Studies, Canberra, 1983
——*Women's role in Aboriginal society*, Australian Institute of Aboriginal Studies, Canberra, 1970
Galligan, D. J. *Discretionary powers: a legal study of official discretion*, Clarendon Press, Oxford, 1986
Gamble, A. *An introduction to modern social and political thought*, Macmillan, London, 1981

Bibliography

Geertz, Clifford *Local knowledge: further essays in interpretive anthropology*, Basic Books, New York, 1983

Gerritsen, R. 'Cause for hope? Self-management and local government in Australia', Royal Commission into Aboriginal Deaths in Custody discussion paper, October 1990

Gilligan, Carol *In a different voice*, Harvard University Press, Cambridge, Mass., 1982

Golder, Hilary 'An exercise in unnecessary chivalry: the New South Wales Matrimonial Causes Act Amendment Act of 1881', in *In pursuit of justice: Australian women and the law 1788-1979*, eds Judy Mackinolty & Heather Radi, Hale and Iremonger, Sydney, 1979

Goldring, John 'Babies and bathwater: tradition or progress in legal scholarship and legal education' (1987) 17 *University of Western Australia Law Review* 216

Goldsmith, A. J. 'An unruly conjunction? Social thought and legal action in clinical legal education' (1993) 43 *Journal of Legal Education* 415

Goodrich, Peter 'Critical legal studies in England: prospective histories' (1992) 12 *Oxford Journal of Legal Studies* 195

——*Reading the law: a critical introduction to legal method and techniques*, Blackwell, Oxford, 1986

Gordon, R. W. 'Critical legal studies as a teaching method' (1989) 1 *Legal Education Review* 59

——'Historicism in legal scholarship' (1981) *Yale Law Journal* 1017

——'New developments in legal theory', in *The politics of law*, ed. D. Kairys, Pantheon Books, New York, 1982; rev. edn 1992

Grabosky, Peter, Braithwaite, John and Wilson, Paul 'The myth of community tolerance of white collar crime' (1987) 20 *Australia and New Zealand Journal of Criminology* 33

Gramsci, Antonio *Selections from the prison notebooks*, Lawrence & Wishart, London, 1971

Graycar, Regina 'Hoovering as a hobby: the common law's approach to work in the home' (1985) *Refractory Girl*, no. 28, 22

——'Women's work: who cares?' (1992) 14 *Sydney Law Review* 86

Graycar, Regina and Morgan, Jenny, *The hidden gender of law*, Federation Press, Sydney, 1990

Green, L. C. and Dickason, O. P. *The law of nations and the New World*, Alberta, University of Alberta Press, 1989

Greenberg, Judith G. 'Introduction', in Mary Joe Frug, *Postmodern legal feminism*, Routledge, New York, 1992

Greig, D. W. 'Sovereignty, territory and the international lawyer's dilemma' (1988) 26 *Osgoode Hall Law Journal* 127

Griffith, J. *The politics of the judiciary*, Fontana, London, 3rd edn, 1985

Gross, Elizabeth 'What is feminist theory?', in *Feminist challenges: social and political theory*, eds Carole Pateman and Elizabeth Gross, Allen & Unwin, Sydney, 1986

Hand, Gerry *Foundations for the future*, AGPS, Canberra, 1987

Hannum, H. 'New developments in indigenous rights' (1988) 28 *Virginia Journal of International Law* 649

Hansen, Lynne 'Feminist jurisprudence in a conventional context: is there room for feminism in Dworkin's theory of interpretive concepts?' (1992) 30 *Osgoode Hall Law Journal* 355

Haralambros, M. *Sociology: themes and perspectives*, University Tutorial, Slough, 1980; 3rd edn 1990

Harding, Sandra *The science question in feminism*, Cornell University Press, Ithaca, 1986
Harris, Angela P. 'Categorical discourse and dominance theory' (1989–90) 4 *Berkeley Women's Law Journal* 181
——'Race and essentialism in feminist legal theory' (1990) 42 *Stanford Law Review* 580
Harris, D. et al. *Compensation and support for illness and injury*, Clarendon Press, Oxford, 1984
Harris, J. W. *Law and legal science*, Clarendon Press, Oxford, 1979
——*Legal philosophies*, Butterworths, London, 1980
——'Unger's critique of formalism in legal reasoning: hero, Hercules and humdrum' (1986) 11 *Bulletin of the Australian Society of Legal Philosophy* 199
Harris, Mark 'Jeff Kennett, *Mabo* and the *Land Titles Validation Bill*' (1993) 3/64 *Aboriginal Law Bulletin* 22
Hart, H. L. A. *Essays in jurisprudence and philosophy*, Oxford University Press, Oxford, 1983
——*The concept of law*, Oxford University Press, Oxford, 1961
Hatty, Suzanne *Male violence and the police: an Australian experience*, School of Social Work, University of New South Wales, Kensington, 1988
Hawke, R. J. 'The Commonwealth arbitration court—legal tribunal or economic legislature?' (1956) 3 *University of Western Australia Annual Law Review* 422
Hawkins, Keith *Environment and enforcement: regulation and the social definition of pollution*, Oxford University Press, Oxford, 1984
——'On legal decision-making' (1986) 43 *Washington and Lee Law Review* 1161
Healy, Chris '"We know your mob now": histories and their cultures' (1990) 49 *Meanjin* 512
Hegel, G. W. F. *Philosophy of history*, Oxford University Press, Oxford, 1952
Heilbroner, R. L. *The making of economic society*, Prentice-Hall, Englewood Cliffs, NJ, 9th edn, 1993
Henderson, L. 'Legality and empathy' (1987) 85 *Michigan Law Review* 1574
Henley, Kenneth 'Abstract principles, mid-level principles, and the rule of law' (1993) 12 *Law and Philosophy* 121
Henry, S. *Private justice: towards integrated theorising in the sociology of law*, Routlege & Kegan Paul, London, 1983
Higgins, H. B. 'A new province for law and order' (1915) 29 *Harvard Law Review* 13
Hocking, Barbara ed. *International law and Aboriginal human rights*, Law Book Co., Sydney, 1988
Holtmaat, Riki 'The power of legal concepts: the development of a feminist theory of law' (1989) 17 *International Journal of the Sociology of Law* 481
Hooker, M. B. *Legal pluralism: an introduction to colonial and neo-colonial laws*, Clarendon Press, Oxford, 1975
House of Representatives Standing Committee on Legal and Constitutional Affairs, *Half way to equal: report of the inquiry into equal opportunity and equal status for women in Australia*, AGPS, Canberra, 1992
Human Rights and Equal Opportunity Commission, *Report of the national inquiry into racist violence*, AGPS, Canberra, 1993
Hunt, Alan 'Marxism and the analysis of law', in *Sociological approaches to law*, eds A. Podgorecki and C. J. Whelan, Croom Helm, London, 1981
——'The big fear: law confronts postmodernism' (1990) 35 *McGill Law Journal* 507

Bibliography

—— 'The ideology of law: advances and problems in recent applications of the concept of ideology to the analysis of law' (1985) 19 *Law and Society Review* 11
—— *The sociological movement in law*, Macmillan, London, 1978
Hunter, Rosemary 'The representation of gender in legal analysis: a case/book study of labour law' (1991) 18 *Melbourne University Law Review* 305
Hutchinson, Allan *Dwelling on the threshold: critical essays on modern legal thought*, Carswell, Toronto, 1988
Hutchinson, Allan and Monahan, P. 'Law, politics and critical legal scholars: the unfolding drama of American legal thought' (1984) 36 *Stanford Law Review* 199
Hutson, Jack *Penal colony to penal powers*, Amalgamated Engineering Union, Sydney, 1966
Hutter, Bridget M. 'Variations in regulatory enforcement styles' (1989) 11 *Law and Policy* 153
Iorns, Catherine J. 'A sexed Bill of Rights for New Zealand?' (1987) 17 *Victoria University of Wellington Law Review* 215
—— 'Indigenous peoples and self-determination' (1992) 24 *Case Western Reserve Journal of International Law* 199
Implementation of Commonwealth Government Response to the Recommendations of the Royal Commission into Aboriginal Deaths in Custody, *First annual report 1992–93*, AGPS, Canberra, 1994
Ingleby, Richard *Family law and society*, Butterworths, Sydney, 1993
—— *Solicitors and divorce*, Oxford University Press, Oxford, 1992
James, Margaret 'Not bread but a stone: women and divorce in colonial Victoria', in *Families in colonial Australia*, eds Patricia Grimshaw, Chris McConville and Ellen McEwen, Allen & Unwin, Sydney, 1985
Jameson, Frederic *Postmodernism, or, the cultural logic of late capitalism*, Duke University Press, Durham, 1991
Jennett, Christine 'Aboriginal affairs policy', in *Hawke and Australian public policy: consensus and restructuring*, eds C. Jennett and R. G. Stewart, Macmillan, Sydney, 1990
Johnson, Alex M. Jr 'Think like a lawyer, work like a machine: the dissonance between law school and law practice' (1991) *Southern California Law Review* 1231
Johnstone, Richard 'Aboriginal land rights', in A. Bradbrook, S. MacCallum and A. Moore, *Australian real property law*, Law Book Co., Sydney, 1991
—— *The court and the factory: the legal construction of occupational health and safety offences in Victoria*, unpublished PhD thesis, University of Melbourne, 1994
Kairys, D. 'Freedom of speech', in *The politics of law*, ed. D. Kairys, Pantheon Books, New York, 1982; rev. edn 1992
—— 'Legal reasoning', in *The politics of law*, ed. D. Kairys, Pantheon Books, New York, 1982; rev. edn 1992
Kairys, D. ed. *The politics of law*, Pantheon Books, New York, 1982; rev. edn 1992
Karst, K. 'Woman's Constitution' (1984) *Duke Law Journal* 447
Katz, Martin F. 'After the deconstruction: law in the age of post-structuralism' (1986) 24 *University of Western Ontario Law Review* 51
Keating, Paul 'Redfern park speech', in (1993) 3/61 *Aboriginal Law Bulletin* 4
Kelman, Mark 'Trashing' (1984) 36 *Stanford Law Review* 293
Kennedy, David 'Critical theory, structuralism and contemporary legal scholarship' (1985–86) 21 *New England Law Review* 209
Kennedy, Duncan 'Legal education as training for hierarchy', in *The politics of law*, ed. D. Kairys, Pantheon Books, New York, 1982; rev. edn 1992

——'Legal formality' (1973) 2 *Journal of Legal Studies* 351
——'The structure of Blackstone's Commentaries' (1979) 28 *Buffalo Law Review* 205
Keon-Cohen, B. A. 'Some problems of proof: the admissibility of traditional evidence', in *Mabo, a judicial revolution: the Aboriginal land rights decision and its impact on Australian law*, eds M. A. Stephenson and Suri Ratnapala, University of Queensland Press, St. Lucia, 1993
Kerr, Sir John *Matters for judgment: an autobiography*, Macmillan, Melbourne, 1978
King, Michael and Israel, Mark 'The pursuit of excellence, or how solicitors maintain racial inequality?' (1989) 16 *New Community* 107
Kirkby, Diane 'Arbitration and the fight for economic justice', in *Foundations of arbitration*, eds Stuart Macintyre and Richard Mitchell, Oxford University Press, Melbourne, 1989
Klare, Karl 'Judicial deradicalisation of the Wagner Act and the origins of modern legal consciousness, 1937–1941' (1978) 62 *Minnesota Law Review* 265
Klevorick, A. K. 'Law and economic theory: an economist's view' (1975) 65 *American Economic Review* 237
Kohlberg, Lawrence *The philosophy of moral development: moral stages and the idea of justice*, Harper & Row, San Francisco, 1981
Korpi, W. *The working class in welfare capitalism*, Routledge & Kegan Paul, London, 1978
Krygier, M. 'Humdrum, hero and legal doctrine: a comment' (1986) 11 *Bulletin of the Australian Society of Legal Philosophy* 220
Lacey, Nicola 'Legislation against sex discrimination: questions from a feminist perspective' (1987) 14 *Journal of Law and Society* 411
La Trobe/Melbourne Occupational Health and Safety Project, *Victorian occupational health and safety—an assessment of law in transition*, National Centre for Socio-Legal Studies, La Trobe University, Bundoora, 1989
Law Institute of Victoria *Career patterns of law graduates*, Law Institute, Melbourne, 1990
Le Brun, Marlene and Johnstone, Richard *The quiet (r)evolution. Improving student learning in law*, Law Book Co., Sydney, 1994
Leff, A. 'Economic analysis of law: some realism about nominalism' (1974) 60 *Virginia Law Review* 451
Lenman, B. and Parker, G. 'The state, the community and the criminal law in early modern Europe', in *Crime and the law: the social history of crime in western Europe since 1500*, eds V. A. C. Gatrell, B. Lenman and G. Parker, Europa Publications, London, 1980
Lerman, Lisa 'Mediation of wife abuse cases: the adverse impact of informal dispute resolution on women' (1984) 7 *Harvard Women's Law Journal* 57
Letwin, W. *The origins of scientific economics: English economic thought, 1660–1776*, Methuen, London, 1963
Lindley, M. F. *The acquisition and government of backward territory in international law: being a treatise on the law and practice relating to colonial expansion*, New York, Negro University Press, 1969
Little, Archbishop Frank 'Religion and discrimination: the archbishop responds', the *Age*, 14 June 1993
Littleton, Christine, 'Equality and feminist legal theory' (1987) 48 *University of Pittsburgh Law Review* 1043
Llewellyn, Karl *Jurisprudence: realism in theory and practice*, University of Chicago Press, Chicago, 1962

Bibliography

——*The bramble bush: or our law and its study*, Oceana Publications, New York, 1951
Lloyd-Bostock, Sally 'The psychology of routine discretion: accident screening by British factory inspectors' (1992) 14 *Law and Policy* 45
Lord Lloyd of Hampstead and Freeman, M. D. A. *Lloyd's introduction to jurisprudence*, Stevens, London, 5th edn, 1985
Lukes, S. 'Can a marxist believe in human rights?' (1982) 1 *Praxis International* 344
Lukes, S. and Scull, A. *Durkheim and the law*, Martin Robinson, Oxford, 1983
Lumb, R. D. 'The Mabo case—public law aspects', in *Mabo: a judicial revolution*, eds M. A. Stephenson and Suri Ratnapala, University of Queensland Press, St. Lucia, 1993
Lyotard, Jean-Francois *The postmodern condition: a report on knowledge*, Manchester University Press, Manchester, 1984
MacCormick, Neil *Legal reasoning and legal theory*, Oxford University Press, Oxford, 1978
Macintyre, Stuart *A colonial liberalism: the lost world of three Victorian visionaries*, Oxford University Press, Melbourne, 1991
——'Neither capital nor labour: the politics of the establishment of arbitration', in *Foundations of arbitration*, eds Stuart Macintyre and Richard Mitchell, Oxford University Press, Melbourne, 1989
Macintyre, Stuart and Mitchell, Richard eds *Foundations of arbitration: the origins and effects of state compulsory arbitration 1890–1914*, Oxford University Press, Melbourne, 1989
MacKinnon, Catharine A. 'Feminism in legal education' (1989) 1 *Legal Education Review* 85
——'Feminism, marxism, method and the state: toward feminist jurisprudence' (1983) 8 *Signs* 635
——*Feminism unmodified: discourses in law and life*, Harvard University Press, Cambridge, Mass., 1987
——'From practice to theory, or what is a white woman anyway?' (1991) 4 *Yale Journal of Law and Feminism* 13
——*Sexual harassment of working women*, Yale University Press, New Haven, 1979
Maddock, Kenneth 'Aboriginal customary law', in *Aborigines and the law: essays in memory of Elizabeth Eggleston*, eds Peter Hanks and Bryan Keon-Cohen, Allen & Unwin, Sydney, 1984
Magarey, Kirsty 'Discrimination and the church' (1991) *Reform* no. 62, 101
Malinowski, B. *Crime and custom in savage society*, Routledge & Kegan Paul, London, 1926
Mann, K. *Defending white collar crime: a portrait of attorneys at work*, Yale University Press, New Haven, 1985
Mansell, Michael 'The court gives an inch but takes another mile' (1992) 2/57 *Aboriginal Law Bulletin* 4
——'Treaty proposal: Aboriginal sovereignty' (1989) 2/37 *Aboriginal Law Bulletin* 4
Marcuse, Herbert 'Repressive tolerance', in *A critique of pure tolerance*, eds Herbert Marcuse, Barrington Moore Jr and Robert Paul Wolff, Cape, London, 1965
Markey, Ray 'Trade unions, the Labor party and the introduction of arbitration in New South Wales and the Commonwealth', in *Foundations of arbitration*, eds Stuart Macintyre and Richard Mitchell, Oxford University Press, Melbourne, 1989
Marshall, Geoffrey *Constitutional theory*, Oxford University Press, Oxford, 1971
Marx, Karl *Capital*, 1894, repr. Lawrence & Wishart, London, 1970

Marx, Karl and Engels, Friedrich 'The German ideology', in Karl Marx, *The essential writings*, ed. F. L. Bender, Harper & Row, New York, 1972
Mason, Sir Anthony 'Putting *Mabo* in perspective', *Australian Lawyer*, July 1993, 23
Matsuda, Mari J. 'Looking to the bottom: critical legal studies and reparations' (1987) 22 *Harvard Civil Rights–Civil Liberties Law Review* 323
——'Voices of America: accent, antidiscrimination law, and a jurisprudence for the last reconstruction' (1990) 100 *Yale Law Journal* 1329
Matsuda, Mari J., Lawrence, Charles R. III, Delgado, Richard and Crenshaw, Kimberley Williams *Words that wound: critical race theory, assaultive speech and the First Amendment*, Westview Press, Boulder, 1993
McBarnet, Doreen J. *Conviction: law, the state, and the construction of justice*, Clarendon Press, Oxford, 1981
——'Pre-trial procedures and the construction of conviction', in *Sociology of law*, ed. Pat Carlen, Sociological Review Monograph no. 23, University of Keele, Keele, 1976
McCorquodale, John 'Judicial racism in Australia? Aboriginals in civil and criminal cases', in *Ivory scales: black Australians and the law*, ed. Kayleen M. Hazlehurst, University of New South Wales, Kensington, 1987
McGinley, G. 'Indigenous peoples' rights: *Mabo and others v State of Queensland*: the Australian High Court addresses 200 years of oppression' (1993) 21 *Denver Journal of International Law and Policy* 311
McGrath, Ann, 'History and land rights', in *Law and history in Australia, vol. III*, ed. Diane Kirkby, La Trobe University, Bundoora, 1987
McGuinness, P. P. 'High court's role now irrevocably politicised', the *Australian*, 13–14 November 1993
——'Legal creation science', *Financial Review* 1 February 1989
McRae, H., Nettheim, G. and Beacroft, L. *Aboriginal legal issues: commentary and materials*, Law Book Co., Sydney, 1991
Mead, G. H. *Mind, self and society*, University of Chicago Press, Chicago, 1934
Mednick, M. T. 'On the politics of psychological constructs' (1989) 44 *American Psychologist* 1118
Menkel-Meadow, Carrie 'Portia in a different voice: speculations on a women's lawyering process' (1985) 1 *Berkeley Women's Law Journal* 39
Merlan, Francesca, 'Gender in Aboriginal social life: a review', in *Social anthropology in Australian Aboriginal studies: a contemporary overview*, eds R. M. Berndt and R. Tonkinson, Aboriginal Studies Press, Canberra, 1988
——'Review of D. Bell, "Daughters of the dreaming"' (1984–85) 55(3) *Oceania* 225
Mitchell, Richard 'State systems of conciliation and arbitration: the legal origins of the Australasian model', in *Foundations of arbitration*, eds Stuart Macintyre and Richard Mitchell, Oxford University Press, Melbourne, 1989
Mill, John Stuart *On liberty*, edited by G. Himmelfarb, Penguin, Harmondsworth, 1974
Mills, C. Wright, *The sociological imagination*, Oxford University Press, Oxford, 1959
Minow, Martha 'Interpreting rights: an essay for Robert Cover' (1987) 96 *Yale Law Journal* 1860
——'Partial justice: law and minorities', in *The fate of law*, eds A. Sarat and T. Kerns, University of Michigan Press, Ann Arbor, 1991
Mnookin, Robert H. and Kornhauser, Lewis 'Bargaining in the shadow of the law: the case of divorce' (1979) 88 *Yale Law Journal* 950
Morgan, Jenny 'Equality rights in the Australian context: a feminist assessment', in

Bibliography

Towards an Australian bill of rights, ed. Philip Alston, Oxford University Press, Sydney, forthcoming 1994

Morgan, Wayne, 'Identifying evil for what it is: Tasmania, sexual perversity and the United Nations' (1994) 19 *Melbourne University Law Review* 740

Morris, Barry 'Frontier colonialism as a culture of terror', in *Power, knowledge and Aborigines*, eds Bain Attwood and John Arnold, La Trobe University Press, Melbourne, 1992

Morrison, Toni ed. *Race-ing justice, en-gender-ing power: essays on Anita Hill, Clarence Thomas and the construction of social reality*, Chatto & Windus, London, 1993

Mowbray, M. and Shain, K. 'Self-management: one Northern Territory experience' (1986) 11 *Legal Service Bulletin* 106

Mulvaney, D. J. and White, J. Peter eds *Australians to 1788*, Fairfax, Syme & Weldon, Sydney, 1987

Murray, Tim 'Aboriginal (pre)history and Australian archaeology: the discourse of Australian prehistoric archaeology', in *Power, knowledge and Aborigines*, eds Bain Attwood and John Arnold, La Trobe University Press, Melbourne, 1992

Naffine, Ngaire *Law and the sexes*, Allen & Unwin, Sydney, 1990

Nails, D. 'Social scientific sexism: Gilligan's mismeasure of man' (1983) 50 *Social Research* 643

National Women's Consultative Council and Labour Research Centre, *Pay equity for women in Australia*, AGPS, Canberra, 1990

Navarro, V. 'The determinants of social policy. A case study: regulating health and safety at the workplace in Sweden' (1983) 14 *International Journal of Health Services* 517

Neate, Graeme 'Power, policy, politics and persuasion' (1989) 6 *Environment and Planning Law Journal* 214

Nelken, D. *The limits of the legal process: a study of landlords, law and crime*, Academic Press, London, 1983

Nettheim, Garth 'Indigenous rights, human rights and Australia' (1987) 61 *Australian Law Journal* 291

——'Little evidence of uncertainty to justify Kennett's Mabo Bill', the *Australian*, 28 July 1993

——'"The consent of the natives": Mabo and indigenous political rights' (1993) 15 *Sydney Law Review* 237

Nietzsche, Frederick *A Nietzsche reader*, ed. R. Hollingdale, Penguin, Harmondsworth, 1977

Norris, C. 'Law, deconstruction, and the resistance to theory' (1988) 15 *Journal of Law and Society* 166

——*What's wrong with postmodernism: critical theory and the ends of philosophy*, Johns Hopkins University Press, Baltimore, 1990

Nozick, Robert *Anarchy, the state and utopia*, Blackwell, Oxford, 1974

O'Donovan, Katherine *Sexual divisions in law*, Weidenfeld & Nicolson, London, 1985

Okin, Susan Moller *Justice, gender and the family*, Basic Books, New York, 1989

Olsen, Frances E. 'Feminism and critical legal theory: an American perspective' (1990) 18 *International Journal of the Sociology of Law* 199

——'Feminist theory in grand style' (1989) 89 *Columbia Law Review* 1147

——'Statutory rape: a critique of rights analysis' (1984) 63 *Texas Law Review* 387

——'The myth of state intervention in the family' (1985) 18 *University of Michigan Journal of Law Reform* 835

O'Malley, Pat *Law, capitalism and democracy*, Allen & Unwin, Sydney, 1983
O'Shane, Pat 'Launch of the Australian Feminist Law Journal, August 29 1993, The University of Melbourne' (1994) 2 *Australian Feminist Law Journal* 3
Otto, Dianne 'Violence against women—something *other* than a violation of human rights?' (1993) 1 *Australian Feminist Law Journal* 159
Pashukanis, Evegeny *Law and marxism*, Ink Links, London, 1978
Pateman, Carole 'Feminist critiques of the public/private dichotomy', in *Public and private in social life*, eds S. I. Benn and G. F. Gaus, Croom Helm, Canberra, 1983
Patterson, D. 'Postmodernism/feminism/law' (1992) 77 *Cornell Law Review* 254
Pearce, D. C. *Australian law schools: a discipline assessment for the Commonwealth Tertiary Education Commission*, AGPS, Canberra, 1987
Pearson, Noel '200 years of invisible title', in *Mabo: a judicial revolution*, eds M. A. Stephenson and Suri Ratnapala, University of Queensland Press, St. Lucia, 1993
——'Reconciliation: to be or not to be' (1993) 3/61 *Aboriginal Law Bulletin* 14
——'The deed of grant in trust and Hope Vale Aboriginal community, north Queensland' (1989) 2/38 *Aboriginal Law Bulletin* 12
Pepper, Phillip *You are what you make yourself to be: the story of a Victorian Aboriginal family 1842–1980*, Hyland House, Melbourne, 1980
Pettman, Jan 'Gendered knowledges: Aboriginal women and the politics of feminism', in *Power, knowledge and Aborigines*, eds Bain Attwood and John Arnold, La Trobe University Press, Melbourne, 1992
Plowman, David 'Forced march: the employers and arbitration', in *Foundations of arbitration*, eds Stuart Macintyre and Richard Mitchell, Oxford University Press, Melbourne, 1989
Plowman, David and Smith, Graham 'Moulding federal arbitration: the employers and the High Court, 1903–1935' (1986) 2 *Australian Journal of Management* 203
Polinsky, A. *An introduction to law and economics*, Little, Brown & Co., Boston, 2nd edn, 1989
Posner, R. *Economic analysis of law*, Little, Brown & Co., Boston, 4th edn, 1992
Poulantzas, N. *Political power and social class*, Humanities Press, New Jersey, 1973
——*State, power and socialism*, New Left Books, London, 1978
Pritchard, Sarah 'The right of indigenous peoples to self-determination under international law' (1992) 2/55 *Aboriginal Law Bulletin* 4
Quinlan, Michael '"Pre-arbitral" labour legislation in Australia: its implications for the introduction of compulsory arbitration', in *Foundations of arbitration*, eds Stuart Macintyre and Richard Mitchell, Oxford University Press, Melbourne, 1989
Rawls, John *A theory of justice*, Oxford University Press, Oxford, 1973
——*Political liberalism*, Columbia University Press, New York, 1993
Raz, Joseph, *The authority of law*, Oxford University Press, Oxford, 1979
——'The politics of the rule of law' (1990) 3 *Ratio Juris* 331
Read, Peter, *The stolen generations: the removal of Aboriginal children in N.S.W. 1883–1969*, NSW Ministry of Aboriginal Affairs, Sydney, 1982
Report of the Committee on Safety and Health at Work 1970–72, HMSO, London, 1972
Resnick, Judith 'On the bias: feminist reconsideration of the aspirations for our judges' (1988) 61 *Southern California Law Review* 1877
Reynolds, Henry 'Mabo and pastoral leases' (1992) 2/59 *Aboriginal Law Bulletin* 8
——'Native title and pastoral leases', in *Mabo: a judicial revolution*, eds M. A. Stephenson and Suri Ratnapala, University of Queensland Press, St. Lucia, 1993
——*The law of the land*, Penguin, Ringwood, 1987; 2nd edn 1992

Bibliography

―――*The other side of the frontier*, Penguin, Ringwood, 1982
Rhode, Deborah L. 'Feminist critical theories' (1990) 42 *Stanford Law Review* 617
Rifkin, Janet 'Mediation from a feminist perspective: promises and problems' (1984) 2 *Law and Inequality* 21
Roach Anleu, Sharyn 'Women in the legal profession' (1992) 66 *Law Institute Journal* 162
Rorty, Richard 'The intellectuals at the end of socialism', *Harper's Magazine*, May 1992, 16
Rosaldo, M. Z. 'Women, culture, and society: a theoretical overview', in *Women, culture and society*, eds M. Z. Rosaldo and L. Lamphere, Stanford University Press, Stanford, 1974
Rowntree, Derek *Assessing students: how shall we know them?*, Kogan Page, London, 1977
Rowse, Tim 'Top-down tensions', *Modern Times*, no. 4, June 1992
Royal Commission into Aboriginal Deaths in Custody *Final Report*, AGPS, Canberra, 1991
Russell, D. and Van de Wen N. eds *Crimes against women: proceedings of the international tribunal*, Frog in the Well, East Palo Alto, 1984
Sadurski, W. 'Equality before the law: a conceptual analysis' (1986) 60 *Australian Law Journal* 131
Sampford, Charles 'Law, institutions and the public/private divide' (1991) 20 *Federal Law Review* 185
―――'Reconciling responsible government and federalism', in *The emergence of Australian law*, eds M. P. Ellinghaus, A. J. Bradbrook and A. J. Duggan, Butterworths, Sydney, 1989
Sandel, M. *Liberalism and its critics*, New York University Press, New York, 1984
Sanders, Doug 'Towards Aboriginal self-government: an update on Canadian constitutional reform' (1992) 2/58 *Aboriginal Law Bulletin* 12
Sarat, Austin and Felstiner, William L. F. 'Law and strategy in the divorce lawyer's office' (1986) 20 *Law and Society Review* 93
Sargent, N. 'Law, ideology and corporate crime: a critique of instrumentalism' (1989) 4 *Canadian Journal of Law and Society* 39
―――'Law, ideology, and social change: an analysis of the role of law in the construction of corporate crime' (1990) 1 *The Journal of Human Justice* 97
Scales, Ann 'The emergence of feminist jurisprudence: an essay' (1986) 95 *Yale Law Journal* 1373
Schelling, T. C. *Choice and consequences: perspectives of an errant economist*, Harvard University Press, Cambridge, Mass., 1984
Schwartz, R. and Miller, J. C. 'Legal evolution and societal complexity' (1964) 70 *American Journal of Sociology* 159
Scott, Joan W. 'Deconstructing equality-versus-difference: or, the uses of poststructuralist theory for feminism' (1988) 14 *Feminist Studies* 33
Sedley, S. 'Freedom of speech for Rupert Murdoch?', *London Review of Books*, vol. 13, no. 24, 19 December 1991
Selznick, P. 'Dworkin's unfinished task' (1989) 77 *California Law Review* 505
Shapland, J. *Between conviction and sentence*, Routledge & Kegan Paul, London, 1981
Sharp, Nonie 'No ordinary case: reflections upon Mabo (No. 2)' (1993) 15 *Sydney Law Review* 143
Sheehy, Elizabeth 'Feminist argumentation before the Supreme Court of Canada in *R v*

Seaboyer; R v Gayme: the sound of one hand clapping' (1991) 18 *Melbourne University Law Review* 450

Sheleff, S. 'From restitutive law to repressive law: Durkheim's *The division of labour in society* revisited' (1975) XVI *European Journal of Sociology* 29

Sherry, Susanna 'Civic virtue and the feminine voice in constitutional adjudication' (1986) 72 *Virginia Law Review* 543

Singer, Peter *How are we to live?*, Text Publishing, Melbourne, 1993

'Sit down girlie' (1994) 19 *Alternative Law Journal* 86

Smart, Carol *Feminism and the power of law*, Routledge, London, 1989

———'Feminist jurisprudence', paper given at seminar at La Trobe University, December 1987

———*The ties that bind: law, marriage and the reproduction of patriarchal relations*, Routledge & Kegan Paul, London, 1984

Smith, Adam *An inquiry into the nature and causes of wealth of nations*, edited by Edwin Cannan, Random House, New York, 1937

Soper, E. Philip 'Legal theory and the obligation of a judge: the Hart/Dworkin dispute' (1976) 75 *Michigan Law Review* 512

Spitzer, S. 'Punishment and social organisation: a study of Durkheim's theory of penal evolution' (1975) 9 *Law and Society Review* 613

Stang Dahl, Tove and Snare, A. 'The coercion of privacy', in *Women, sexuality and social control*, eds Carol Smart and Barry Smart, Routledge, London, 1978

Stone, Julius *Legal system and lawyers' reasonings*, Maitland, Sydney, 1964

———*Precedent and law: dynamics of common law growth*, Butterworths, Sydney, 1985

———*Province and function of law*, Maitland, Sydney, 1950

Sumner, Colin *Reading ideologies: an investigation into the marxist theory of ideology and law*, Academic Press, London, 1979

'Symposium on the Makarrata' (1982) *Aboriginal Law Bulletin* no. 5, 5

Thompson, E. P. *Whigs and hunters: the origins of the Black Act*, Penguin, Harmondsworth, 1977

Thornberry, P. *International law and the rights of minorities*, Oxford University Press, Oxford, 1991

Thornton, Margaret 'Feminist jurisprudence: illusion or reality?' (1986) 3 *Australian Journal of Law and Society* 5

———*The liberal promise: anti-discrimination legislation in Australia*, Oxford University Press, Melbourne, 1990

Tomasic, Roman ed. *Lawyers and the community*, Law Foundation of New South Wales, Sydney, 1978

———*Understanding lawyers: perspectives on the legal profession in Australia*, Law Foundation of New South Wales, Sydney, 1978

Toyne, Phillip and Vachon, Daniel *Growing up the country: the Pitjantjatjara struggle for their land*, McPhee Gribble/Penguin, Melbourne, 1984

Troup, Magdalen 'Rupturing the veil: feminism, deconstruction and the law' (1993) 1 *Australian Feminist Law Journal* 63

Trubek, D. 'The handmaiden's revenge: on reading and using the newer sociology of civil procedure' (1988) 51 *Law and Contemporary Problems* 111

Tucker, D. 'Unger on liberalism' (1986) 11 *Bulletin of the Australian Society of Legal Philosophy* 174

Tucker, E. 'Worker participation in health and safety regulation: lessons from Sweden' (1992) 37 *Studies in Political Economy* 95

Bibliography

Tushnet, Mark 'A marxist analysis of American law', *Marxist Perspectives*, Spring 1978, 96
——'An essay on rights' (1984) 62 *Texas Law Review* 1363
——'Critical legal studies: an introduction to its origins and underpinnings' (1986) 36 *Journal of Legal Education* 505
——'Following the rules laid down: a critique of interpretivism and neutral principles' (1983) 96 *Harvard Law Review* 781
——'Rights: an essay in informal political theory' (1989) 17 *Politics and Society* 403
——'Scenes from the metropolitan underground: a critical perspective on the status of critical legal education' (1984) 52 *George Washington Law Review* 272
Unger, Roberto M. *Law in modern society: towards a criticism of social theory*, Free Press, New York, 1975
——*Politics: a work in constructive social theory*, Cambridge University Press, Cambridge, 1987
——'The critical legal studies movement' (1983) 96 *Harvard Law Review* 561
Updike, John *A rabbit omnibus*, Penguin, London, 1981
Veljanovski, C. *The economics of law: an introductory text*, Institute of Economic Affairs, London, 1990
——*The new law and economics*, Oxford University Press, Oxford, 1982
Victorian parliamentary debates, Legislative Assembly, 20–22 July 1993
Walker, Geoffrey de Q. *The rule of law: foundation of constitutional democracy*, Melbourne University Press, Melbourne, 1988
Warren, C. 'Aboriginal power over cultural heritage' (1991) 16 *Legal Service Bulletin* 6
Weber, M. *Economy and society: an outline of interpretive sociology*, eds G. Roth and C. Wittich, Bedminster Press, Totowa, NJ, 1968
——*On law and economy in society*, trans. E. Shils and M. Rheinstein, Harvard University Press, Cambridge, Mass., 1954
Weisbrot, D. *Australian lawyers*, Longman Cheshire, Melbourne, 1990
West, Robin 'Jurisprudence and gender' (1988) 55 *University of Chicago Law Review* 1
Whitlam, Gough *The truth of the matter*, Allen Lane, Ringwood, 1979
Williams, Nancy M. *Two laws: managing disputes in a contemporary Aboriginal community*, Australian Institute of Aboriginal Studies, Canberra, 1987
Williams, Patricia J. 'Alchemical notes: reconstructing ideals from deconstructed rights' (1987) 22 *Harvard Civil Rights–Civil Liberties Law Review* 401
——*The alchemy of race and rights: diary of a law professor*, Harvard University Press, Cambridge, Mass., 1991
Williams, Susan H. 'Feminist legal epistemology' (1993) 8 *Berkeley Women's Law Journal* 63
Willis, E. *The sociological quest: an introduction to the study of social life*, Allen & Unwin, Sydney, 1993
Wilson, Madam Justice Bertha 'Will women judges really make a difference?' (1990) 28 *Osgoode Hall Law Journal* 507
Windeyer, W. J. V. *Lectures on legal history*, Law Book Co., Sydney, 2nd edn (rev.), 1957
Winterton, George 'Appointment of federal judges in Australia' (1987) 16 *Melbourne University Law Review* 185
Wolff, D. *In defence of anarchism*, Pantheon, New York, 1978
'Women in law–the statistical picture' (1992) *Law Institute Journal* 161

Wood, David 'Adjudication and community values: Sir Anthony Mason's recommendations', in *The emergence of Australian law*, eds M. P. Ellinghaus, A. J. Bradbrook and A. J. Duggan, Butterworths, Sydney, 1989

Yngvesson, Barbara 'Re-examining continuing relations and the law' (1985) *Wisconsin Law Review* 623

Index

Abel, Richard, 167
Aboriginal deaths in custody
　Royal Commission into, 31, 35, 35–6
Aboriginal history
　compared with European history, 7–8
　depiction of law in, 6
　determination of validity within, 5–6
　method of transmission, 5
　preservation of, 6
Aboriginal law, 4, 7, 9–10, 17, 26
Aboriginal society
　compared with European, 4–5
　recognition of by European, 28
　relationship with police, 161–2
Adams, John, 178
Airo-Farulla, Geoff, 130
Althusser, Louis, 97
anthropology, 8–10
　association with colonialism, 9
　limits of, 9–10
　methodology of, 9, 159
archaeology, 8–9
　methodology of, 7–8
assumptions, 160
　functionalist compared with critical, 99, 102

　underlying economic analysis, 61, 63–5
　underlying feminism, 110–11
　underlying functionalism, 61
　underlying liberal thought, 102
　underlying Marxist thought, 89–90
　underlying postmodernism, 123–4
　see also method
ATSIC, *see* self-management
autonomy of law, relative, *see* Marxism

Balbus, Isaac, 95, 96–7
Baldwin, John, 172
Barthes, Roland, 127–8
Beccaria, Cesare, 62
Behrendt, Larissa, 111
Bell, Diane, 9–10
Bennett, J.M., 139, 139–41, 142
Bentham, Jeremy, 62
Berns, Sandra, 105, 118
Bird, Greta, 161–2
Blackstone, William, 13, 101
Blumberg, Abraham, 172
Boyle, Christine, 114–5
Boyle, James, 108
Braithwaite, John, 165–6
Brennan, Frank, 32
Brereton, David, 146–7

Brooklyn, Bridget, 139, 141–2
Brownsword, Roger, 178

Cain, Maureen, 169–70, 184
Calabresi, Guido, 63
Carrington, Paul, 109
Carson, Kit, 149–50, 162, 163–4, 169, 172
Cicourel, Aaron, 160–2
Coase theorem, 66, 71
colonialism, 155
   divorce law in time of, 139, 140–41
   High Court response to, 17–18
   impact of on Aboriginal society, 10, 14–8
   legal system and, 10–15
commodity form of law, see Marxism
common law, 20, 135
   colonisation and, 13
   decision making in, 63–4, 100, 107, 178–9
   fiction of *terra nullius*, 3
   rationality of, 77, 106
   see also judges
conciliation
   and arbitration in industrial relations, 143–8
   see also industrial relations
corporate crime, 149, 163–5, 171
Cotterrell, Roger, 138–9, 155–6
courts, see decisionmaking, judges
criminal law, 72, 73–4, 94
   see also police, discretion
criminology, 160–1
critical legal studies, 87–8, 179
   approach to law reform, 138, 152
   critique of, 105, 110
   critique of rights talk, 104–5
   culture of, 100
   law as politics in, 86, 101–2, 106
   origins of, 100–1
customary law, 10, 27, 28–9, 35
   see also pluralism

Dalton, Clare, 113
Davies, Margaret, 126
decisionmaking, see discretion, judges
deconstruction, 101, 126–9, 182
   see also postmodernism, poststructuralism, structuralism
Derrida, Jacques, 128
de Saussure, 127
discretion, 103, 158, 172–3, 184–7
   decision frames and, 162–3, 173
   empirical examination of, 183–6
   in the enforcement of legislation, 163–5
   judicial, 174ff
   to invoke the law, 167
Dismissal, the, 42, 55–6
disputes, 10, 167–9
divorce, 120
   empirical observation of, 185–6
   legal profession and, 170
   reform in nineteenth century, 139–43
Dodson, Pat, 6
Doran, Jenny, 148
Dreamtime, 5–6
Durkhein, Emile, 61, 71–4, 80, 83, 84, 117
Dworkin, Ronald, 101, 180–1

Easterbrook, Frank, 68
economics, see law and economics, Marx, Marxism
education
   legal, 105–9
enforcement, 162, 163–5, 186–7
Engels, Frederich, 91–2, 93, 97
English law, 12, 21, 77
Enlightenment, 42, 62, 74, 123, 128
equality, 25, 44, 59, 111, 117, 123, 138, 151–2
   formal, 15, 20, 48, 112, 153–4
   other models, 15, 48
   see also commodity form of law
event-focused nature of law, see translation into legal system
evolutionary theories, 11–12, 22, 72, 74, 75–7, 80

family law, see divorce
federalism
   approaching centenary, 41
   Australian constitution, 57–9
   conciliation and arbitration in, 143
Felstiner, William, 167, 170

Index

feminist legal theory, 87, 166
  approach to law reform, 137–8, 143
  concerns of, 110–11
  cultural, 113–15
  liberal, 111–13
  radical, 115–17
  relationship with postmodernism, 117–19
Finnis, John, 48, 52, 124
Fish, Stanley, 182
Fiss, Owen, 110
Foley, Gary, 4, 7
Foucault, Michel, 124, 125, 125–6
Frank, Jerome, 93
Frazer, Andrew, 145–6
Friedman, Milton, 69
Frug, Gerald, 108
Fuller, Lon, 47–8, 50
functionalism, 79–84, 99, 151–2, 159
  approach to law reform, 137, 151, 155
  see also assumptions

Galanter, Marc, 94, 158, 166
Geertz, Clifford, 101, 187
Gilligan, Carol, 113–14, 115
Golder, Hilary, 139, 142–3
Goodrich, Peter, 182
Gove case, 15–17, 18, 20, 21–2, 29
Grabosky, Peter, 165–6
Gramsci, Antonio, 97

Hansen, Lynne, 181
Harding, Sandra, 112
Harris, Jim, 181
Hart, H. L. A., 48, 50, 51, 124, 179–80
Hawke, R. J., 145
Hawkins, Keith, 162
Hayek, F., 69
Healy, Chris, 7
Henenberg, Cathy, 149–50, 164
historical materialism, *see* Marxism
history, 24–5
  Aboriginal, *see* Aboriginal history
  of Factory Acts, 149
  of law reform, 139–41, 143–5, 148, 151–2
  oral, 5, 6, 19

Hume, David, 62
Hunt, Alan, 87, 88, 93, 171
Hutchinson, Allan, 49
Hutter, Bridget, 164

ideology, 91, 97–9, 101
  of common law decision making, 178, 178–9
  of law, 77–8, 99, 155–6, 173, 184
  of occupational health and safety, 149, 164
industrial relations, 69, 143–8
  see also occupational health and safety
Ingleby, Richard, 170, 185–6
interactionism, 159–60
  critical interactionism, 160, 164–5
  participant observation and, 9, 162–3
international law, 10–11, 52
  colonialism and, 11–12
  evolution of, 11
  use of by Aborigines, 33–5
interpretation
  and deconstruction, 74, 126–9
  and judicial reasoning, 54, 176, 180–3
  and sociology, 75
  in legal education, 108

James, Margaret, 139, 141
Johnstone, Richard, 171, 186–7
judges
  first instance, 183–7
  importance of, 176–7
  modes of reasoning, 174–6
  see also common law, discretion, interpretation
judicial power, 53, 54–5
jurisprudence, 43–4

Kennedy, Duncan, 101, 104, 107, 108–9
Kooris, *see* Aboriginal
Kornhauser, Lewis, 168

Lacey, Nicola, 113
land rights, 130
  cases, 15–18
  legal recognition of, 29–30, 150–5

see also Aboriginal society,
   Murray Islands case, native title,
   130
law and economics, 89
   concept of efficiency, 70
   concept of opportunity cost, 65–7
   Kaldor-Hicks efficiency, 70
   limitations of, 70–1, 124
   marginal analysis, 67–8
   nature of, 67
   normative analysis, 69
   Pareto optimality, 70
   positive compared with impact
      analysis, 68–9
   purpose of, 63
   structural analysis, 68–9
   supply and demand in, 67–8
   welfare economics, 69–70
   see also utilitarianism
law reform, 83
lawyers, 10, 64, 103, 167, 169–70,
   176–7, 183
legal domination, see ideology of law
legal profession, see lawyers
   Leff, Arthur, 71
Levi-Strauss, Claude, 127
liberal, 86–7, 92, 99, 129, 145
   approach in feminist legal theory,
      111–13
   critique of, 124
   definition of, 41
   laissez-faire, 42–3, 69, 146
   libertarian, 42–3, 46, 49, 69
   notions of legal reasoning, 179–82
   promotions of conciliation and
      arbitration, 145, 146
   welfare, 45, 46, 49
Llewellyn, Karl, 93, 93–4
Locke, John, 62

McBarnet, Doreen, 171–2
McConville, Michael, 172
MacCormick, Neil, 181–2
MacIntyre, Stuart, 145
MacKinnon, Catherine, 87, 111, 115,
   115–17, 118, 119, 137, 170
Marcuse, Herbert, 98
marginal analysis, see law and
   economics

Marx, Karl, 78, 79, 83, 88, 89–92,
   93, 97, 117, 124
Marxism, 87, 104
   approach to law reform, 136, 137,
      147, 152, 155
   commodification and, 96, 99
   concept of relative autonomy, 78,
      94–7
   doctrine of historical materialism
      in, 90–1
   influence of, 88–9
   instrumentalism, 92
   social control and, see also
      ideology of law, 92–4
Mason, Sir Anthony, 177–8
method
   empirical, 141, 158, 159, 165–6,
      184, 186
   jurisprudential, 43–4
   see also anthropology, archaeology
Mill, John Stuart, 42, 62
Mills, C. Wright, 160
Minow, Martha, 105
Mnookin, Robert, 168
morality
   inner morality of law, 47–8
   relationship with law, 50–3
Morgan, Jenny, 122
Mulvaney, D. J., 8
Murray Islands case, 3, 4, 6, 103,
   138, 151, 153, 155
   High Court reasoning in, 19–24,
      174–6, 176–7, 180
   transformation of claim into legal
      system, 18–19
   see also Aboriginal society, land
      rights, native title

native title, 16–18, 103, 138, 150,
   182
   compared with customary title,
      152–3
   compensation for loss of, 23–4
   extinguishment of, 22–4
   legal basis of, 21, 25
   legislative recognition of, 25–7,
      28, 150–5
   see also land rights, Murray
      Islands case
natural law, 50–2, 77

Index

Nietzsche, Frederick, 124
Nozick, Robert, 43, 69, 124

objectivity, 5, 61, 75, 84, 86, 88, 106, 112, 114, 125–6, 177–8
  standpoint theory compared with, 113, 115–16
occupational health and safety, 148–50, 157
  and the courts, 186–8
  community attitudes to, 165–6
  empirical observation of regulation of, 186–8
  enforcement of rules relating to, 162–5, 167–8, 171
O'Donovan, Katherine, 121
Okin, Susan Moller, 121
Olsen, Frances, 120
out-of-court activity
  advantages of repeat players in, 158, 168, 172
  compared with formal law, 157–9, 172–3
  construction of guilt in, 171–2
  framework for analysis of, 168–9
  see also discretion, translation into legal system

parliamentary sovereignty, see sovereignty
Parsons, Talcott, 61, 74, 79–84, 117, 127, 169
Pashukanis, Evegeny, 95
philosophy of law, see jurisprudence
Pitjantjatjara, 9, 26
pluralism, 27, 28, 35, 76, 146–8, 148–9, 150, 167
  approach to law reform, 136, 136–7, 147, 151, 155
policing, 144, 160–2
political economy, 160
  approach to conciliation and arbitration, 144, 149–50
  approach to occupational health and safety, 163–5
positivism
  approach to law reform, 135–6, 139–40, 148
  legal, 50–1
  sociological, 72, 159

postliberalism, 54, 102–4
postmodernism, 87, 88, 160
  approach to law reform, 138, 152
  assumptions underlying, 129–31
  definition of, 123–4
  see also deconstruction, Derrida, Foucault, poststructuralism, structuralism
poststructuralism, 126–9
  see also deconstruction, postmodernism, structuralism
precedent
  and Privy Council, 15–17
private property, 42, 43, 91, 102, 153
public/private distinction, 9–10, 46, 102, 113, 120–1, 166, 169, 184

Quinlan, Michael, 144

rationality, see objectivity, law and economics
Rawls, John, 44
realism, 93, 100
  see also discretion, judges
responsible government
  doctrine of, 55–7
Reynolds, Henry, 13, 14, 176
rights, 114
  Bill of, 46, 55
  critical legal studies critique of, 102, 104–5
  feminist critique of, 115, 121–3
  individual, 42, 44–5, 46
  to divorce, 140, 142
Robinson, Roland, 6
Rorty, Richard, 125
rule of law, 47–50, 56, 59, 82, 94–5, 101, 103, 153–4, 156, 179

Sarat, Austin, 167, 170
Scott, Joan, 117
self-determination, 35–6
  compared with self-management, 30
  in international law, 12
self-management
  ATSIC, 30–2
  definition, 30
separation of powers, 41, 46, 53–5, 59, 103, 176

253

Sherry, Susannah, 115
Smart, Carol, 87, 118, 119, 122, 126
Smith, Adam, 62
sociology of law, *see* discretion, interpretation, method
solidarity
  organic, 73, 83–4
  social, 73
sovereignty, 16, 19–20, 32–3
  parliamentary, 41, 45–6
  retention of by Aborigines, 32
Stone, Julius, 93
structuralism, 127

terra nullius, 3, 12, 13–14
  and common law, 13, 16–17
  and Murray Islands case, 19–22, 24–25, 27
Thompson, E. P., 94–5
transaction costs, 66, 168
  see also law and economics
translation into legal system, 157

event-focused nature of, 166, 170–1, 187
invocation of law and, 166–9
Murray Islands case, in, 18–19
Troup, Maggie, 129
Tushnet, Mark, 87

Unger, Roberto, 102–4, 110
United Nations, 12, 33
universality
  rejection of, 111–17, 124
utilitarianism, 43–5
  see also law and economics

Weber, Max, 61, 74–9, 83, 117, 159, 169
Western Sahara case, 12
Williams, Patricia, 87, 118, 130–1
Williams, Susan, 130
Wilson, Paul, 165–6
Wood, David, 178

Yngvesson, Barbara, 169

For Product Safety Concerns and Information please contact our EU
representative GPSR@taylorandfrancis.com
Taylor & Francis Verlag GmbH, Kaufingerstraße 24, 80331 München, Germany

www.ingramcontent.com/pod-product-compliance
Lightning Source LLC
Chambersburg PA
CBHW070557300426
44113CB00010B/1297